The Pursuit of Equality
in American History

Jefferson Memorial Lectures

But to Adam in what sort
Shall I appeer? shall I to him make known
As yet my change, and give him to partake
Full happiness with mee, or rather not,
But keep the odds of Knowledge in my power
Without Copartner? so to add what wants
In Femal Sex, the more to draw his Love,
And render me more equal, and perhaps,
A thing not undesirable, sometime
Superior: for inferior who is free?

Milton, *Paradise Lost*, Book IV

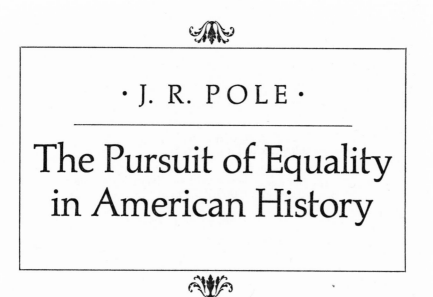

· J. R. POLE ·

The Pursuit of Equality
in American History

University of California Press

BERKELEY · LOS ANGELES · LONDON

University of California Press
Berkeley and Los Angeles, California

University of California Press, Ltd.
London, England

Copyright © 1978 by
The Regents of the University of California

ISBN 0–520–03286–1
Library of Congress Catalog Card Number: 76–20020
Printed in the United States of America

1 2 3 4 5 6 7 8 9

In memory of
Richard Hofstadter

Contents

Preface

"A nation, conceived in liberty, and dedicated to the proposition that all men are created equal"—Lincoln's words are a masterly fusion of the two central commitments of the American Republic. The equal legal and moral status of free individuals was America's reason for independent existence. Yet only at comparatively rare—and then generally stormy—intervals has the idea of equality dominated American debates on major questions of policy. Equality is normally the language of the underdog, and habitually loses some of its magnetism on the attainment of a sufficient degree of success—a conclusion no less true of groups than of individuals. But the discrepancy between the public commitment and the public concern to translate commitment into policy can hardly be explained on the comfortable ground of an achievement that had at any particular period left little room for further advance. My aim in this book has been to explore the historical sources and character of this discrepancy, together with the circumstances in which ideas of equality have come to the surface, the meanings of equality in American ideology, and the operative effect of egalitarian ideas in American history. In all this, a work of history, not of philosophy and still less of advocacy, I have tried to be true to the intellectual context of each period and to the meaning and intention of each contributor, on all sides, to a continuing debate whose intellectual interest certainly loses nothing from the intense seriousness of its subject.

[ix]

Despite this disclaimer, my own interpretations tend to reflect an assumption as to the proper and normative object of egalitarian thought. I see egalitarian principles in the light of a Western tradition in which they are legitimised by a profound, not a merely perfunctory, respect for individuality, and which emphasises the distinctions among people as well as their similarities; and I regard this emphasis as logically consistent with the requirements of the United States Constitution, more especially since the Fourteenth Amendment. These views come somewhat more clearly into focus with the advance of the twentieth century. But although they are deceptively easy to present as though they were merely respectable truisms, they are so far from being self-evident that in one important sense they have probably never been sanctioned by majority opinion. The tension arises over the conflict between the demand for uniform principles which hold the rights of the individual consistent throughout the Union, and the structure of American federalism. Contention can easily develop over the question of whether federal—that is, diffusionist—principles are being used for the protection of legitimate local preferences and interests, or as a shield for practices which conflict with the national responsibility for equal rights. This is the most obvious and direct form of such conflicts, which are further complicated by widely diffused if vaguely defined ideas of pluralism; and these views have thoroughly respectable sources in American constitutional law and custom. When Stephen Douglas accused Abraham Lincoln of trying to take the United States off its original mixed basis, he was charging his rival with destroying the balance among different entities whose voluntary adherence alone had brought the federal Union into existence.

In order to understand the political meaning of such arguments it is not enough diligently to trace their historical authenticity or to satisfy ourselves of their internal consistency; it is indispensably necessary to reveal the *function* of the argument by analysing its historical context as well as its logical structure and by comparing it to the alternatives to which it was exposed in its own time. This is the method I have tried to follow, and if my own interpretations bear some signs of an individualistic preference, I hope at least that my methods are consistent and that I have subjected all the arguments, on all sides of the question, to equal treatment. To have done less would hardly be fair to my theme.

The focus of this study is equality as an issue in public policy. While I am well aware of the risks of having failed to do full justice to the enormous literature, I have not sought to trace the reflections of private individuals, I have used literary evidence only when it is specific in its public implications (and even then very sparingly), and I have allowed the nature of American public preoccupations to dictate the distribution of my own treatment. Some of the most glaring inequalities in American life have always been economic; and yet, on the whole, a remarkably small proportion of the debates on equality recurring throughout American history has been taken up by such questions as the redistribution of wealth or any effective re-evaluation of the criteria by which economic rewards are allotted. I do not mean that the subject has been ignored; the Granger laws, the Populist programmes, certain aspects of the Progressive Movement, federal policies in income tax and welfare, and the New Deal were all expressions of protest against inequalities which had blown up into inequities, and in that sense an idea of equality has been present throughout the turbulent history of economic and social protest. To the extent that it has been the dominant legitimating element in the protest, I have tried to take note of its presence as an expression of the American pursuit of equality. But it must be admitted that the strains of protest often seem to have been muted by the partial acceptance of assumptions which in themselves conflict with the ideal of achieving an equal society.

Another book could well be written with this theme as its central problem. In the process of writing this book I have seen enough alternative approaches, and have changed my mind often enough, to be reasonably aware that others might see the problem of equality along lines marked by different perspectives. To take a further example, another very marked inequality has been regional. As C. Vann Woodward has pointed out, regions of the United States differ from one another in wealth as widely as some of the more widely differing countries of Europe. Yet until Franklin Roosevelt described the South in 1938 as "the nation's Number One problem" this aspect hardly ever presented itself as requiring national attention. I suppose the creation of the Tennessee Valley Authority might be considered the first step in that direction; but it was only in the 1950s that the federal government deliberately fed wealth and multipliers of wealth into the South by establishing all the five space programme bases in Southern states.

This brings me to another question. At certain critical phases in the development of the argument I have touched on the problem of equality in the special context of Southern society. But I have long believed that the literature of American history needs a much more exhaustive analysis of the effects of slavery on Southern society as a whole, of the development of those effects over a long period, and of the consequences of the racial problem for the post Civil War South than it has ever yet received, and until that work has been done there will be some inadequacy in our understanding of the South and the meaning of equality for its people. When that work has been done I trust that my own appreciation will impel me to rewrite this book to take account of it; meanwhile I hope that what I have written will be found to point in the right direction.

Being a study in the history of ideas, and of the relationship of those ideas to social structures and political policies, this work has required a method which it will be helpful to explain. When I first formulated the problem for the Jefferson Memorial Lectures at Berkeley, I broke down the idea of equality into three categories; equality before the law, equality of opportunity, and equality of esteem. I also used a chronology, long since discarded, which assigned these categories broadly to the eighteenth, nineteenth, and twentieth centuries respectively. Analytical categories, like essentials, ought not to be multiplied beyond their uses; but historical analysis must take precedence over logical purity, and I have found it necessary to double the number of categories, whose significance lies in the fact that they represent real levels of awareness of equality as a social issue. Political equality, or equality of power as some political scientists call it, is not quite the same thing as equality before the law; and sexual equality, though logically treatable within the other categories, has established itself separately as a historical issue. So has religious and moral equality, which by defining the individual as an irreducible unit of moral responsibility gives the whole subject a certain unity. When my manuscript was almost complete, David Hackett Fischer kindly presented me with a manuscript of his own[1] suggesting that different age-groups might require similar consideration; future problems may produce other points of view and other categories, but in considering them one should always be careful to compare like with like: Equality before the law and equality of esteem, for example, are not of the same order, and it is theoretically possible (though for obvious reasons unlikely) that equality before the law might exist without equality of esteem. These distinctions will serve to produce a deeper understanding of society if they are kept clear, but not if they are confused. They may serve to do so when by establishing the category into which some claim or grievance falls we may be able to evaluate or perhaps to resolve it; by discovering how such categories arose to past perceptions we can begin to understand how past society perceived its own problems—and how it came to write laws and prescribe customs which have passed into the legal and moral codes of later generations including our own.

When I look into this book's biography I recognise that its roots run deep into my studies in American history and into my observations of both American and British society in our own times. In the middle of the 1950s I began to collect information about American state anti-discrimination and human rights laws, leading to an article in *History Today* in 1958 which may perhaps have been a premonition of the interest in equality. Some of these ideas I collected for a lecture at the University of York in 1968. But it was during my Fellowship at the Center for Advanced Studies in the Behavioral Sciences at Stanford in the winter of 1969–70 that I began to work systematically on equality, and it gives me pleasure to look back on all the help, kindness, and intellectual stimulation that I received through the good offices of Meredith Wilson, Preston Cutler, and Jane Kielsmeyer, and through my colleagues and contemporaries at the Center.

An early product of these efforts took shape in my Jefferson Memorial Lectures, delivered at Berkeley in April 1971. I should like to express my appreciation to the University of California for the

1. Since published as *Growing Old in America* (New York, 1977).

invitation to deliver these lectures (a distinction that I was the first British scholar to receive) and, I must now add, to William J. Mc-Clung of the University of California Press for his tactful combination of encouragement and forbearance in awaiting my many revisions of the manuscript.

During the past few years I have transformed that early draft into something approximating to the present book during lecture courses in my own university; and my efforts to refine the arguments have been assisted by our American Studies seminar at Cambridge and by seminars at several universities in the United States. Successive drafts of this book have been subjected to the scrutiny of friends in the United States and Britain. Apart from the points along the way at which I have noted guidance on special topics, I have profited by the advice of David Yale on English common law and of Judith Hole, who, without accepting some aspects of my argument, helped me to get the women's rights movement into perspective. Early versions were read by James S. Coleman, Paul A. Freund, Alison Gilbert Olson, and Amélie Oksenberg Rorty. While lecturing and writing in Cambridge I have had constant help from Betty Wood, who several times referred me to works I would otherwise have overlooked. Beatrice Hofstadter, Eric McKitrick, and John Zvesper combed right through the first of my full-length drafts, leading me to a series of revisions which in turn were most attentively read by Stanley Katz and C. Vann Woodward. While all of these critics have contributed to the present shape and texture of the book, all, I feel sure, would wish to disclaim at least some of my arguments or emphases. Some of the material in Chapter 12 has previously appeared in *A Tug of Loyalties*, edited by Esmond Wright (London, 1975), and in my B. K. Smith Lecture in *Social Radicalism and the Idea of Equality in the American Revolution* (University of St Thomas, Houston, 1976).

The greatest and most enduring debt, which it is too late now to repay, is to one who passed from our sight before I had begun to write this book, but who had been and in some ways will, I think, remain the closest personal inspiration of my historical work. In casting my mind back over the years, and particularly to the summer of 1970 when with his own time running short he seemed to have

more of it to give than ever before, I can only take the risks of sentiment by borrowing again from *Hamlet* the words that I quoted in
my first lecture before the audience at Berkeley:

> He was a man, take him for all in all
> I shall not look upon his like again.

J. R. P.

Cambridge, England
26 September 1976

Chapter One

The Idea of Equality in
a Hostile World

The people of Britain's North American colonies were the first subjects of any of Europe's colonial empires to claim their independence of the Old World. They justified that claim by an appeal to the principle of human equality, to which they accorded the status of a "self-evident truth". The concept of equality, thus proclaimed in the rhetoric of American independence, entered into the principles of government, where it linked forces with demands arising from newly released sources of popular power. It must be admitted, however, that self-evident truths, whatever the influence they may exert on mankind's opinions at particularly impressionable moments, never succeed in commanding concentrated attention over long periods. An abstract concept based on the unverifiable proposition that "all men are created equal", which is not even in principle capable of being translated into political reality, appeared to stand little hope of transforming the character or affecting the operations of the nation's most powerful material interests. The evolutionary survival of the idea of equality in America has owed much to its proven ability to adapt to varied and often hostile environments by meaning different things to different minds, and furnishing rival interests with equally satisfying terms of moral reference—all of which throws some doubt on the immutable character claimed by the Republic's founders for human rights determined forever by the laws of nature.

Only in circumstances of social upheaval—or the imminent threat of it—has the idea of equality been able to stamp an unmistakable and lasting imprint on social institutions. The Great Awakening, within certain very marked limits and with correspondingly limited consequences, was probably the first such period after colonial institutions had taken a settled shape. Accordingly it is chronologically the first to appear in the pages that follow; and because its religious character merges with the theme of the attitude of the state towards the individual's moral identity, giving the subject an inherent unity which bears on all other aspects of equality, two separate chapters are devoted to that problem. The American Revolution and its aftermath constituted another period of upheaval. For all the rhetoric and invocations of principle that accompanied the election of Thomas Jefferson in 1800, and the policies of Andrew Jackson from the early campaigns for his election through his veto of the Bank bill and other pronouncements to his retirement in 1837, the administrations of these publicly dedicated reformists did little to deflect the advancing inequalities that characterised the distribution of wealth and all that followed from it. The Jacksonian affirmation could be described in terms of the comparatively new concept of equality of opportunity, an imperfectly digested notion which actually conflicted with other egalitarian precepts, held by some of Jackson's contemporaries to be of even more urgent importance.

It was only with the tremendous upheaval wrought by the Civil War—and then after more moderate policies had failed for political reasons—that the principle of the equal protection of the laws, with all that it could be held to require in making sure that the laws themselves were genuinely equal, was written into the Constitution and converted from a general and insubstantial ideal into a positive obligation of government. The language of equal protection, however, soon proved to be as flexible as the vague idea of equal opportunity. Soon after achieving the modest and, as it seemed, short-lived triumphs of the Fourteenth and Fifteenth Amendments, egalitarians lost their grip on American development more completely than ever before.

Yet the idea of a national commitment refused to die, because the underprivileged sections of the American community refused to accept defeat, and fought back by using as a weapon the egalitarian principles already implanted in American ideology and in the Constitution itself. One of the most remarkable features of the period that began to develop out of the Depression, the New Deal, and more particularly the Second World War was the prolonged attention to equality as a central and definitive object—a social aim to be achieved through various combinations of exhortation, legislation, and constitutional law. The fate of earlier demands to translate the egalitarian spirit into law would not have appeared to make this effort likely to last more than perhaps two or three presidential terms; but the war was swiftly followed by a new and more prolonged threat to America's moral reassurance and physical stability—Korea and the Cold War. To these influences were added a civil rights movement of exceptional vitality and a Supreme Court of equally exceptional vision.

The idea of equality thus revealed over the two hundred years of the nation's independent existence a tenacity which afforded a peculiar kind of glamour to American claims and pretentions, and a kind of justification to the offer—or threat—of social justice which America had always seemed to hold out to the common people in face of the empires, monarchies, priesthoods, and social hierarchies of the Old World. This tenacity of egalitarian principles owed a great deal to the historical structure of American institutions and to the formal and constitutional origins of the American nation; and similarly the idea owed much of its vitality to the fact that equality had entered into the language of justice in a more explicit and more public manner than in most contemporaneous political systems. The movement in this direction, through which equality began to define the obligations of government to the people, had its deeper origins in seventeenth-century England, gained power to affect the character of religious, legal, and political institutions in the middle of the eighteenth century, and emerged in the higher reaches of popular thought as a successor to the idea of the Great Chain of Being.

Chain and Locke

The human race was only one link in the Great Chain which bound the whole order of the Universe downwards from God to the lowest of his creation in a series of interdependent gradations. It was a concept of superb aesthetic harmony which enabled people to think

[3]

about the cosmic order with far greater comfort, and moreover with more clarity and certainty, than they have been able to do in more recent times. By the force of a powerful analogy it also provided an explanation for the necessity of rank and authority in the kingdoms of the world.[1] Mankind was believed to occupy a special position in the Great Chain, halfway between the angels and the beasts, incorporating some of the qualities of each, but actually superior to the angels in his power of independent reason. This imagery stencilled in people's minds a picture which reflected the structure of political authority, with power descending from the king and his court through different ranks marked off from one another by birthright and title.

Arthur Lovejoy's magnificent exposition of this cosmic picture includes a clear explanation of the Great Chain's political implications.[2] The Universe had been constructed by its Creator on the principle of plenitude, which meant that everything in existence had its use to the whole and that everything that could be of use to the whole already existed, an admirable state of affairs which clearly left no room for dissatisfaction and no possibility of improvement. This cosmology could therefore be used as a weapon against social discontent "and especially against all equalitarian movements". Since the best of possible systems had been fashioned "by means of inequality", any tendency towards equality could be considered not only subversive but even tinged with implications of heresy. The whole scheme was epitomised by Pope's *Essay on Man*, whose harmonious pentameters and pungent couplets, which themselves seemed to examplify the virtues of order, inculcated into educated minds the principle that hierarchy was in all things required by divine Reason.[3] But this was not all: To that Reason, the happiness of the humble, in their station, was every bit as important as that of the mighty; which of course was another argument against envy and discontent.

> Order is Heav'n's first law, and this confest,
> Some are, and must be, greater than the rest,
> More rich, more wise; but who infers from hence

1. Arthur O. Lovejoy, *The Great Chain of Being* (Cambridge, Mass., 1948).
2. Ibid., pp. 183–207.
3. Alexander Pope, *Essay on Man*, IV, 49–56. The poem appeared in two parts published in 1733 and 1734.

That such are happier, shocks all common sense.
Heaven to mankind impartial we confess,
If all are equal in their happiness:
But mutual wants this happiness increase;
All nature's difference keeps all nature's peace.

This exposition of the grounds for material inequality naturally required an equitable justification, and Pope significantly provided that happiness—the *result* of unequal distribution of fortunes—was itself to be equally distributed. The theory could hardly have appeased social envy or economic discontent. But it hinted at a need to explain social order on the principle that each person's needs were to be given equal consideration, a theme capable of stronger development in the hands of political reform. Lovejoy, who used this passage to underline the theme of hierarchy, undervalued this point when he broke off the quotation in the middle of the third line. Yet by virtue of its very completeness, the theory had in the most obvious sense nowhere to go. It could answer no new questions except by positing further subdivisions of its own orders; and while it undoubtedly exerted considerable power to stifle the formulation of new questions, when early geological speculation began to suggest that some parts of nature might have been formed later than others, the Great Chain of Being was doomed; it constituted a perfect example of an exhausted scientific paradigm.

This was a glacially gradual process, complicated by many intellectual and theological cross-currents. The cosmic picture had in truth never been linked with the order of human affairs by any strictly logical connection; it did not follow from the Great Chain of all Being, of which mankind was one sector, that an identical system must exist among the creatures within that sector. It would have been possible to think of all men as being equals within their allotted sphere. The analogy with divine authority, however, served very well the interests of the secular powers, who were also able to have recourse to the Pauline doctrine that secular power was invested with divine authority. There was no one of equal weight to confute these views, emanating as they did from the oracles of Church and State, from New England magistrates and divines no less than from those of the Old World. The idea of equality thus had to struggle for existence in an almost entirely hostile world, for it was subversive of all received and almost all conceivable ideas of order. It was not for nothing that the early Christians were regarded as subversive or that when the Church came to terms with the State it arranged itself in an elaborate hierarchy which in important ways reflected those of the secular world. Equality was an intuition rather than a doctrine, and had no comparable suggestions to offer on such questions as how civil society was to meet the needs of supply and demand, provide military defence, or organise systems of administration and justice. If ideas of equality were to survive, their proponents had the task of convincing the rest of the world that they were compatible with effective economic and political institutions (in which they have never fully succeeded). Desperate spirits among the peasantry, an occasional discontented earl, or a disgruntled region might resort to rebellion, and even kings did not invariably survive such manifestations; such movements, however, were rarely egalitarian at heart— or for long. With one short and fatal exception in English history, the crown always survived, and rebellion seldom resorted to an alternative cosmology.

The Great Chain did not enjoy absolute possession of the field throughout all the ages before the Enlightenment. Yet ideas of equality as the rightful relations among men seldom seem to have occurred except to special groups or in unusual circumstances. When, in fifth-century Athens, the Sophists argued against all prevailing thought that all men were equal in sharing the faculty of reason, they hit on a theme that could have been developed separately from the more general principle of equality but which never afterwards failed to become entangled with it. To say that all men shared the faculty of reason was not to say that they all shared it in an equal degree. The importance of the Sophists' observation was that it insisted on a common humanity made explicit through a common faculty. It meant that men owed one another whatever was required of reasonableness, and it was egalitarian because it cut across the much more conventional belief that different endowments of reason, or virtue, and of other qualities constituted precisely the differences between those who ruled by right and those whose duty was to obey. Aristotle on the other hand was sure that all men possessed reason, but thought that the distinguishing mark of slaves was that they possessed only so much of the power of reason as to enable them to

[6]

understand their masters, without being able to reason for themselves; and he concluded that manual workers ought not to participate in government on the ground that their lives denied them the opportunity to cultivate the qualities essential to wisdom.[4]

In the ancient world, philosophers attached great importance to the human capacity for reason.[5] Christians were bound together, and to all mankind, by the concept of the common fatherhood of God, whose will was expressed in the laws of nature and apprehended through the God-given faculty of reason. The truth that all men were capable of virtue and of experiencing happiness was perceived by Stoics and by Epicureans as a kind of equality; but it appears to remain true that these opinions stood out either as rare perceptions, maintained against the general current of the age, or as generalities at a level which had very little binding application to the rights and wrongs of government or of private forms of authority. None of them challenged the right of the naturally superior to rule the naturally inferior, an assumption which passed without question until the writings of Marsilius of Padua and Nicholas of Cusa, who contributed to the development of an idea of equality not by maintaining that people were by nature equally endowed, but by the belief that all could and should in some way participate in law and government, through councils and elections, to the extent of their capacities. But it was compatible with these views, and in fact necessary to them if they were to hold any plausibility, to maintain that the ignorant should consent to the rule of the wise—a position not far distant from Samuel Stone's characterisation of the early Massachusetts Congregational Church as governed by "a speaking *Aristocracy* in the face of a silent *Democracy*".[6]

Equality can be the principle of a closely knit community. The early sixteenth century Anabaptists, led by Thomas Muntzer, drew doctrines of communal life from the Reformation, but only the spiri-

---

4. Aristotle, *Politics*, books VII, *ix*, 1, I, *v*, 8.
5. For this passage, see Sanford A. Lakoff, *Equality in Political Philosophy* (Cambridge, Mass., 1964), pp. 12–59.
6. The phrase is quoted by Perry Miller, *The New England Mind: The Seventeenth Century* (Cambridge, Mass., 1954), p. 452. Stone (1602–1663) was educated at Emmanuel College, Cambridge, and migrated to New England in 1633, where he became pastor of the church at Newton, later called Cambridge. Thomas Hutchinson, *The History of the Colony and Province of Massachusetts-Bay*, ed. Lawrence Shaw Mayo (Cambridge, Mass., 1936), I, 31–2.

tually perfect could join in their enterprise; only the elect would be equal among themselves, and then, if necessary, after exterminating or expelling the impure. These views, which reflected a significant turn in the history of Protestant theology, contributed little to the development of any egalitarian doctrine in politics or society. It has been very generally the case in Western history that, with exceptions to be made for monastic communities and theological extremities, thinkers who have tried to develop ideas of equality have had to do so in the context of strongly hierarchical social orders and political institutions. Ideas of equality became articulate in the great struggles of seventeenth-century England; but even among the Levellers, there were those who would have excluded almstakers and servants from participation in political life, because such people were wholly dependent on the will of others.[7] Independence was a criterion, if not for ultimate spiritual equality, then for the safe exercise of equality in public affairs. The egalitarianism of the seventeenth-century Levellers' great contemporary, Hobbes, was that of total submission, in his view the only sure way to safety in the terrible war of all against all. Yet the severe theological embroilments of the seventeenth century also gave rise to a weariness of Puritanism and with it a new, undogmatic mood, characterised by the Latitudinarian interest in—and optimism about—human nature.

This new philosophy of benevolence, which profoundly influenced the third Earl of Shaftesbury and the Scottish philosopher Francis Hutcheson, contained the seeds of a more systematic theory of equality.[8] For Shaftesbury, as for his grandfather's famous teacher John Locke, the state of nature that was thought to have preceded civil society offered no protection for the rights of property, which were themselves of natural, not of civil, origin; civil law therefore incorporated the law of nature but could never supersede it. The function of civil law was rather to give security to existing natural rights by establishing forms and procedures. Just government could come into existence only by the consent of those who voluntarily entered into it, and who lived under it, for the protection of rights already recognised by natural law. It is clear that two very distinct

7. This aspect is discussed in Chapter 2.
8. David Brion Davis, *The Problem of Slavery in Western Culture* (Ithaca, 1966), pp. 348–64. Justification by benevolence is also one of the themes of Pope's *Essay on Man*.

themes of great future significance, were implicit in these views. One of these is often called "voluntarism", because of the basis of personal motive and independent action called for by the structure of the argument; and in later generations, after the emergence of the doctrine of laisser-faire and the development of theories of competitive enterprise, this would be extended to the "individualism" of nineteenth-century America. Individualism in fact received its name in France, and became a leading characteristic of entrepreneurial economics and society in Western history, but it did get its earliest favourable connotation in the United States, and its harder, more atomised forms became more characteristic of the United States than of Europe.

The second theme was that of equality. For if people decided, voluntarily, to enter into a compact to form a civil society, then at least to the extent of being signatories to the agreement, they were equals. They might have brought with them unequal amounts of property and unequal attributes of other sorts, but they brought equal voices, equal wills. This approach was fortified by Locke's belief that God had given the world to men to enjoy in common and that no one was entitled to possess more than he could actually use. The difficulties in reconciling this position with Locke's attributed plans for the extremely hierarchical distribution of land, status, and political power in Carolina, and with other aspects of his views on property, are familiar, but do not detract much from the impulse of moral legitimation which he gave to the more positive doctrines about equality which became precepts for Thomas Jefferson. In the Declaration of Independence, where Locke's "Life, liberty and estate" became "Life, liberty and the pursuit of happiness", the whole statement rested on the natural foundation of equality in human rights. For Locke the postulates of this condition were in a residual sense more theological than for Jefferson; his views descended from the Calvinistic doctrine of the Calling. "The Calling", as John Dunn has said, "is thus a summons from God, but it is a summons for the interpretation of which each adult individual is fully responsible".[9] But Locke was writing a treatise on civil, not ecclesiastical, government; and it would have been inconceivable that his successors would

9. John Dunn, *The Political Thought of John Locke* (Cambridge, 1969), p. 223.

[9]

take the rights which he affirmed without the principles of equality which made them good for the individuals who consented to live under civil government.

The ideas of equality as they came to hand in the era of the American Revolution thus bore an ancient lineage, but a lineage which had never provided them with more than a minority position. Writers who proposed theories of equality seldom made them into programmes for social reform; the more revolutionary implications of Locke's general theory were muffled by his acceptance of the order, and the important inferences for his own time really had to do in concrete terms with the rights of kings and peoples rather than with the relations among the estates of the realm or with individuals in their relations to one another.

Yet for Locke as for his successors the social and economic order effectively dominated these relations. It was against a background of extreme social privilege that most reforming thinkers of the eighteenth century were obliged to work out the alternative of social equality. In a context of crippling taxation and total subordination imposed on the masses of the people, the French *philosophes* confronted the problem of social justice, and a demand for equality of burdens and duties came to light as the elemental answer. The demand for equality emerged in circumstances which exactly correspond to Giovanni Sartori's description of it as a "protest ideal",[10] for which reason it was not a clearly defined objective. The immense reforms which would be the least possible remedy for the gross inequalities of Europe could be administered only by powers even stronger than those of the existing nobilities, so that in general the *philosophes* were ready to accept a strengthened monarchy as a prerequisite of reform. The French monarchy, never able to nerve itself to the task, eventually disappeared in the avalanche which buried the orders, ranks, privileges, and abuses of the *ancien régime*. In Britain's American colonies the social situation was profoundly different. A variety of different structures had grown up in relation to several regionally differing economies, influenced in their style, interests, and ideals by various differences of policy and circumstances. No single hierarchy unified the continent, which could not be said to have a single social structure; and the great moulding and uni-

10. Giovanni Sartori, *Democratic Theory* (New York, 1967), pp. 325–6.

fying tendency of the monarchy itself was conspicuous by its absence from colonial soil and politics. Colonial societies had their distinct characters, and each was held together by sanctions which included the power of property over the laws, and a traditional deference for visible authority and social status. Men of the more ambitious kind of individual aspiration could often also find their outlets in a society which offered fewer heights to scale than that of Britain, but probably also more open access to those that were in view.

Being heirs to the heritage of English common law and subjects to British statutes, the American colonials received in common a great fund of similar legal and moral ideas. The general reception of these ideas may well have been a necessary condition of the American Revolution; they provided Americans with a common legal discourse. That discourse, however, was not based on assumptions of social equality, and can only in a limited sense be thought to have laid foundations for an egalitarian social order. The same assumptions, rules of procedure, and laws in Britain sustained a society which, though it gave some remarkable forms of protection to the liberty of the subject, did not rest his liberties on anything remotely resembling a society of equals. Even the widely held ideas of natural law were too vague and speculative to make any noticeable impression on colonial law or legislation. It was the quarrel with Britain that forced Americans to reach upward and bring natural law down from the skies, to be converted into a political theory for use as a weapon in constitutional argument; in that capacity it was directed against British policies and was never intended as a method of analysing the rights and wrongs of colonial life. That was a process awaiting the quickening of American political self-consciousness which British policy and British criticism unwittingly did so much to precipitate.[11]

11. I am not arguing that mid-eighteenth-century British policy was alone responsible for making American colonists sensitive to ideas of equality. On the contrary, David Lovejoy has convincingly demonstrated that the issue of equality for the colonies in the context of membership of the British nation was a prominent aspect of their discontent in the era of the Glorious Revolution. But although the grievances of small farmers, small tobacco planters, and others in economically subordinate positions played a large part in the disorders of the period, the demand of colonial leaders for equality within the empire never seems to have spread over into the rhetoric of internal discontent

or to have given rise to a philosophically co-ordinated demand for equality as a matter of domestic colonial justice. Neither in political structure nor in political philosophy were the late seventeenth century colonial societies in any condition to produce a general demand for equality. The differences between this situation and that of the 1760s and 1770s represented a long lifetime of economic growth, political adaptation, and of an increasingly mature interest in political ideas. For the earlier period, see David S. Lovejoy, *The Glorious Revolution in America* (New York, 1972), pp. 39, 116, 229, 358, 377–8. For the influence of "Commonwealth" ideas descending from the seventeenth century, see Bernard Bailyn, *Ideological Origins of the American Revolution* (Cambridge, Mass., 1967).

Chapter Two

The Meanings of a
Self-Evident Truth

English Common Law as Carrier
of Egalitarian Principle

The American Revolution introduced an egalitarian rhetoric to an unequal society. The culminating expression of egalitarian sentiments, through which they were most brilliantly transmitted to succeeding generations, resulted from the literary craft of Thomas Jefferson, who was invited to compose the Declaration of Independence because of the "peculiar felicity of expression" which characterised his writings.[1] In a society that recognised sharp—and often keenly felt—differences in wealth, rank, and esteem, one effect of this rhetoric was to compel the people of different colonies to direct their thoughts to their own social inequalities and to the politics which reflected them. These impulses of conscience and considerations of theory brought consequences in ideology, law, and social relations which many of the Revolution's progenitors could not foresee, and did not always approve; in a strong sense, the egalitarian consequences were the very substance of the Revolution. Yet their ultimate reach was muted and restrained by the sources from which they had sprung. The Declaration's resounding preamble conveyed different meanings to different minds. It won its widest appeal as romance, as the glancing flash of a bright illusion. The illusion of

1. Charles Francis Adams, ed., *Works of John Adams* (Boston, 1850), II, 514.

equality among all people, capable of attainment and translation into the everyday life of political institutions, economic policies, and personal relations, was thenceforth to remain as one of the most vital and magnetic forces in American life—a source of constantly renewed hope and repeatedly embittered disappointment. But the men who subscribed to the Declaration in 1776 did not feel themselves thereby mandated to transform American life. Many no doubt saw the vision and for awhile were uplifted by it; but the majority were probably more interested in the Declaration's long catalogue of grievances and in the legal and moral arguments by which the Continental Congress justified American resistance to British authority. These arguments, which had brought them to the point of independence, would have convinced them of the justice of their cause even if a different hand had written a different preamble.

From the beginning of the colonial argument, the American case rested on the assumption that Britain's colonial subjects had rights and privileges identical with those at home. But when Americans began to grasp the fact that the British, whom they regarded not as their masters but as fellow subjects, were systematically treating them as unequals, they recognized the corollary that differences did exist between the colonies and the home country in fact if not in constitutional status. This difference of fact gave rise to the need for assertions of equality. The rights in respect of which the inhabitants of the colonies claimed equal treatment were rights which they believed their forebears had carried with them and which they themselves had inherited, continuing to be as fully protected by the British constitution as those who remained in Britain. The Glorious Revolution of 1688–1689 had made all this so clear that no argument seemed to be required—which helps to explain why many colonials quickly came to suspect the British of bad faith.

British taxation policies following the end of the wars in 1763 aroused controversy that turned on fundamentals of constitutional law. But from an early stage there were colonial spokesmen who held that even the British constitution was inferior to the ultimate authority of natural law. This thesis seemed of very slight importance, however, because Americans generally considered themselves happy in living under the protection of the British constitution and common law which embodied all the sanctions required by just government, owing their validity to the fact that they actually protected and enforced the rights derived from the laws of nature. James Otis, whose pamphlets gained early celebrity from their learning as well as their expository power, was not attracted by the appeal to natural law: "The truth is . . . men come into the world and into society at the same instant," he observed. Thus the idea of a state of nature could be used to illustrate and explain natural and original rights, but Americans lived under civil law—and it was civil law to which they should attend.[2] Any question of what would happen if English law departed from natural law simply did not arise; the whole crisis had been created by British measures which violated precepts of constitutional and common law. Otis thus significantly dismissed even such great continental jurists as Grotius and Pufendorf and preferred to draw his opinions from "our English writers, particularly from Mr *Locke*, to whom might be added a *few* of other nations . . .".[3] The importance of equality in this argument was not diminished by the fact that it was restricted to specific counts in a lawyer's brief. The really natural thing about Americans' rights was not that they descended from God-given laws of nature, but that they belonged to Americans because they were true-born or "natural-born" Englishmen; and in making this assertion the colonial spokesmen claimed all they needed about doctrines of equality. The connection was clearly explained by the learned Virginian lawyer Richard Bland: "I am speaking of the *rights* of a people: *rights* imply *equality*, in the instances to which they belong. . . . By what right is it, that parliament can exercise such a power over the colonies, who have as natural a right to the privileges and liberties of Englishmen, as if they were actually resident within the Kingdom?"[4]

In the first instance it was by virtue of the deprivation of common law rights that Americans were made conscious of the problem of inequality. So clear were the principles involved that future loy-

2. James Otis, *The Rights of the British Colonies Asserted and Proved* (Boston, 1764), in Bernard Bailyn, ed., *Pamphlets of the American Revolution* (Cambridge, Mass., 1965), I, 438–9.
3. Ibid., I, 436–7.
4. Richard Bland, *An Enquiry into the Rights of the British Colonies* (Williamsburg, Va., 1769).

alists concurred with future whigs in holding that English common law was crucial to their rights.[5] The common law, though respectable in its antiquity, was diffuse in substance. Its name derived from its origin as the law that was common to the whole kingdom of England in the twelfth century when Henry II strove to extend royal authority throughout his realms at the assizes of Clarendon in 1166 and Northampton in 1176.[6] Common law was case law; it developed from precedent to precedent and by extrapolation from case to case. Its principles were thus independent of statutes, though statute law could occupy ground held by common law. Statutes had power to abrogate common law precedents, but when this happened the tendency of the courts was to treat the statute in question as an exception, and if any choice were left to them the courts would be unlikely to reinterpret related common law cases in the light of such a statute. The common law was a fundamental part of the English constitution, which is why James Otis could argue that it was superior to and could control statute law.[7] This point would have been more accurately stated as an ability to interpret rather than as a power to control; but most jurists would have agreed that the constitution existed not only that the monarch should reign in his realm but also that the common law rights of his subjects should be protected. The most prominent colonial grievance, taxation without representation, displayed this continuity of principle between constitution and common law. Taxes were voted in Parliament, where the colonies sent

5. For example, Daniel Dulany, *Considerations on the Propriety of Imposing Taxes in the Colonies* (1765), in Bailyn, *Pamphlets*, I, 638; Martin Howard, Jr., *Letter from a Gentleman at Halifax* (Newport, R.I., 1765), in Bailyn, *Pamphlets* I, 532–44, and Otis, *Rights*, in Bailyn, *Pamphlets*, I, 452; Bailyn's comment, ibid., I, 409.

6. William Stubbs, *The Constitutional History of England* (Oxford, 1903), I, 505–12; F. W. Maitland, *Constitutional History of England* (Cambridge, 1919), pp. 22–3; G. D. Sayles, *Medieval Foundations of England* (London, 1948), p. 343. Mark De Wolfe Howe has argued that the common law in which Americans found their rights was spurious: "Building upon legend which Coke had dignified with spurious annotation and English Puritans had sanctified with pious pedantry, the Americans discovered that the rights that really mattered to them had their roots in common law." See his essay in A. L. Goodhart, ed., *The Migration of the Common Law* (London, 1960). He then attacks "the Jeffersonian myth of the common law as Saxon, desecrated by successive parliaments and kings". But common law defences of the liberty and property of the subject were very much alive, as this chapter will show; and what mattered was not the antiquity but the legality of these defences.

7. Otis, in Bailyn, *Pamphlets*, I, pp. 449–50.

no representatives; but a man's right to his own property was common law right, from which it followed that only the owner or his appointed deputy could grant any portion of it to the king.

The first serious challenge to colonial equality in common law rights arose in Massachusetts before anything was heard of parliamentary taxation. It was not planned in Britain, and had only a remote connection with any aspect of British policy towards the colonies; yet for largely accidental reasons, the course of the dispute brought vividly to light the differences between common law practices in Britain and the colonies. The trouble began over the so-called writs of assistance, which were issued at the request of customs officers as a legal form of protection against lawsuits or direct resistance incurred when their very unpopular duties led them to enter and inspect warehouses, stores, or even private homes. These writs, which since 1757 had been issued by the Superior Court of Massachusetts, were not returnable to the Court after the execution of a specified task but remained in force throughout the lifetime of the reigning monarch. Officers armed with them thus had alarming powers, which merchants resented as a threat to their privacy and security. The writ, in fact, closely resembled a general warrant, under whose authority the king's messengers had powers to search and examine anything that they found in a suspected person's house. The question of legality of writs of assistance was tested and affirmed in Massachusetts, with only marginal reference to the Crown; that of general warrants, however, was brought before the English Court of Common Pleas only a short time afterwards and with strikingly different results.

All things done in the king's name, including legislative assemblies summoned and writs issued, came to an end within six months of the reigning monarch's death; when George II died in 1759, the Boston merchants seized their opportunity, briefed James Otis, Jr., and Oxenbridge Thacher to represent them, and filed a suit before Chief Justice Thomas Hutchinson to stop the renewed issue of the detested writs in the new reign. The two lawyers denounced the writs as grants of unlimited power over people's homes. The common law principle that an Englishman's home is his castle was no mere cliché but an article of the case, as was soon to be powerfully proved in England; and Thacher argued further that by act of Parliament, only the English Court of Exchequer had the power to issue this kind of writ. Hence the Massachusetts Superior Court, a subordinate body, could not do it. According to John Adams's oft-quoted report, written out some time after the hearings, Otis proceeded to a fiery denunciation of these tyrannical powers; he admitted that the old books gave certain precedents for general warrants, but "in more modern books you will find only special warrants to search such and such houses specially named, in which the complainant has before sworn that he suspects his goods are concealed; and you will find it adjudged that special warrants only are legal". The general nature of the writ was precisely what made it illegal. Otis went further to declare, as he was to do in later pamphlets, that an act against the constitution was void; officers of the plantations were under the same limits as those at home.[8]

Hutchinson, although new to the bench, was well informed in these matters, for it was he who as lieutenant governor in 1757 had been instrumental in preventing the governor from issuing these writs on his own authority, with the result that the power was lodged in the Superior Court acting as a local court of exchequer. Hutchinson knew that general warrants were in use in England, that they had been issued previously to eight customs officers in Massachusetts, and that there was no issue of legal substance to decide.[9] He prevailed on the bench to defer a decision until the province's agent in London, William Bollan, could be consulted on English practice, after which the Superior Court again issued writs of assistance late in 1761.[10] That comparable events were about to take place in England was due to different circumstances having no connection with New England; but the colonists were bound to be impressed by the similarities of the attitudes of the ministry and its officers in both cases, and by the profound dissimilarity of the outcomes.

In 1762 John Wilkes, who had earlier purchased a parliamentary seat at Aylesbury, began to publish a satirical paper, *The North*

8. Lyman H. Butterfield, ed., *The Adams Papers: Diary and Autobiography of John Adams* (Cambridge, Mass., 1961), I, 211–12; Works, II, 124; Nelson B. Lasson, *The History and Development of the Fourth Amendment*, Johns Hopkins University Studies, LV, no. 2 (Baltimore, 1937), pp. 55–7.

9. Bernard Bailyn, *The Ordeal of Thomas Hutchinson* (Cambridge, Mass., 1974), pp. 54–6.

10. Lasson, *Fourth Amendment*, pp. 59–63.

Briton, in which he excited London society by his attacks on the court and the ministry. Number Forty-Five, on 23 April 1763, denounced a passage in the King's speech as a falsehood and alleged that it had been written by the unpopular Earl of Bute. The ministry decided to prosecute for sedition, and the Earl of Halifax, secretary of state for the Southern department, acting in magisterial capacity, issued a general warrant "to make strict and diligent search for the authors, printers and publishers of a seditious and treasonable paper entitled, The North Briton, No. 45 ... and them, or any of them, to apprehend and seize, together with their papers". No one was named, but in three days forty-nine persons including the journeymen printers, were arrested. While Wilkes himself was under arrest in the Tower, his papers were rifled by Robert Wood, Lord Halifax's secretary.[11] Within a fortnight Wilkes appeared to sue for damages in the Court of Common Pleas. The resulting case of *Wilkes* v. *Wood*, better known as the *Case of General Warrants*, led to a celebrated vindication of the liberties of the subject against the powers of the state.

Fortuitous circumstances had brought about judicial trials of similar principles in Boston and Westminster. But Sir Charles Pratt, Chief Justice of the Common Pleas—who had formerly served as attorney general under Pitt—had no doubts as to the principles at stake, and was quick to recognise them in the American colonies; from the Stamp Act down to Independence, he remained the best British friend of the American cause. In 1766, recently elevated to the peerage by the Rockingham ministry and known since then as Lord Chief Justice Camden, he used his seat in the House of Lords to denounce the Declaratory Act (which declared the power of Parliament to legislate for the colonies "in all cases whatsoever") as a bill, "the very existence of which is illegal, absolutely illegal, contrary to the fundamental laws of nature, contrary to the fundamental laws of this kingdom".[12] American newspapers enthusiastically reported Camden's speeches in their defence; in 1774 it was reported that in the debate on the Boston Port bill "Lord Camden exerted himself nobly in the House of Lords".[13] In the summer of 1775 he was re-

11. Ibid., p. 43.
12. Rind's *Virginia Gazette*, 4 February 1768.
13. Purdie and Dixon's *Virginia Gazette*, 9 June 1774.

corded as defending the Americans on the principles of the Revolution—meaning of course that of 1688. "To say that no violation of charters, no infraction of civil compacts, no erasure of rights would justify resistance, was to give up the cause of the revolution," he told the Lords, and concluded, "As an Englishman I cannot wish harm to my mother country; but I wish most sincerely that the Americans may *preserve their liberty*".[14]

Wilkes's case and the allied case of *Entick* v. *Carrington*, which arose from a search of the publisher John Entick's papers by a king's messenger, Nathan Carrington, on a warrant which named the person but not the specific papers, presented the courts with a rare opportunity to declare fundamental principles protecting the rights of British subjects. Reviewing the powers of search and seizure claimed by the Secretary of State, Chief Justice Pratt held in *Wilkes* that "If such a power is truly invested in a Secretary of State, and he can delegate this power, it may certainly affect the person and property of every man in this kingdom, and is totally subversive of the liberty of the subject".[15] Wilkes was awarded £1,000 damages, the journeyman printers received from £200 to £300 for their lesser injuries, and the administration was notably humiliated. When *Entick* v. *Carrington* came on two years later the newly elevated Lord Chief Justice, grounding himself firmly in the common law of England, administered an even more resounding rebuke to the former administration. He remarked at one point in his judgment that he could have wished on this occasion that the Revolution had not been considered the only basis for English liberties—the point being that the Revolution had merely restored the Constitution to its original principles. It was the books of common law that held the key: "If it be law, it will be found in our books. If it is not to be found there, it is not law". The Licensing Act of Charles II had been allowed to lapse; there was therefore no statutory authority for the power of censorship before publication, or of search to prevent publication. "And with respect to the argument of state necessity, or a distinction that has been aimed at between state offences and others, the common law does not understand that kind of reasoning, nor do our books take notice

14. Dixon and Hunter's *Virginia Gazette*, 10 June 1775.
15. T. B. Howell, ed., *State Trials*, (London, 1816), XIX, 1159 ff.

of any such distinctions".[16] The administration, appealing from the Common Pleas, could find no more comfort even from the King's Bench, where Lord Chief Justice Mansfield, who did not share Camden's taste for rhetoric, agreed with him as to the law. In fact he held so strongly that general warrants were illegal that when the House of Commons itself passed a resolution to that effect Lord Mansfield, speaking in the Lords, remarked that if Parliament could declare general warrants illegal it could presumably declare them legal, but he would hold them to be illegal whatever either House of Parliament might say![17]

It was Camden whose judgments read like political manifestoes to the liberty of Britons. Toasts were drunk, the freedom of cities conferred, portraits painted (Dr Johnson even wrote an inscription for one of them) and—a significant mark of public favour—taverns were named after him. In 1766 Chatham made him Lord Chancellor, an office he held until 1770, when he proved incompatible with Lord North's administration.[18]

The Wilkes affair was closely followed in the American colonies, and many of his other adventures were reported in the colonial press. Reports arriving from England were first printed in the seaport newspapers and then reprinted verbatim in other parts of the colonies. The importance of Camden's part in these events, and in his opposition to the Stamp Act, was not lost on Americans, who drank his health in many celebrations when the Stamp Act was repealed; the newspapers carried frequent favourable references to his conduct and principles. Perhaps even more significant of American favour was the naming of towns and counties, which still bear testimony to America's gratitude to the great English Whig judge.[19]

16. Ibid., XIX, 1038–73.

17. Sir Charles Grant Robertson, *Select Statutes, Cases and Documents* (London, 1947), p. 455.

18. *Dictionary of National Biography* (London, 1896), XLVI, 285–8.

19. Colonial newspapers in which these events were relayed to American readers included the *Connecticut Courant, New York Gazette, New York Mercury, Boston Gazette, Massachusetts Gazette, South Carolina Gazette*, and the several versions of the *Virginia Gazette*, to name only a few. John Wilkes and Isaac Barré had their names linked in a town in Pennsylvania, an association which drew disapproval from Namier, who felt that Barré's reputation deserved better treatment. L. B. Namier, *England in the Age of the American Revolution* (London, 1930), p. 263, n. 2.

The decisions making general warrants illegal in England had important implications for the colonies. In October 1766 the British attorney general, William De Grey, advised the customs commissioners to use a strict construction of the statute of William III under which they had been entering houses and warehouses, by which he meant that they must conduct their searches with great restraint. The obvious inference was that many recent searches and seizures might prove to have been illegal; but when the House of Commons condemned general warrants it excepted such cases as might be provided for by act of Parliament, thus giving itself freedom of action of which it soon took advantage. In 1767 Parliament passed the Townshend Act, which not only imposed a new round of tariffs on imports into the colonies, but formally legalised the American writs of assistance and designated the superior court of each province as the court of issue. Nothing could have more forcibly demonstrated to Americans that in Parliament's view they did not share equally in the rights and privileges which protected the liberties and properties of Englishmen at home.[20]

The Townshend Act caused acute difficulties for American judges. If, as Otis held, the common law could control statute law—and if, as even Lord Mansfield had said, general warrants were illegal despite the resolutions of Parliament—then the law itself was doubtful;[21] but so, unfortunately, might be the future of a judge who defied the laws of Parliament. American judges, with some exceptions, faced these difficulties with remarkable consistency and determination. One of the exceptions was in South Carolina, where after some years of resistance the judges gave way, as late as April 1773, to the demand to issue writs of assistance—though it is not known whether the court there was persuaded by legal argument or political pressure. Customs collectors started to make requests to the courts in 1768 and repeated them in face of a steady, if often anxious, series of rejections by the bench. In nine colonies—including Florida—the judges considered and refused these requests despite English pressure, to which De Grey added the force of his own au-

20. Lasson, Fourth Amendment, p. 65, n. 50.
21. Mansfield, however, was speaking of declarations or resolutions of either House of Parliament; his observation would probably yield to statute. Many American judges ignored this distinction in order to deny the legality of the writs.

thority. The answer of Chief Justice William Allen of Pennsylvania to John Swift, collector of the port of Philadelphia, gains weight from the fact that Allen later remained loyal to the crown: "Though my duty and my inclination would lead me to do everything in my power to promote the King's service, yet I conceive that I am not warranted by Law to issue any such Warrant", he wrote. Unsure of his own opinion, he had consulted the attorney general and another eminent lawyer, "who both concur with me in opinion that such a general writ as you have demanded is not agreeable to Law".[22] The issue was pressed hardest by the crown in Virginia in 1769 and again in 1772 and 1773, but the court firmly refused to grant the writs, and intimated on the final occasion that it did not wish to hear of them again. In Connecticut Judge Trumbull consulted judges in other colonies before giving an opinion, and it seems likely that this correspondence was intended to concert colonial resistance.[23]

The personal right of freedom from official powers of search and seizure continued to be of central importance throughout the revolutionary and constitutional periods. The invidious distinction between Englishmen and Americans in respect of these rights was a theme of number IX of John Dickinson's *Letters from a Farmer in Pennsylvania*,[24] probably the most influential publication on colonial rights before 1776. A formal safeguard against such violations of private property became common form in the new state constitutions. Virginia adopted such a provision in 1776; it was copied exactly by Pennsylvania and included by Massachusetts in the Constitution of 1780.[25] When Patrick Henry opposed the ratification of the Federal Constitution by Virginia he specifically attacked the omission of a safeguard against general warrants, particularly fatal in a vast country with "no judge within a thousand miles to issue a writ of habeas corpus".[26] The conclusion of the story of general warrants—until

22. O. M. Dickerson, "Writs of Assistance as a Cause of the American Revolution", in Richard B. Morris, ed., *The Era of the American Revolution* (New York, 1939; repr. 1965), pp. 40–75. Grant Robertson, *Select Statutes*, pp. 454–5.
23. Dickerson, "Writs", p. 59.
24. Purdie and Dixon's *Virginia Gazette*, 10 March 1768.
25. J. R. Pole, ed., *The Revolution in America: Documents on the Internal Development of America in the Revolutionary Era* (London, 1970), pp. 482, 520 (Virginia, in which "general warrants" are mentioned), 531.
26. Hugh Blair Grigsby, *The History of the Virginia Federal Convention of 1788* (Richmond, 1890), I, 308.

new questions of police powers arose to perplex a free society in the twentieth century—was written into the federal constitution with the adoption of the Fourth Amendment, forbidding "unreasonable searches and seizures" and guaranteeing security to people in their own homes. It may fairly be said that this amendment virtually enacts Lord Camden's opinions as the supreme law of the land.

Inequality in respect of common law rights made an even more dramatic invasion of colonial shores when the British Revenue Act of 1764 established a new vice-admiralty court, not as it happened in the old colonies but at Halifax. Vice-admiralty jurisdiction had first been established in the colonies by the Navigation Act of 1696; these courts, equipped to deal with technical questions of marine law, were popular with British merchants, who did not wish to submit themselves to the interminable complexities of common law in disputes that arose over their transactions. But they sat without juries. In the atmosphere generated by mounting controversy over parliamentary taxation, Americans were quick to perceive that in the extension to their provinces of a judiciary that dispensed with that ancient English principle, the British government was unfolding its plans to reduce them to slavery. Trial without juries was not a procedure from which many Americans suffered serious inconvenience or injustice. It attracted attention, however, on certain notorious occasions; through the winter of 1768–1769, the vice-admiralty court trial of John Hancock for the illegal unloading of his sloop *Liberty* gained public acclaim for him and for the cause for which his vessel was named. John Adams, Hancock's counsel, added to the political tenour of the case by telling the court that his client had never consented to the laws imposing the duties which he was alleged to have tried to evade—and this was yet another case of the unequal treatment from which the Americans suffered.[27]

Only civil cases would be heard by the vice-admiralty courts; but a much more serious threat appeared after the angry altercations in 1768 between the Massachusetts assembly and the governor, when the Duke of Bedford introduced into the House of Lords a resolution proposing that Americans be made liable to be removed to England

27. Carl Ubbelohde, *The Vice-Admiralty Courts and the American Revolution* (Chapel Hill, 1960), pp. 15, 63, 64, 72–4, 90, 94; chap. 7; pp. 208–9. *Diary of John Adams* in *Works*, II, 215–16.

for trial under the statute of treasons dating to the reign of Henry VIII.[28] This threat was never translated into action. But it was periodically discussed, and it aroused the most bitter resentment among Americans, many of whom became convinced that it was part of the malevolent designs of British administrations; every petition from that time forth and almost every attack on British policy included a reference to the impending deprivation of that most inestimable of English privileges, the right to trial by a jury of one's peers, drawn from the vicinity. Since Americans could not be persuaded to accept the absolute supremacy of Parliament over all matters touching their lives and fortunes, and since their remonstrances constantly implied the risk of violence, the mere mention of treason was to be taken seriously. When colonial lawyers, planters, merchants, and editors heard that the British government contemplated seizing its victims, transporting them to England, and trying them for their lives, they became convinced that they were being treated not as freeborn Englishmen but as inferiors and slaves.

British provocations increasingly pricked colonial writers into making this bitter comparison of their own condition with that of slavery. The word itself came to be widely used in colonial protests. But this somewhat hyperbolic language had its repercussions: Americans had only to look about them to take their own black slaves as their point of comparison, whose loss of natural liberty was founded on a condition of total, permanent, and irremediable state of inequality. When Americans later gained their national liberty they coped in different ways, reflecting in each case an interplay between conscience and interest, with the crisis of conscience which these observations frequently brought about. Some became convinced emancipationists; many more felt worried but helpless; but others, notably in the Southern states, were entirely satisfied—for reasons resting on their own reading of the Lockeian contract—that slaves and their descendants had never been parties to the contractual system and that the rights due to English subjects did not extend to them. But this accentuated awareness of the horror of slavery thenceforth served to emphasise the contrasting importance of the equality of those who were within the political community, an idea which never

28. T. B. Hansard, *Parliamentary History of England* (London, 1813), XVI, 479–80, 494–5, 510.

completely lost its grip on the American sense of political justice.[29] The quarrel between Britain and her colonies raised the ultimate question of sovereignty. In theory, Americans could have exchanged sovereigns without recourse to any theory of equality beyond that which gave them the right to overthrow a king who had broken his contract with the people. It was because of the issues on which this quarrel turned that equal rights were forced into the public mind. If the argument had not broken out as it did and had not taken the course that it did—if, for example, the British had modified their policies in the light of better information and more conciliatory attitudes at an earlier date—there is no reason to suppose that any great declarations of egalitarian principle would have emanated from America, or that any more definitive formulations of egalitarian theory would have been attempted there than in other countries of the Western world in the Age of the Enlightenment. Yet when such formulations of principle did emanate from American declarations, from state constitutions, and the public statements of private individuals, they gained credibility because of their affinity with familiar sentiments, and because they reflected attitudes in which many Americans took pride. This paradox had its origins in the confused and contradictory conditions of late colonial society and that society's relationship to its own political ideas.

A Flattering Mirror:
The Self-Image of a Mixed Society

Colonial Americans, like most other people, were ready to believe the best of themselves. The best, in an opinion widely shared throughout the colonies, was represented by the idea and practice of equality. The note was easy to catch, and William Eddis, a well-connected young Englishman living in Maryland, reflected it when he concluded a letter in early 1772 by saying, "An idea of equality seems generally to prevail, and the inferior order of people pay little but external respect to those who occupy superior stations".[30] If he had travelled more widely he could have found strikingly similar

29. Duncan J. MacLeod, *Slavery, Race and the American Revolution* (Cambridge, 1974), pp. 14–31.
30. William Eddis, *Letters from America*, ed. Aubrey C. Land (Cambridge, Mass., 1969), p. 65.

expressions in use in all the provinces to the north and to a lesser extent in those to the south; but closer enquiry would have revealed that they did not always mean the same things.

Late colonial America was a nest of paradoxes. The romantic French sojourner J. Hector St Jean de Crèvecoeur conveyed a vivid and beautifully written impression of a free, prosperous, and tolerant society by dwelling mainly—though not by any means exclusively— on those characteristics which appealed most forcibly to his own imagination and which constituted what he most wished to believe to be true of the whole.[31] Crèvecoeur's description drew generously from two observations that were to be of continuing importance for American political thought. In his opinion the mixture of peoples, already a distinguishing feature of American society, was producing a new and distinctive type, a "new man"; and among these new men there prevailed a high degree of economic and social equality. Enjoying their own freedom, they treated one another with amity and respect. The vision anticipated Israel Zangwill's "melting pot" of the early twentieth century, and was based on the same implicit theory. This new society of equals was in important respects of mind, aim, and character a homogeneous society; and its homogeneity was a necessary condition of equality.

The first condition for this and the other glowing portraits reported by visitors and exulted in by Americans was the fact that certain elemental needs were generally supplied more fully by the economy of the colonies than by those of the Old World. Very few people starved in America. In the countryside food was generally plentiful, and the marketplaces of the towns were never far from the countryside. Farms of different sizes throughout New England, New York, and Pennsylvania yielded a wide range of produce, and while they afforded their owners or tenants substantial differences of personal wealth, they gave a livelihood to all who worked on them. Most New England towns did their best to maintain a version of the old English poor law restrictions to keep vagrants and unsupported people out of the town limits; they voted funds to relieve unmerited distress among their inhabitants, but offered no external charities, and saw little poverty. This policy of the country towns may help to

31. Crèvecoeur, Michel Guillaume, called St. John de, *Letters from an American Farmer* (London, 1908).

explain the sharp rise in the statistics of poor people in Boston, whose much larger, more mixed, and fluid population included a sector virtually without property whose proportion increased fourfold between 1687 and 1771 while the city's population only doubled; on the eve of the Revolution no less than 29 percent were too poor to be taxed.[32] These figures probably show that Boston was unlike other towns, but if that is true they also show that Boston was collecting a poor population that other towns could not accommodate. The prosperity and rapid economic changes brought about by the War of Independence do not seem to have altered this urban aspect of the situation for the better; philanthropic societies multiplied in postwar years and acted as agencies through which wealthier citizens could direct their resources to the relief of the persistent problems of poverty and distress. These needs caused widespread and constant calls on public policy and private charity.[33]

These conditions never appeared to reporters of the American scene as typical, however. Americans liked to see their social image depicted in the style which foreign observers and British officials reported with often more mixed feelings. The cheerful prosperity, simple but robust health, and equally robust self-respect of ordinary people, their lack of servility, and their sense of responsibility were features on which Americans were pleased to dwell. Twenty years before independence the Philadelphia Presbyterian leader, the Reverend Francis Allison, told his congregation of the virtues of equality in a sermon which also seemed to suggest that some of these condi-

32. James A. Henretta, "Economic Development and Social Structure in Colonial Boston", *William & Mary Quarterly*, 3rd ser., XXII (1 January 1965), 75–92.

33. Allan Kulikoff, "The Progress of Inequality in Revolutionary Boston", *William & Mary Quarterly*, XVIII (3 July 1971), 376; Raymond A. Mohl, *Poverty in New York, 1783–1825* (New York, 1971), passim. The evidence for social and economic stratification remains subject to debate, and differs in value as between different cities and between city and countryside. See Gary B. Nash, "Urban Wealth and Poverty in Pre-Revolutionary America"; G. B. Warden, "Inequality and Instability in Eighteenth Century Boston: A Reappraisal"; Jacob M. Price, "Quantifying Colonial America: A Comment on Nash and Warden", all in *Journal of Interdisciplinary History*, vi:4 (Spring, 1976). None of this seems to me likely to detract from the argument that differences were increasingly conspicuous and correspondingly resented by the classes who felt themselves disadvantaged by the trend, though I think the evidence does also suggest that this trend was much more acute in Philadelphia and New York than in Boston. For further comment, see citations under notes 54 and 55.

tions remained to be fulfilled: He wanted "equal laws, equally executed", for all were equally entitled to protection, to reap the benefit of honest industry, with equal access to public honours and places of profit and trust according to their abilities and qualifications to serve the public. Equal rights and privileges went with equal burdens.[34] There was a warning here that privileges were not to be taken for granted or abused. But Americans liked to hear that they had already achieved the principal characteristics of an equal society. In 1772 the Anglican cleric, the Reverend Jacob Duché, declared in a sermon in Philadelphia that "the poorest labourer upon the shore of the Delaware thinks himself entitled to deliver his sentiments in matters of religion and politics with as much freedom as the gentleman and the scholar. Indeed, there is less distinction among the citizens of Philadelphia, than among those of any civilized city in the world. Riches give none. For every man expects one day to be on a footing with his wealthiest neighbour".[35] However much truth there may have been in this observation, it was clearly the sort of thing that his parishioners liked to believe, and Duché, who later became pro-British when royal troops occupied the city, was probably a good weathervane, if not the most penetrating of social analysts. Not everyone in Philadelphia was quite so easily satisfied. As late as the April elections of 1776, a contributor to the *Pennsylvania Evening Post* remarked sarcastically, "A poor man has rarely the honor of speaking to a gentleman on any terms, and never with familiarity but for a few weeks before the election. How many poor men, common men and mechanics, have been made happy within this fortnight by a shake of the hand, a pleasing smile, and a little familiar chat with gentlemen who have not for these seven years past condescended to look at them. Blessed state that brings all so nearly on a level! In a word, electioneering and aristocratical pride are incompatible".[36]

Quotations such as these from either side of the question prove nothing about the actual distribution of wealth or opportunity; but even the complacent remarks of Duché reveal the existence of wide

34. Francis Allison MSS, Presbyterian Historical Society, Philadelphia; Sermons, Folder 5, V: 1756.
35. Daniel J. Boorstin, *The Americans: The Colonial Experience* (Harmondsworth, 1965), p. 349.
36. *Pennsylvania Evening Post*, 27 April 1776.

social and economic divisions accompanied by understood distances of rank and approachability. The important and characteristically American feature of these distinctions seems to have been that although inferior classes existed, they were not denied all possibility of self-respect; in fact their more politically alert representatives resented the assumed grandeurs of the gentry with a social consciousness that sprang directly from their American background: "Is not half the property in the city of Philadelphia owned by men who wear LEATHERN APRONS?" demanded a writer in another of the city papers; "Does not the other half belong to men whose fathers or grandfathers wore LEATHERN APRONS?"[37] The possibility that correct answers to these questions might have been negative hardly matters: The questions could be asked, and contributed to the rise of the spirit that made possible the internal revolution in Pennsylvania.

Farther south, the great landowner and slaveowner George Mason of Virginia made his own contribution to the mystique of American equality with his "Remarks on Annual Elections to the Fairfax Independent Company", seemingly written in April 1775 about the local defence organisation.[38] "Upon this generous and public-spirited plan", Mason observed with satisfaction, "gentlemen of the first fortune and character among us have become members of the Fairfax Independent Company, have submitted to stand in the ranks of common soldiers, and to pay due obedience to officers of their own choice". This company, limited to not more than one hundred members, was formed at a meeting of "a Number of Gentlemen and Freeholders of Fairfax County" with Mason himself in the chair; they were not subjecting themselves to much risk of taking orders from the common people, and it seems exceedingly likely that the gentlemen chose officers of appropriate rank. Mason's memorandum contains the famous statement, "We came equals into this world and equals we shall go out of it," which carries a distant echo from Ecclesiastes, but does not preclude all possibility that we might become unequal at some point between these salient events. His political principles were consistently republican throughout his life, but his pride in equality was that of a republican aristocrat.

37. *Pennsylvania Packet*, 18 March 1776.
38. *The Papers of George Mason, 1725–1792*, ed. Robert A. Rutland (Chapel Hill, 1970), I, 229.

Concepts of social rank appeared much more clearly when the Congress took up the task of fixing the scales of soldiers' pay. Feelings on this issue exposed the differences, not only between social classes, but still more keenly between New England and the South. Under strong pressure from the Southern magnates, the Congress determined on steep differentials between the ranks, marked by an unmistakably Old World notion of the difference between a commissioned officer and the common soldier. There is nothing more revealing about a society than the way it organises its armed forces. New England delegates were well aware of the hostility these rates of pay would arouse at home. "The pay which has been voted to all the officers, which the Continental Congress intends to choose, is so large, that I fear our people will think it extravagant, and be uneasy," wrote John Adams from Philadelphia as soon as the decisions had been taken; and added, "Those ideas of equality, which are so agreeable to us natives of New England, are very disagreeable to many gentlemen in the other colonies. . . . They think the Massachusetts establishment too high for the privates, and too low for the officers, and they would have their own way. . .".[39] Public opinion was indeed hostile in New England, and in November 1775 Adams again explained the difficulties to an influential correspondent at home. Joseph Hawley had warned him that there would be no winter army unless more was done to encourage the privates. The New England delegates were only too well aware of the problem but, as John Adams wrote, "We cannot suddenly alter the temper, principles, opinions, or prejudices of men. The characters of gentlemen in the four New England colonies, differ as much from those in the others as that of the common people differs; that is, as much as several distinct nations almost. Gentlemen, men of sense or any kind of education, in the other colonies, are much fewer in proportion than in New England. . . . Gentlemen in other colonies have large plantations of slaves, and the common people among them are very ignorant and very poor. These gentlemen are habituated to higher notions of themselves, and the distinction between them and the common people, than we are".[40]

39. Edmund C. Burnett, Letters of the Continental Congress (Washington, D.C., 1921), I, 136.
40. Ibid., I, 259–60.

These remarks left plenty of room for real differences between gentlemen and common people even in New England; Adams was well aware of such distinctions. They also reflected a somewhat high-minded and puritanical sense of the superiority of New England's ways of life. But the basic evidence on which they rested was firm enough. Southern gentlemen did insist on high pay and a high style for the officers; New Englanders resented the process of building consciousness of social rank into the conditions of military service and seriously feared that their farmers and common men would refuse to serve under such conditions. Washington's unflattering opinion of the Massachusetts soldiery under his command in the autumn of 1775 confirmed both sides in their prejudices.[41]

Where, as in Philadelphia, resentful consciousness of class distinctions occurred, it was obvious evidence of economic mobility; but not that the opportunities presented by such mobility were fairly or evenly distributed, or that they were tending towards greater equality. Throughout most of the northern provinces, a substantial class of comfortable property owners gave society its characteristic features of stability based on personal independence; the small proportion of owners of very large estates and fortunes did not constitute a dominating aristocracy. Yet the comparatively broad distribution of successful farmers, merchants, and artisans in no way alleviated and may have added to the difficulties of the still considerable numbers of the genuinely poor. As much as one-fourth or one-fifth of the population of Massachusetts had little beyond immediate personal belongings, and when indentured servants are included—as they properly should be—the proportions of the poor in the North as a whole rose to nearly one-third of the white population.[42] The more prosperous a farming society was, the more likely it was to carry a large population of landless agricultural labourers, as was the case in some of the richest counties of New Jersey.[43] William Eddis, who noted the preoccupation of Maryland people

41. And of the numerous men who deserted or failed to enlist: Even Ramsay's discreet narrative fails to conceal the ill-feeling. David Ramsay, M.D., *The Life of George Washington* (London, 1807), chap. 2.
42. Jackson Turner Main, *The Social Structure of Revolutionary America* (Princeton, 1965), pp. 41–2.
43. Ibid., p. 33.

with "an idea of equality", also commented with distress on the wretched conditions of the servants, and assured his correspondent that their situation was no better than in Britain. The traffic in indentured servants and the treatment they received shocked him.[44] Eddis had entered a society of widely differing fortunes, but his own social surroundings generally concealed from him the narrow circumstances in which the majority of Maryland planters got their subsistence from the soil and the livestock on it. Some 60 percent of them, with estates of £100 or less, had only enough income from them to support the cruder necessities of life.[45] In Virginia about a quarter of the white male population possessed no land and little personal property; when the slave population is added, however, the proportions rise to 40 percent. In the richer parishes of South Carolina, the inclusion of slaves in the ranks of unpropertied labourers brings their proportions up to nearly 90 percent.[46]

It is a popular but profound error to disregard the slave population when estimating the success with which white society solved the problems of combining economic subsistence with representative government. The free sector of society could never have achieved its way of life without the support of the unfree; to appreciate the force of this point it should only be necessary to consider the possibilities that would have been open to white ambitions if black labour had been unavailable. In all probability a much more massive unfree or limited service labour force would have been drafted into the plantation colonies from the ranks of white convicts and other social outcasts—in which case the planters' privileges would unmistakably have rested on the labour of landless workers with small hope of advancement for themselves or their children. Such a society would probably not have appeared to later generations—even perhaps to itself—as such a conspicuous example of the satisfactory operation of republican, still less of democratic principles. Even Jefferson would hardly have advocated giving freehold land with voting rights to the mass of landless labourers on whose toil depended the upkeep of the entire plantation economy. It was not the nature of the agri-

44. Eddis, *Letters from America*, p. 40.
45. Ibid., Introduction by Aubrey C. Land, pp. *xvi–xviii*.
46. Main, *Social Structure*, p. 57.

[33]

cultural labourer's occupation but the pigmentation of his skin that so effectively concealed the true character of his relationship to republican society.[47]

Considerations such as these, however, were seldom far beneath the surface when slavery was under discussion. At the time of the Revolution, the open attack on slavery was still of fairly recent origin. It began rather sporadically some thirty or forty years earlier with the tracts and sermons of individuals, notably Benjamin Lay and John Woolman, but gathered momentum from the Quakers during the great mid-century wars. The Society of Friends in Pennsylvania, in conformity with their pacifist ideals, refused to support the war and their members resigned from the assembly, but their course of action placed a severe strain on their consciences; a new commitment to antislavery seems to have been one result. Reviled once more—as they had been in their origins—as fanatics and now as traitors, the Pennsylvania Quakers rediscovered their sympathy for other victims of persecution. Moving in close association with the London Meeting for Sufferings, which in 1757 decided to investigate Quaker involvement in the slave trade, the Philadelphia yearly meeting resolved next year to exclude from business meetings all members who bought or sold Negroes and to refuse their money. During the next few years American Quakers moved in increasing numbers to set their slaves free.[48]

Within a very short time, the American quarrel with Britain gave the question a new twist. It was common coin of the American defence that Britain intended to reduce the colonies to slavery; the word acquired a new currency, inducing many colonials to ask themselves

47. I do not infer from this, as argued by Edmund S. Morgan in *American Slavery, American Freedom, The Ordeal of Colonial Virginia* (New York, 1975), that Virginians set the American example by developing a republican ideology at the indispensable cost of slave labour and racism. Jefferson's own political principles would have been satisfied in a republic of small, independent farmers supporting themselves by their own labour. I have examined these questions at greater length in a review article, "Slavery and Revolution: The Conscience of the Rich", *The Historical Journal*, Vol. 20 no. 2 June 1977.

48. David Brion Davis, *The Problem of Slavery in Western Culture* (Ithaca, 1966), pp. 330–2, 434–43. But see also Adam Smith's ironical comment, "The late resolution of the Quakers in Pennsylvania to set at liberty all their negro slaves may satisfy us that their numbers cannot be very great. Had they made any considerable part of their property, such a resolution could never have been agreed to". Adam Smith, *An Enquiry into the Nature and Causes of the Wealth of Nations*, London, 1776 (Chicago, 1952), p. 167.

not only what they meant by it, but what right they had to enslave others. Southern planters, who were as well versed in republican doctrines as their contemporaries to the northeast, and certainly in some cases as uneasy about the conflict of principles, tended to ease their consciences with criticism of the African slave trade. During the political discussion of the period from the early protests against British policy to the making of new state constitutions, criticism of slavery and the slave trade attested to the misgivings of American consciences, but never posed the slightest threat to the safety of the institution. Most of the adverse comment came from New England, where James Otis scathingly condemned the pretexts for slavery in an early pamphlet,[49] and where certain town meetings demanded emancipation on the strength of the liberties that the colonists claimed for themselves.[50] There seems to have been no comparable criticism of indentured white servitude. Considering the cruelties and miseries inflicted by the operation of the system, this silence is impressive testimony to the continuing demand for various forms of cheap labour. Indentured service was imposed for limited terms, involved certain obligations which were honoured more or less faithfully by the master depending on his nature and circumstances, and the servant was sometimes discharged with a grant of land or money. This was not a system of absolute slavery; but it was subject to very inadequate controls and often fitted the servant only to become a lifelong subordinate. Indentured servitude contributed heavily to the cluster of anomalies and inconsistencies which characterised large sectors of colonial America.

Late colonial America can best be understood when its own confident self-image, in which robust ideals of equality were freely described as accomplished facts yet were often denied by the evidence people could see around them, is itself regarded as part of the evidence requiring interpretation. The comparison made both then and afterwards with the condition of the common people of many parts of Europe was both fair and flattering; Americans were proud of the contrast, and visiting Europeans tended to concur with them. This contrast in the observable facts helped to explain why America proved fertile ground for new ideas of social justice. The ideas that

49. James Otis, *Rights of the British Colonies* . . . ; Bailyn, *Pamphlets*, I, 439.
50. For examples, Massachusetts Archives 156/347, 156/389, 277/44.

were beginning to coalesce into an American concept of republicanism were not especially American in origin: In parts of the Old
World, notably in France and Scotland, philosophers had already developed the idea that the purpose of government was to promote
the happiness of the people—the whole people. But America differed
from Europe: Differences of wealth and rank and social style it did
indeed have—but these were not built on laws of privilege. No one
claimed that colonial society was composed, like that of Europe, of
different "estates" or upon a legally implanted hierarchy of rights.
In America, as John Adams remarked, there was "but one order".[51]
In Scotland Francis Hutcheson had coined the idea that the object of
government was to achieve the greatest happiness of the greatest
number;[52] in America, much more clearly than in the Old World,
the fires of revolution could forge a link between a government's
success in promoting the happiness of the people, and its legitimacy.
Neither under colonial law nor in the new state constitutions was
this aim completely translated into practice. But it emerged as a
principle by which government could be judged.

Ideas of equality were not popular only with the artisans or mechanics or small farmers who could be expected to read the public
prints. They were evidently acceptable to much more substantial
members of society who normally held positions of authority in
courts and legislatures as well as in business, the law, and in their
country communities. Except in the monarchy, which for most of
the time was little more than a name, Americans acknowledged no
rights of hereditary rulership. They had confirmed by experience
what the republican principles of the seventeenth century had taught
them by precept: Rulers should gain their position by virtue of the
confidence of the ruled, expressed in open elections. These elections,
however, normally produced very predictable results. The voters
seldom deviated from expressions of confidence in their social superiors. They acquiesced voluntarily in the political authority of the
men whom they recognised by virtue of wealth, family, and rank.
This class of gentry could make no claim to rule by principles of

51. John Adams, *Defence of the Constitutions of Government of the United
States* (1787), in *Works*, IV, 434.
52. Francis Hutcheson, *System of Moral Philosophy*, 2 vols. (London, 1755).

inheritance even if they had wanted to make it. The idea of a prevalent condition of equality, if not pursued in too much detail, therefore did them a particularly valuable service, which goes far to explain why members of the colonial leadership class were so willing to take their bearings in political discourse from an egalitarian rather than from any traditionally hierarchical standpoint. It served to satisfy them that their dominant—or at any rate prominent—positions in society were earned. Birth, family, and social standing entered quite easily into this accounting because they were accepted as conventional by most of the lower orders just as they were expected to be by the leaders. But it was comfortable for the gentry of merchants, landowners, and lawyers, as they settled into their accustomed seats in assemblies and other places of power, to accommodate themselves to the notion that they owed their positions to the public recognition of personal merit.

It would have been premature to speak of any formal theory of equality of opportunity. But no one who had known the colonies over the previous generation or more could doubt that Americans were capable of exhibiting extreme economic competitiveness whenever they could seize the opportunities for advancement in land, ships, stores, professional services, or credit. This urgent quest for private gain, however, raised obvious problems of conscience, especially for descendants of Puritans. Self-interest released with no other end but self-advancement was hard to justify either to community or God. During the late colonial period it became increasingly common to claim that commercial prosperity sought through personal enterprise made a true contribution to the public interest, and the popularity of this thesis suggests the very real need to alleviate the strains of conscience by introducing a justificatory psychology of economic success.[53] Self-interest released in the service of community involved no dereliction of duty to God or calling. And beneath this doctrine a primitive form of the idea of equality of opportunity could be faintly discerned. Feelings of guilt, of having earned a retribution which society might have a duty to inflict, could be assuaged by resort to ideas of equality. If it were true that self-interest was pursued under

53. J. E. Crowley, *This Sheba, Self: The Conceptualization of Economic Life in the Eighteenth Century* (Baltimore and London, 1974), pp. 76–85.

equal and therefore just laws, then the society that made those laws would ratify the results of the pursuit. Men of wealth, rank, and advantage could rest content with the unequal effects of their efforts.

Personal Independence and Collective Self-Esteem: The Discovery of Political Equality

The observations of travellers and the inferences drawn from statistical analyses clearly yield no single or consistent pattern. The colonies differed in too many respects to make any such consistency likely. But when the historical perspective is deepened the picture begins to grow at least a little clearer, and trends beginning some half a century before the Revolution, which reflected large-scale advances in population, international trade, and the opportunities for individual enrichment, tend to be reproduced under the differing circumstances of several colonies. The great landowners, including the proprietors of Pennsylvania and Maryland and heirs of great estates like Lord Halifax in the Northern Neck of Virginia and the patroons of the Hudson Valley in New York, exerted themselves to extract more and more wealth from their lands by a process which has been appropriately called a "feudal revival."[54] But this new feudalism was a bastard sort that knew nothing of the old mutuality of obligations; it was the worst kind of all, an absentee or at best a purely extractive system, which can be called any form of feudalism only at the risk of obscuring the origins of the term in forms of reciprocal service and protection.

These trends were not historical accidents. They resulted from deliberate policies which increased the burdens of rent, widened the distinctions of economic power and social rank, and made the corresponding sense of personal importance on the one side and impotence on the other more pronounced and more oppressive. But they did not pass unchallenged. By the end of the mid-century wars, and in some instances earlier, they were beginning to provoke sharp, sometimes violent reactions among tenants and other victims over an extremely wide area ranging at least from the Hudson Valley to

54. Rowland Berthoff and John M. Murrin, "Feudalism, Communalism and the Yeoman Freeholder" in Stephen G. Kurtz and James H. Hutson, eds., *Essays on the American Revolution* (Chapel Hill and New York, 1973).

the western Carolinas. In the summer of 1768 the Regulators of North Carolina, in a state of incipient revolt against their rulers, cited as a basic cause of their discontent "the unequal chances the poor and the weak have in contentions with the rich and the powerful".[55] Thus although the pattern contains so many cross-currents and contradictions, it seems reasonably clear that the increasingly inegalitarian distribution of wealth and power in the late colonial era was already exciting scattered manifestations of determined opposition, in which the dissidents attributed their grievances to certain forms of inequality. It is not clear that they demanded much more than a return to conditions which they felt had belonged to them in the past; but as some of their landlords and leaders grew uneasily aware with the advance of the quarrel with Great Britain, these demands reflected a new social consciousness, which was disposed to question the authority of the established powers.

In this unstable domestic situation within many of the colonies, the rising controversy with Britain stoked up a hothouse of discontent. The riots and mobs that followed the Stamp Act disturbed all established conventions of order and authority in the colonies. In Massachusetts Governor Bernard complained repeatedly of the disorder and what he denounced as a "democracy" that prevailed in the town meetings.[56] The observation in fact was a commonplace of communications among members of the governing orders, who were painfully aware that the clash with established authority was unsettling the habit of subordination which they expected from the common people. "A Spirit of Levillism Seems to go Through the Country," as Thomas Cushing wrote plaintively to the lieutenant governor of Massachusetts, Thomas Hutchinson, "'and Very little distinction between the highest and the lowest in Office".[57] The mood was not consistently maintained, and had a tendency to subside when lacking immediate provocation; but after the Continental Congress had opened in Philadelphia in September 1774, assertions

55. Marvin L. Michael Kay, "The North Carolina Regulation, 1766–1776: A Class Conflict", in Alfred F. Young, ed., *The American Revolution: Explorations in the History of American Radicalism* (DeKalb, 1976), p. 88; and see this volume, passim.

56. Robert E. Brown, *Middle-Class Democracy and the American Revolution in Massachusetts, 1689–1780* (Ithaca, 1955), pp. 57, 58, 223–4, 245.

57. Cushing to Hutchinson, 15 December 1766. Hutchinson Letterbooks transcripts, Massachusetts Historical Society, xxv, 119.

of equality became more strident and rapidly spilt over from collective assertions of the colonial relationship to Britain to expressions of the demands of the lower orders in the colonies themselves.

It was in the collective form, however, that the colonial interest in equality was both earliest and most sustained. Consciousness of unequal treatment by Parliament raised for colonial spokesmen, especially—as was usually the case—when they were lawyers, acute problems of both theory and loyalty. There existed in political science no grounds for denying that a single political entity must have a sovereign somewhere—and Americans made a point of the claim that they were members of the British nation. From a legal point of view it could even have seemed easier to take the step that placed the Americans outside the Empire than to invent a system of dual sovereignty inside it. That step was a matter of temperament rather than law, and few responsible public men were willing to take it even in 1775. By that time, however, certain tough minds had worked their way to the view that the colonial assemblies had all the constitutional power within their several provinces that Parliament exercised in the British Isles. James Wilson, the Scottish-born Philadelphia lawyer who was to have a decisive role in defining political equality under American law, reached this conclusion, much against his own original expectations, when he wrote an essay on the subject in 1770; but the rapid decline of the quarrel over the Townshend tariffs led him to withhold it from publication; there seemed no point in advancing so bold and unsettling a theory when relations with Britain were returning to normal. It was not until 1774 that renewed troubles led him to publish it in pamphlet form.[58] At the same time, John Adams was advancing the same views in his newspaper controversy with Daniel Leonard, conducted under the pseudonyms respectively of Novanglus and Massachusettensis. The arguments on both sides were learned and heavily freighted with old law, running back to the earlier relations between England and Scotland. Whether parliamentary powers extended beyond the immediate boundaries of the realm and by what law settlers on other shores were bound, whether Parliament had ever legitimately exercised power over charter colonies deriving their rights from the king,

58. James Wilson, *Considerations on the Nature and Extent of the Legislative Authority of the British Parliament* (Philadelphia, 1774).

were questions not easily resolved either then or now. In deploying their arguments, always couched in legal reasoning, the colonials were clearly driven by something more urgent than the logic of the law.

The emotional force arose from two sources: a sense of danger from the extension over their own affairs of an uncontrollable parliamentary power, and injured self-esteem. The latter sentiment was both personal and collective. No American felt or exemplified it more deeply than George Washington, whose distinguished service as a militia officer during the French and Indian War was soured by his disappointed desire for a royal commission. If he were appointed a militia colonel, as at one time suggested by Governor Sharp, but with only the pay and powers of a captain, "Every Captain bearing the King's Commission, every half-pay Officer, or other, appearing with such a commission would rank before me. . .".[59] This, of course, was a very personal feeling; but in the future commander of the Continental armies, a man particularly distinguished for his high sense of honour as well as his obvious personal ambition, its symbolic importance can hardly be overrated. Many years later, after the first Continental Congress had already dispersed, the Tory Daniel Leonard put his finger on the point in more general terms: "The Whigs flattered the people with the idea of independence", he accusingly said; "the tory plan supposed a degree of subordination, which is rather an humiliating idea".[60]

In a very true sense, the American Whigs were right. The British position did require them to accept a degree of subordination, though not one that would in fact have much effect on their daily lives. The independence-minded radicals, in hammering incessantly at the theme of colonial rights, were whipping up the sentiment of American self-esteem by inculcating the sense of injury. The difference between them and the loyalists was that the latter accepted the idea of subordination within a larger whole. But the conflict meant agony of mind for many colonials whose self-respect was involved with and depended on the British connection.

59. Bernhard Knollenberg, *George Washington, the Virginia Period, 1732–1775* (Durham, 1964), p. 25.
60. Massachusettensis, 19 December 1774. Bernard Mason, ed., *The American Colonial Crisis* (New York, 1972), p. 12.

Equality of esteem had thus emerged as a category of American aspiration at a crucial phase of collective self-identification. But in this sense it had little bearing on the problem of personal equality. A nation or community claiming equal rights or status with others does not thereby make any admission as to the relations among its own members. Leonard, a Tory having no sympathy with what was happening, was freer than such whigs as his anonymous opponent John Adams to say what he thought on that issue too. "The disaffected", Leonard wrote, "begin by reminding the people of the elevated rank they hold in the universe, as men, that all men are by nature equal; that Kings are but the ministers of the people; that their authority is delegated by the people for their good. . . ".[61] By these means, the seeds of sedition were sown, and real liberty was soon lost in licentiousness—a process which Leonard, who had lived through these times with his enemies, traced through the measures pursued in the general court and the courts of common law. There was an ironical appropriateness in his addressing these remarks to John Adams. Though Leonard did not know his adversary's identity, Adams was in fact almost equally alarmed by the prospects of innovation in government, and bent as much time and energy as he could spare from his congressional duties to advising the makers of state constitutions against radical political reform. Adams, imbued with the political thought of James Harrington, was convinced that power followed the distribution of property; for a person of republican sentiments, this meant that property—especially land—should be widely distributed. But it also meant that those without property should be kept at a safe distance from any exercise of political influence, for such people lacked judgment and the independence which could alone secure them against influence and corruption.

All men were assuredly equal in the right to hold property which they lawfully owned, in their rights before the law, and in their religious consciences. The problem, however, was to construct a political order in which these rights would be safe. The essential foundation of any such order was public virtue—a genuine dedication among the people at large to the principles of their own government, strong enough to resist the temptations of personal ambition

61. Ibid., p. 14.

and the guiles of mischievous demagogues. One could never expect to find this virtue in men without property—in those who did not begin with the things that attached them to the principles of the society. Writing to John Sullivan, who sought his opinion as to the future constitution of Massachusetts in May 1776, John Adams outlined the views that he was to hold with considerable consistency though perhaps with diminishing optimism over the following years. The suffrage should not be tampered with; once that happened, "new claims will arise; women will demand a vote; lads from twelve to twenty-one will think their rights not closely enough attended to; and every man who has not a farthing will demand an equal voice with any other, in all acts of state".[62] Similar reflections, prompted by the need to stall the democratising influence of Thomas Paine's *Common Sense*, led Adams to compose his *Thoughts on Government*, in which he exerted his own considerable influence in favour of a marked institutional conservatism and continuity with the forms of the old colonial governments.[63]

Adams came back to the crucial point when he drafted a constitution for consideration by the Massachusetts convention in 1779. He wanted to use the preamble to declare that "All men are born equally free and independent"—thus avoiding the vague and dangerous statement that all were born "equal". After Adams's departure for Europe, the convention deleted "equally" and returned to the Jeffersonian formula.[64] This difference of emphasis carried an important doctrinal implication, from which different long-term policies could reasonably have developed. The language adopted by the convention dispensed with the idea that rights depended on specified attributes such as property, themselves subject to civil law; if all were equal by birth, no law which denied the consequences of equality could be just. Other aspects of the constitution of 1780, such as the property qualifications for voting and office, revealed that members of the convention did not adhere to the full implications of their

62. John Adams to James Sullivan, 26 May 1776, in *Works*, IX, 375–8; John R. Howe, Jr., *The Changing Political Thought of John Adams* (Princeton, 1966), pp. 7–11; 79–101.

63. John Adams, *Thoughts on Government* (1776), in *Works*, IX, 189–202.

64. Page Smith, *John Adams*, 2 vols. (New York, 1962), p. 441; Massachusetts Constitution of 1780, in Pole, *Revolution in America: Documents*, p. 480.

own formula, and were not far removed from the thinking of their unofficial mentor John Adams.[65] But it was Adams who consistently stuck to the keynote of personal independence as the criterion for political equality.

Adams's view that good government was best assured by personal independence, and that the independent man was free of domination by the will of another, was drawn from the central principles of the English republican tradition. An earlier generation had debated the same issues during the English Civil Wars. The lines run remarkably clear from the famous debates on Putney Heath in the autumn of 1647, when the Levellers in the New Model Army met their generals, Ireton and Cromwell, to challenge them about the forms of government for which they had been contending, right down to the Boston, Philadelphia, and Richmond of America in the formative days of the American Revolution.

The Levellers were by no means wholly of one view. Most of them recognised a need for some limits on the suffrage. But one of their most democratic assertions of principle, drawn up by John Wildman, demanded that in elections to Parliament, "all free-born men at the age of twenty-one years and upwards be the electors, excepting those that have or shall deprive themselves of that their freedom, either for some years or wholly, by delinquency".[66] In an earlier pamphlet, John Lilburne declared, "That only and sole legislative law-making power *is originally inherent in the people, and derivatively in their Commissions chosen by themselves by common consent, and no other.* In which the poorest he that lives hath as true a right to give a vote, as the richest and greatest . . .".[67] But these strong affirmations of principle proved difficult to maintain in detail, or in face of Ireton's impressive powers of argument. Even Maximilian Petty, who said at one point, "We judge that all inhabitants that have not lost their birthright should have an equal voice in elections", later admitted that "apprentices, or servants, or those that take alms" should be excluded—and for precisely the same reason that

65. John Adams, *Works*, IV, 220.
66. John Wildman, "The Case of the Army Truly Stated", in A. S. P. Woodhouse, ed., *Puritanism and Liberty* (Chicago, 1951), p. 433.
67. John Lilburne, *The Charters of London*, quoted by C. B. Macpherson, *The Political Theory of Possessive Individualism* (Oxford, 1962), pp. 3–4.

[44]

was to reappear in John Adams, George Mason, and their contemporaries: "They depend upon the will of other men and should be afraid to displease them. For servants and apprentices, they are included in their masters . . .".[68]

General Ireton, who carried the main burden of the fight against the radical Levellers, returned again and again to the defence of property—and by tactical skill worthy of his military abilities, he exposed the rift among the Levellers themselves. Property itself defined the character of the state. "I think," Ireton declared, "that no person hath a right to interest or share in the disposing of the affairs of the kingdom, and in determining or choosing those that shall determine what laws we shall be ruled by here—no person hath a right to this, that hath not a permanent fixed interest in this kingdom, and those persons together are properly the represented of this kingdom, and consequently are (also) to make up the representers of this kingdom, who taken together do comprehend whatever is of real or permanent interest in the kingdom".[69]

True Levellers could not agree to define the purposes of the state by the protection of property. " . . . The chief end of this government," said Major William Rainborough, "is to preserve the persons as well as estates, and if any law shall take hold of my person it is more dear than my estate".[70] But Ireton's stand was plain: "All the main thing that I speak for is because I would have an eye to property". A man on a two years' rack rent could not have "a fixed or permanent interest". Such men might vote to destroy all property.[71] When in 1655 the Virginia legislature for the first time ordained a property qualification for the suffrage, the principles were the same: "The laws of England", declared the preamble, "grant a voice in such election only to such as by their estates real or personal have interest enough to tie them to the endeavour of the public good".[72] More than a century later, when George Mason wrote the Declaration of Rights that propounded the basis of the government of the new State of Virginia, the language had hardly changed: "that all

68. Woodhouse, ed., *Puritanism*, pp. 53, 83.
69. Ibid., p. 57.
70. Ibid., p. 67.
71. Ibid., pp. 53–4, 62–3.
72. Hening, *Statutes of Virginia*, II, 280.

men, having sufficient evidence of permanent common interest with, and attachment to the community, have the right of suffrage".[73]

The system of politics which these views reflected had always excluded those for whom fortune had cast a role outside the bounds of propertied society. They included the numerous class of servants composed of house servants and labourers, those who depended on charity, and casual or wandering labourers as well as the vagrants and beggars so feared in Tudor England. In England these classes were numerous and vaguely menacing; in America they were comparatively few. But in either case the system which excluded them in principle had no innate tendency towards self-correction. The best that men like John Adams or his cousin Samuel, who wrote the Address to circulate to the Massachusetts towns with the draft Constitution of 1780, could suggest was that the fortunate circumstances of American life would soon enable all hardworking men to acquire enough property for political participation.[74] This justification rested not on principles but on circumstances; and circumstances could change for the worse as well as the better—a truth which John Adams was soon to appreciate as he watched the deterioration of his countrymen's political morals.

These prudential and circumstantial arguments seem a long way from natural rights. Yet John Adams himself was a strong proponent of natural rights when rallying the colonial cause against Britain, and regarded it as a significant triumph when the first Continental Congress included a reference to them along with the usual appeals to constitutional principles in the Congressional Association of October 1774. The fact that Adams could hold these different views without sensing inconsistency makes it important to distinguish between the principles to which he and his associates appealed against British encroachments on colonial interests, and those which leading men were prepared to put into practice at home. This is not to suggest that there was anything insincere or half-hearted about Adams's own commitments. In 1765 he wrote the most outspoken of early American tracts against feudal inequalities in his *Dissertation on the Canon and Feudal Law*—his first public contribution to the developing de-

73. Pole, ed., *Revolution in America: Documents*, p. 520.
74. Massachusetts Archives, State House, Boston, vol. 276. W. V. Wells, *The Life and Public Services of Samuel Adams*, 3 vols. (Boston 1865), III, 89, 90–96.

bate on American rights. He denounced "feudal" dignities as an affront to the true dignity of human nature, and bitterly attacked "all that dark ribaldry of heredity, indefeasible right,—the Lord's annointed,—and the divine, miraculous original of Government, with which the priesthood has enveloped the feudal monarch in clouds and mysteries, from which they have deduced the most mischievous of all doctrines, that of passive obedience and non-resistance".[75] He struck the same note again during the War of Independence when he was an American commissioner in France. A missive, apparently originating from no less a source than George III himself, offered the Americans a settlement under which their restored allegiance would be rewarded with the ennoblement of leading Americans. "An Aristocracy of American Peers!" Adams contemptuously exclaimed in his autobiography: "hereditary peers I suppose were meant, but whether hereditary or for Life, nothing could be more abhorrent to the general Sense of America at that time, which was for making every Magistrate and every Legislator eligible and that annually at least".[76]

Even as early as 1765 this attack on hereditary privilege in government carried a veiled criticism of the principle of monarchy. But Thomas Paine's *Common Sense*, published anonymously in Philadelphia in January 1776, was the first tract to attack the monarchy itself from an American base. (Paine himself had been resident only some two years in Philadelphia at the time.) It did more, for the attack on monarchy cut at the roots of all hereditary pretensions and offered Americans some of the ideas that would be needed for an alternative theory. "Mankind being originally equals in the order of creation, the equality could only be destroyed by some subsequent circumstance: the distinctions of rich and poor may in great measure be accounted for, and that without having recourse to the harsh and ill-sounding names of oppression and avarice. Oppression is often the *consequence*, but seldom the *means* of riches; and though avarice will preserve a man from being necessitously poor, it generally makes him too timorous to be wealthy".[77] In these observations Paine disclosed some of the shortcomings of his knowledge of history

75. John Adams, *Works*, III, 447–55, 454.
76. Butterfield, ed., *Adams Papers*, IV, 149–52.
77. *The Writings of Thomas Paine*, ed. Philip S. Foner (New York, 1945), p. 9.

and human affairs; but he followed with the real aim of his attack, "the distinction of men into KINGS and SUBJECTS", a distinction which, unlike that between male and female, could not be naturally accounted for. Paine's statement that mankind were "originally equals in the order of creation" was not different in sense from Jefferson's "All men are created equal". Even John Adams, who disliked Paine's style, was antagonised by his irreligion, and feared the democratising consequences of his rhetoric, was bound to agree with the central tenent that no man was born with a right to rule over others. Such views were held by all the emerging makers of the American republics of the several states.

The forcing house of revolutionary argument began in these ways to disclose certain points of agreement. No American could be found to argue that hereditary status conferred an indefeasible right to make laws. Americans generally seem to have accepted that such a state of affairs was appropriate to the realm of England, and seldom if ever directly criticised the English constitutional structure. They did assert at times that the republican—meaning the representative —part was the best of the constitution; however, the House of Lords impinged little on colonial life, and might be thought to uphold certain values of permanence, propriety, and a tradition of service which American leaders could hardly despise. But its traditions were wholly alien to American experience and irrelevant to American needs.

The Declaration of Independence encouraged Americans to stake their ideas of social justice on the belief that each individual possessed certain rights in which he stood independent of all others: They were well expressed as the right to life, liberty, and the pursuit of happiness. The last item added a distinct flavour of individual experience and personal choice to the theory of government, implying strongly that individuals should be free to find happiness in their own several ways. Government existed to bring about the best conditions for the preservation of these rights. But it did not follow that all had an equal right to participate in making the laws—that would depend on specific qualifications appropriate to the needs of society, and men of influence generally agreed that the interests of society as a whole were still safest in the hands of the owners of property. The corollary to this position of political privilege was that men of property should make it their business to ensure through just laws that worthy individuals had the opportunity to acquire property; since men were believed to have entered into society in order to secure this property, these views were joined to a voluntarist theory of the origins of the state. Several new states put these theories into official form with declarations preceding their constitutions. "All men," stated Virginia, in George Mason's words, "are by nature equally free and independent, and have certain inherent rights, of which, when they enter into society, they cannot by any compact deprive or divest their posterity; namely, the enjoyment of life and liberty, with the means of acquiring and possessing property, and pursuing and obtaining happiness and safety".[78] The makers of the Massachusetts constitution, as we have seen, discarded the statement that all men were independent in favour of the word "equal". Their preamble then stated, as though it were a matter of ascertained fact, "The body politic is formed by a voluntary association of individuals: It is a social compact, by which the whole people covenants with each citizen, and each citizen with the whole people, that all shall be governed by certain laws for the common good".[79] It is worth observing that the voluntarily associating individuals were immediately spoken of as "citizens". This might have meant that all inhabitants were considered as citizens, but that usage would have been not only highly unusual but patently false to the facts. By common consent, citizenship was less than coextensive with the whole population; citizens were invariably persons invested with certain privileges. The theory of the Massachusetts constitution allowed for inclusion under the laws of persons who did not enjoy these privileges, whether by reason of dependence, sex, race, or religion. Opin-

---

78. Pole, ed., *Revolution in America: Documents*, p. 519; Rutland, ed., *Papers of George Mason*, p. 283.

79. Pole, *Revolution in America: Documents*, p. 479. See also Jack P. Greene, *"All Men Are Created Equal"*: *Some Reflections on the Character of the American Revolution*, An Inaugural Lecture (Oxford, 1976). While I entirely agree with the main thrust of Professor Greene's argument (the pamphlet reached me during the copy-editing of this book), I think he makes his point at the expense of under-emphasising the connection which many contemporaries caught, between the rhetorical and the literal commitments to equality in Jefferson's language—and not in his only. On citizenship, see the first edition of the *Encyclopaedia Britannica* (Edinburgh, 1768–1771), which emphasises the privileged status of citizens as distinct from mere inhabitants. A citizen of Rome could not be scourged.

ions might differ as to the extent to which such secondary inhabitants might aspire to quality for full citizenship. For many, the promise of the Declaration of Independence and the Revolution could be fulfilled only by the progressive extension of the concept of citizenship. With these limitations and in these deliberate and self-conscious expressions the constitution-makers committed themselves to a theory of political equality.

It was, therefore, a theory of very limited scope—a foundation rather than a structure. Different convictions as to the obligations of government were buried in it from the beginning, and different systems might conceivably arise from those convictions. The most effective steps towards the implementation of a positive politics of electoral equality were taken for practical rather than theoretical reasons, though it must be recognised that they would have been impossible if a groundwork of theory had not existed. The elements of the majority principle, which crept into American political practice during the Revolution, required that political representation should be based on the votes of equal electors—equality being assured by the establishment of electoral constituencies of equal numbers. This process was a new departure from the unequal town and country constituencies that generally prevailed. It was not due to whig theory that America took this particular opportunity to put majoritarian principles into practice; whig theorists, had they been so minded, could have made more vigorous efforts in that direction in earlier years. As is usual in cases of major political advance, the new principle got its strength from that fact that it served powerful existing interests. Where, as happened in Massachusetts between 1775 and 1780, in other states at different times, and in the larger arena of Federal government in 1787, strong concentrations of property were allied with the largest concentrations of numbers, the interest of property had little to fear and much to gain from the introduction of majority rule.[80] To argue that true American whigs introduced majority rule as a matter of principle would do less than justice to their demonstrated capacity for political realism.[81] But once their perception of

80. For this development, see J. R. Pole, *Political Representation in England and the Origins of the American Republic* (London, 1966; Berkeley, 1971), pp. 170–2, 248, 317, 372–3, 535–6.
81. As maintained by Gordon S. Wood, *The Creation of the American Republic* (Chapel Hill, 1968), pp. 170–2.

political realities had enabled them to grasp this strand and weave it firmly into the new constitutional fabric, the formalistic element of voluntarism in whig theory was toughened and enlarged into a prominent theme in American political—and indeed social—thought. In conjunction with the majority principle it thus became a far more active principle in America than it had ever been in England.[82]

It would be a mistake to treat the majority principle as standing alone in the American political system. State sovereignty, which competed with it as a principle of loyalty as well as a method of counting voters, formed a cover for alternative interests. Moreover, numerically equal constituencies could be drawn in favour of private or party interests; the early enunciation of majority rule began rather than ended a process of interpretation. But it could not be dislodged, and contained an inner logic which could overcome the reasoning by which local or private interests protected their own claims to representation. This logic owed most of its force to the simple fact that the majority principle incorporated the idea of political equality.

The Meanings of a Self-Evident Truth

The Declaration of Independence was neither the earliest nor the clearest American affirmation of the idea of equality, but from the moment of its promulgation it was undoubtedly the most central; it was the one statement in relation to which all others had to take their bearings. In view of these formidable consequences it is not out of place to ask exactly what its words meant. The Preamble described its own crucial proposition as "self-evident"; but what does that mean?[83] As it could not mean that the truths in question were

82. In this connection, see the masterly analysis of Yehoshua Arieli, *Individualism and Nationalism in American Ideology* (Cambridge, Mass., 1964), especially pp. 158–80.

83. Carl L. Becker, *The Declaration of Independence* (1922; repr. New York, 1959), pp. 141–2. Fortunately, Jefferson's original work in composing the draft Declaration comes to our help. From the copy known as the Rough Draft it appears that he first intended to describe these truths as "sacred and undeniable", and that the alteration to "self-evident" is in a hand that resembles Franklin's. The change, moreover, is typical of Franklin, and suggests something more than a mere verbal preference, for as with all significant differences of style it conveys a different meaning. Jefferson's use of the word "sacred" may have carried little more than an echo of the idea that human reason was implanted by divine power, but it does bear a direct reference to that power.

evident to themselves, it must be taken to mean "evident to the senses", which must include moral apprehension. Even if the overt meaning was "evident on sight", this reading must clearly be correct, since it is the mind, not the eye, that perceives truth. Every member of the human race was therefore held to be provided with his own equipment of moral apprehension; and this statement could be of value only if the truth is universal. It follows that no one could be equipped with the normal moral sense without being accessible to the truth that all men are created equal. This helps to explain why the Declaration was to be of such future potency. It told every individual that he was capable of seeing these things for himself, just as it forbade governments to deny the consequences of that vision. The analogy with religious doctrine was close, and significant because politics borrowed from its theological counterpart. Not only the Calvinists but all religious instructors taught that each person bore throughout his life a primary responsibility to God; in much the same way, the Declaration of Independence told people that each of them bore a responsibility for a continuous relationship to his government. This was in the first instance little more than a symbolic statement, a gesture; complex changes in institutions and in personal attitudes would have to take effect to give it political force. But the gesture did deposit the full responsibility on men, for making government respond to the kind of lives they wanted to live. To the Puritans, liberty had not been designed for the hedonistic pursuit of one's own earth-bound aims and gains; it meant only liberty to serve Christ. When those high purposes had been dismissed, and human happiness promoted to a place not only of profit but of honour in men's values, then it surely fell to the human race to determine those values.

Nothing very concrete followed immediately from this statement.

There is a difference between rights that are sacred, like the divine right of kings, and rights that are secular, like those embodied in the writ of habeas corpus. Small though this change may have been, it has a symbolic place in the transition from the theological to the secular in the basis of modern politics. It did not complete that transition; many future writers, including lawyers, were to make the state rest on some form of theological principle; but in the language of Jefferson and in that of his successors, the rights of the individual would in no way depend on, or be respected as a manifestation of, his personal relationship to God, or of the state's responsibility to God. *The Papers of Thomas Jefferson*, ed., Julian P. Boyd (Princeton, 1950), I, 426–8, n. 11.

Individuals could bear these responsibilities quite adequately within the existing organisation of government; state constitutions were made anew during the first phase of independence, but they were made generally on the lines that continued, while broadening, that organisation. The concept of consent was central to the case made by the Declaration of Independence against the British, but only in Massachusetts and New Hampshire was the concept put to the test of a formal ratification by the people of their state constitution. The Declaration rested on principles too general to imply specific institutional consequences; moreover, when subjected to exegesis, even these principles disclosed underlying ambiguities. It soon appeared that different individuals did have differing moral apprehensions. The first difficulty arose over Jefferson's denunciation of the slave trade, which is not the less celebrated for having been suppressed. The form Jefferson devised was an indictment of George III, which minimised any American guilt by laying all the blame squarely, if not quite fairly, at the door of Britain. Jefferson concluded by denouncing the British for inciting the enslaved Negroes to rise against their American masters, who emerged as the doubly injured victims of this complicated plot. Despite these reservations, his language was felt by his colleagues to be too provocative for powerful interests in Congress, and the entire paragraph was excised.

The approved passages are not free from problems of interpretation. Certainly Jefferson himself did not believe that all men had been created with equal endowments of virtue, intelligence, or natural skills. Yet his statement in its clearest sense was undoubtedly universal; it spoke of men as individuals, not as groups or nations. Only in respect of certain rights could they be thought of as equals, and it was no part of the business of a declaration of national independence to enter into a philosophical disquisition on the concept of rights. Rights could be thought of as a sort of invisible essence, as attributes inseparable from the persons to whom they adhered; but while people differed from one another in shape, size, skill, colour, and every conceivable attribute, their rights remained utterly constant, unchanged and unaffected by these differences among the people they lived in.

There were strong contemporary reasons for regarding the Declaration as a universal pronouncement. Ideas of equality among individuals had been common currency for years—as Daniel Leonard had remarked in disapproval. The sheer lack of qualification lent this meaning to Jefferson's language. And yet, although the universalist interpretation was in many ways the most obvious and easiest to the common mind, and was consonant with much current popular philosophy, its claims were remarkably bold. It swept away all considerations of time, place, and circumstance. It ignored differences of culture, religion, or morals and presupposed that individual members of different civilisations in different historical periods shared the same values and moral perceptions. Jefferson aimed, as he remarked half a century later, to express "the common sense of the subject".[84] But it was not the only philosophically available common sense. More than a quarter-century had elapsed since the publication of Montesquieu's *De l'esprit des lois*, possibly the most influential work of modern political science known to Jefferson's generation. Both in this book and in his *Lettres persanes*, Montesquieu had diffused among cultivated readers a new kind of moral and cultural relativism, which related laws, customs, and morals to circumstances specific to different civilisations. Alternative views were thus certainly available; and the forms of cultural relativism would soon revive in the new United States of America with the advance of an increasingly ominous differentiation between North and South.

The universalist sense of the Declaration of Independence was the easiest, the most popular, and with the passage of time the only sense in which it was commonly understood. Reformers from that time forth made it their own. From its earliest beginnings in the national period, the antislavery movement adopted the Declaration and held it forth as the definitive American principle, the justification for the independent existence of the United States. The popularity of this interpretation was attested by the fact that when nineteenth-century apologists for slavery attacked the doctrine of human equality, they denied the assertions with which the Declaration began. But they did not as a rule deny that the language carried a universalist and individualist meaning.[85]

84. Quoted in Becker, *Declaration of Independence*, p. 25.
85. Duncan J. MacLeod, *Slavery, Race and American Revolution* (Cambridge, 1974), pp. 21, 59, 99, 182.

A less universal version of the Preamble was available to contemporaries, however. The signers of the Declaration could reasonably have been considered to have committed themselves to nothing more sweeping than the view that one people was the equal of another; and this view had the advantages not only of uniting Americans against Britain without committing them to dangerous innovations at home, but of being consistent with recent American arguments on legislative power. Once British policies had forced Americans to admit that they no longer formed a part of the British people, and that by virtue of their history and their own choice they constituted a people among themselves, it followed that the British could no more make laws for the colonies than the colonies could for Britain—or, to take a popular example, than the Scottish Parliament could have done for England before the Act of Union. There are good reasons for thinking that in spite of its less explicit and more limited implications, this alternative reading of the views that were expected to have practical consequences would have been accepted by Jefferson and his colleagues. Jefferson's own pamphlet, *A Summary View of the Rights of British America*, had recently made this very point; John Adams and James Wilson had independently arrived at the same conclusion. The opening sentences of the Declaration of Independence gave support to this reading by specific reference to the separation of one people from another and to their assumption of a "separate and equal station". That was the practical issue, and it was to justify that step that Congress appealed to "the opinions of mankind".

Despite its flamboyant rhetoric, the Preamble was in some ways a vulnerable instrument of revolutionary policy. It had the fault of being easy to take too literally. Jefferson's phrases, in both the universalist as well as the more limited sense, referred only to an equality of rights; if all men had been equal in other respects there would have been no cause to declare the fact, and little likelihood that anyone would do so. But they were easily intelligible and more attractive in a much broader sense, and enemies of equality, determined to destroy the psychological power exerted by Jefferson's language, found it easy to discredit this apparently literal meaning. When Southern writers used this argument against the Abolitionist opponents, the Declaration of Independence was itself invoked to divide the American people about their founding principles.[86]

Jefferson's moral universalism conformed with his deism. But he lived in an age when the unbending truths of former religious dispensations were giving way before the milder and more rationalistic idea that God might have timed his revelations for the advancing stages of man's understanding. "God the educator", as David Brion Davis has said, "replaced God the engineer".[87] Jefferson's own expression, "the pursuit of happiness", suggested the influence of the Scottish philosophers and of other popularisers of the philosophy of benevolence whose works were read during his youth and education. Whether or not it was so intended by Jefferson, this phrase was highly susceptible to interpretation in the light of the more recent and benevolent views of God's aims for man, and as such it may be said to have given the Declaration a cutting edge into the future of political philosophy. Jefferson himself was fond of a stance of strong social egalitarianism, which he pursued by his studied informalities when holding high office rather than through any alteration in his patriarchal style of life at Monticello. His proposals for suffrage extension and his efforts to reform the constitution of Virginia as well as his attack on primogeniture and entail were his own political witness to the egalitarianism that he deeply felt to be in tune with the needs of a republican government. To the end of his life he disliked forms of government based on monarchy, aristocracy, or priesthood, and believed that the people, properly educated and well led by their own "natural" aristocracy, could be trusted to govern themselves. His views called for reforms in Virginia's political structure and would have increased the number of small farms without disturbing the settled estates and wealth of the great planters.[88]

Many members of the revolutionary generation, however, were inspired by an egalitarian and still more by a libertarian impulse. In fighting against enslavement by the British Empire, they felt they had

86. Becker, *Declaration of Independence*, 245–55; Northern anti-abolitionists used similar arguments.

87. Davis, *The Problem of Slavery in the Age of Revolution, 1770–1823* (Ithaca and London 1975), pp. 527–31.

88. For examples of Jefferson's style of what may after Cromwell be called "russet-coated" egalitarianism, see Jefferson to Judge William Johnson, 12 June 1823 (*Memorial Ed.*, XV, p. 439). John Zvesper kindly supplied me with this reference.

learnt what the word meant. This desire to transmit the blessings of liberty to others led to a wave of slave manumissions, assisted also by deep impulses of religion, and on some occasions by the fear that a slave population would menace its masters. The Abolitionist societies that soon sprang up drew their inspiration from the Revolution and their rhetoric from the Declaration of Independence. Even in some states with genuine slave economies, these sentiments had a surprisingly long life; their survival over a period of twenty-five years was revealed in the sympathetic attitude of the courts of Maryland and Virginia to slave claims for liberation on grounds, usually supported only by hearsay, of having had free mothers or forebears. These judicial acts of emancipation died out towards the close of the century; by then, for other reasons, notably the horrors of the slave rising in St Domingue, the climate was changing for the worse with regard to race while in other respects it was opening towards wider ideas of opportunity.[89]

The emotions released by the Revolution left many Americans deeply dedicated to the aim of keeping in being a society whose members, whatever their differences in wealth, education, fortune, or social style, would respect one another as equals. The force of this feeling was easy to sense but not easy to fix. It emerged most clearly when threatened by presumptions of aristocracy, as seemed to have happened when certain officers of the former continental army formed themselves into a select society. The ominous feature of this Society of the Cincinnati was that its membership was thenceforth to be hereditary—a recrudescence of aristocratic principles on American soil. George Washington was naturally invited to be its first president, and made the mistake of accepting. The Society came into being in May 1783, but was promptly denounced by a South Carolina judge who, in the lengthy title of his pamphlet, accused them of creating a "Race of Hereditary Patricians, or Nobility". The uproar that followed was widespread and damaging; town and county meetings denounced the Cincinnati in New England, in Massachusetts a committee of both houses of assembly expressed disapproval, in Rhode Island there were suggestions of disfranchising the members and in North Carolina of preventing them from taking seats in the legislature. When the Society convened in May

89. MacLeod, *Slavery, Race and Revolution*, chap. 3 and pp. 153–7.

1784, it reviewed its reputation and decided to abandon the idea of hereditary membership at least on the national level. Its funds were to be placed in the keeping of state legislatures.[90] The storm was more furious because of the Society's admitted object of supporting the government and the union, a policy which, in a body of officers, was suspected of concealing nationalistic designs. In fact the Society continued to exist and to enlist influential members; twenty-seven of them were members of the Constitutional Convention of 1787.[91] But the intense reaction against the idea of hereditary status was truly characteristic of popular feeling, and was reflected in the new Constitution's clause forbidding Congress to grant any title of nobility.

The Revolution had released great passions and high but inconsistent ideals. Men had been required as never before to ask themselves, and tell their neighbours, where they stood with regard to government and the principles on which it rested. As the Convention assembled in Philadelphia, the idea of equality would clearly not stand alone as a theoretical basis for future American government, but it was also clear that no American government could dispense with the morality of equal political and legal rights.

90. Merrill Jensen, *The New Nation* (New York, 1950), pp. 261–5.
91. Ibid., p. 264.

Chapter Three

Religion and Conscience:
Do Good Fences Make Good Neighbors?

*Sectarians and Rationalists: The Serpentine Foundations
of Religious Liberty*

Thomas Jefferson once described the effect of the religious clause
of the First Amendment to the United States Constitution by a powerful but misleading metaphor. "I contemplate with sovereign reverence that act of the whole American people", he wrote to the
Baptists of Danbury, Connecticut, "which declared that their legislature should make 'no law respecting an establishment of religion,
or prohibiting the free exercise thereof', thus building a wall of
separation between Church and State".[1] This pronouncement acquired such authority that as late as 1947, in a case arising from
the repayment of bus fares for children attending Catholic parochial
schools, the justices of the Supreme Court addressed themselves to
Jefferson's language in order to satisfy themselves as to the meaning
of the Amendment.[2]

Yet Jefferson's meaning was more ambiguous than his language
seemed to suggest. His words distantly but distinctly echoed a more
carefully articulated metaphor of Roger Williams, who had spoken
of the wall placed by God to separate the garden of his church from

1. *Complete Works of Thomas Jefferson*, ed. H. A. Washington (New
York, 1854), VIII, 113.
2. Everson v. Board of Education, 330 U.S. 1 (1947).

contamination by the wilderness of the world[3] In Williams's experience, government could not be trusted to protect the true interests of religion, and any form of establishment was likely to become a form of oppression; the true policy was therefore to free religion from any danger of political interference. This was a view which more recent history had so fully confirmed that Jefferson could have no difficulty in approving it; his immediate clients in the struggle for religious liberty in Virginia had been the Baptists, a persecuted minority in the state. His own reasons however, were more distinctively secular. He believed that the liberties of the people were the gift of God, and that a conviction to that effect was their only secure basis;[4] but his horror of moral or physical coercion in matters of faith and his profound conviction that truth could be discovered only by the play of free minds coloured his thought with reflections of the anticlericalism that was rampant in France. While all religions should be equally free to flourish under the protection of the First Amendment, they must never be allowed to attach the powers of government to their purposes. The wall of separation was there to protect government from the influence of religion just as surely as to protect religion from the oppressions of government. Both sides of the argument could have agreed that, as Mr. Justice Frankfurter was to say one and a half centuries later, "If nowhere else, in the relations between Church and State, good fences make good neighbours".[5]

The course of religious liberty, whose ultimate meaning came to depend on the equality of individual consciences, can be plotted along the line of Jefferson's wall of separation. The wall eventually crumbled under the pressure exerted by the changing composition of American society and by the conflicting values of powerful ingredients, which, on the whole, have not been as Jefferson would have wished them. He would therefore have been disappointed that his metaphor had failed to define the position for the indefinite future, and that it did not prove to be the conclusion of the persecutions

3. Mark De Wolfe Howe, *The Garden and the Wilderness: Religion and Government in American Constitutional History* (Chicago and London, 1965), pp. 6–7.
   4. Thomas Jefferson, *Notes on the State of Virginia*, ed. Wm. Peden (Chapel Hill, 1954), p. 163.
   5. Anson Phelps Stokes, *Church and State in the United States*, 3 vols. (New York, 1950), II, 520.

and controversies which he looked on as lying in the past. He was entirely correct, however, in his belief that events of definitive importance had already determined much of the shape of the relationship between church and state in America.

The story can be understood in three phases, the first of which begins with the Great Awakening and concludes with the First Amendment, handing on to the future both the constitutional doctrine of separation, and the social character of American religious pluralism. The second phase, during which the doctrine of separation continues to be subsumed under a generally unquestioned Protestant aegis, is marked by the emergence of a positive challenge from the Roman Catholic hierarchy. There is no strict terminal point to this phase, only a series of uneasy and not strictly logical adjustments between principle and expediency. But a third, overlapping with the second, can be discerned as emerging in the Second World War when the state began to lose its power to enquire into the validity of claims to religious faith, to be eventually deprived of authority to distinguish between religious and irreligious moral convictions. The real meaning of neutrality was under a course of profound re-examination. That re-examination, and the principles that emerged, were the work of the Supreme Court under Chief Justice Warren.

Foundations of Jefferson's Wall: the Sectarian Struggle for Religious Liberty

The early American Puritan ministry did not face the problem of accommodating itself to the exigencies of government, since it enjoyed the benefit of a political system which existed in large measure to provide for the purposes of a Puritan ministry. During the course of some two generations, however, it did have the uncomfortable experience of accommodating itself to a decline in the religious fervour of the people themselves; a seriously decreasing proportion of inhabitants showed the necessary disposition to become members of the church, and this in spite of the fact that church membership was a desideratum of political privileges. The seriousness of the situation multiplied with the advance of population for the obvious reason that the children of nonmembers were all the less likely to present themselves for admission to the churches. It was to meet this situation and offer the possibility of redemption to the children that the Half-Way Covenant was devised and first adopted in 1662.

By this arrangement, persons who had been baptised in infancy, though not themselves professing Christians, could present their children for baptism if they, the parents, were upright and would "own the covenant", which meant accepting the spiritual authority of the church; but as they were not allowed to partake of the Lord's supper or vote in church affairs, they were only "half-way" members. The intention, urged by an anxious clergy on a hesitant and reluctant laity, was to bring such persons back into a connection which would encourage them to become full members. It was not the Half-Way Covenant, however, but a series of disasters beginning with King Philip's War in 1675 that revived the fears of the people and with them the search for religious comfort. Then they came flooding back into the churches. But the clergy could renew the bridge between church and community only by admitting compromises in the original covenant of grace and recognising that unregenerate persons possessed capabilities which had previously been denied.[6] A generally more secular frame of mind continued to pervade those affairs which were not the strict province of the church, and to define the limits of those that were.

This drift was countenanced, even encouraged, by many of the Congregational clergy of Massachusetts during the early eighteenth century. In Connecticut, the adoption in 1708 of the Saybrook Platform, implemented as it was by legislative authority, brought that province closer to the Presbyterian churches of the middle colonies and marked what has been called a "parting of the ways" of the churches of Connecticut and Massachusetts.[7] Connecticut was thenceforth to have a more closely co-ordinated system under more explicit legislative authority. Massachusetts remained highly federal, with a system of independent congregations, each of which was allowed to levy taxes to support its local establishment. It was in Massachusetts that the Arminian tendency, which meant not merely a generally increasing tolerance of diversity, but a positive

6. Roger G. Pope, "New England versus the New England Mind: The Myth of Declension", *Journal of Social History*, vol. 3, no. 2 (winter 1969/70).
7. C. C. Goen, *Revivalism and Separatism in New England* (New Haven, 1962), p. 3.

rejection of the strict Calvinist doctrine of human depravity, appeared to be receiving most encouragement from civil society. To resist these teachings Jonathan Edwards, minister of Northampton, in 1734 preached five sermons insisting on the doctrine of justification by grace alone. Edwards discerned heresy in the increasing willingness of Congregational clergy to tolerate ideas of human capability in dealing with basic spiritual problems; but there was no dearth of texts for the doctrine that all depended on the will and grace of God, and that the presumption of human influence was a form of heretical arrogance.

From these sermons to the Great Awakening there was no single or straight progression. A remarkable revival shook Northampton and neighbouring towns during 1736, affecting, on Edward's own account, "all sorts, sober and vicious, high and low, rich and poor, wise and unwise. It reached the most considerable families and persons, to all appearance, as much as others".[8] A few years later, in the years 1740 to 1742, the English settlements were shaken by the greatest spiritual upheaval in their entire history.

When the Calvinist clergy turned their attention to worldly affairs, they were apt to deprecate the accumulation of riches and to draw peoples' minds back to the primal rule and condition of equality among men. But the Calvinistic "Rule of Equity", which forbade envy of one's neighbour's birth or fortune, clearly permitted a basic acceptance of the ways in which the goods of this world happened to be distributed in civil society. Calvinists were not concerned with any programme of social action or even of prescriptive social judgments; Edwards himself treated the distribution of worldly goods as a matter for contentment.[9] Calvinism had little encouragement to offer to those who resented the social status of their apparent superiors; a system which declared that some were elect and the rest were damned might disclaim all official knowledge of the exact distribution of these attributes, but it seemed unlikely that the magisterial teachers of the doctrine would prove to be among its most unfortunate victims. The unspoken implications of Calvinist teaching had from its beginnings at least not been inconsistent with

8. Jonathan Edwards, "A Narrative of Surprising Conversions" (1736), in *Select Works of Jonathan Edwards* (London, 1965), I, 19.

9. Alan Heimert, *Religion and the American Mind from the Great Awakening to the Revolution* (Cambridge, Mass., 1966), pp. 304–8.

notions corresponding to hierarchy in the social order. As John Winthrop himself had said in an earlier period of the settlement of Massachusetts, "In all times some must be rich some poore, some highe and eminent in power and dignitie; others meane and in subieccon".[10] The compromise of the Half-Way Covenant, with its more secular mentality, was itself hardly conducive to ideas of equality; for it conferred advantages of the highest spiritual importance on the children of those who had once been baptised. The politics may have been those of persuasion, but the genetics of salvation were decidedly aristocratic.[11]

Jonathan Edwards was the first influential minister of his generation to attack the Half-Way Covenant and to insist on the immediacy of God's grace; both emotionally and intellectually he made a powerful and sustained contribution to the sense of the importance of the individual. Other ministers maintained and diffused the same message. George Whitefield, who laid greater stress on God's love and grace than did some of his contemporaries, travelled so widely and became known for the same mission to so many provinces that he has been appropriately described as America's first "national" figure[12]—a remark which would ordinarily presuppose the existence of a nation. Any egalitarian implications in these teachings depended on the thrust of an individual preacher and on their reception by his individual hearers; the passion of Edwards and his leading contemporaries was directed towards saving souls, which meant that the social or political consequences, whatever they might be, were of secondary importance.

The new light struck where it would, without regard for social station. An intense preoccupation with one's own soul might teach the believer that all were equal in the sight of God, or at the worst that all people shared a grim equality in depravity; but it did not require people to question social institutions, still less to reform

10. John Winthrop, "Modell of Christian Charity", *Winthrop Papers*, 5 vols., ed. A. B. Forbes (Boston, 1929–1947), II, 282.

11. A point that could hardly have been more clearly put than by Increase Mather when he said that "God has so cast the Line of Election that for the most part it runs through the Loins of Godly Parents . . . ". *Pray for the Rising Generation* (1678), quoted by Edmund S. Morgan, *The Puritan Family*, (New York, 1966), p. 183.

12. H. Richard Niebuhr, *The Kingdom of God in America* (New York, 1956), p. 126.

them. The new light separated its beneficiaries from the old, unillu-
minated ministry and their congregations, and called them to form
"Separate" churches. But Separatism was never simply a religion
of the disinherited, and in the Awakening, as noted by Edwards in
the earlier phase, the evidence suggests that a fairly representative
social segment was swept up by the movement.[13] Numerous poor
and humble adherents were balanced, in proportions that seem to
have related to the normal structure of the community, by members
of the most prominent local families.

By the very nature of their faith, the Separates questioned established authority. Nothing could make the matter plainer than the
title of Gilbert Tennent's sermon of March 1740, *The Danger of an
Unconverted Ministry*.[14] Though Tennent's own aims were far from
being socially subversive, the implication was clear: Education and
learning, a knowledge of Hebrew, Greek, and Latin, an established
position of spiritual and social authority—none of these attributes
could give a man the knowledge that came from the light itself, none
of them could remotely compare with the knowledge given by the
light. It followed that the educated ministry simply did not possess
the power to speak to the people upon the authority of their education. This challenge to religious establishment could not but carry
social consequences, although such consequences formed no part
of their original intentions. The Separates wanted to set up their
own churches and naturally wanted to support their own ministers
without being taxed to support those whom they had renounced;
but this was not the only way in which Separates and other evange-
lists disturbed the peace, for those who had experienced conversion
soon felt impelled to carry the message to the people of other neighbourhoods. Many newly converted preachers felt that itineracy was
not merely a possibility but a duty. It is easy to see it as more than
that; it must have expressed a certain restlessness which the quiet
communities of New England, and other areas whether more or
less recently settled, did little in themselves to alleviate. Itinerant
preachers, however, threatened the tranquility of existing congregations in a manner which we have learnt to associate with "invasions

13. Goen, *Revivalism*, pp. 188–91.
14. Gilbert Tennent, *The Danger of An Unconverted Ministry* (1740), in
Richard L. Bushman, ed., *The Great Awakening: Documents on the Revival of
Religion, 1740–1745* (New York, 1970), pp. 87–93.

[65]

of territory", and often met with bitter resistance. Itinerant evange-
lists who succeeded in attracting audiences against the will of an
established minister—and the minister could hardly be expected to
welcome the brotherly aid of an uninvited visitor who made a point
of being his superior in God's grace—naturally reduced the standing
of the clergy and, by consequence, of the social order which sustained that clergy. Itineracy also tended to break down the limits
imposed by one's own community and to weaken the sense of collec-
tiveness which generally governed the lives of New Englanders.

Nothing more emphatically demonstrated the Separate rejection
of established religion than their insistence on lay ordination; to them
it was the necessary consequence of the fact that a man who had
experienced divine truth was superior in knowledge to a learned
minister who had never experienced true conversion. The same was
true of women. If the new light did not respect social rank, it was
soon clear that it did not practice sexual favouritism: What was true
for men was true for women, and although women did not become
ministers, they took a much more conspicuous and influential part
in the activities of Separatist congregations. Edward's own earliest
observations were of the influence of pious—or reformed—young
women on the moral conduct of their communities.

Separate churches were formed by new light congregations who
could no longer accept or agree to support orthodox ministers. But the
laws extracted tax payments to support ministers of the established
church. Under laws dating from 1728 to 1729, Quakers and Baptists
—or Anabaptists as they were called—were formally exempt from
these requirements. The earliest Separatist movement towards Baptism seems to have come as a device for escaping "double taxation"—
for the orthodox ministers as well as their own. In its own merits,
however, the Baptist argument had the force of an insistent inner
logic. If it was true that conversion depended on the light, and that
only a person who had experienced true conversion could be properly
baptised, then baptism without conversion was an empty ceremony,
and the practice of baptising infants was a hollow and blasphemous
practice. In August 1751, Isaac Backus, the young new light minister
of Titicut, Massachusetts, who was to become the greatest Baptist
spokesman in American history, overcame three years of misgivings

over these difficult questions and allowed himself to be immersed.[15] This was a departure from all the orthodoxies of his training that Jonathan Edwards was never able to make.

The new light community, meanwhile, was by its nature or by God's grace a closed and select community, whose claims might challenge the authority of the learned ministry but which itself made no significant advances towards general social equality. "We believe", declared the Confession of the Mansfield Separates in 1745, "that we are of that Number who are Elected of GOD to eternal Life, and that Christ did live on Earth, die and live again for us in particular . . .".[16] Among themselves they were entirely democratic and egalitarian; but it would have been quite as possible to follow their reasoning to a new kind of moral hierarchy as that of the orthodox Calvinists. In one important sense, the revival, by shaking the old congregations until in many cases they split into separate churches, did in fact influence the old lights as well as the new. Wherever the revival spread, it forced ordinary people to question the authorities to which they had habitually deferred. Whatever the outcome of this questioning, the process required individuals to make up their own minds. The very nature of the Pietist challenge detracted from the old clergy's ability to command obedience on the basis of authority alone. Individuals claimed conversion and formed alternative associations, and it fell to others, as individuals, to decide whether to go, or remain. But these effects in themselves might have receded within a couple of years if they had been left alone. The dispute began to get its political dimension when ministers, with support from town officers, fought—sometimes physically—to keep itinerants out, just as they invoked the law to enforce tax payments. Behind them, the General Court maintained the old connection between spiritual and political authority.

Like all great religious movements, the Awakening had disturbing effects on the social order. But also in common with other revivals of religion, however massive, the spiritual effects of the Awakening

15. William G. McLoughlin, *Isaac Backus and the American Pietistic Tradition* (Boston, 1967), p. 58; William G. McLoughlin, ed., *Isaac Backus on Church, State and Calvinism: Pamphlets, 1754–1789* (Cambridge, Mass., 1968), p. 29.
16. Quoted in Goen, *Revivalism*, p. 151.

ran out like a receding tide; the shore was marked and freshened by the incursion, but after some two years of activity the main effort was spent. By 1744 the dejected clergy had no news to report.[17] Many later revivals occurred, but the devoted and hard-working itinerants of many sects knew human nature too well to expect the effects of their labours to survive without repeated visitations and ever-renewed exhortations.

A movement whose aims were spiritual rather than either social or—still less—political, and whose primary impulse faded some thirty years before the first Continental Congress, does not seem to stand forth strongly among the social or political influences leading to the American Revolution. Pietist doctrine concerned the salvation of souls; it was not a political theory. By teaching that each individual ought to have a personal relationship to God, and that this relationship was incomparably more important than those that belonged to the world, Pietism enhanced the self-esteem of its adherents and gave the humblest among them a sort of lifeline of spiritual escape from any troubles or oppressions they might suffer under the social system. Among its adherents, the revival encouraged a new and intense spiritual intimacy to which rank and precedence were entirely irrelevant; but this intimacy did not spread itself beyond the focus of the new light. Some Pietist preachers openly defied the authorities and provoked breaches of the peace; but Pietism had no theological message that required its initiates to disregard such institutions as the courts, the legislatures, or the laws of property. If it were true, as many historians have maintained, that a linear connection had developed from the religious revivals to the democratisation of American society and the formation of a revolutionary national consciousness, it would be necessary to explain the effects of those revivals on the large proportion of Americans whom they left unmoved, or even hostile. When the matter is put in this way, it can hardly be said that arguments based on the social consequences of pietistic theology have established the connection.[18] The argument

17. Nathan O. Hatch, "The Origins of Civil Millenianism in America", *William and Mary Quarterly*, vol. XXXI, no. 3 (July 1974), p. 414.
18. The numerous arguments which do run on these lines tend to assume the connection without adequate examination of the implicit social process. They vary widely among themselves. Alan Heimert reaches the conclusion

leaves too much unexplained; if those in sympathy numbered half the population—which is only a guess—then as many stayed with the old faith, or with none. Boston, the leading centre of intellectual influence, shifted in the early nineteenth century towards Unitarianism and Universalism, both of which were in some ways just as typically American in character as Baptism, to which they bore no other resemblance.

Pietists challenged the existing social order, and in some cases broke the law, not because Pietism was a form of social or political theory, but because the law supported the social order in trying to suppress them. The law against itineracy stood directly in their path. In their defiance, it seems altogether likely that the Separatists drew to their side some people who had private causes for discontent; and the old lights certainly felt threatened by a general spirit of rebelliousness which the limited police powers of the parish might find it hard to contain.[19]

The connection between theology and the emergence of a more egalitarian view of society was in truth a connection between the specific experience of religious conversion on one hand, and the society within which that conversion took place on the other. This much must be agreed. But these colonial societies actually differed widely from one another in their religious policies, and responded with corresponding difficulties to the rise of Pietism. Pennsylvania

---

that "What was awakened in 1740 was the spirit of American democracy". Alan Heimert and Perry Miller, eds., *The Great Awakening: Documents Illustrating the Crisis and Its Consequences* (Indianapolis, 1967), p. *lxi*; Heimert completed this introduction after Miller's death. An influential book by Clinton Rossiter asserts that doctrines of equality (rather than liberty or fraternity), beginning with what he called "personalized religion" in the Great Awakening, led to Jacksonian democracy. Clinton Rossiter, *Seedtime of the Republic* (New York 1953), p. 57. Heimert makes the substance of a large book out of the socially "democratic" consequences of the Awakening and their effects on national consciousness. Alan Heimert, *Religion and the American Mind*. William G. McLoughlin, whose studies are indispensable to an understanding of the Baptists, also dramatises this argument: "The evangelical movement laid the ground work for the Revolution. It played a major role in the breaking down of the static, aristocratic, class-stratified and carefully controlled social order of the old colonial society". McLoughlin, *Backus and the Pietistic Tradition*, p. 231.

19. Richard L. Bushman, *From Puritan to Yankee: Character and Social Order in Connecticut, 1690–1765* (Cambridge, Mass., 1967), pp. 235–7.

offered no resistance, and although the province was embroiled in much politically charged dispute about religious affiliations, no attempt was made to suppress the free exercise of religion by any sect. It is significant that the rise of egalitarian and democratic attitudes in Pennsylvania has not generally been attributed by historians to the social consequences of the Great Awakening. The point, though a negative one, helps to explain the more positive developments in New England and to a lesser extent in the South. It was political oppression, carried out as government policy, and maintained over long years of repeated distraints, imprisonments, and nagging persecutions, that forced the survivors of the Awakening to turn to politics, making them conscious that equality of religion must be advanced as a political cause to be safeguarded by laws as well as by conscience.

Religious intolerance was nothing new in New England, where official policies were sharply out of keeping with the tenour of the British Act of Toleration. The Massachusetts Congregational Church had never had much taste for the compromises which formally exempted Quakers and Baptists. No doubt need exist but that in religious matters New England was demonstrably more repressive than Britain; except in Rhode Island, the rulers of New England provinces had no inclination to follow the British preference for coexistence between rival religions and a deprecation of persecution. After the fading of the Awakening, Separation went into an early (though not a complete) decline, partly because of painful internal differences over the theory of infant baptism, but partly because the coercive measures employed by the state were very effective. Separates who refused to pay taxes assessed for the official clergy had their homes invaded and their goods seized and sold at auction, while they themselves were often thrown into jail. In Connecticut the town of Windham added a new story to its jail in 1753 to make room for the expected new inmates.[20] In Massachusetts the General Court imposed new obstacles to Baptist exemptions. By a law of 1753, the procedures by which a Baptist could get a legally authorised certificate of his religious affiliation, as required for tax exemption, were made tortuous, humiliating, and in many cases almost impossible to fulfil. Despite bitter protests, this act was

20. Goen, *Revivalism*, p. 195.

renewed in 1757, and survived until 1770. In Connecticut the legal disabilities were even more severe.[21]

It was these repressions that forced the Baptists to turn their attention to politics, and led Isaac Backus to reflect on the consequences of placing power over religious conscience in the hands of the state. The Massachusetts Baptists replied to the act of 1753 with a *Memorial and Remonstrance* drawn up in 1754 and presented to the General Court by a committee "on behalf of several societies of the people called Baptists". This pamphlet represented an important step in the clarification of Baptist attitudes to church and state, and to the right relationship between churches. The legislature was warned that the Act of 1753 was contrary to the laws of England— a serious line to take in Massachusetts where legislative autonomy had always been regarded with exceptional jealousy. The Baptist committee not only hinted at their preference for Britain's broader tolerance, but implied that oppressed colonial minorities might seek the shelter of parliamentary or royal protection. They went on to assert their right to equal freedom from persecution with any religious group—a claim based at least nominally on the English Act of Toleration.

These were the beginnings of a political argument. But the egalitarian practices which the Baptists are often said to have contributed to the character of American social assumptions were far from being the only kind that could be fairly drawn from Christian teaching. The liberal Calvinist minister Jonathan Mayhew—soon to be one of Backus's political opponents—explained another view, when he said in a sermon in 1754, quoting Luke 12:48, "It is an established maxim of God's equal government that 'Unto whomsoever much is given, of him much shall be required'."[22] Equality here became a doctrine of service; but it made no pretence that men were equally endowed, nor did it quarrel with the unequal distribution of things. Equality in this reading is indistinguishable from concepts of proportion and fairness.

The Baptists' struggle for religious liberty was to be prolonged into the period when the Assembly of Massachusetts became increas-

21. Ibid., p. 269.
22. A. W. Plumstead, ed., *The Wall and the Garden: Selected Massachusetts Election Sermons, 1670–1775* (Minneapolis, 1968), p. 298.

ingly occupied with the quarrel with Britain. The advance of that conflict gave the Baptists no cause for comfort when American liberties were taken under protection by the Congregationalist majority. It was far from certain that religious minorities would be able to gain effective protection if Massachusetts ever became an independent state.

Baptist congregations had ideological doubts about forming larger organisations, but in 1767, in face of the relentless persistence of the tax laws and of much hostility amounting to persecution in some country towns, twenty churches sent representatives to the Massachusetts town of Warren, where they began the association bearing that name. From 1770 the Warren Association's grievance committee, with Backus as its most influential and eloquent member, was busy in defence of Baptist interests. The general problem posed by the requirement of certificates for tax exemption had taken an acute form in the recently settled town of Ashfield, where an act of the legislature vested power in the proprietors rather than the inhabitants. Upon the nonpayment of religious taxes by Baptists in the town, the proprietors used their owers to sell at auction 398 acres of landed property owned by Baptists, valued at £363.13s., for a paltry £19.3s. Failing redress at home, the grievance committee resolved to take the whole issue to the Lords of Trade in London; they seem to have had some indirect assistance from Governor Hutchinson, who did not like Baptists but was willing to see the General Assembly's authority questioned. The outcome was that in July 1771, the Crown disallowed the law objected to by the grievance committee, thus relieving the Baptists and demonstrating that persecuted minorities might seek royal protection against local oppression.[23]

The Baptists' procedure in seeking relief from the Crown was subject to obvious risks; the least lack of enthusiasm for the more popular notion of American liberties, the least expression of sympathy with Britain, exposed them to grave suspicions of treachery to the American cause in the rising struggle against Crown and Parliament. Yet the legislature, which persisted in renewing the tax laws, left the Baptists little choice but to show equal persistence in opposition.

23. Isaac Backus, *Church History of New England from 1620 to 1804* (Philadelphia, 1853), pp. 192–3; McLoughlin, ed., *Backus on Church, State, and Calvinism*, pp. 11–12; McLoughlin, *New England Dissent, 1630–1833*, 2 vols. (Cambridge, Mass., 1971), I, chap. 29, 531–46.

An incidental irony noted by Backus was that the fee of fourpence local money or threepence sterling was the same as the tea tax which had provoked the Boston Tea Party![24] In 1773, in default of remedies, the grievance committee proposed to individual Baptists that they should refuse to comply with the tax requirements—a policy of virtual civil disobedience. This plan was not translated into action by enough churches to make an immediate impression, but the discontent of so significant a faction had in turn to be pondered by the legislators as questions of loyalty became increasingly urgent.

Equality had not been an initial issue in these disputes. But in fighting against a determined form of persecution and repression, American religious minorities could demand nothing less than equality for themselves. Yet Backus's arguments did not proceed from the premises of the Anglo-American whig tradition. In an important pamphlet, *An Appeal to the Public for Religious Liberty*, published in connection with the campaign for civil disobedience, Backus explained that God had appointed two kinds of government, ecclesiastical and civil, and his point was made by asserting that "they ought not to be confounded together". It is clearly implicit in this argument that the free exercise of religion would stand to benefit from separation between religion and government. In the matter of taxation and representation, the Baptists agreed with their legislators, he was careful to say; the question they raised was whether their civil legislators were their representatives in religious affairs. "They [our opponents] often talk about *equality* in these affairs", exclaimed Backus in a revealing comment, "but where does it appear!"[25] His argument did not rest on natural rights, however. Backus was quite satisfied with those granted in the charter, and was therefore not obliged to allow himself to be drawn into the theological or philosophical problems that would arise from asserting the natural rights of a creature whose condition, since the Fall, was known to be one of fundamental depravity. He denounced the Congregationalists for using the word "equality" as an excuse for taxing Baptists to support Congregational ministers. Natural rights, however, did find their way back into the argument when Backus came by a different route into a surprising proximity to the position

24. Backus, *Church History*, p. 192.
25. McLoughlin, ed., *Backus on Church, State, and Calvinism*, p. 334.

of his Whig opponents in describing "equal liberty of conscience" as "that dearest of all rights"—a right given by God.[26] Backus on the other hand could have no sympathy with philosophers who were prepared to talk of the laws of nature as though God himself were subject to them, as though he were, in truth, "nature's God"; but the effect in terms of rights with which people were equally endowed, and which in consequence were morally binding, was apparently the same.

The meeting of the Continental Congress in September 1774, gave the Massachusetts Baptists the opportunity for a new and more spectacular stage for their claims. At the suggestion of certain western members of the Warren Committee, Backus and two colleagues agreed to travel to Philadelphia with a memorial from about twenty Baptist churches. The memorial gave a summary of the oppressions suffered under the tax exemption laws with special emphasis on Sturbridge and Ashfield, and concluded, "It may now be asked— What is the liberty desired? The answer is; as the kingdom of Christ is not of this world and religion is a concern between God and the soul with which no human authority can intermeddle . . . we claim and expect the liberty of worshipping God according to our consciences, not being obliged to support a ministry we cannot attend, whilst we demean ourselves as faithful subjects".[27]

The Baptist deputation presented this memorial at a meeting with the Massachusetts delegation on the evening of 14 October. John Adams replied with a speech about the mildness of the Massachusetts arrangements for religious establishment. Then Israel Pemberton, the elderly and distinguished Philadelphia Quaker (of whose presence Backus makes no mention), intervened with a forthright speech about religious persecution in Massachusetts which Adams regarded as "quite rude". Adams told him that the people of Massachusetts were as religious and conscientious as the people of Pennsylvania and their consciences dictated to them that it was their duty to support their existing laws—an assertion which clearly satisfied him but must have seemed to his opponents like a very special case of special pleading. Samuel Adams, who had been present in the legislature when the particular issues complained of were debated, gave

26. Ibid., p. 338.
27. McLoughlin, *New England Dissent*, I, 558–60.

the meeting an account of those events and satisfied his colleagues
that no oppression had occurred. But John Adams developed a strong
suspicion that they were witnessing a Quaker plot, to which the
Massachusetts Baptists were lending themselves, to sew disunity in
the American cause. Robert Treat Paine, another delegate, snarled
at Backus that they were only contending against paying a little
money, not about conscience; to which the Baptist minister replied
with another affirmation of faith: "It is absolutely a point of conscience with me", he said; "for I cannot give in the certificates they
require without implicitly acknowledging that power to man which
I believe belongs to God". This statement, together perhaps with the
obvious dangers of disunity, seems to have made an impression; the
meeting ended with assurances that the Massachusetts delegation
would see what could be done for the Baptists' relief.[28]

Imputations of disloyalty to the colonial cause exposed the Baptists to serious risks, accentuated by the fact that they had actually
obtained relief from the Crown against their own legislature over
the matter of Ashfield. Backus later claimed that not one Baptist had
been listed by the General Court among the 311 who were banned as
traitors from returning to Massachusetts.[29] Yet the prospect of being
ruled by an unrestrained Massachusetts legislature, from whose laws
no appeal would lie to any higher authority, was an equally serious
cause of anxiety to the Baptists, who had quite enough experience of
religious majorities to have their own doubts about the merits of majority rule. Independence did nothing to relieve these anxieties; in
1777 the legislature passed a further tax exemption law which still
required Baptists to pay for copies of certificates to be issued by town
clerks to prove their exemption from religious taxes.

When the legislature presented the towns with a new constitution
in 1778, Backus renewed the attack with a powerful assertion that
civil rulers could not represent the Baptists in religious affairs. As to
the fee for exemption certificates, he echoed the tones of colonial resistance to parliamentary taxation: "It is not the PENCE but the POWER
that alarms us". Backus snatched his sharpest tactical weapon in this

28. L. H. Butterfield, ed., *Diary and Autobiography of John Adams* (Cambridge, Mass., 1961), II, 152–4; III, 311–13; Backus, *Church History*, pp.
192–3; McLoughlin, *New England Dissent*, I, 558–61.
29. Backus, *Church History*, p. 196.

argument from the grasp of the liberal Congregational clergyman, Charles Chauncy, who had forged it ten years earlier against the threat of an Anglican bishopric in America. In that dispute, Chauncy had declared, "We are, in principle, against all civil establishments in religion"; and he concluded, "By the Gospel-charter all Christians are vested with precisely the same rights . . ."—views which Backus had only to quote in order to demonstrate his opponents divergence from their own principles.[30]

When a Baptist elder, Noah Alden, was elected to the State's Constitutional Convention in 1779 he sought Backus's advice, to which Backus replied with a long letter giving a proposed "Declaration of the Rights of the Inhabitants of the State of Massachusetts, in New England". His exposition closely followed those rights announced by George Mason in Virginia, but in the religious article Backus emphasised God, revelation, religious worship, and the soul, where the Virginian Anglican was more temperate in style and latitudinarian in theology.[31]

These struggles revealed significant differences of principle between Isaac Backus and his Whig-republican contemporaries about the origins and necessity of government. The latter tended, with differing degrees of emphasis and inclination, to regard government as a disagreeable phenomenon, though not all would have accepted Thomas Paine's rhetorical statement that it was "a badge of lost innocence". The concept of innocence, however, was extremely important, for American Whigs had accepted the idea of a state of nature in which rights already existed and held as an article of faith that property belonged among those rights. These views and the disposition to regard them as fundamental, had very little in common with the thought of the Pietists, for whom heresy began when people forgot or denied the consequences of original sin. Backus took a less sanguine view of any suppositious state of nature and recognised clearly that there could be no liberty worth having without government; the only alternatives to civil government were tyranny and licentiousness. The crucial need that emerged from these prolonged disputes was to break down not only religious monopolies but all

30. McLoughlin, ed., *Backus on Church, State, and Calvinism*, pp. 350–65.
31. McLoughlin, *New England Dissent*, pp. 600–01. For Mason's version in full, see p. 25.

vestiges of religious privilege. The equality of religious conscience that Backus and his fellow Baptists, in common with the Congregationalist majority, believed in, was limited to equality among Christians. These views did not imply equality for fundamentally differing religions, or between religion and irreligion. Yet these arguments did attack the principles of religious establishment. With the memorial which Backus took to Philadelphia in 1774, they constituted the early steps towards the eventual political solution of complete neutrality which was at least nominally implied by the adoption of the First Amendment.

Isaac Backus probably never took the social implications of his faith as far as did his Massachusetts colleague John Leland, who travelled farther than Backus and did much of his mission work in Virginia. In a sermon delivered in 1804, Leland spoke in terms of popular political sympathies:

As far as church government on earth is the government of Christ, it is of democratical genius. Church governmnet is congregational, not parochial, diocesan, not national. Each congregated church disclaims the power of Popes, kings, bishops, parliaments, kirks, or presbyteries, and claims the right and power to govern itself according to the laws of Christ. And it must be confessed that the spirit and rule by which the subjects of Christ's kingdom are to live one among another, greatly resemble the genius of a republic, and as greatly confronts the inequality and haughtiness of monarchies.[32]

Leland in effect was arguing by analogy from principles that were already known and approved to those he was advocating—from republican politics to pietistic religion. This, however, came on the tide that flowed after the second great revival of 1798 which began in Kentucky and was much more consciously political than its predecessors. Its preachers regarded themselves in part as agents for Jefferson's election, and treated the federalists as religious and political enemies. By now political victories had been won and political solutions reached. In the long and harrowing period of their earlier trials, the Baptists, who were not the only persecuted religious minority but were the most numerous, and who by virtue of their descent from established New England religion were also the great-

32. Edwin Scott Gaustad, "The Backus-Leland Tradition", in W. S. Hudson, ed., Baptist Concepts of the Church (Philadelphia, 1959), p. 123.

est threat to orthodoxy, were never committed by their principles to any general idea of religious equality.

The importance of this partly successful struggle, as a result of which the Baptists did gain a grudging toleration and a gradual acceptance of their independence, lay in the clarification of the issues. Isaac Backus and his colleagues had forced their contemporaries to define the objects and terms of the relationship between church and government and had gone far to demonstrate that no form of establishment for one religion could be wholly compatible with equality for others. It was important, too, that Backus had defined the moral basis of the claim for equality of conscience, for that claim did not rest exclusively on the Whig idea of social contract. The rights of religion were clearly prior to those of society.

These distinctions emerged in the same period in Virginia. The Baptist Separates disturbed the spiritual tranquility of the Valley of Virginia during the late 1760s; the small but settled Baptist communities were startled by these incursions; the Anglicans were often enraged. As in New England, the hostility of existing parishes and congregations was social as well as theological in origin. The Baptists' claims on other peoples' souls, and their own claims to recognition, stopped far short of any interest in controlling the political system. In Virginia no more than in New England did they seek a new political order or a redistribution of worldly goods, and in this sense their contribution to the spread of ideas of equality was less than has often been claimed for them; it was not in any case a contribution for which they wished to claim credit. Yet in spite of these limitations, the Separates and the more militant Baptists did challenge the existing social order. The equality of relationships in the conduct of their own affairs contrasted sharply with the preoccupation with rank, etiquette, and formalities of style and procedure which did much to give Virginian society its character. The Separates held themselves together in a community which by its existence, by its withdrawal from the world, questioned the values of the rest.

The formal privileges of the Anglican church were extensive, but they were exercised with little severity or determination. The main instrument at hand for restraining the excesses of the new invaders was a requirement that preachers obtain a licence to preach only in specific places. Itineracy defied this restriction even where the preachers might have been able to comply with the regulations. The noise made by the Separates seems to have been disproportionate to their numbers, which, together with official Baptists, were not reckoned above five thousand at the outbreak of the War of Independence.[33] It was the noise that mattered, however, partly because of the force of the argument, but partly because of the patronage they gained in the House of Burgesses.

The intellectual heritage of Thomas Jefferson and James Madison was entirely different from that of the Baptists, whose cause they adopted in the Virginia legislature. They believed in liberty of thought and conscience with a conviction as intense as the Baptists' belief in salvation. Although Jefferson and Madison, in common with their colleagues in Virginia political life, were religious men, and perceived an ultimate connection between the reasons for religious belief and the reasons for liberty of conscience, it would nevertheless have been possible for them to hold that belief without faith in personal salvation.

Both men were heavily in debt to Locke's *Letter on Toleration*; but for them, toleration was never enough, and they preferred the stronger concept of religious liberty. The rationalist thinking of their age drew on a considerable heritage from the seventeenth century, which had gained enormous subsequent vitality from Newton's demonstration that the universe was co-ordinated by mechanical and rationally explicable laws. For generations, various works of the phases of European Enlightenment had crossed the Atlantic, colouring the attitudes of enquiring American minds, who were ready to make their own contributions to the development of science. These interests were easily compatible with the Anglican affiliations of many American leaders, especially those in the southern provinces and in New York, whose outlook was tinged with a worldliness that sometimes passed into deism. In America as in Britain, such men— Jefferson in this was something of an exception—rarely became subject to the violent anticlericalism that affected French intellectuals after springing from similar philosophical sources; the kind of politi-

---

33. Wesley M. Gewehr, *The Great Awakening in Virginia, 1740–1790* (Durham, N.C., 1930), passim; and for further estimates, Rhys Isaac, "Evangelical Revolt: The Nature of the Baptists' Challenge to the Traditional Order in Virginia, 1765–1775", *William and Mary Quarterly*, vol. XXXI, no. 3 (July, 1974), p. 346, n. 2.

cal anticlericalism that was active in parliamentary circles in eighteenth-century England was often consistent with faithful exercise of the religious duties prescribed by the church itself. American consciences took their colour from the English attitude, and in any case those Americans who subscribed to the religions established in their provinces encountered nothing to terrify them in the forms of powers of the church.

Jefferson's mind and temperament were in keeping with this intellectual background. He was far from irreligious; his deepest moral convictions would have been shattered by the denial of a religious explanation of the world. But his deism reflected an earnest rejection of dogma. He was horrified by the cruelty and the sheer absurdity of religious persecution, for which he blamed the priesthood and suspected New England. The truth—an abstraction to which he had the most profound devotion—could never be discovered, nor could people be led to it, by coercion. "The legitimate powers of government extend to such acts only as are injurious to others", he declared in a famous passage. "But it does me no injury for my neighbour to say there are twenty gods, or no god. It neither picks my pocket nor breaks my leg". The only way to seek the truth, and the only way to convince others, was by reason and persuasion. "To make way for these, free enquiry must be indulged".[34]

Although many of the best political minds of the time remained convinced that some form of established religion was indispensable to social order, this conviction did not extend to the benefits of moral coercion, on which Jefferson's scepticism was widely shared. The point was that religious understanding could simply not be reached through persecution or coercion; and outward observance was not the same thing as true religious feeling. One did not have to be a revivalist to see the fruitlessness of compulsion. It was in keeping with these views that the Virginia Declaration of Rights of 1776 was drawn up to include a straightforward statement of the generally agreed latitudinarian principles of religious freedom: "That religion, or the duty we owe to our Creator, and the manner of discharging it, can be directed only by reason and conviction, not by force or violence; and therefore men are equally entitled to the free exercise of

34. Jefferson, *Notes on Virginia*, pp. 159–60.

religion, according to the dictates of conscience; and that it is the mutual duty of all to practice Christian forbearance, and love, and charity towards each other".[35]

This language, however, was compatible with various possible forms of religious establishment. The one guiding condition was that of Christianity; in common with nearly all American states of the new Republic, Virginia expected not only Christianity, but its Protestant variety, to lie at the base of all religious observance as recognised or fostered by the state. But both local and provincial government had long been in the hands of men who regarded the established church as a symbol of their own habitual predominance. Jefferson's campaign to overturn the establishment of the Episcopal Church—as the Church of England was now called—therefore met with deeply entrenched and widespread opposition. The moderate but convinced Anglicans who dominated the legislature, led and rallied by Edmund Pendleton, put up a resistance which later caused Jefferson to reflect that the movement for disestablishment "brought on the severest contests that I have known".[36] When Jefferson became governor of Virginia in 1779, the management of his bill for religious liberty passed into the hands of the younger Madison, who until that time had been personally little known to Jefferson.

The struggle was prolonged over several years. Many sectarian interests could have been satisfied by a general act requiring taxation in support of religion while leaving individuals to decide which sect to support; and in 1784, Patrick Henry helped to promote two legislative measures, one to incorporate the Episcopal Church, and the other to assess and raise taxes for the support of all sects without discrimination. With Jefferson now serving as American minister in France, Madison undertook the task of parliamentary and public opposition. The incorporation bill was passed in December 1784; but Madison, by delaying legislative action until he had been able to arouse public opinion through a widely circulated petition, succeeded in bringing about the defeat of the more important assess-

35. J. R. Pole, ed., *The Revolution in America: Documents on the Internal Development of America in the Revolutionary Era, 1754–1788* (London, 1970), p. 521.
36. *Autobiography*, quoted in Bernard Mayo, *Jefferson Himself* (Charlottesville, 1942), p. 79.

ment bill; and he then called up Jefferson's Bill for Establishing Religious Freedom, which passed into law in January 1786. Jefferson, moving now in French court and salon circles, had reason to boast of the achievement; it was one of the three things that he caused to be engraved on his tombstone.[37]

The Memorial and Remonstrance,[38] written by Madison in 1785, was the centerpiece of the campaign against the bill for religious assessments. When its persuasive reasoning had had time to penetrate into the country, support for Henry's project fell away quite remarkably. The *Memorial* is a striking example of Madison's art of combining philosophical and political argument into a single piece of political propaganda, in which he was soon to excel as a contributor to *The Federalist Papers*; and as with that later document, the recourse to fundamental principles gives the *Memorial* a general character as a commentary on the meaning of religious freedom.

Much of this carefully worded pamphlet was acceptable to the Baptists, who had played such an important part in fighting for sectarian autonomy, and were among Madison's own political constituents. Madison's faith, reinforced by the theological studies in which he had steeped himself as a student at Princeton, disposed him to make a political principle of the precept that man's duty to God was prior to any duty he owed to the state. Any civil government was necessarily subordinate to that of God, for which reason no man's right in religion could be abridged by the establishment of civil government. But Madison's position, as developed in the *Memorial*, was still distinctly to the secular side of the Baptists. They held that no government could come between the individual and his conscience because the kind of knowledge with which the conscience worked was given by God and was not answerable to human government. Madison was close to this when he said that men owed a prior duty to God. But his concept of human judgment owed slightly more to the idea of the autonomy of reason. The right to follow one's own religious convictions was unalienable—"because the opinions of men, depending only on the evidence contemplated by their own minds,

37. Elwyn A. Smith, *Religious Liberty in the United States: The Development of Church-State Thought since the Revolutionary Era* (Philadelphia, 1972), pp. 11–13.

38. Saul K. Padover, ed., *The Complete Madison* (New York, 1953), pp. 299–306.

cannot follow the dictates of other men". This rationalistic view of the effect of evidence in the formation of opinion (not here called faith) was then appropriately followed by a reference to man's duty to his Creator. Further down, Madison developed a lucid expression of the basically humanistic rationality of the Enlightenment: "Whilst we assert for ourselves a freedom to embrace, to profess and to observe, the Religion which we believe to be of divine origin, we cannot deny an equal freedom to those whose minds have not yielded to the evidence which has convinced us. If this freedom be abused, it is an offence against God, not against man". The divine and human elements were nicely balanced, and it would be hard to say which led the argument. Madison would have said that each was incomplete without the other; it is more doubtful whether he would have wanted to pursue these thoughts to purely secular conclusions. Nevertheless, he had charted a course which, in the intellectual and social climate of the mid-twentieth century, would lead further than he could easily have foreseen.

The *Memorial* carried conviction with the Virginia electorate on other and more political grounds. "Who does not see", Madison argued, "that the same authority which can establish Christianity, in exclusion of all other Religions, may establish with the same ease any particular sect of Christians, in exclusion of all other sects?" The assessment bill violated "that equality which ought to be the basis of every law"—an affirmation that could be supported by simply quoting the Virginia Declaration of Rights. The reasoning and rhetoric of Madison's appeal to public opinion ran straight back to Jefferson's in the Declaration of Independence; equality in religion was "held by the same tenure with all our other rights. If we recur to its origin, it is equally the gift of nature . . .".

Madison was well aware that religious freedom rested on other, and securer, foundations than those supplied by arguments of finely spun rationality. Individual states might retain their religious establishments, but no single establishment could ever be expected to dominate the nation. The Union was developing with a curiously mixed and uncommitted kind of religious pluralism. States differed widely in their policies; Connecticut retained its Congregational system until 1818; and when Massachusetts finally ended its residue of support for the Congregational churches in 1833, it was not on the strength of anti-establishmentarian convictions, but because the spread of Unitarianism was taking control of the churches away from the Congregationalists themselves.[39] In neither state did the movement for disestablishment draw its impetus directly from the Revolution. But Madison already saw clearly that the variety of religious affiliations in the United States would constitute a safeguard against any national establishment of the European kind. Speaking on this theme in the Virginia ratifying convention in June 1788, he explained, "This freedom arises from the multiplicity of sects, which pervades America, and which is the best and only security for religious liberty in any country".[40] In *The Federalist Number Fifty-One* he gave a slightly fuller exposition of the same theme, in this case by extension from his argument in *Federalist Ten* that political freedom was secured by the existence of various independent interests operating within the same political system: "In a free government", he argued, "the security for civil rights must be the same as for religious rights. It consists in the one case in the multiplicity of interests and in the other, in the multiplicity of sects. The degree of security in both cases will depend on the number of interests and sects; and this may be presumed to depend on the extent of the country and the number of people comprehended under the same government".[41]

The sectarian need for security in a world where power was always considered untrustworthy formed one of the most effective impulses in the demand for a constitutional amendment to safeguard religion against state intervention. But many people who wanted some such safeguard were still willing to support provisions by which the government could give assistance to religious organisations, provided such assistance was equally distributed. These differences caused prolonged debate during the drafting of the First Amendment. Madison, who was engaged in these debates as a member of the House of Representatives, would have liked a specific safeguard for conscience. This moral autonomy of the individual was a basic ingredient of Madison's idea of republican principles; but it

39. Howe, *Garden and Wilderness*, p. 36; Stokes, *Church and State*, IV, 377–8.
40. Padover, ed., *Complete Madison*, p. 306.
41. Jacob E. Cooke, ed., *The Federalist* (Middletown, Conn., 1961), pp. 351–2.

was difficult to frame a statement that committed the government to complete neutrality without seeming more hostile to religious sentiments than was true of the feelings of most members of Congress, and also of the people they represented. It was this that explained the ambiguity that has always lain coiled within formal American doctrines of separation between church and state. Representative American spokesmen wished at heart for a system that would be neutral but hospitable to religion, as opposed to the alternative of a neutrality that would seem positively unhospitable. But even so mild a concept as hospitality might leave the irreligious conscience on an unequal footing. The dilemma has never yielded a completely satisfactory solution.

The First Amendment emerged in its final form from a three-man committee of which Madison was a member. Its clause on religion stated simply but with a high degree of condensation that "Congress shall make no law respecting an establishment of religion, nor prohibiting the free exercise thereof". The reference to "conscience" had gone, no doubt to Madison's disappointment.[42] But the language imposed a sweeping ban on federal government intervention in religious activities; the interpretation of this language was to exercise the highest ingenuity of lawyers and judges in later centuries.

As presidents of the United States, Jefferson and Madison both viewed their duties as calling for a strict application of the First Amendment. Jefferson refused to declare any religious observances; Madison vetoed a bill to incorporate the Protestant Episcopal Church in Alexandria, and another bill reserving a parcel of land in the Mississippi Territory for the use of Baptist churches.[43] He condemned both these measures as involving the federal government in the activities of religious bodies in a manner prohibited by the Constitution. The principle was clear. Real religious freedom must also mean religious self-sufficiency; state intervention to assist a church in any way was a denial of the self-sufficiency of that church, and to that extent an encroachment on the basic neutrality, not only of the state towards the church—which was Madison's concern as president—but of the church towards the state. For the most part, however, Americans were unable to reconcile this degree of constitutional purity with

42. Smith, *Religious Liberty*, pp. 45–57.
43. Padover, ed., *Complete Madison*, pp. 307–8.

their very real and far-reaching religious commitments. The constitutional history of the issue of separation was to be not only prolonged, but intensely complicated. The First Amendment had set up the standard by which the issue was to be judged; but Jefferson, who had not been a party to the framing of that amendment, added further complexities to the language of constitutional argument by erecting a metaphysical wall to keep church and state apart, without admitting any possibility that it might ever be scaled from either side.

Chapter Four

The Emergence of
Religious Pluralism

The Protestant Aegis Challenged

George Washington's farewell address is not usually considered a religious statement, which makes his one reference to the subject all the more instructive. Congratulating his fellow countrymen on their advantages, Washington told them, "with slight shades of differences, you have the same religion, manners, habits, and political principles".[1] The assumption was that the similarities in their religious beliefs disposed people towards agreement in matters affecting their more material interests. In the absence of those passions that had broken out in European civil and religious wars, the people of the different states could settle such differences as arose between them within their existing institutions.

Washington's own state of Virginia had repealed its restrictive laws against Roman Catholics in 1785.[2] But his generation handed on to their successors the fundamental conviction that the American people were Protestant. Their broad lands and spacious circumstances gave room for minorities whose practices held no threat to the republican character of the Union. But that character, a declared attribute of the Constitution itself, was permeated with Protestant

1. James Richardson, comp., *Messages and Papers of the Presidents, 1789–1897* (Washington, D.C., 1896), I, 213–24.
2. W. W. Hening, *The Statutes at Large of Virginia, 1619–1792* (Richmond, 1809–23), XII, 120.

[87]

assumptions about history and society. It is no exaggeration to say of some of the leading Americans of that generation, including Thomas Jefferson and Washington himself, that they were better Christians in their politics than in their religion.

The elemental Christianity to which Washington had referred was no merely passive inference: It exerted a force in the interpretation of the laws, and was assumed on several occasions to have passed into that part of the common law which the United States had received from England. Early state reports contain plentiful cases in which this assumption was made. In 1811, Chief Justice Kent of New York punished an atheist for blasphemy against the Christian religion, declaring that "the case assumes we are a Christian people, and the morality of the country is deeply engrafted upon Christianity, and not on the doctrines and worship of these imposters"—meaning Mohamet or the Grand Lama. The reception through common law was confirmed by the Supreme Court in 1844, when the United States was again referred to as "a Christian nation". The basically religious character of the American people continued to inform the opinions of the Supreme Court, without express reference to Christianity, when in 1892 it was held that contract labour laws could not exclude a minister of religion who had been summoned from abroad: "No purpose or action against religion can be imputed to any legislation", declared the court, "because this is a religious people. This is historically true. From the discovery of this continent to the present hour, there is a single voice making this affirmation".[3] Such different foreign observers as Tocqueville in the 1830s and James Bryce some half a century later regarded Christianity as a national though not an established religion.[4] The pervasiveness of this assumption exerted a controlling effect on the interpretation of the First Amendment. Its nationally secular implications were at a heavy discount against the principles attached to it by those who wanted to protect the interests of religion rather than to curtail them. Until nearly the middle of the nineteenth century, moreover, the essence of American religion

3. Mark De Wolfe Howe, *The Garden and the Wilderness: Religion and Government in American Constitutional History* (Chicago and London, 1965), pp. 28–9.
4. Alexis de Tocqueville, *De la démocratie en Amérique* (1840), ed. J.–P. Meyer (Paris, 1961), II, 308–15; James Bryce, *The American Commonwealth*, 2 vols. (Chicago, 1891), II, 560, 570–99.

was a Protestantism whose reserves of strength and numbers were so immense that no rival seemed capable of challenging either the tenure of Protestant theology, or the Protestant character of the sectarian diversity which flourished under the protection of the Constitution.

The creed that grew alongside this elemental Protestantism was that of laisser-faire capitalism. While it remained to periodic generations of evangelical or fundamentalist preachers to lament the growing national obsession with material gain, popular religious teaching had little difficulty in reconciling the Sermon on the Mount with *The Wealth of Nations*. The spirit of individual economic enterprise, under the peculiar American advantages of self-government and democracy, was celebrated by ministers of religion as well as by Fourth-of-July orators for its power to make America a beacon to less exemplary nations. The Reverend Lyman Beecher, perhaps the most prominent of the Unitarian clergy of the Jacksonian era, urged in this spirit that with the aid of education, America could do its duty to the world by extending the missionary combination of Protestantism and self-government.[5]

The ministry's misgivings about human depravity seemed to be nicely balanced by their manifest satisfaction with the American combination of liberty and Protestantism. Horace Bushnell, a young man in 1835, explained in a sermon that pure religion had to begin again at the beginning in a new world, "and call up around it all its own proper institutions. And He who apportions all events to their times with sovereign wisdom had reserved such a world unknown . . . a vast continent of forests still in the wilderness of nature. . . . It was Protestantism in religion that produced republicanism in government".[6]

All the leading branches of Protestant theology in the growing Republic placed intense emphasis on the worth of the individual. In the Universalist and Unitarian forms, an optimistic and positive view of human achievements displaced the increasingly unacceptable

5. Lyman Beecher, *A Plea for the West*, cited by Yehoshua Arieli, *Individualism and Nationalism in American Ideology* (Cambridge, Mass., 1964), pp. 254–5.
6. Horace Bushnell, *Crisis of the Church* (Hartford, 1835), quoted in Elwyn A. Smith, *Religious Liberty in the United States: The Development of Church-State Thought since the Revolutionary Era* (Philadelphia, 1972), pp. 11–13.

Calvinist insistence on depravity; where Calvinists deprived their subjects of hope for any form of salvation through their own efforts, the newer and more humanistic faiths gave them reasons for believing that they could contribute to their own salvation.[7] Calvinism declined not only in such urbane centres as Boston and New York but on the Midwestern frontier, where hardworking men and women were determined to place their faith in more hopeful doctrines.[8]

None of these attitudes offered any grounds for resistance to the growth of private wealth. After the Mexican War and the Compromise of 1850, Northern ministers of religion lent themselves increasingly to the moral crusade against slavery; any faith which valued the individual could hardly do less, once the issue had been opened, and the only cause for surprise lay in the hesitation with which the Northern churches had opened their fire. But few similar voices were raised against the morals or the effects of the dominant preoccupation with acquisitive business enterprise. The concern with individual worth reflected a kind of withdrawal from areas of public policy in which churches had often taken part in the past. During and for a generation after the Revolution it was a common complaint of the clergy that the virtues of simplicity of life and dedication to religion were getting lost in a welter of lust for private gain. But it was not until the late nineteenth century, when questions of the social accountability of wealth emerged once again, that the Protestant churches showed any appreciable concern over the moral implications or consequences of the economic system. With the rise of great corporations and vast accumulations of wealth, Protestantism became a sort of moral caretaker for the methods and consciences of businessmen.[9] It was in keeping with this spirit that the Reverend Henry Ward Beecher, probably the most celebrated cleric of his time, could declare in 1879 that "God intended the great to be great and the little to be little".[10]

Calvinistic theology did not stand still in face of the emphatic individualism unleashed in the early Republic. A school of Connecti-

7. W. W. Sweet, *Religion in the Development of American Culture, 1765–1840* (New York, 1952), pp. 234–5.
8. Ibid., p. 210.
9. Sidney E. Meade, *The Lively Experiment* (New York, 1963), pp. 138–42.
10. David H. Montgomery, *Beyond Equality: Labor and the Radical Republicans, 1862–1872* (New York, 1967), pp. 230–1.

cut theologians, all born in the eighteenth century, worked to adapt a belief in the divine authority of government to the conditions of popular sovereignty. The eldest, Timothy Dwight (1752–1817), was president of Yale; his pupil, Lyman Beecher (1775–1863) practiced the belief that Christians ought to endeavour to influence events; and Nathaniel W. Taylor (1786–1858), Professor of Divinity at Yale, became the most subtle theoretical exponent of the new Calvinism. When Taylor developed the argument, certainly heretical by earlier standards, that man was the author of his own sin and was correspondingly responsible for his own salvation, his doctrine displaced the efficacy of grace and came full circle with the power of works.[11]

Differences among Protestant sects were deep and often bitter. But all of them accepted a basic compatibility between Protestantism and the republican ideals of the Constitution. This self-conscious identification was no mere exuberance of the national spirit, however. Centuries of English and American history taught Protestants to regard the Church of Rome as an inveterate enemy. Many of the revolutionary state constitutions specified the Protestant branch of Christianity when prescribing qualifications for political office; in Massachusetts, the omission of this provision from the qualifications for the governorship caused more objections than any other article of the Constitution of 1780.[12] When Catholic immigrants from Ireland and Germany began to establish a conspicuous and growing foothold in the early nineteenth century, Protestants almost everywhere regarded them as ideological aliens. So far as the sources of faith were concerned, moreover, American Protestants were not entirely misguided in taking this ominous view of the mixture of religious affiliations which threatened to become a feature of American society. When Pope Gregory XVI in 1832 issued an encyclical which denounced liberty of conscience as an "absurd and erroneous doctrine, or rather raving", flowing from the "polluted fountain of indiffer-

11. Nathaniel W. Taylor, *Concio ad Clerum, A Sermon Delivered in the Chapel of Yale College* (New Haven, 1828); *Lectures on the Moral Government of God*, 2 vols. (New York, 1859), I, 258–9; II, 162; Sweet, *Religion*, pp. 199–200; Smith, *Religious Liberty*, pp. 70–90.

12. The town meeting records on which this statement is based are in Massachusetts Archives, State House, Boston, vols. 276 and 277. They have been edited by Oscar and Mary Handlin as *The Popular Sources of Legislative Authority* (Cambridge, Mass., 1966).

ence", he did not make it easy for American Catholics to explain their dual attachment to the principles of the Republic and to the faith of Rome. "The pontiff", declared the Reverend J. F. Berg of Philadelphia, "is clearly committed against the first principles of American freedom and regards them as unmitigated abominations".[13] This, without the slightest doubt, was a highly representative expression of opinion.

The emergence of a substantial body of American Catholic citizens exposed the doctrine of separation to questions that had not previously been asked. The truth was that Washington's quiet assurance as to the homogeneity of American religion had reflected the widespread and largely unquestioned assumption that political stability did indeed rest on certain religious foundations. The idea of separation between church and state was far more daring in 1791 than it has seemed to have been in the light of subsequent history. No one could really be sure that a political system would have the moral resources to survive without the support of any officially recognised religious system.[14] Even those who believed in separation in a clearer and more doctrinal sense than most—and Jefferson and Madison, to name two, had thought their way through the problem —could still count on the overwhelming stability of Protestant sentiment as a fact of American life, which took up the ground left vacant by the absence of political experience.

The American system rested on the ultimate autonomy of individual conscience and therefore on freedom of individual choice. This view was no more attractive to genuine Pietists than it had been to Puritans; it was at the best a distasteful and theologically dubious consequence of the existence of religious pluralism; the members of a church covenant were bound by an extremely strong bond of spiritual community which effectively permitted very little independence to the individual.[15] But individual choice was a fact of political and increasingly of religious life. The Roman Catholic Church, on the other hand, did not share the first assumptions that lay deep in

13. Smith, *Religious Liberty*, pp. 103–4.
14. This point is persuasively argued by Sidney E. Meade, *Lively Experiment*, p. 59.
15. Larzer Ziff, "The Social Bond of Church Government", *American Quarterly*, winter 1958.

Protestant history. People had once chosen to be Protestant; but Catholics had merely continued to be Catholics. The training and indoctrination of Catholics was part of a complete programme at home and school. For Catholic priests, the idea of a secular education was a contradiction in terms; there could be no education without the teaching of religious truths. Yet American education was based on the assumption of the religious neutrality of the state. The state might set aside land for churches, or even exempt them from taxation; but it could not enter into the process of education without taking sides with religion, and by implication with one religion in preference to others.

These were difficult problems for Protestants as well as Catholics. The full rigour of religious abstention had never been systematically practised by the United States. After all, the Ohio Valley had been settled in the early years of the nineteenth century under the great Northwest Ordinance of 1787, repassed by the first Congress, which had explicitly linked "religion, morality, and knowledge" as "necessary to good government and the happiness of mankind" in providing for "schools and means of education",[16] and no one seems to have regarded that as a contradiction of the First Amendment. American policy often protected religious interests, and sometimes encouraged them; and in any case it was only the federal government, not the states, that was restrained from entering into the activities of religion. Moral precepts were normally given a religious base, and Bible readings were often included in school hours—an inherently Protestant procedure. In view of the vital importance of religious principle in the very nature of a Roman Catholic education—and on the other side, of the Protestant assumptions about the formal neutrality of American schooling—it is not surprising that the doctrine of "separation" was subjected to its most prolonged scrutiny by the sometimes fiery light of controversies over education. The heat became more intense after the separation enjoined on the federal government was held, though the operation of the Fourteenth Amendment, to apply to the states as well. As Mr Justice Jackson observed in 1947, it was no exaggeration to say that the whole historic controversy between

16. The Northwest Ordnance of 1787, in J. R. Pole, ed., *The Revolution in America: Documents on the Internal Development of America in the Revolutionary Era, 1754–1788* (London, 1970), p. 386.

Catholics and non-Catholics in temporal policy came into focus in their respective school policies.[17]

When Protestants living in Eastern cities began to comprehend that the Catholic presence was both permanent and increasing, their hostility to Catholic communities sometimes made the public schools into unpleasant places for Catholic children. The normal Catholic desire for parochial schools was accentuated by the attitudes prevailing in mixed communities. Bishop John Hughes, Roman Catholic diocesan of New York, brought the issue to a head in 1840 when he applied for a share of the public funds appropriated for education. When liberal Protestants found their traditional respect for the manifestly free and democratic system of religious individualism opposed by Catholics on principle, they could not believe that Catholics had any faith in free institutions—a discovery which only confirmed their previous suspicions. But the hierarchy, who did not believe that religion was acquired by free individual decisions, knew that they needed parochial schools to maintain the body of their faith. They regarded the official view as actually hostile to them. On this ground they could meet and surprise the Protestants with the charge that the practice of separation was not neutral at all, but favoured the prevailing Protestant majority.

After much wrangling, the State of New York resolved the problem of Bishop Hughes's challenge by imposing a more rigorous secularisation of its educational system. In 1842 a state commission observed that the population of New York City was "by no means homogeneous" and that the attempt to provide a homogeneous system assumed an end which the various communities did not share.[18] The answer was to drive all religious teaching out of the schools in receipt of public support, an outcome that gave Hughes no satisfaction beyond that of having forced the state to redefine its policy of neutrality and to recognise the truth that its population would never again be homogeneous in religion. New York meanwhile moved very slowly towards a legal position which gave the Catholic hierarchy a satisfactory tenure of church property. An act of 1813 had vested trusteeship in the lay community—a procedure on the whole characteristic of the temper of the period, but highly objectionable

17. Everson v. Board of Education, 330 U.S. 1 (1947).
18. Smith, *Religious Liberty*, pp. 111–16.

to religious orders whose structure of authority was hierarchical rather than diffuse. Not until 1863 did New York indicate the lines on which American society might begin to come to legal terms with its own religious heterogeneity. The law of that year made each church and congregation a body corporate. Under these provisions, known as the "corporate aggregate" plan, the archbishop, bishop, vicar-general and pastor of the diocese, with two laymen, were to sign a certificate showing the title by which the corporation was to be known. The church was able to retain effective legal control in the hands of its superior officers.[19] Many states, however, were less hospitable to the Roman Catholic Church and continued to place legal obstacles in the way of ecclesiastical concentrations of power.[20] The rise of a permanent and evidently increasing Catholic element in America's population had a toughening rather than an ameliorating effect on the Protestant majority's determination to keep formal religious teaching out of the domain of public education. President Grant, in his seventh annual message in 1875, recommended to Congress a constitutional amendment providing for public education, and including a provision to ban all teaching of "religious, atheistic, or pagan tenets", and went on to exclude any kind of aid or exemption, direct or indirect, for any religious sect or denomination.[21] The force of this amendment, if it had been adopted, would have fallen equally on all religions. Grant's intention may have been to prevent the schools from becoming the grounds of a new wave of public controversy; but the effect would have been to deprive Catholics of any prospect of public support for their own educational system, and this was a situation in which Protestants expected to flourish, as they had in the past. Although the Grant's proposal did not lead to an amendment to the federal Constitution, many states adopted constitutional provisions of their own, most of which forbade the use or appropriation of public funds or state property for the benefit of sectarian schools.[22]

19. Stokes, *Church and State*, III, 406–10.
20. Smith, *Religious Liberty*, gives a table of references, pp. 118–19.
21. Richardson, *Messages and Papers*, VII, 334–5. Grant also proposed taxation of church property and suggested that people would soon lose patience with exemptions granted to ecclesiastical bodies while property taxes were rising. There is an anticlerical ring to his words.
22. Smith, *Religious Liberty*, p. 117–19.

American Catholics were obliged to maintain a delicate balance between their American and their Roman loyalties—a position periodically upset as a result of the Vatican's chronic difficulties in trying to understand the concept of religious neutrality in a republican state; European experience, of which plenty existed, taught it to believe that the state could not be neutral, and that a state which was not friendly was hostile. The phase of religious policy that took its formal inauguration from the adoption of the First Amendment in 1791 was based on the assumption that religious pluralism was safe for the Republic because it was safe for Protestants—a Catholic presence was hardly even contemplated; but that phase disintegrated gradually with the disappearance, not so much of the Protestant majority, as of the unchallenged nature of that majority's ascendency. The rise of the Roman Catholic Church in America posed the question as to whether religious pluralism and competition might eventually undermine the traditional ascendency which had freed Protestants to indulge the liberties of other sects or creeds. Catholic leaders such as Bishop Hughes perceived the doctrine of separation as a disguised form of official hostility and attacked it in order to establish a Catholic foothold under the protection of public policy. This attempt failed, and the failure marked the limits of one form of Catholic compromise with American constitutional principles. A long time was to elapse—virtually another lifetime—before in the twentieth century the Catholic Church was to perceive advantages in the American doctrine of separation. Strictly construed and enforced, it could at least protect it from hostile local majorities, and spare the children the indoctrination they might have suffered from hearing school assembly readings from the English Bible. But when towards the middle of the twentieth century, state governments began to provide benefits to the recipients of their school policies, not as religion but as education, the Catholics could hope to share them not as Catholics but as citizens. This subtle development helped to give them a friendlier view of the now much-disputed line traced by the wall of separation.

While these difficulties exposed some of the deeper hostilities between different sections of American society, the doctrine of separation also presented problems which required judicial solutions. Religious bodies are notoriously susceptible to disputes on points of doctrine, and when such disputes, or even broad changes of sentiment, led to schism within a sect or congregation, the passions of faith were quickly translated into demands for the control of church property and the power to appoint ministers. The first case of this kind to require close judicial determination arose in 1820 from the slow drift of the majority of the parishioners of Dedham to the newly fashionable doctrines of Unitarianism, while the nucleus of the church had remained with the old Congregational faith. The Massachusetts Supreme Court decided that a church had no legal existence except in connection with "some regularly constituted society", and that the whole parish was the legally constituted owner of the meeting house.[23] Fifty years later, and after a civil war, questions of religious doctrine turned on deep sectional loyalties. The General Assembly of the Presbyterian Church had declared for the Constitution and the Union in opposition to the wishes of the church's Southern members; the Westminster Confession of Faith, to which they adhered, made it improper for the General Assembly to make pronouncements on political problems.

The doctrinal questions could not be averted in a situation where the majority held slavery to be impious and required persons seeking ordination to denounce it. The Supreme Court deciding the question in *Watson* v. *Jones*, however, conscientiously averted its formal attention from the doctrinal issues and pronounced a ringing declaration of the American principle of separation. In drawing a sharp contrast with an opinion in which Lord Eldon, when Lord Chancellor of England, had determined a case by entering into theological doctrine, Mr Justice Miller declared, "In this country the full and free right to entertain any religious belief, to practice any religious principle, and to teach any religious doctrine which does not violate the laws of morality and property, and which does not infringe personal rights, is conceded to all. The law knows no heresy, and is committed to the support of no dogma, the establishment of no sect". The case was decided in favour of the General Assembly on grounds determined by the structure, not the doctrine of the Presbyterian Church: "Where the local congregation"—in this case the Southern-inclined church in Louisville, Kentucky—"is a member of a larger and much

23. Howe, *Garden and Wilderness*, pp. 32–60; Stokes, *Church and State*, III, 376–8.

more important religious organisation, and is under its government and control and is bound by its orders and judgments, its decisions are final, and binding on legal tribunals". The court's reasoning proceeded from the premise that courts, having no ecclesiastical jurisdiction, could not revise or question acts of church discipline: The judicial power arose from the conflicting claims of the parties to church property and the use of it.[24]

The exceptions noticed by Mr Justice Miller might prove more spacious than his language suggested, since "the laws of morality and property" were those of Christian morality and capitalist property. The severest possible test of this definition was inevitably posed when a religious sect claiming allegiance to a different set of religious, moral, and economic principles established itself within the territorial bounds of the United States. The Mormons believed that polygamy was a religious duty; the United States charged them with bigamy, and in the resulting case of *Reynolds* v. *United States* in 1879 the justices gave short shrift to the defence that religion constituted a claim to exemption from the criminal law. It was in this case that Chief Justice Waite first introduced Jefferson's metaphor of the wall of separation into the language of the court, and this was clearly understood to give religion no liberty of exercise the lawful limits of civil conduct.[25] Whatever may have been the merits of the case for a uniform law of marriage—and it is perhaps noteworthy that Poland and Edmunds, two of the senators who were responsible for legislation against Mormon practices, were also strong proponents of civil rights in the era of Reconstruction—the government was not prepared to leave the Mormons alone. The series of laws passed in 1862, 1874, 1882, all strengthened federal authority in the territories and culminated in the Tucker-Edmunds Act of 1887. But this was not confined to the proprieties of matrimony; passing into law without President Cleveland's signature, this final measure pursued the Mormons to the virtual destruction of their institutions. The Corporation of the Church of Christ of Latter-Day Saints was dissolved, all its property was declared forfeit, female suffrage in Utah was abolished, and the children of plural marriages were disinherited. The Mormons had not confined their departures

24. Watson v. Jones, 13 Wallace 679–738 (1871).
25. Reynolds v. U.S., 98 U.S. 145 (1879).

from conventional American precepts to polygamy but had established a society whose church was its central institution of political and economic life. The dissolution of the corporation meant the destruction of the most ambitious and successful of American attempts at a collective economy, and the return of the people of Utah to the economics of private business. These measures were upheld by the Supreme Court in 1890 over the dissents of Chief Justice Fuller and Justices Field and Lamar.[26]

Once the Mormons had agreed to conform to American morals as expressed in American laws, they were treated with tolerable leniency and Utah was admitted to the Union as a state in 1895. But the legislation which destroyed the foundations of their order passed far beyond the considerations which might have been ordinarily conceived of as essential to a uniform morality, where morality was the result of religious conviction. In cases which touched the central nerves of American public morals less closely, the judiciary continued to observe the principle that its jurisdiction extended to matters of organisation but not to doctrine. The line could be a fine one, however. In the curious case of *Gonzalez* v. *Roman Catholic Archbishop of Manila*, decided in 1929, the court had to adjudicate on the merits of the claims of a child to succeed to a chaplaincy which had been founded with provisions requiring a family succession. The Archbishop of Manila's objections were based on canon law provisions which had not existed when the trust was founded. The Supreme Court denied the archbishop the satisfaction of a determination under the authority of the canon law, but awarded him the judgment on the secular grounds that he was competent to decide the theological qualifications of a candidate for the chaplaincy under the will which founded that office.[27]

A more politically charged case came before the court after the opening of the Cold War. The Russian Orthodox Cathedral Church of St. Nicholas had been incorporated by an act of New York in 1925, and continued like the Church of Rome, to acknowledge a spiritual head abroad, in this case, however, in Moscow. Since the

26. The Late Corporation of the Church of Christ of Latter-Day Saints v. United States, 136 U.S. (1890); Leonard J. Arrington, *Great Basin Kingdom: An Economic History of the Latter-Day Saints* (Cambridge, Mass., 1958), pp. 353–75.
27. Gonzalez v. Roman Catholic Archbishop of Manila, 280 U.S. 10 (1929).

rapprochement between the Soviet government and the Russian Church, a number of American adherents were unwilling to recognise Moscow as the third Rome, and prevailed on the state to transfer to them the control of the property of the church. But the Supreme Court could find here no issue over which the state could exercise lawful control. "There is no charge of subversive or hostile action by any ecclesiastic", observed Mr Justice Reed for the court. "Here there is a transfer by statute of control over churches. This violates our rule of separation between church and state". He cited *Watson* v. *Jones*; "the law knows no heresy", and pointed out that the record showed no schism over faith between the Russian Church in America and the Russian Orthodox Church. The move, in other words, was political, but even if it had been based on theological dissension, the precepts which bound the court would seem to have obliged it to find in favour of the Russian patriarch. This was a notable vindication of the independence of religion from the state. But the judgment drew a powerful dissent from Mr Justice Jackson, who argued that New York had done nothing to interfere with the free exercise of religion; the law complained of touched property, not liberty.[28] This distinction received little attention in the history of religious cases, in which the court held consistently that the clauses respecting either establishment or free exercise were of critical importance. If attention had been concentrated on liberty of speech, press, and association, also protected by the first batch of constitutional amendments, and the question of what constituted an "establishment" had been treated with greater indulgence, much acrimonious and expensive controversy might have been avoided. These problems reappeared in the third phase of the subject, which emerged to overlap with the second and to probe the outer limits of its logic.

The Crumbling of Jefferson's Wall

Jefferson and Madison knew that religious persecution was a sin against God as well as man. They placed all their confidence—faith, one might say—in the reasonableness of tolerance; but the circumstances of their own times did not oblige them to decide what ought

28. Kedroff v. St Nicholas Cathedral, 344 U.S. 94 (1952).

to be done when religion itself required people to take actions that conflicted with prevailing laws or customs. The problem of religious assessments was no exception to this statement; the Baptists were willing to support their own ministers, and if they had simply been left to themselves, they would have had no need to disobey the laws. When, as with the Mormons, sincerely held religious beliefs resulted in acts that clearly broke the criminal law, the Supreme Court in a manner that was consciously consistent with Jefferson's own principles had no difficulty in defending the principles of civil society against not the beliefs but the acts that flowed from them.

There were two sides to this coin, however. Just as religion was not allowed to dictate a breach of the law, so it was also true that civil society itself might not impose laws which interfered with the "free exercise" of religion. This thesis was clearly defined in 1925, when Oregon tried to banish parochial or sectarian schools and to bring all secondary education under the direct tutelage of the state. The celebrated case in which this issue was tried resulted in the declaration that the child was not "a mere creature of the state"; it was a high duty of those who nurtured him and directed his destiny to prepare him for additional obligations. The individuality of persons was confirmed as a matter of fundamental law; all the states of the Union rested on a theory of liberty which excluded any power in the state "to standardize its children".[29]

This recognition of the right of diversity in educational choice, and of the corresponding right of different doctrinal bodies to the educational observances required by their very existence, was to reappear in much stronger form with the bitterly contested issue of concessions to parochial schools; but it did not touch directly on the more intricate questions that would arise when the obligations of conscience came into conflict with ceremonial observances ordained by public authorities. The observances in question, though purely civil, had about them an almost religious quality because they involved the flag of the United States. In 1940 the Supreme Court upheld the right of the State of West Virginia to compel children attending its schools to salute the flag and recite an oath of allegiance; Mr Justice Frankfurter's opinion noted that the dissent of some chil-

29. Pierce v. Society of Sisters, 268 U.S. 510 (1925).

dren, if permitted, might undermine the conviction of others.[30] This remark betrayed a suggestion that the court assimilated the social aims of the school board and the state to the issue of constitutional liberties. Three years later, in the *Barnette* case in the same state, the court reversed itself. As in the earlier case, the objectors were members of the sect of Jehovah's Witnesses, who took literally the biblical injunction against graven images.

It seems likely that the justices had by this time been unfavourably impressed by the consequences of government-compelled conformity of allegiance abroad. The year was 1943; four local groups had objected to the prescribed salute on the grounds that it resembled Hitler's. The decision was notable for Mr Justice Jackson's opinion, written in a style as powerful as John Marshall's. "It is not clear", he observed, "whether the regulation contemplates that pupils forego any contrary convictions of their own and become unwilling converts to the prescribed ceremony or whether it will be acceptable if they simulate assent by words without belief and by a gesture barren of meaning. It is now a commonplace that censorship or suppression of expression of opinion is tolerated by our Constitution only when the expression constitutes a clear and present danger of action of a kind the Sate is empowered to prevent and punish. It would seem that involuntary affirmation could be commanded only on more immediate and urgent grounds than silence". Later he added, "There are village tyrants as well as village Hampdens, but none who acts under color of law is beyond the reach of the Constitution". The consequences of coercion were far more serious than those of permitting dissent. "Those who begin coercive elimination of dissent soon find themselves exterminating dissenters. Compulsory unification of opinion achieves only the unanimity of the graveyard". Jackson then added a statement which distantly echoed Madison's warning that "it is proper to take alarm at the first experiment on our liberties". Turning directly to the First Amendment, Jackson pointed out that "it was designed to avoid these results by avoiding these beginnings. There is no mysticism in the American concept of the State or of the nature or origin of its authority. We set up government by the consent of the governed, and the Bill of Rights denies those in power any legal

30. Minersville School District v. Gobitis, 310 U.S. 586 (1940).

opportunity to coerce that consent. Authority here is to be controlled by public opinion, not public opinion by authority".[31]

The case was also notable for a powerful dissent by Mr Justice Frankfurter, who held that the aims of the ceremony were fully within the legitimate competence of the state authorities, were consistent with the needs of a civic education, and belonged to the jurisdiction of the legislature and not of the courts. "The constitutional protection of religious freedom terminated disabilities, it did not create new privileges", he said. "It gave religious equality, not civil immunity. Its essence is freedom from conformity to religious dogma, not freedom from conformity to law because of religious dogma.... Otherwise each individual could set up his own censor against obedience to laws conscientiously deemed for the public good by those whose business it is to make laws".[32] Frankfurter anticipated correctly the complex of issues that would arise over such matters as the provision of textbooks, lunches, and transport by public authorities for children attending private or parochial schools. It was in this opinion that he adverted to the general thesis, which occupied much of his judicial life, that "our constant preoccupation with the constitutionality of legislation rather than with its wisdom tends to preoccupation of the American mind with a false value".[33]

Frankfurter, whose reasoning was as consistent with the First Amendment as the majority's, showed that political neutrality towards religious convictions could be maintained without impairing the authority of the state in matters of law and policy. The court's argument, for all the toughness of Jackson's language, disclosed the beginnings of a softening of attitude towards individual conscience as the arbiter of personal conduct in matters within the traditionally public domain. Jackson did not follow this course; but the court was to pursue it to a conclusion which diverged from much of the subject's previous history.

The modern state provides its citizens with many forms of protection and benefit in the ordinary course of its duty. They include such things as police protection, schools, and public transport. The beneficiaries of these services are of all religions and of no religion;

31. W. Virginia State Board of Education v. Barnette, 319 U.S. 624 (1943).
32. Ibid.
33. Ibid.

their beliefs have nothing whatever to do with their rights as equal citizens to equal shares in the state's services. When, however, individual states began to respond to the shifting distribution of population, with its attendant voting power, by including in their benefits such institutions as existed for religious purposes, they opened a new direction in American practice. As early as 1930 the State of Louisiana was challenged to justify the provision of free school textbooks to the children attending Catholic parochial schools—a policy as formally "neutral" in that part of the country as the provision of a King James Bible would have appeared in New England. The court recognized these realities. It struck out along the line of citizenship rather than religion. The doctrine of the judgment was that of "child benefit"; it was not the schools but the children, and in due course the state, that gained the benefit from education.[34] But a far more controversial case came to a head soon after the Second World War in New Jersey. The state's laws authorised local school districts to arrange for the transport of children to and from schools; a township board of education followed this by authorising reimbursement to parents of money spent on their children's school transport, and some of this money was used to reimburse parents of children attending Catholic schools. To this procedure a local taxpayer objected, filed a suit, and carried the matter to the Supreme Court.

Mr Justice Black, in delivering the opinion of the court, resurveyed Jefferson's wall, punched holes of considerable magnitude in it, and concluded by satisfying himself that it stood completely unchanged. Yet his opinion was notable for a strong statement of the prohibitions of the "establishment" clause in the First Amendment. The basic tenet of the judgment was that the Catholic beneficiaries of these funds were beneficiaries in their capacity as citizens, not in their capacity as Catholics; all were equally entitled to receive the benefits of public welfare legislation, and there was nothing to prevent the authorities from offering these to individuals who made a sectarian use of them so long as the use accrued to the individuals and not to the sect.

This decision in *Everson* v. *Board of Education*,[35] which was carried by five votes to four, provoked a series of cogent dissenting

34. Cochran v. Board of Education, 281 U.S. 370 (1930).
35. 330 U.S. 1 (1947).

opinions, of which Mr Justice Jackson's soon became famous. The First Amendment, he observed, "was intended not only to keep the state's hands out of religion, but to keep religion's hands off the state, and above all, to keep bitter religious controversy out of public life by denying to every denomination any advantage from getting control of public policy or the public purse. Those great ends I cannot but think are immeasurably compromised by today's decision".[36] The other dissenting justices took the historically interesting step of appending the full text of Madison's *Memorial and Remonstrance* of 1785 to their opinion. There could be no clearer statement of the basic principles of separation, and no clearer demonstration that the court's judgment represented a profound departure from those principles.

The problems arising under the First Amendment were now becoming more crowded and complex than ever before. They would have been easier to deal with if the federal and state governments had always chosen the path of strict neutrality that was most clearly consistent with the establishment clause. The great difficulty that confounded the Supreme Court when it first distinguished firmly between the concepts of "establishment" and of "free exercise", both of which lived in the short wording of the religious clause of the amendment, was that history confuted logic. American governments had long displayed a hospitality to religion that obviously conformed to popular preferences. It seemed pedantic to quarrel with the phrase "In God We Trust", which had first appeared on the coinage in 1864,[37] to object to the use of the expression "So help me God" on solemn occasions, or—as soon came to be pointed out—to find religious establishment in the words with which the Supreme Court itself was declared open: "God Save the United States and This Honorable Court!" As religions of deeply different kinds revealed their permanence and voting power, it was much easier to accept their presence in the same spirit in which the Protestant presence had once been almost unquestioningly accepted than to adopt a new rigour. A streak of sentimental religiosity may also have popularised the notion of hospitality to religious observances. "We are a religious people, whose institutions presuppose a Supreme Being",

36. Ibid.
37. Stokes, *Church and State*, III, 602.

declared Mr Justice Douglas, when, speaking for the court in 1952, he validated the practice of releasing school time for children to go elsewhere for religious attendance.[38]

The weakness of this apology perhaps helped to make the distinctions clear. It was true that American institutions owed much to the theory of natural rights, and that natural rights derived their force in the eighteenth century from a concept of deity. But Whig ideas of the justification of government did not really demand such beliefs and could have survived without them; the whole practical force of the American Constitution was drawn from the actual registration of political consent. This being the case, Douglas's dictum was irrelevant, and the remark that the Americans were "a religious people" was devoid of constitutional interest.

While the Cold War made people in American public life visibly anxious to affirm their godliness in face of the avowed national enemy in the form of atheistic communism, the sectarian issue became extremely bitter. Protestants objected with increasing vehemence to the provision of public support to Catholic schools; but believers in other faiths, and unbelievers, objected to any form of state-sponsored religious observance, especially in schools, where the issue could not be kept down. The State of New York tried to find a nonsectarian form of prayer acceptable for all faiths attending its public schools; but when this procedure was challenged in the Supreme Court in *Engel* v. *Vitale* in 1962, it fell under the axe of the "establishment" clause. "When the power, prestige, and financial support of the government is placed behind a particular religious belief, the indirect coercive pressure upon religious minorities to conform to the prevailing officially approved view is plain . . .", declared the court. In this case, too, Mr Justice Douglas disposed of *Everson* as being "in retrospect . . . out of line with the First Amendment".[39] It is odd, however, that although these opinions dealt with the susceptibilities of children, they did not notice the difficulty for the irreligious or nonconformist teacher, who might be given the duty of leading the class in prayer.

Pennsylvania tried to meet the problem by allowing dissenting children to be excused. A Unitarian family whose children attended

38. Zorach v. Clauson, 343 U.S. 346 (1952).
39. Engel v. Vitale, 370 U.S. 421 (1962).

an Abington Township school considered the offer and decided that it was not good enough because the request might prejudice their children in the eyes of their teachers and classmates. The Supreme Court agreed: "In the relationship between man and religion, the State is firmly committed to a position of neutrality". As Mr Justice Brennan commented, once it was found that the exercises were essentially religious, the availability of excusal or exemption had no relevance to the question of "establishment". But even under the more difficult heading of "free exercise of religion", they could not require people to profess disbelief, and children might be reluctant to be stigmatised as atheists or nonconformists.[40] These judgments were not unanimous. But the sharp sectarian divisions of the period reopened issues that had been present when the idea of separation was planted in the laws of Virginia and the Bill of Rights; it was not pedantry, not a taste for antequarian survivals, that tempted the justices to quote Madison's *Memorial and Remonstrance* in their opinions in these years. They were driven back to the doctrine of state neutrality by an inexorable logic without which the concept of separation would soon have lost its meaning.

The problem of conscience, of the meaning to the individual of his own experience, and of the state's right to interpret that meaning, was at the centre of these problems. It came up in a slightly perverse form when a self-styled religious group claimed to be able to cure diseases through the good offices of St. Germain. Members of this "I AM" movement were arrested and convicted of fraud. But the Supreme Court struck down the conviction on the ground, essentially deriving from *Watson* v. *Jones*, that "the law knows no heresy and is committed to the support of no dogma"; as earlier cases had shown, the First Amendment forestalled compulsion to observe any creed and safeguarded the free exercise of any chosen form of religion.[41] There was sharp disagreement on the court about this case. "The state of one's mind is a fact as capable of fraudulent misrepresentation as one's physical condition or the state of his bodily health", observed Chief Justice Stone in a dissent strongly marked by the reasoning of common sense; but Jackson replied that truth or falsity could not be determined in religious beliefs, and the

40. School District of Abington Township v. Schempp, 374 U.S. 203 (1963).
41. Cantwell v. Connecticut, 310 U.S. 296 (1940).

trial judge had been mistaken in telling the jury to make up their minds whether the beliefs were honestly held or not.[42]

If the government had no right to establish or favour religious beliefs, it followed that it had no right to determine and had no appropriate machinery for determining whether a particular person's conscience was or was not religious. It seems strange, therefore, that in the most serious test of national tolerance, that of conscientious exemption from military service, the government made a habitual practice of granting exemptions only on grounds of religious conviction. The war in Vietnam brought out the most intense challenge to these policies; and in the decisive case, concluded in 1970, the defendant resolutely declined to claim exemption on grounds of religion. His objections to war were humanistic; but they were as firm as those of a fundamentalist standing—as few fundamentalists have done—on the Sixth Commandment. The court had to decide whether his nonreligious conscience had equal claims with religious consciences making the same profession. The accumulated weight of the doctrine of neutrality, together, perhaps, with increasingly widespread feelings that the war itself was immoral, contributed to the judgment, which upheld the defendant's right to conscientious exemption.[43] The ground had shifted from religious faith—which under the establishment clause the state had never been clearly competent to try—to the seriousness with which the convictions were held. It is not difficult to discern a line leading from Jackson's earlier argument that the government cannot enquire into other people's religious experiences to the further conclusion that it cannot look into the state of their secular consciences; but that way lies something like anarchy—as Frankfurter had discerningly warned in his *Barnette* dissent in 1943.

The manifest tendency of these cases was to leave the state with only secular means by which to foster civic virtues and political loyalties; it might not invoke religion as an engine of support. State neutrality was seen in both *Engel* and *Abington* as the only posture wholly compatible with the central doctrine of nonestablishment. It is true that justices disclaimed the view that neutrality need mean hostility; but people who believed that religion formed an intrinsic

42. U.S. v. Ballard, 322 U.S. 78 (1944).
43. United States v. Elliott Ashton Welsh II, 398 U.S. 333 (1970).

part of education, or that it was essential to civic consciousness, could only feel that steely neutrality was inherently inimical. No resolution of this problem can give equal satisfaction on all sides.

The religious clause of the First Amendment contained in its brief, enigmatic language an irony not only of logic but of genuine historical meaning. The strictest and most consistent interpretation of that language could have steered the American government away from any form of concession or exemption to religious institutions, whose property and practices would have ranked with those of business, theatres, and warehouses. To argue this is to overlook, or override, the view that the First Amendment may have been more important for its federalism than for its libertarianism, and that the restraint imposed on federal action was expected by many people to enable state government to encourage and assist their own religious establishment.[44] Only when the Fourteenth Amendment extending to states the civil rights ensured by the national government had been adopted, and having been adopted was held in the 1940s to apply the religious clause of the First Amendment,[45] could this argument be pursued with absolute conviction. But many states had indicated a willingness to take it up on their own initiatives by adopting state constitutional amendments of a rigorously separationist character. The contradiction between steely political neutrality and a way of life which took many of its moral and social precepts from the Bible was thus written into the public policy of many of the states long before the federal judiciary had any occasion to take cognisance of the problem. The emergence of religious orders which did not owe their faith to the Bible, and the claims of secular consciences, threw the basic logical difficulties into still sharper relief and clarified the case for a policy of total political abstention. That case had always existed and by strong implication had often been confirmed. The powerful language of *Watson* v. *Jones*—"the law knows no heresy"—reappeared to make its impression on judgments in the twentieth century.

The history of the subject, however, reflected the very real diversity of popular and legislative sentiments, which had still more

44. This is the central thesis of Howe's brief but masterly essay, *The Garden and the Wilderness*; see especially, pp. 10–19, 29.
45. 310 U.S. 296.

often been translated through tax exemptions and other favours into positive commitments by government to the churches. (And the fact that it might be as charities rather than as churches that they gained these favours could hardly conceal the real need to compromise politics with religion.) The alternative method of reasoning, which might have permitted these obviously popular and widely desired concessions without the entanglement resulting from the repeated attempts of state governments to square them with the religious clause, would have lain along the line of those other clauses which guaranteed the liberties of person, speech, press, association, and property protected by the First and Fifth Amendments. In an analogous connection, when the Supreme Court needed the instrument to extend the equal protection clause from the state to the District of Columbia, it had done so by way of the Fifth Amendment.[46] That judgment made clear that when the court was determined to protect the equal rights of citizens, it would do so by way of the principle of equal liberty if the technicalities of the Constitution closed the road by way of the equal protection clause of the Fourteenth Amendment. It is at least arguable that the rights of free speech and press, allied perhaps to the defence of "the free exercise" of religion, could have averted the fearful confusions raised by the questions which were soon to follow in the matter of state aid to religion in education.[47] Economic stringencies in the 1960s made state legislators more willing to assist parochial schools, which were actually educating children who would otherwise have fallen into the public school system and onto the finances of the states. In a new set of cases the Supreme Court attempted to steer between "excessive entanglement", which it discerned when striking down state statutes designed to finance the teaching of secular courses in private schools, and on the other hand permissable aid to the children as distinct from religion when textbooks were lent to them but not to their schools.[48] The doctrinal complexities created by these and other

46. Bolling v. Sharpe, 349 U.S. 497, 98 (1954) re D.C.

47. Howe, *Garden and Wilderness*, p. 157, takes the view that the protection of free speech and press alone is adequate to the protection of religious conscience without invoking the machinery of anti-establishment.

48. Lemon v. Kurtzman, 403 U.S. 602 (1971); Robinson v. Dicenso, 403 U.S. 672 (1971); Tilton v. Richardson, 403 U.S. 672 (1971); Donald A. Gianella,

rulings admit of no clear line of reasoning or prediction; alterations in public attitudes evidently found some response in the lessened stringency, and perhaps also in the relaxed intellectual rigour, of the court itself.

A fair rule of neutrality has eluded the court, not so much because it is wholly unattainable as because it has been sought along lines which require, for their fulfilment, a rigour which public and even judicial sentiment have been unwilling to countenance permanently. Professor Kurland, however, has suggested the formula for such a rule: "The state may not use religion as a basis for classification for purposes of governmental action, whether that action be for the conferring of rights or privileges or the imposition of duties or obligations".[49] This position need not have interfered with the doctrines which, whatever the refinements of the school cases, left the individual alone with his conscience. In safeguarding the free exercise of religion, the government treats all individuals as equals; in avoiding establishment, it makes the irreligious conscience equal to the devout.

The concept of equality of conscience, which began as a claim for equal treatment between warring sects, thus ends by forming a perfect unity with the political equality of individuals. Whatever an individual's heritage, convictions, or associations, the government's only legitimate knowledge of him or her is as the sovereign possessor of autonomous moral being.

"Lemon and Tilton: The Bitter-Sweet of Church-State Entanglement", *Supreme Court Review*, 1971, pp. 146–200.

49. Phillip B. Kurland, *Religion and the Law* (1962), p. 18.

Chapter Five

The Constitutional Aegis and the
Emergence of Individualism

A Community of Principles

The political society formed by the peoples of the United States between 1774 and 1788 was an artifact; the early Republic was a kind of anthology of communities. The prolonged struggle to get agreement among the states over the Articles of Confederation and the success of the smaller states in checking the moves towards a more powerful and unified government, revealed, long before the successful outcome of the War of Independence, the difficulties of the makers of this new anthology in finding their own unifying principles. The form of the Articles permitted the states to retain almost all their local preferences, which ranged from the total exclusion of certain parts of the population from any form of membership of political society except obedience to its laws, to the conferment of the normal rights of citizenship on all who paid taxes. The Confederation itself came into being as an indispensable necessity of the war; its existence required Americans to define the common principles and outer limits of their political community.

Although each state remained responsible for its own rules of citizenship, a more collective purpose was also clearly envisaged in the article which declared, "The better to secure and perpetuate mutual friendship and intercourse among the people of different States of this Union, the free inhabitants of the different States, paupers, vagabonds, and fugitives from justice excepted, shall be entitled to all privileges and immunities of free citizens in the several States; and the people of each State shall have free ingress and egress to and from every other State, and shall enjoy therein all the privileges of trade and commerce, subject to the same duties, impositions, and restrictions as the inhabitants thereof respectively . . .".[1] The corresponding section of the Constitution, Article IV, came to be known as the Comity Clause, in which the ancient restrictions on paupers and vagabonds disappeared, and the tortuous phrasing of the Articles was condensed by the arts of superior parliamentary draftsmanship into the words, "The Citizens of each State shall be entitled to all the Privileges and Immunities of Citizens in the several States". But states retained the power to determine their own rules of citizenship, though not of naturalisation.

The search for equality as embodied in national institutions had thenceforth to be carried to the Constitution itself. Apart from the sense in which the Constitution equalised its citizens by making no differentiation among them, its chief instruments, before the adoption of the Reconstruction amendments, were the Comity Clause and the guarantee to each state of a republican form of government. The Comity Clause has always been interpreted narrowly by the Supreme Court; it has been held to mean only that a state must afford to citizens of other states all such privileges as it gives to its own—and the effect of this is to forbid discrimination in favour of its own and against others.[2] Any possibility of converting the Comity Clause into an instrument for the development of a nationally enforceable standard of equality has been not merely neglected but carefully restrained.

The Guarantee Clause had its origins in the cession of Virginia's western land claims to the Continental Congress. In accepting the

1. S. E. Morison, ed., *Sources and Documents Illustrating the American Revolution 1764–1788 and the Formation of the Federal Constitution* (Oxford, repr. 1962), p. 178.

2. The notion that a citizen carries with him through any state he may visit all the rights that he may enjoy as a citizen of his own state has been specifically rejected: Detroit v. Osborne, 135 U.S. 492 (1890); Dred Scott v. Sanford, 19 Howard 393 (1857); McKane v. Durston, 153 U.S. 684 (1894). For discussion, see *The Constitution of the United States of America, Analysis and Interpretation*, Library of Congress, Legislative Reference Service (Washington, D.C., 1952), pp. 686–92.

cession, the Congress adapted an earlier formula of Jefferson's to provide that the states to be created "shall not be incompatible with republican principles, which are the basis of the constitutions of the respective states in the Union", which probably meant little more than that they should not be monarchies. The Northwest Ordinance of 1787 had the more dramatic effect of transforming republican government into civil and religious liberty. But the meaning of its appearance in the Constitution remained so obscure as to cause John Adams to reflect that he had never understood what it meant—"and I believe no man ever did or will".[3] The Supreme Court has been diffident about the exercise of any powers of its own, the leading case being that of *Luther* v. *Borden*, in 1849, which arose out of the claims of rival governments in Rhode Island resulting from the Dorr rebellion in that state. The court decided that only Congress could "determine what government is the established one in a State. For as the United States guarantee to each State a republican government, Congress must necessarily decide what government is established in a State before it can determine whether it is republican or not".[4] This decision did not absolve the court from having to determine fundamental questions affecting the relationship of individual citizens to their state governments. The concept of a "state" as found in the Constitution can be held to include its territory, but can never be divorced from its citizens, a doctrine laid down in the post-Civil War case of *Texas* v. *White*.[5] To this extent, the Guarantee Clause imposes uniformity, and uniformity must mean equality, not only among the citizens of a specified state, but among the citizens of all states. The United States cannot tolerate a situation in which some citizens are governed by unrepublican governments; but the Constitution is silent as to what exactly constitutes a republican government. Since all the states were obviously held to have republican governments in 1789, the problem arose when new departures appeared to violate republican precepts.

Opinions on these questions could not be held eternally fixed at the point from which the Constitution was launched. The rise of the

3. William M. Wiecek, *The Guarantee Clause of the United States Constitution* (Ithaca and London, 1972), pp. 13–17.
4. 4 U.S. Howard 1 (1849).
5. 7 Wallace 700 (1869).

great controversy over slavery led to a reopening of the question of the meaning of the Guarantee Clause. In 1820, during the bitter dispute over the admission of Missouri to the Union as a slave state, opponents of slavery in Congress were already maintaining that slavery was incompatible with republican forms of government; whatever might have been the case at the founding of the Constitution, according to this argument, the United States could admit no new states which permitted slavery. Thenceforward, no new slave state was admitted without an attack on its government as unrepublican.[6] Yet the Guarantee Clause in fact proved an ineffective instrument for shaping constitutional policies. It was resurrected in the crisis of authority that followed the Civil War, when Charles Sumner told the Senate that it was "a clause which is like a sleeping giant in the Constitution, never until this recent war awakened, but now it comes forward with a giant's power. . . . There is no clause which gives to Congress such supreme power over the States as that clause". The Radical Republicans in pressing for the adoption and ratification of the Fourteenth Amendment were able, if only briefly, to use it as a weapon of some potency.[7] Yet there were obvious difficulties, as emerged in a Senate clash between Sumner and William Pitt Fessenden of Maine—who was himself to emerge later as an architect of Congressional Reconstruction. Sumner wanted to use the clause to underwrite political as well as civil rights in the former Confederate states; Fessenden could not see how the clause could be held to apply to those states without extending to the North, where Sumner was content to rely on the much weaker implications of the Thirteenth Amendment, the abolition of slavery.[8] The difficulties were again illustrated in a case unconnected with race, but closely connected with the principles of political equality, when in 1875 a woman brought a suit claiming a right to register as an elector. The Supreme Court dismissed her claims under the Fourteenth Amendment but proceeded to consider them under the Guarantee

6. Charles O. Lerche, Jr., "Constitutional Interpretations of the Guarantee of a Republican Form of Government during Reconstruction", *Journal of Southern History*, XV (1944).

7. Arthur E. Bonfield, "The Guarantee Clause of Article IV: A Study in Constitutional Disuetude", *Minnesota Law Review*, XXXXVI (1962), 546–7. Sumner's quotation is included in this article.

8. *Congressional Globe*, 39th Cong., 1st sess. (1866), pp. 702–08.

Clause. All citizens had plainly not been invested with the rights of suffrage: "Under these circumstances it is certainly now too late to contend that a government is not republican, within the meaning of this guaranty in the Constitution, because women are not voters". Since 1867, in brief, the Guarantee Clause has never done more than stir in its prolonged sleep.[9]

The Constitution in its original form remained open to a wide variety of interpretations as to the lawfully permissible relations between citizens; but the complete omission by its founders of any declaration of rights and privileges aroused deep misgivings among many people throughout the states who believed that any new form of government must be controlled by the ideological inspiration of the Revolution. That inspiration was a varied and complex affair; but the first ten amendments, adopted before the end of 1791, gave it a degree of concreteness which it had never so clearly had before. This restraint on unfair treatment of individuals by the federal government left the states free to do as they chose, and most of them adopted their own similar bills of rights. The Fifth Amendment stated briefly that no person was to be deprived of life, liberty, or property without due process of law, which meant fair and equal procedures in courts. The Supreme Court held in 1833 that the Fifth Amendment restrained the federal government but did not apply to the states. Very rarely before the Civil War did the Supreme Court— notably in the *Dred Scott Case* of 1857—adopt the view that confiscatory legislation could violate the concept of "due process". When it did so, it introduced a virtually new doctrine—that of "substantive due process", whose operations were too vague and unpredictable to be described as an extension of any rigorous ideas of equality.

Few strict rules were enjoined on the states under the ægis of the Constitution. Despite the powerful nationalism of John Marshall's stewardship as chief justice from 1801 to 1835, the rapid growth of geographical sections with their own interests, laws, and principles made the Constitution into a guardian of a form not only of political but of moral pluralism. Where the issues at stake involved liberty itself, moral pluralism could not endure forever; yet even the collapse of that experiment in civil war did not lead immediately to a new

9. Minor v. Happersett, 21 Wall. 262; Wiececk, *Guarantee Clause*, p. 292.

and clearer set of uniform rules. The Civil War ended slavery; not until 1868 and 1869 did the Fourteenth and Fifteenth Amendments rewrite the terms of citizenship and declare the constitutional status of even the minimum of corresponding political rights. These amendments translated the Constitution into a document that could not conceivably have been ratified, and could hardly have been proposed, in eighteenth-century America. To understand the development of ideas of equality under the original Constitution it will be necessary to return to the beginnings of the Republic.

Equality versus Incentive in Early Republican Thought

The Constitution provided Americans with a very loose-fitting frame in which to grow. It was clear already that no idea of equality could survive as an end in itself; its value and indeed its meaning existed in connection with some identified need or aspiration—equality before the law, equality of religious conscience, equality of political participation, equality of opportunity. The Constitution was as fully capable of growing to accommodate this last conception as of mounting the defence needed by individual citizens against the encroachments of government. The unspoken doctrine protected by the Constitution, if not definitely embodied in it, was that of incentive. The voluntaristic idea of Whig political thought had long borne an implicit debt to the importance of incentive, if only to the extent that individuals in a state of nature were assumed to have needed incentives to enter the social contract. That story at best was an allegory. But personal incentives were real; they had been active in the founding of the colonies—it did not require the Revolution to release ambitions towards personal acquisition in America, but the Revolution advanced, sanctioned, and provided formal cover for the advance of a vast range of private aspirations. Only the concept of equality of opportunity could reconcile them to the formal requirements of equality in law and politics.

By the middle of the nineteenth century the concept had become a commonplace. To the Republicans whose vivid enthusiasm perceived the obliteration of class and the rise of universal prosperity, it was the theme by which the great American experiment fused doctrine and achievement into a way of life which justified the Republic's very existence.[10] It is more difficult to put one's finger on an early formulation of the specific concept, but Noah Webster came very close to it when in an anti-slavery tract of 1793 he contrasted the advantages of freedom to the inevitable tendency of slavery to breed tyranny, savage customs, and sloth. "Here", he said, speaking of the best in the United States as opposed to the rather mixed picture of society in Great Britain, "the equalizing genius of the laws distributes property to every citizen". There were no commercial or corporate monopolies and no religious tests (which was not entirely correct) but, "Here every man finds employment, and the road is open for the poorest citizen to amass wealth by labor and economy, and by his talent and virtue to raise himself to the highest offices of the State".[11] This was a work of persuasion, not of research, but it showed a marked continuity with earlier as well as later expressions of American enthusiasm, all of which revealed the same tendency to translate material aspirations into moral accomplishments. Jacob Duché's sermon of 1772 in Philadelphia had referred to the humblest labourer's expectation of rising; and even such a document as the Address of the Massachusetts Convention of 1780, which sought to justify the property restrictions on political rights, maintained that every man who worked could earn the requisite property—an incomplete formula in every way, but an intimation of a connection between equality of opportunity and the nature of the state constitution. After the formation of the federal Constitution, the same principle acquired national extension. The first chief justice of the Supreme Court, John Jay, one of the authors of *The Federalist Papers* and a consistently conservative influence during his political life, expounded the duty of upholding the laws as the indispensable security for civil liberty; addressing the grand juries of the Eastern Circuit in 1790, he explained that civil liberty consisted "in an equal right to all the citizens to have, enjoy and to do, in peace, security, and without molestation, whatever the equal and constitutional laws of the country admit to be consistent with the public good".[12]

10. Eric Foner, *Free Soil, Free Labor, Free Men: The Ideology of the Republican Party before the Civil War* (London, New York, 1970).

11. Noah Webster, Jr., Esq., *Effects of Slavery on Morals and Industry* (Hartford, 1793), pp. 31–2.

12. *The Charge of Chief Justice Jay to the Grand Juries on the Eastern*

The problem of reconciling the equally legitimate aspirations of innumerable individuals with the needs of fairness, or of a public accountability also conceived of in terms of equality, was to provide the central tension of American political consciousness. Thomas Jefferson was well aware of a republican government's need to reconcile personal opportunity with public interest, a problem that presented itself in his own state as soon as Virginia had declared its statehood. Jefferson used his seat in the House of Delegates to dismember the land systems of primogeniture and entail, and he initiated the famous law of religious liberty. But that was not all. At this beginning of the Republic's history, Jefferson also discerned the importance of serving both the individual's capacity for self-fulfilment and the country's need for intelligence through public education. As despotism depended on fear, monarchies on the spirit of honour, and aristocracies upon moderation based on virtue, so republics could not survive without virtue; all readers of Montesquieu knew these rules, and Jefferson believed that republican virtue must be cultivated by education. Educated people could regulate their own affairs and live better lives than those who possessed no schooling; and the system that Jefferson offered his state, when in 1778 he was placed on the commission to revise and codify its laws, was designed to harmonise equality of opportunity with public interest— a problem that had lost none of its urgency two centuries later.

Jefferson's Bill for the More General Diffusion of Knowledge avowed two aims, as defined in its preamble: first "to illuminate, as far as practicable, the minds of the people at large"; and further, to ensure "that those persons, whom nature has endowed with genius and virtue, should be rendered by liberal education worthy to receive, and able to guard the sacred deposit of the rights and liberties of their fellow citizens, and that they should be called to that charge without regard to wealth, birth or other accidental condition or circumstance".[13] Jefferson proposed a general system of education, arranged in three grades, based on the local communities and rising from three years of free education for the children of the masses,

---

Circuit (Portsmouth, N.H. [1790]), pp. 13–14. John Zvesper kindly supplied me with this reference.

13. Merrill Peterson, *Thomas Jefferson and the New Nation* (New York, 1970), p. 146.

through a grammar school grade for the select few, to the College of William and Mary for the genuine elite. The whole conception does much to clarify Jefferson's views on equality both natural and social.

By means of a system of selective examinations, Jefferson remarked in a letter describing the scheme, "twenty of the best geniuses will be raked from the rubbish annually, and be instructed, at public expense, as far as grammar schools go".[14] A modern politician would hardly have risked that limited encomium on the sovereign people; Jefferson plainly had no illusions about equality of endowment, but he did believe that the state should use its powers in the public interest to equalise opportunity; knowledge was indispensable to the stability of a republic, which had no ultimate security other than the virtue and talents of the people. Hence the selective principle joined individual rights to public policy in a consistent chain. Although Jefferson's bill never became law, he persisted successfully in later years with his grand design for the University of Virginia. In 1817 the state legislature had to consider two plans for spending public money on education, and the contest between them showed where Jefferson's deeper sympathies now lay. Charles Fenton Mercer, a respected Federalist politician, was backing a plan for public education through a school system compatible with Jefferson's own earlier design; but Jefferson supported Joseph C. Cabell's rival plan, which would have left elementary education to local initiative while spending state money on the university.[15] This emphasis does not imply that Jefferson had lost all sight of his earlier enthusiasm for public schools: Local communities at least had it in their power to do something about local education; it was probably true that only the state could maintain a university on the scale he desired. It was higher education which engaged his deeper interests. Even in the earlier period, Jefferson was aware that most of the entrants to the proposed grammar schools would in fact be the sons of parents "in easy circumstances" (and could therefore be charged for tuition and board). His assumptions about the distribution of intellectual ability (which, incidentally, he seems to have linked with virtue, though

14. Ibid., p. 148.
15. Rush Welter, *Popular Education and Democratic Thought in America* (New York, 1962), p. 32.

both qualities needed to be carefully trained) after all were not far out of keeping with the existing distribution of social advantages. His plans for a public school system would have taught the poor to read, write, and figure, and would have given state support for the most part to the advancement of the sons of planters, merchants, and lawyers. This expectation—which looked more palatable and more economical from the point of view of the legislators who would have to vote the money—did not exclude all possibility that genius would be found in what he called the rubbish. Whatever its limitations and the felicity of style in which he described them, Jefferson's scheme was the most advanced of the time, and its rejection by the Virginia legislature shows how little they were prepared to follow the author of the Declaration of Independence into practical policy.

Jefferson's political persuasion was not without economic foundations. In his vision of a republic of independent farmers, their independence was more important than the precise size of their farms. Considerable variations in wealth could be safely accommodated without impairing the indispensable consideration of self-sufficiency. But Jefferson was much more concerned about political equality, as he showed in his severe strictures on the unequal distribution of power reflected in the basis of legislative representation in the Virginia Constitution of 1776, in which he left the distribution of property unscathed. Such questions as that of a republican optimum for the distribution of property, or the role of public money, engaged more attention among some of his contemporaries. It was Madison who perceived danger in disparities of property. When discussing the sources of faction in the tenth essay of *The Federalist Papers*, Madison argued their "most common and durable source" arise from "the unequal and various distribution of property", which he had just explained resulted from the "protection of different and unequal faculties of acquiring property" that was the government's duty. Writing to support the new Constitution, he needed to assure his readers that the new frame of government would hold a balance between factions.[16] But it was no part of his purpose to propose a policy of equalisation. And Madison's reference to inequality of

16. Jacob E. Cooke, ed., *The Federalist* (Middletown, 1961), pp. 58–9.

property was the only explicit reference to equality in the entire series[17]; Jay said little; and Alexander Hamilton, the third voice in the composite personality of the author Publius, had altogether higher and more enthralling aims in view. When, four years later, Madison was occupied with concerting opposition to Hamilton's conduct as Secretary of the Treasury, his share in the personality of Publius marched off in a different direction, and he suggested in the recently founded *National Gazette* that legislative measures might be needed to establish "political equality among all". In one of a series of articles published in 1792, Madison advanced the view that new laws should be enacted to withhold "*unnecessary* opportunities from the few to increase the inequality of property by an immoderate, and especially unmerited, accumulation of riches". Moreover, laws should be passed so as silently to "reduce extreme wealth towards a state of mediocrity, and raise indigence towards a state of comfort".[18] Madison's aims were not to propose a system of state regulation, but rather to restrain those vastly unequal accumulations that threatened the stability of the state, and thwarted further opportunities. In this sense his views were compatible with the advancing columns of laisser-faire economics, and he made a point that government should refrain from aiding one interest at the expense of another. But it is perhaps still more significant that he already saw these problems as requiring the attentions of government, a thought that would probably have struck him as irrelevant before the Hamiltonian programme began.

There is no reason to suppose that Madison differed seriously from Jefferson in these matters. Although they played perhaps a less salient part in his thought, Jefferson had made a similar analysis in 1787 when, writing to Madison from Paris, he remarked that gross inequalities of property could cause society to lose its stability, thus provoking revolution. It hardly seemed that he could disapprove such results on such a provocation. But France was not Virginia; and the real victims of the Virginian system, the Negro slaves, who were themselves a form of property, had no hope of revolution. Their

17. I depend here on the index to Cooke's edition; glancing references may have been overlooked.
18. *Writings of James Madison*, ed. Gaillard Hunt (New York, 1900–1910), VI, 86, 87, 104–5, 106–23.

salvation would lie in an act of providential intervention, a "revolution in the wheel of fortune", to use his own words,[19] which Jefferson did in fact believe possible, but which could hardly be said to fall within the realms of political science.

Nothing in Madison's or Jefferson's philosophies need have been expected to lead to a sweeping programme of domestic reform, and despite the horrified forebodings of the Federalists, the Republican party's victory in 1800 was largely barren of social or economic consequences. The Bank of the United States remained in being, but even if it had been dismantled, the relentless drive towards economic expansion and individual aggrandisement through banking and credit would undoubtedly have continued. When federal and state governments could be prevailed upon to grant charters to private groups in return for undertaking to perform some public service, and then those private groups became corporations with permanent and exclusive privileges, the forces of economic change were reshaping both the structure of society and its assumptions. Hamilton with his funding system had charged the whole process with energy, giving it both the sanction and the encouragement of the federal government. Jefferson's victory failed to check this process, still less to reverse it. John Taylor of Caroline County, Virginia, a political ally of Jefferson since he entered into the pamphlet war about parties early in the 1790s, contemplated these developments with deepening dismay. It was not until long after Jefferson's retirement that Taylor published his first systematic treatise, which was also probably the first large-scale attempt to examine the operation of the American system of government from the standpoint of a formal philosophy.

Despite his laborious redundancies of style, Taylor's thesis was, and remains, important. In his earnest, systematic thoroughness, he was in one sense a purer Jefferson than Jefferson himself. His aim was to establish an alternative, non-Hamiltonian position on which he believed that American society could still stand. Taylor's attempt was inspired by two somewhat different developments. One of these was what he called the system of paper and patronage; he saw with

19. In *Notes on the State of Virginia*, ed. Wm. Peden (Chapel Hill, 1954), p. 163.

dismay the rise of a new aristocracy, based on unworthy dealings in credit and paper money, but without roots in the country's real agricultural wealth. This insidious process was a direct result of legislative policies, which in turn placed legislatures in the grip of the new corporations and banks. Taylor's other inspiration was a retarded reaction to John Adams's *Defence of the Constitutions of the United States*, actually written as long previously as 1786, and first published before the federal Constitution had come into force. Taylor was deeply antagonised by Adams's insistence on the division of all societies, including America's, into social orders, and by his conviction that safety had to be sought in some arrangement which converted them into political institutions. In contradistinction to Adams, Taylor placed the whole weight of his own beliefs on the integrity of the individual. In this respect his position was akin to James Wilson's, and was wholly consistent with the school of thought and political practice which treated the equal representation of individual citizens, unadorned by considerations of wealth or other qualifications, as the only proper foundation of politics. "The sovereignty of the people arises, and representation flows, out of each man's right to govern himself", he laid down; and it followed that the true principle of government was representation of the majority by equal districts.[20] Men like Taylor were important converts to the pure principle of political equality at a period when, despite recent advances, it still had to share the field with other views of earlier vintage.

The case against Adams also had a moral dimension. "Mr Adams's political system, deduces government from a natural fate; the policy of the United States deduces it from moral liberty", Taylor explained, making clear that a correct understanding of the principles which animated the American Constitution would go a long way to solving the problem. In his view the Constitution left property where it belonged, in the hands of those who had gained it "fairly . . . by talents and industry."[21] When, therefore, the legislature effected transfers of property through the agencies of paper and patronage,

20. John Taylor, of Caroline County, Virginia, *An Inquiry into the Principles and Practice of the Government of the United States* (1814; London, 1950), pp. 35–57, 101, 365.
21. Ibid., p. 124.

such measures were as unconstitutional as those for re-establishing king, lords, and commons—a sharp thrust at Adams's belief in the inevitability of aristocracy and his reputation for monarchist principles. Taylor's economics, however, were unequal to the demands made on them by his political opinions. Instead of proposing an economic alternative, he was perfectly satisfied with the distribution of property before the poison of paper and credit had got to work. He offered no theory of political economy, nor did he support his views with statistical information. His considerable reading in the literature of political economy had failed to disturb a rather elementary agrarianism. Agriculture was for him the source of all other wealth and the centre of all interests. He was at his weakest when he discountenanced any danger from a landed aristocracy by arguing that "aristocracy is nowhere agrarian" and that a landed monopoly in England was "hardly felt as a political principle".[22] It seemed that an agrarian economy contained some self-correcting mechanism to forestall the rise of a monopolistic aristocracy. Taylor's conviction that his principles of "moral liberty" were superior to Adams's belief in the value of historical experience did not serve him well; for the moral principles which Taylor regarded as fundamental to good government simply did not establish the actual superiority of his system, and his appeals to English and colonial American experience did, in fact, constitute an appeal to historical knowledge rather than moral intuition. He was not nearly inquisitive enough about the real distribution of lands and goods, and the real consequence of that distribution, even in the recent history of his own state of Virginia. He rejected the idea that the free creation of property would tend to produce new forms of monopoly, and sharply disapproved of laws for equalising either property or knowledge. "They pretend to keep property equal among evanescant beings, and to supersede mental inequalities", he declared; and later, "a Law has never been able to produce an equality of property where industry exists; but it can produce its monopoly".[23]

Broadly, then, Taylor was not dissatisfied with the state of affairs that existed at the outbreak of the Revolution, nor did subsequent changes infringe on his general principles, until the Hamiltonian

22. Ibid., p. 477.
23. Ibid., pp. 472, 544.

machine began to work. Although he did severely criticise the Constitution, he thought it embodied right principles, which he wanted to impose as absolute rules of policy. Political equality played a vital part in those principles. The new aristocracy of wealth could gain power through a corrupt use of the natural desire for property, but it could never serve the interests of the majority. Its methods were therefore those of patronage and favour. It was clear to Taylor, given these premises and these observations, that the country was sliding headlong from its own basic postulates. It is not difficult to see a sectional dimension to his anxieties about the future. The landed interests which he had so deeply at heart were primarily Southern, and were losing ground to those of the bankers, the merchants, the monopolists, and the manipulators, whose seats could most easily be discerned in the cities of the North.

In the frenetic race for wealth many fell by the wayside, while more still were overtaken; it was of small comfort to them that John Taylor faced resolutely in the opposite direction. Thomas Skidmore, writing in the very different atmosphere of New York reformist politics early in Andrew Jackson's presidency, made a still more radical attempt to set the country back on its foundations, and in the process to correct the defects of those foundations. Skidmore based his political science on the absolute irreducibility of equal rights. "Rights are like truths, capable of being understood alike by all men;—as much so, as the demonstration of Euclid", he asserted.[24] This statement, an alternative formulation of the concept of the self-evident truth, would have been acceptable to Jefferson. Skidmore, however, was not satisfied with the credentials which Jefferson had conferred on the young Republic. He was under no doubt as to the central position of the preamble to the Declaration of Independence in staking out the ideological territory to be held, and he rebuked its author for losing the most valuable item in the vague rhetoric of "the pursuit of happiness". The item in question was property; for without property, happiness was impossible, and Jefferson was accused of evading the issue.[25] Skidmore thus differed

24. Thomas Skidmore, *The Rights of Man to Property!* (New York, 1829), p. 31.
25. Ibid., pp. 11, 58–60.

from Taylor in that he could never be satisfied with the position which Americans were intent on defending in 1776. Not only the American government, but all governments, had begun on wrong foundations when they accepted the unequal distribution of property in the origins of society—for he recognised quite clearly that there was no society before government.[26]

Skidmore's ideas about property, which with most contemporaries he founded on the produce of labour, were not unlike Taylor's; but he complicated the issue by maintaining that the materials out of which goods were made still belonged to the community.[27] Skidmore was more thorough and more radical than Taylor, and probably than any of his American predecessors, in cutting through to the logical foundations that his principles required. He was scornfully irreverent about all claims to property as sanctified by law. The purpose of laws of property was in the main to sanction the infractions of equal rights which the unequal possession of property necessarily entailed. The difficulty lay not only in the possession of property but in the manner of its distribution, and his argument therefore turned on inheritance. In identifying this question, Skidmore was theoretically correct. He was not interested in half-measures or merely tolerable accommodations but was determined to advance a coherent plan, primarily to be put into force in the State of New York, which would equalise all existing property and forestall any possibility of the occurrence of new inequalities.

Wills and inheritances were the proper concern of government action because they derived their force in law from official recognition. The argument of this point was lengthy, and perhaps more technical than anything devised by Taylor. Skidmore held that it was necessary to put a complete stop to the practice of transferring property at death; all must revert to the state; children, he argued, were the responsibility of the community, not of their parents.[28] He naturally demanded the abolition of slavery but, with a clarity of vision that reappeared only among some of the later Radical Republicans, he also emphasized that the freed slaves ought to be given

26. Ibid., pp. 76, 126–7.   27. Ibid., pp. 33–5.
28. Ibid., pp. 61–2.

the land and goods they would need to earn their own living in freedom.[29] In order to bring about the equality of property he believed to be necessary as a starting point for the future, Skidmore proposed that all existing property be surrendered to the state and then reapportioned in a "General Division". Beyond this, he believed that education was the most important consideration in the minds of the people of New York, and he therefore proposed a new arrangement (in place of the existing School Fund, which was connected with the retention by the state of the public lands) by which the Treasury would pay equally for all schooling.[30] These views reflected a more radical vision of society than that of John Taylor, who was thoroughly opposed to any idea of state plans for equalising knowledge and evidently regarded such matters as falling within the private domain, to be left alone by the government. But Skidmore joined Taylor in his attack on every aspect of the system of legislative charters and privileges, which he developed at great length. He quoted Paine with approval in arguing that charters did not confer rights but on the contrary took them away from the people at large.[31]

Skidmore has been dismissed as a fanatic, of whose "errant influence" the emerging workingmen's movement of New York did well to purge itself.[32] Skidmore's contemporary, Langdon Byllesby, who published *Observations on the Sources and Effects of Unequal Wealth* in 1826,[33] regarded Jefferson's Declaration as establishing the "universally admitted" principle of individual rights. Like John Taylor, he regarded the growth of banking and financial institutions—to which he added insurance companies—as a corruption of the natural sources of wealth, and also attacked labour-saving machinery and manufactures, which, he argued, reduced purchasing power by reducing the labour force. Byllesby wanted to promote equality through labour associations for "Securing Equal (or Mutual) Advantages (or Interests)" which would share among members

29. Ibid., p. 270.   30. Ibid., pp. 157–8.
31. Ibid., pp. 160–88.
32. Arthur M. Schlesinger, Jr., *The Age of Jackson* (Boston, 1950), p. 184.
33. L. Byllesby, *Observations on the Sources and Effects of Unequal Wealth, with Propositions towards Remedying the Disparity of Profit in Pursuing the Arts of Life, and Establishing Security in Individual Prospects and Resources* (New York, 1826).

the wealth derived from their activities. Skidmore had touched only lightly on education; Byllesby—whose name does not seem to reappear—wanted to use it to promote individual accomplishment and usefulness in place of "factious distinctions of merit or honour between the members of different callings or trades".

Skidmore's intellectual significance is not merely nugatory, however. He was one of those who showed that in a period which for many elements of a somewhat disjointed society was one of redefinition, of a very uneasy searching for both social and political identity, it was possible to recur to the nation's founding principles, and from that standpoint to view the American social order as a whole. John Adams had once believed that there was "but one order" in American society; no one seems any longer to have held that view in the Jacksonian period, but Skidmore was unusually clear in the view that there ought to be but one order. Nor did he accept the moral completeness of the founders' principles; he aimed to go further than they, and to complete them. Even in the workingmen's movement which they tried to influence, Skidmore and his group were out of place, and their very failure gives him a further significance. It makes inescapably clear that concepts of equality could survive only in forms of adaption to the aspirations of an age dominated by economic development. Equality of opportunity was the chief meaning that Americans could now hope to extract from a tradition which had been handed down to them as equality of rights.

For a group of their more influential contemporaries, who were both colleagues and rivals in the workingmen's and reformist movements, education was the key to the social problem. The leading figures were all recent British arrivals. Robert Dale Owen was the son of Robert Owen, founder of the paternalistically organised co-operative factory at New Lanark in Scotland and of the New Harmony community in Indiana; George H. Evans was an anticlerical English printer who later threw himself into the movement for making land grants to would-be farmers; Frances Wright, the brilliant Scot who dominated them through the force of her intellect and personality, was one of the most energetic social thinkers of her time and an early influence in the feminist movement. Frances Wright developed a scheme for general school education under the complete guardianship and control of the state; all children would be brought up in boarding schools where conditions of rigorous equality would eliminate all vestiges of privilege and thus suppress the very consciousness of class.[34] These views did not derive primarily from Jefferson's kind of belief in the need to teach republican virtues along with the elements of intellectual training; Wright and her supporters had grasped the fact that education was part of the social process which both reflected and formed the individual's social consciousness and fed him or her out into appropriate positions. They wanted by remodelling the system as a whole to change the mould in which American citizens were formed.

Skidmore, for all his defects, held that the injustices of a competitive economic order could be remedied only by considering society as a whole, under the guiding principle of total equality. All of them worked within a single state, New York, and Skidmore took a position close to state rights in arguing that the state had authority to enact his General Division and to enforce laws abolishing inheritance.[35] These reformers, with their differing remedies, shared a consciousness of crisis. The crisis they perceived had many aspects, and the realities they sought to control were extremely complex. Viewed as they were by different observers from many angles and with differing expectations, the conditions of Jacksonian America gave rise to a bewildering variety of intense but inharmonious impressions.

Threatened Dignities: Labour and Gentility

All later knowledge of American society in this period has been coloured by the most eloquently written of these impressions in Alexis de Tocqueville's *Democracy in America*. Tocqueville had no difficulty in discovering that "equality of conditions" which his reading had led him to expect. It was for him America's prevailing and most significant characteristic; and his discovery of America was a prevision of the future that he discerned for Europe. In this vision it was impossible to disentangle the strands of liberty, individualism, and equality, not because they were incapable of separate definition, but because they were threads of a single fabric. The "equality of

34. Schlesinger, *Age of Jackson*, pp. 181–4.
35. Skidmore, *Rights of Man*, p. 329.

conditions" to which Tocqueville attached such critical emphasis was a state of affairs which he felt as the dominant feature of social and economic relations; but it is clear from his language that this material manifestation, which made farmers and tradesmen, merchants and professional persons one another's social equals, and apparently did not exclude labourers from some kind of social access to their obvious superiors, was animated by the ideals and aspirations of equality. "Equality", he wrote, "every day gives every man a multitude of little delights. The charms of equality are felt every hour and are within everyone's reach; the noblest hearts are not insensitive to them and the commonest souls delight in them. The passion to which equality gives birth must thus be at once energetic and general".[36] Tocqueville thus saw equality as both a fact and an ideal— a fact dominating American life, representing the actual achievement of America's animating ideal. These observations are too vivid to be brushed aside as a result of more recent discoveries that social equality was not all that it seemed and that economic inequality had struck firm roots. Yet his remarks permit the suggestion that his American contemporaries of a social standing that would not have ranked high in the Old World may have been more interested in asserting equality with their superiors than in accepting it from inferiors. Equality and self-esteem were not easy partners in such a highly competitive society.

During the same period, the theme of political equality was also repeatedly asserted. State constitutional conventions revised the basic conditions of political participation until white male suffrage, with corresponding access to elective office, became an almost universal rule; and a wide range of public offices was brought within reach of the electorate. Even judges were increasingly being judged by the voters. But this rage for equality did not affect everyone equally. Old Federalist critics could sardonically observe that the benefits of these reforms were not extended to Indians, who lay outside American political society but not outside its power, or to Negroes, whom the tide of Jacksonian democracy subjected to increasing disenfranchisement and victimisation.

The fragmented society of white America did display certain

36. Alexis de Tocqueville. *De la démocratie en Amérique*, ed. J.-P. Meyer (Paris, 1961), pp. 101–4.

common characteristics and tendencies. In the aims which people avowed, in their choice of where to live, where to worship, and whom to live with as well as in the drive for wealth, individual personality and its ambitions were displacing the values normally associated with place, community, and even with kin. These tendencies had no single or national source; but cheap land, rising ambitions, and the loosening of conventions of authority gave them their American forms. As with many new phenomena, the new style was first named by its opponents, who called it "individualism". The word seems to have been unknown before 1826, when it made its appearance in France.[37] Jefferson, it is true, had used it in 1814 to characterise the nominalist ideas of Buffon, of which he disapproved; and when it emerged in the vocabulary of St Simon's school of French socialists it was also an expression of disapproval. For socialists, individualism disrupted the foundations necessary for co-operative action. The St Simonians took it to mean individual antagonism in the struggle for gain, and denounced laisser-faire as thinly disguised exploitation; but they took care to distinguish rootless and destructive individualism from individuality, which stood for dignity and man's capacity to grow in reason and morality. Romantic conservatives, who treasured the profusion with which the past had bestowed its institutions, beliefs, and languages on the present, regarded individualism as a disintegrating force, hostile to the fabric of faith, custom and social order. This was the tenour of Edmund Burke's indictment of the French Revolution, in which sense he used the word "individuality".[38] American usage was equally hostile, and as late as 1847 *Webster's Dictionary* defined it as   self-interest and selfishness, which, whatever one might think of those qualities, had never been far from the truth. But American usage gradually softened towards the merits of a word which conveyed so accurate an intimation of the cherished values of American society, and whose propriety seemed at least to have been hinted by a founding reference to "the pursuit of happiness".[39]

37. Yehoshua Arieli, *Individualism and Nationalism in American Ideology* (Cambridge, Mass., 1964), p. 404, n. 84.
38. These remarks depend on ibid., pp. 221–32. Tocqueville regarded America's free institutions as the best safeguard against the corrosive aspects of individualism; Tocqueville, *Démocratie en Amérique*, II, pp. 105–12.
39. Arieli, *Individualism*, p. 198.

Manifestations of this new mood, of individual dissociation from older structures of authority, were discerned long before the age connected with the name of Jackson, and should not be ascribed to his presidency merely because historians have so often found it convenient to date them from the time when Tocqueville first noticed them. In 1806 Benjamin Latrobe, America's first professional architect, reflected on the advanced stage these changes had already attained. "Ever since the Revolution," he observed, "the internal state of the United States has been undergoing a regular and gradual change. That deference of race which, without existing titles of nobility, grows out of the habits and prejudices of the people, was bequeathed to Americans by English manners and institutions which were established before the Revolution. These manners could not be suddenly altered nor did the institutions of the country undergo any very great or sudden change. After the adoption of the Federal Constitution, the extension of the right of suffrage in all the states to a majority of adult male citizens, planted a germ which has gradually evolved and spread actual and practical equality and political democracy over the whole union. . . . Every man is independent".[40] At the time of these comments Latrobe, an Englishman by birth, had lived some ten years in the United States. His perspective was advantageous, but it did not give him the only word on the subject, and his observations were probably more accurate for the older states than for some of the newer ones. In the Southwest, men of the stature of William Blount and John Sevier dominated successive governments of Tennessee with an assurance that owed a great deal to the habit of command and very little to the exigencies of social equality or electoral politics. Thomas P. Abernethy, the first modern historian of Tennessee's early life, reached conclusions never superseded by more recent research when he demonstrated the immense political and economic power of the great land speculators and natural leaders, who treated public office as their inheritance, secured the votes of the common people by their prestige, and felt no need to stoop to campaigning for election.[41] But in Tennessee as elsewhere, this stable

40. Mathew Page Andrews, *History of Maryland* (Garden City, N.Y., 1929), p. 410. The word *race* was here used to mean a family or group connected by kinship. See Dr Johnson's *Dictionary* (London, 1773).
41. Thomas P. Abernethy, *From Frontier to Plantation in Tennessee* (Chapel Hill, 1932), especially chaps. 10 and 22.

order was assailed by the groundswell that brought James K. Polk to Congress in 1825 and was soon to be linked indissolubly with the name and image of Jackson. In face of this social insurgency Judge Emmerson, a retired justice of the state's supreme court, exclaimed with more passion than clarity, "Had I the power, no exertion of which I was capable would be wanting to arrest the progress of that wild and furious democracy which has long threatened to overwhelm our country at no distant date in the vortex of anarchy".[42]

In many parts of the country, the democracy which alarmed Judge Emmerson was less wild than he imagined, but had rather more grounds for alarm. Before the rise of major industry, fortunes accumulated by earlier generations in commerce and land speculation had brought about conspicuous disparities in the distribution of wealth, education, social standing, and consequently opportunities for security and personal advancement. The fluidity which impressed Tocqueville—who was aware that social mobility also had a downward direction[43]—was not a merely superficial manifestation, but its extreme visibility was deceptive. City wealth, especially in the Northeast, was concentrating in families who derived their initial advantage from wealthy forebears of high social status. Even when they had been less wealthy, the antecedents of such families seem to have been well-to-do; poverty or subsistence incomes were extremely rare foundations for the rise to riches.[44] Different patterns may have been in process of development in the Northwest, but there is little reason to suppose that the cumulative processes which inequalities of goods and social position normally introduced into the development of the economic order were materially different elsewhere. In the South, population movements and economic growth drew the best lands into the hands of the greater planters and slaveowners.

In Eastern cities, the growing concentration of industrial plant, together with the separation of capital and management from the work force, was bringing about the beginnings of resentfully self-conscious urban skilled working class. The artisans of New York and

42. Charles G. Sellers, *James K. Polk, Jacksonian, 1795–1843* (Princeton, 1957), p. 99.
43. Tocqueville, *Démocratie en Amérique*, II, 106.
44. Edward Pessen, "The Egalitarian Myth and the American Social Reality: Wealth, Mobility and Equality in the 'Era of the Common Man'", *American Historical Review*, vol. xx, no. 4 (1971).

Philadelphia sensed a new alienation between their skills and the capital that controlled them as a threat to their livelihood and dignity. Workingmen's political parties, though of recent growth, were strong enough by 1830 to cause anxiety among the major parties—after which the New York Workingmen's party drifted against its own wishes towards the Democrats.[45] Five years later began the first American steps towards a combined movement of trades unions in America.

It was at the regular monthly meeting of the delegates of the General Trades' Union of the City of New York and its vicinity, held on Wednesday, 26 March 1834, that the decision was made to propose a national union to the several trades unions of the country.[46] The meeting, after a delay caused by an outbreak of cholera, assembled in New York City on 25 August. Its proceedings resulted in the adoption of a series of resolutions, preceded by a statement of the general ills and injustices of the era. The committee to which the convention referred the task of drafting "resolutions expressive of the views of the National Trades' Union Convention on the social, civil, and intellectual condition of the labouring classes of these United States, and the like classes of all countries" deplored the fact that these conditions exhibited "the most unequal and unjustifiable distribution of the produce of labor, thus operating to produce a humiliating, servile dependency, incompatible with the inherent, natural equality of man". There followed a brief declaration of the principles on which political economy ought to be founded, which included the statement that property could be justly acquired only by production, equal exchange, or gift (the last being a method precluded by the Skidmore system). A peroration whose emotive force was greatly impaired by its turgid composition and excessive length ended by calling on the workers to bark the tree of corruption and nourish that of liberty and equality.

The influence of Frances Wright and her group emerged at once in the resolutions on education. The first of these viewed existing systems as "destructive of that Equality which is predicated in the

---

45. Walter Hugins, *Jacksonian Democracy and the Working Class* (Stanford, 1960), pp. 15–23.

46. John R. Commons and Associates, *A Documentary History of American Industrial Society*, 10 vols. (Cleveland, Ohio, 1910), VI, 194–5.

Declaration of Independence, because of their exclusive character in giving instruction to the wealthy few at the expense of the industrious many, fostering, by means of Colleges, Universities, Military and Naval Academies, &c, a professional Monopoly of Knowledge, thereby drawing a line of demarcation between the producers of all the wealth, and other portions of society which subsist on the fruits of the Working Man's industry".[47] It is an impressive indication of the thinking of the convention that education should have taken pride of place in their general picture of the institutions whose character determined the structure of society. There followed resolutions on public lands, hours of labour, the legality of trade unions, and the need to revise bad legislation. It was also necessary that every labourer inform himself of his equal rights "to promote the good of the whole community, rather than to confer privileges on the favored few". The movement continued in existence for a few years, but without gaining strength; its early interest in education was soon lost in more urgent issues, and at the Convention of 1836 the committee deputed to report on education itself became preoccupied with the currency, economic necessities, and the important proposal that cooperative trade associations be formed in order to secure for the mechanic "sole and absolute control over the disposal of his labor".[48]

The trades union movement, which at its best was obliged to pass resolutions expressing concern about the apathy and indifference of the workers, failed for many years to recover from the ruinous effects of the economic panic of 1837. Unions were depleted of funds at the very moment when their members needed support; ideas of equality played little part in rebuilding either class solidarity or trade union action. Yet equality stands out as the central intellectual commitment of the working-class movement of the Jacksonian era. Spokesmen for working-class interests—not usually themselves working-class people—clearly saw how privileges in education and social position were eroding the advantages of equality in law and politics, and undermining the formal guarantees conferred by suffrage and representation.

Leaders of the American trade union and workingmen's movements were few in number and far from representative of the classes

47. Ibid., pp. 205–7.
48. Ibid., pp. 291–3.

for whom they claimed to speak. They did represent the highest level at which those classes were able to articulate themselves, both in the theory which inspired their statements and in their perception of the issues calling for political action. Their ideas of equality revealed what they thought the United States, as a political society, ought to be; and they also revealed what the workers felt was being lost. The transatlantic nature of the movement infused ideas that would not have sprung from exclusively American sources and added to their pronouncements a flavour if international brotherhood which may have buoyed their spirits in face of domestic difficulties: They were not alone in the world. For all the intellectual influence of the British element, however, the faith with which the trades union resolutions invoked the Declaration of Independence was no mere rhetorical convenience, but reflected the belief that their American heritage had converted natural rights into legitimate social expectations.

Whigs and Democrats did not fight their political battles on these issues, although the parties assailed each other with expletives drawn from the vocabulary of aristocracy and monarchy. It was for those whose urgent sense of the moral and economic needs of the day was left deeply unsatisfied by the compromises of party politics to continue the fight with insistent reminders of what Americans owed to the idea of equality. Orestes Brownson, whose changeable career spanned the Unitarian ministry and the Roman Catholic Church, was a witness to that problem. Brownson, who spent much of his life in a burning quest for religious satisfaction, threw himself into Jacksonian politics when he beheld at first hand the misery caused by the crisis of 1837.[49] He was under no illusion that America had achieved equality, but unlike most contemporaries he also understood that it had not achieved genuine freedom of competition. Brownson, whose sense of social justice gave him affinities with the French St Simonians, the Fourierists, and the early socialists, struck out from their course towards collectivism by facing firmly in the opposite direction—from which he believed their American disciples had all come. Whatever might have been true of France, Brownson believed that the revolutionary heritage gave Americans their precedents for equality, which meant that the true problem was not to create but to

49. Arthur M. Schlesinger, Jr., *A Pilgrim's Progress: Orestes Brownson* (Boston, repr. 1966), pp. 82–3, 88–111.

restore a genuine state of laisser-faire. This diagnosis rested on two profound errors. The first was the belief that the desired condition had really existed in the revolutionary era; and second was the belief that the advance of industrial economics could be reversed. Yet his sense of social and immediate realities, and his penetration of the pretences which protected them, were far clearer than that of most of his respectable Unitarian contemporaries in Boston, who soon found his radical views alarming and distasteful. In a highly controversial article, "The Laboring Classes" published in 1840, Brownson declared that universal suffrage "is little better than a mockery, when the voters are not socially equal. No matter what party you support, no matter what man you elect, property is always the basis of your governmental action". He brushed aside the fashionable remedies of free trade and universal education and cut straight to the centre of the problem—the need to abolish inheritance.

This programme had been advocated ten years earlier by Skidmore, who had died young. The timing of Brownson's revival of it was far more critical. The Whigs injected his ideas into the campaign of 1840 as typical of what was to be expected from a Democratic victory, causing resentful consternation among the Democrats and weakening their already damaged prospects of electoral success. The crushing Democratic defeat shook Brownson so badly that he lost much of his faith in forms of government that relied so heavily on the wisdom of the people. He would never be quite so close to them again. But his energetic thinking was one of the many American monuments to the heritage of the Revolution. Not only did he believe that the true principles lay there—he also believed that the Founders had practiced the principles that Jacksonian America had lost. This contemporary view was to be completely reversed by historians who united in regarding the Jacksonian era as an advance, even as the logical fulfilment of the ideas of the Revolution.

Robert Rantoul, Jr., of Massachusetts, who worked for the party in the state and in his locality was both a committed partisan of a variety of reforms and a more dependable Democrat than Brownson.[50] For persons of his outlook one of the critical problems was to make sure that the Democrats became and remained the party of

50. Marvin Meyers, *The Jacksonian Persuasion* (1957) (New York, paperback ed. 1960), p. 206.

equal rights. Whatever needed doing could be done with the party in power. Rantoul was probably addressing his own party as well as the public at large when he told an audience at Worcester, Massachusetts, on 4 July 1837, that "the Democracy" was the party of "equal rights, equal laws, equal privileges, universal protection". It was not the party of any faction; it should include both the rich and poor and do justice to all interests, but its greatest strength lay in "the middling interest" and the substantial yeomanry, "for they have seldom any interest adverse to the common good of all".[51] This was a long way from some of the more alarming demands of his left-wing contemporaries, but Rantoul was equally aware of the threat under which the newly conscious working classes were struggling to maintain their economic competence.

They sensed this treat in the increasingly separate and distant control exercised by capitalist employers. The growth of factories in place of workshops and of other features of a competitive and industrial economy diminished the individual worker's feeling of control over his own life. Equality of opportunity, in these circumstances, appealed more strongly to his employers and masters; it meant equality among competing capitalists, not among all classes of the economy, and from the worker's point of view it was already a failure. It is thus significant that the language of their spokesman combined the old insistence on equal rights—which if put into effect as social policy was still meant to convey equality of opportunity— with a general view of the social order in which institutions were to be shaped, and held in shape, so as to maintain an equal order. But the breaking down of the old arrangements meant that this emphatic assertion of the basic theme that America had been founded as a country of equal rights was an assertion charged with increasing anxiety; people who spoke in this way were threatened with an alarming sense of loss.

It was not only in personal economic independence that the artisan felt the threat, but in the personal dignity invested in that independence. Rantoul made this point in an essay "Workingmen", published in 1833, where he listed claims that the workingman could make on society: (1) The right to his faculties, and the products of

51. Ibid., pp. 222–3.

their use; (2) the right to choose the terms on which he will employ his time; (3) the right to steady wages at the highest going rate; (4) the right to education; (5) the right to respect; (6) the right to advancement in life.[52] The rights here insisted on included all that the workers and their allies needed, but the order and emphasis differed from those of some other spokesmen. Opportunity was obviously present in the last item; education was an essential, though not, for Rantoul, an all-inclusive essential. It was the fifth item which struck the moral rather than the practical keynote of the debate. Whatever their fortune or their skills or their income, people wanted respect. This demand was no mere incident of Rantoul's own choice or temperament. The call which went out from New York for a national convention of trades unions in 1834 began by proposing that the delegations should meet "to consult on such measures as shall be most conducive to advance the moral and intellectual dignity of the laboring classes, sustain their pecuniary interests, succor the oppressed . . .".[53] Pecuniary interest was firmly in its place, but first came the dignity of the labouring classes.

The reference to intellect, which might perhaps have struck a less acceptable note in a later century, was apposite, for the leaders of the movement were not only in close touch with Britain but were readers of the great French rebel priest Lammenais;[54] and it was a coincidence of date, but no mere coincidence of principle, that in 1834, the year of the first trades union convention in New York, Lammenais told the labouring masses of France that they must learn an eleventh commandment: "Respect yourselves".[55] In America, the language of self-respect was the language of equality. That was the peculiar gift which Thomas Jefferson and his colleagues had handed down to later generations of their countrymen.

Not all Americans, however, agreed that respect or esteem was something to which everyone was entitled equally. This attitude formed one branch of the central paradox of Jacksonian history which

52. Quoted by ibid., p. 216.
53. Commons, *Documentary History*, VI, 194.
54. H. F. R. de Lammenais, *Paroles d'un croyant*, was available in French; his *Le Livre du peuple* was translated into English as *The People's Own Book* by Nathaniel Greene, a friend of Brownson's, and appeared in Boston in 1839. Schlesinger, *Brownson*, p. 303.
55. A. G. Lehmann, *Sainte-Beuve* (Oxford, 1962), p. 204; Schlesinger, *Brownson*, p. 320.

has not received the attention it has deserved. Historians who occupy themselves with the plight of the urban workers, with the farmers threatened with debt and dispossession, and with the movements for resisting these threats, have had no difficulty in establishing that significant elements both in and to the left of the Jacksonians felt that their world was in danger. But that was almost exactly what their enemies felt. The crowds who proclaimed the age of the common man by trampling on the furniture of the White House at Andrew Jackson's inauguration did not reassure their more conventional opponents that everyone was in his right place. Judge Emmerson of Tennessee had observed events at a considerable distance from the main political centres, but he was far from being alone in his feelings. Tocqueville's famous observations about the equality of conditions were entirely compatible with the disappearance of both social deference and of the influence of aristocracy and gentry in politics, which the losers of these battles regarded as a dreadful and general phenomenon.

James Fenimore Cooper, who used the form of the novel to make a calculated though far from dispassionate analysis of the new situation, was quite sure that America's march to democracy was a march downhill. In two novels, *Homeward Bound* and *Home as Found*—it is the titles, not the books, that rhyme—he described the adventures of the Effinghams, an upper-class New York family who had lived mainly in Europe for the past twelve years. In the second story the whole family returns home and discovers the worst. A friend warns them that "No country has so much altered for the worse in so short a time". The whole novel forms a treatise on the social necessity for rank and dignity. The object of Cooper's satire was the presumption of ill-bred social climbers that their equal rights as freemen or women under the American Constitution entitled them to come and go as equals among all classes of society. Socially uninstructed characters blunder through the story without apprehending the folly or the enormity of their mistakes; one of them characteristically accepts with joy an offer of introduction to his social superior because he "fancied he had the right, under the Constitution of the United States of America, to be introduced to every human being with whom he came in contact".[56] The two nastiest char-

56. *Home as Found* 2 vols. (Philadelphia, 1838), p. 70 and throughout.

acters, Steadfast Dodge the editor and Aristabulus Bragg the agent and land speculator, are caught between their desire to maintain places within the Effingham circle and their need for popularity among the common people. Their dilemma is illustrated by the occasion on which Aristabulus is requested by John Effingham to tell some apprentices to stop playing ball on his lawn, which he is loath to do, fearing that it may cost him votes at some future election; he solves his problem by hitting on the device of telling the boys that it is aristocratic to play ball on a lawn surrounded by roses, but that by playing in the street they can break the law made by the city council —an irresistable argument which produces the desired result. In a debate on the proposal to abolish pews in the rebuilding of the church, and to raise the congregation to the level of the minister, Mr Dodge observes, "To my mind, gentlemen and ladies, God never intended an American to kneel". An important episode turns on the rights to a park, belonging to Effingham, but which he has long allowed the townspeople to use. When he proposes to reclaim it for the privacy of the family, a dispute breaks out which reveals the interesting point that even the rights of private landed property were no longer held sacred where the popular will was aroused. Bragg and Dodge are in an awkward spot, but feel that Effingham is making a bad mistake. "Resisting the popular will on the part of the individual", says their author, "they considered arrogance and aristocracy *per se*, without at all entering into the question of the right or the wrong". The townspeople regard the park as theirs by right; but Effingham knows where he stands. With Cooper's backing, he holds that his generous indulgence in allowing the people to use his land could be retracted at any moment without the slightest injury or injustice.

Cooper was aware of a need to establish that old, propertied, respectable families really existed and really deserved to be held in special esteem. He had also to convey that this exclusive gentility was perfectly compatible with loyalty to republican principles. An English baronet, Sir George Templemore, is appropriately on the scene, available to provide the genuine example, and to elicit information about the nuances of American social class. "All the old families, for instance", the lovely Grace Effingham tells him, "keep more together than the others, though"—she significantly adds—"it is a subject of regret that they are not more particular than they are". This remark almost causes Sir George to forget himself: " 'Old families?' he exclaimed with quite as much stress as a well-bred man could lay in the circumstances". Grace, however, had herself hinted that old families were not always true to their more exclusive obligations, which presumably included self-preservation. Despite the collision of values between the myrmidons of popular democracy and the Effingham family, with their instinctive high breeding, gentle manners, and unruffled dignity, it is reassuring to find an Englishman of noble descent emerging from obscurity to take the heroine's hand, and everyone marrying exactly according to his or her social station.

The niceties of style and form through which this clash of values is transmitted play an entirely different part in these novels from those of their English counterparts. In English novels the existence of class and rank, and the intricacies of behaviour that accord with them, are sometimes the objects of satire; but they are there, as regular as the squares of London and Bath, as indestructible as the courts of chancery. For Cooper, on the contrary, the very fabric was frail, and stood in urgent need of defence against the insulting claims of a crude and presumptious mob. These views do not give an immediate key to Cooper's politics, however. Though the son of a wealthy Federalist squire, he identified himself as a Democrat and seems to have maintained connections with Jacksonians. This is not as paradoxical as it seems; many more political old Federalists hoped for advancement from a Jacksonian alliance, and Cooper, who has been aptly called a Tory Democrat,[57] was repelled by the business morals that he associated with the Whigs; Dodge was his type of Whig editor.

Andrew Jackson, Individualism, and Equal Protection

Andrew Jackson posed a less serious threat to the social order than his enemies feared. He based his opposition to the recharter of the Bank of the United States not on *dirigiste* or centralising doctrines but on the firm ground of equality of opportunity, which meant the rejection of public support for private privilege. On similar principles he turned against the conventions by which posts in the public

57. By Marvin Meyers, *Jacksonian Persuasion*, p. 59.

service had acquired the character of unofficial forms of property in a manner distinctly resembling practices which had not yet disappeared in Britain. Official duties, he told Congress, could be made "so plain and simple that men of intelligence may readily qualify themselves for their performance"[58]—a programme which opened the doors wider than he knew. Jackson ignored the question of how these men of intelligence were to be recruited for the plain and simple duties of public office; the spoils system, operating in the service of political parties, was to supply the answer. Whether or not this process introduced greater respect for equality of opportunity into the selections for public office, it can hardly be said to have made those positions more accountable to the public for the performance of their duties. It was no mere linguistic chance by which the incumbents of public office in the United States came to be called "office-holders" rather than civil servants.

Jacksonian theory was satisfied that government could maintain the basic conditions for equality of opportunity by such measures as the destruction of the second Bank of the United States, and by steps taken in several of the individual states to ensure that charters of business incorporations were made to conform to standard conditions and taken out of the reach of pressure and privilege. This theory had more to offer to those who hoped to rise through the system than to those who were losing ground in the competitive struggle. Beyond the basically defensive types of policy suggested, Jackson had little to offer but a sort of authoritative inactivity; his veto message on the Bank bill expressed the limits as much as it did the scope of his principles: "Distinctions in society will always exist under every just government. Equality of talents, or education, or of wealth cannot be produced by human institutions". So much, then for the policies of the reformers to his left. His aim was to make sure that government remained neutral between these differences; it was no part of his purpose to indulge in distributionist policies or to supervise the operations of the system with paternalistic control. The economy, the social world, and whatever schools or systems of education people chose to adopt were to be free for all comers. Jack-

58. James D. Richardson, comp., *Messages and Papers of the Presidents, 1789–1897* (Washington, D.C., 1896), II, 576–91.

son did affirm very emphatically that everyone was to be equally entitled to the protection of the law,

in the full enjoyment of the gifts of Heaven and the fruits of superior industry, economy and virtue; but when the laws undertake to add to these natural and just advantages artificial distinctions, to grant titles, gratuities, and exclusive privileges, to make the rich richer and the potent more powerful, the humble members of the society—the farmers, mechanics and laborers—have a right to complain of the injustice of their Government. There are no necessary evils in Government. Its evils exist only in its abuses. If it would confine itself to equal protection, and, as Heaven does its rains shower its favors alike on the high and the low, the rich and the poor, it would be an unqualified blessing. In the act before me there seems to be a wide and unnecessary departure from these principles.

This was a rather simple exposition of the problems of political economy. Other good Jacksonians, such as the anti-paper-money theorist William Gouge,[59] were far better aware of the already manifest fact that the specious appearance of equal economic opportunity concealed complex and growing disparities that simply could not be stopped in their tracks, and certainly not by such lofty restraint on the part of the only power in the country that could attempt to act consistently over the whole system. It was still further from any intent of Jackson's to make government accountable for that equality of esteem which the leaders of labour were beginning to advance as an essential element of their idea of American egalitarianism. Yet the mere fact that it had been discerned as a principle with some claim on public policy was a matter of future importance. Once the idea had been let loose into the domain of public consciousness that the basic requirement of an egalitarian society included an equal degree of respect, due to individuals because they were people, without regard to social position, family, wealth, or inheritance, there was no point at which it could logically stop. If it were to include members of different occupations or skills or religions, it could not reasonably be withheld from those of different races.

No lawyer would have denied Jackson's tenet that the laws ought to provide equal protection to all. The differences of opinion were political, not legal, and they turned (once more) on the actual con-

59. Joseph L. Blau, ed., *Social Theories of Jacksonian Democracy* (Indianapolis, 1954), pp. 183–98.

tent of the laws, Jackson and his party maintaining that such institutions as the national bank were endowed with privileges which imported unwarranted inequalities into American life. Thus, in spite of himself, Jackson was involved if only to a limited extent in affirming that social values must influence political policy. At the same time he was well aware that people were born with very different endowments of the gifts of nature, and brought up to different gifts of society, and he believed that a just government would protect the consequences that fairly flowed from these differences.

When Jackson introduced the phrase "equal protection", he probably intended to limit rather than to extend the bounds of government interest in these and kindred questions. But it was to have a momentous history. For this was the crucial expression that reappeared at a vital phase of American history when the Constitution itself was being reconstructed by the Fourteenth Amendment— which guarantees to the citizens of all states the privileges and immunities of American citizens, and to all persons the equal protection of the laws. At that time the specific purpose was to extend the powers of the supreme law to cover the coloured race, as they were then usually called. This turn of events would have astounded Jackson, who would assuredly have disapproved; but the truth is that the new application of equal protection was consistent with its basic principle. It fell to a later generation than Jackson's to extend the obligations owed by government to members of every race or heritage, as it had fallen to Jackson to affirm that these obligations were owed to every social or economic class. Jackson, who never had the slightest concern for racial equality, might have failed to see the line of connection. That difficulty arose from the nature of his vision, not from the nature of the case. From the altered perspective given by the passage of time, the connection is clear, and the line is straight.

In the competitive conditions of economic and geographical, expansion, equality of opportunity, the one unifying theme of the period, was an idea which always exulted in a higher proportion of rhetoric than practical meaning. The social function of the rhetoric was to give hope, thus drawing off discontent even among those for whom the doors would never open. Opportunities did not have to be equal in order to be real, however; wherever business or farming or the professions were reasonably open to talent, and where people's energies and abilities were engaged with some degree of satisfaction, the notion of equality was merely an adornment to their conception of opportunity. It neither described it accurately nor furnished them with causes for discontent. But the national belief in opportunity, and the rhetoric of equality, imparted a distinctive flavour to the American system of incentives, and bestowed an exceptional touch of moral authority on the force of liberated individuality—at first deplored but later exalted under the name of individualism.

Chapter Six

Equality and Political Community: Who Are the People of the United States?

Inequality and the Constitution

On the scorching afternoon of 21 August 1858 in the northern Illinois town of Ottawa, in the presence of some twelve thousand people accompanied by banners, brass bands, and clouds of highway dust, Abraham Lincoln made his first speech in the formal series of debates between himself and Senator Stephen A. Douglas. Douglas opened the debate with a confident assertion of the familiar theme of Negro inferiority, coupled with his old campaign argument that Lincoln and the Republicans believed in the full equality of the races. "I believe", Douglas declared, "this government was made on the white basis. I believe it was made by white men, for the benefit of white men and their posterity for ever, and I am in favor of confining citizenship to white men, men of European birth and descent, instead of conferring it upon negroes, Indians and other inferior races". He charged Lincoln with believing that the Negro was endowed with equality by the Almighty and that no human law could deprive him of rights conferred "by the Supreme Ruler of the universe". "Now", Douglas added, "I do not believe that the Almighty ever intended the negro to be the equal of the white man. If he did, he has been a long time demonstrating the fact", and he proceeded to call in evidence the history of Negro inferiority "in all latitudes and climes".[1] It was to these beliefs and the vast mass of innate prejudice that supported them that Lincoln addressed his carefully guarded reply.

Lincoln conceded that the physical differences between the races "will probably forever forbid their living together upon a footing of perfect equality", and expressed a preference for his own race having the superior position: "I have no purpose to introduce political and social equality between the white and black races", he declared; elsewhere he denied that Negroes ought to be allowed to vote or to serve on juries. He repudiated Douglas's charges against him on these scores, but added that he held, notwithstanding all this,

There is no reason in the world why the negro is not entitled to all the natural rights enumerated in the Declaration of Independence, the right to life, liberty and the pursuit of happiness. I hold that he is as much entitled to these as the white man. I agree with Judge Douglas that he is not my equal in many respects—certainly not in color, perhaps not in moral and intellectual endowment. But in the right to eat the bread, without leave of anybody else, which his own hand earns, *he is my equal and the equal of Judge Douglas, and the equal of every living man.*[2]

The thunder of applause which greeted this affirmation testified to a difference of attitude rather than opinion. Douglas did not approve of slavery and did not want to deprive Negroes of the ability to earn their own living; neither of the antagonists proposed to place in the Negro's hands the political or even the civil powers that were needed to protect his admitted right to economic independence. The difficulties and inconsistencies in Lincoln's position were at least as serious as those which he succesfully exposed in Douglas during the further course of the debates. He plainly held that equality in the rights enumerated in the Declaration of Independence could be guaranteed without conferring the rights normally connected with citizenship. His aim was to change attitudes but not institutions. The immense popular success of his own campaign which, though he lost the senatorial election, raised him to the national position from which he won the presidency two years later, should not obscure the fact that Lincoln was asserting incompatible principles. That, indeed, was

1. Paul M. Angle, ed., *Created Equal? The Complete Lincoln-Douglas Debates of 1858* (Chicago, 1958), pp. 111–12.
2. Ibid., p. 117.

part of the very reason for his success; the problem facing the numerous Republican supporters who wanted to see the Negroes free, who wanted them to support themselves in peace and safety, and who wanted the institutions of the country to ensure these things, but did not want to share those institutions with the African race, was extremely complex and had not yet been fully explored. The process of exploration was due to intensify with great rapidity during the next ten years. It would entail a great civil war, accompanied and followed by intense and frequently bitter disputes about the possibilities of Negro participation in the life of white society, during which the American doctrine of equality was to be catechised, its hidden assumptions and false promises exposed to political conflict as never before in the nation's history.

But in 1858 all this was not yet certain, and the forms to be taken were unknown. For the time being it was clear that equality of opportunity, equality of politics, and equality before the law were not to be extended to Negroes. Equality of esteem, as Douglas's very characteristic language made clear, was totally out of the question. If in these circumstances the Negro was to enjoy the natural rights of the Declaration of Independence, it could be only by living out his entire life on a different and lower plane, protected perhaps from molestation but without hope for better things even in the remote future. Neither Lincoln nor anyone else would have accepted that such deprivation of the norms of civil and political protection could permanently suffice to maintain the rights of any members of the white race, to whatever group they might have belonged. No solution was possible within these terms of reference. If not full equality, then at least a very substantial degree of political participation and of legal rights were indispensable to the true experience and enjoyment and pursuit of happiness, to liberty, and often to life itself.

The Constitution, resting so lightly on the American multitudes, had permitted and protected the form of moral pluralism which Stephen Douglas held essential to its endurance. Lincoln, who understood historical process better than his rival, perceived that moral pluralism could not last forever. In the past, however, that spacious and accommodating attitude to the reception of such diverse peoples into a single political system had been protected not only by the institutions of the country but by the land itself. The land could absorb, and thus to some extent conceal, incipient conflicts whose ideological character made them eventually inescapable. It was for this reason that space gave many Americans the illusion of possessing indefinite time; wherever space ran out, as in the cities had already happened, conflicts between rival beliefs and mutually hostile communities erupted alarmingly. The Eastern cities experienced these eruptions earlier than the wider spaces of the West. In the age whose democratic propensities have so often been associated with the name of Andrew Jackson, enraged mobs could menace the lives and properties of minorities whom they happened to dislike with almost complete freedom from molestation by police or other forces of public order. It was in the light of these disorders that many good citizens repeated a remark made by Henry Clay in an attack on Jackson's Bank veto: "We are in the midst of a revolution". These manifestations of the spirit of the new democracy that seemed to be abroad, unrestrained by forces of law or by the slightest respect for the interests or feelings of members of other groups, exemplified in a terrible manner the worst fears that Tocqueville had expressed about the tyrannous domination of local majorities. All of this had very little to do with anything the founders had in mind when they promised "a republican form of government". Recording these disturbances, Michel Chevalier, another observant French visitor, sardonically remarked how dead the word *equality* fell when a good citizen pronounced it.[3]

There were several white minorities but most notably the Catholic Irish for whom equality in America was at best an aim, at worst a contemptuous joke. Yet people of diverse origin, manners, and religions had shown that they could accommodate themselves to one another's presence, and could work out forms of association in the political parties. The confederation of states which the Republic comprised always from its foundation included a different confederation, that of communities with their own habits, and of regions with their own economic and social characteristics; and American republican government had always been hospitable to wide differences between communities and regions within the compass of a

3. Michael Chevalier, *Society, Manners and Politics in the United States: Letters on North America* (1840), ed. John William Ward (New York, 1967), pp. 371–4.

single system of law—even that system being supple rather than rigid. Ideas of community worked more or less well according to the patterns of population left by the tides of ethnic, national, or religious migration, and were so frequently in flux as to defy exact meaning. But their outlines were more distinctly marked along the boundaries of race. Whatever ideological professions people might make, it was only too clear that the visible facts of skin pigmentation marked out the limit beyond which most Americans were unwilling to carry their public opinions into civic, still less into private, life.

The Republic contained two populations—those who were of the Republic, and those who were merely in it. It was easier to say who was outside the American community considered as a whole than to say who belonged to it. Differences between northern and southern Europeans, differences of sect or religion, could be extremely sharp and intensely cruel; but they did not hold with such stubbornness as the visible differences of skin pigmentation which for the vast majority of European-descended Americans seemed to mark an insurmountable contrast between themselves and the Afro-Americans. In the sense that this contrast helped to define the community of whites, it may well have strengthened the internal bonds of such a highly diffuse society—there are good reasons for supposing that it did in the South. In the period of increasing sectional tension, this heritage of racial distinctness had retrospective effects on the views held by rival parties about the composition of the American community at the time the Constitution was made. The retrospect took on profound constitutional significance in a highly romantic passage of Chief Justice Taney's opinion in the famous case of *Dred Scott* v. *Sanford*, decided in 1857, after the inauguration of President James Buchanan, but before the storm over Kansas and the repeal of the Missouri Compromise had even begun to subside.

Readers with a taste for historical romance will not always be disappointed by the Supreme Court. But facts must precede romance, and the case arose because Dred Scott, a Negro slave, had once been taken by his master from the slave state of Missouri into territories where, under Congressional Ordinance of 1787, slavery was supposed to be forbidden. Subsequently Scott's master, Dr Emerson, had returned to Missouri with Scott and his wife. But the question that remained for the Supreme Court to decide was fraught with significance for Southern owners of slave property. Had Scott and his wife become free by virtue of setting foot on the free soil of the Northwest? And if not, what became of the Northwest Ordinance and all other congressional enactments on slavery in the territories? But if they had been made free by touching free soil, how then could they have been re-enslaved by returning to Missouri? For a free person does not normally become a slave when he enters a slave state.

The Supreme Court answered that because Negroes were not citizens when the Constitution was made, even a free Negro could never be a citizen of the United States and therefore had no power to sue in the courts. There was therefore no case to answer. But it reached the further conclusion, made superfluous by the disclaimer of jurisdiction already made, that Congress had never possessed a constitutional power to exclude slavery from the territories, for which reason the Missouri Compromise of 1820 was held to have been unconstitutional. Chief Justice Taney and the six justices who concurred in the decision reached these important conclusions by different routes, a fact which suggested to a sceptical public that the conclusions to be arrived at had determined their reasoning rather than the other way round.

The Chief Justice was in a mood for broad principles of interpretation. "The Constitution", he declared, "has conferred on Congress the right to establish an uniform rule of naturalization, and this right is evidently exclusive, and had always been held by this court to be so. Consequently, no State, since the adoption of the Constitution, can by naturalizing an alien invest him with the rights and privileges secured to a citizen of a State under the Federal Government, although, so far as the State alone was concerned, he would undoubtedly be entitled to the rights of a citizen, and clothed with all the rights and immunities which the Constitution and the laws of the State attached to that character". And he continued, "It is very clear, therefore, that no State can, by any act or law of its own, passed since the adoption of the Constitution, introduce a new member into the political community created by the Constitution of the United States. It cannot make him a member of this community by making him a member of its own. And for the same reason it cannot introduce any person, or description of persons, who were not intended to be embraced in this new political family, which the Constitution brought into existence, but were intended to be excluded from it".[4]

The robes of the judge should not conceal the hand of the magician. The chief justice had in mind two different, but imperfectly separated, themes. The first was simple: Only the Congress could make citizens under the Constitution, for which reason a state had no power to make an alien into a citizen under federal law. This view, which followed from the face of the Constitution, was obviously correct. His second theme involved a subjective judgment about the kind of political community that existed in 1788. In addition to his statement that a state could not make a citizen, which was true, Chief Justice Taney argued that a state could never make a citizen of someone who, by his definition, was excluded from the political community when the Constitution was formed—meaning, of course, a person of African descent. To make this argument consistent Taney would have been obliged to exclude *all* persons who were not represented in the population in 1787–1788, a ban which would probably have extended to eastern, central and possibly Mediterranean Europeans. But in view of what had already been said, it was wholly superfluous to declare that no state could introduce into "this new political family" any "description of persons who were not intended to be embraced" in it. The exclusive power of Congress was already sufficient to enable it to decide what description of persons might be made citizens. The chief justice had committed an act of rhetorical embezzlement. He had appropriated the plain constitutional rule which restrained the states from making new citizens and had invested it in a new constitutional doctrine. That doctrine had nothing to do with the law of the Constitution either at the time of its foundation or later; it was a specific social theory about the composition of the people—"the political family" —covered by that Constitution. Taney did not actually lay down that the Congress had no constitutional power to alter this position, though it was all too clear that he would have liked to have said so. As it was, he came precariously close to a usurpation of legislative power, for the Constitution is clear that the legislature, not the ju-

4. 19 U.S. Howard 393 (1857), 405–6.

diciary, decides questions of citizenship. He went about as far as the case of *Dred Scott* v. *Sanford* would allow him towards declaring that the Constitution was itself a racial document, that the admission of Negroes as citizens would violate its spirit and character and the intentions of its makers. That is the whole point of his homily, which is mere *obiter dictum*, about these limits of state powers.

Taney's reasoning was answered by Justices Curtis and McLean. The central weakness in Taney's opinion lay buried, but not buried very deep, in his use of historical evidence; and Mr Justice Curtis was able to show conclusively that Negroes had actually enjoyed the privileges of citizenship in several states at the time of the Constitution. Under the Comity Clause, which here came back into the constitutional argument, the citizens of each state were to enjoy the privileges and immunities of citizens in the other states; but only the federal government could make citizens, from which it followed that all state citizens must have been taken up into United States citizenship when the Constitution came into force. Moreover, Negroes actually voted in many states at that time. Taney had tried to deal with this by drawing a distinction between the right to vote and the rights of citizens; but his difficulty, as Curtis pointed out, was that Negroes could have voted for the ratification of the Constitution itself, which therefore owed its existence in part to the consent of the blacks.[5] The lines which Chief Justice Taney and the court tried to draw were soon to prove untenable. They had made a significant attempt, however, to define the Constitution in terms of the structure of the American population, to create a system of caste by constitutional law.

Science and Inequality

If the idea of equality may be considered as a successor in human affairs to the Great Chain of Being, it must be recognised that it was not in itself a universal theory. Belief in equality of rights rested on moral intuition which did not require the confirmation of observable facts. But daily conduct is intimately connected with daily observations, which together contribute more than moral intuition to the

5. Ibid., 572–88.

way people treat one another. Ordinary Americans felt no incentive to divest themselves of beliefs which seemed to reflect the common sense of race relations. Observation everywhere showed the blacks among them in inferior and often degraded conditions, defective in education, and wanting in ambition or ability. There was little by way of example, leadership, or ecclesiastical authority to alter these comfortable and basically self-protective views. Neither did the early probings of schematic anthropology give any obvious support to the moral intuition that the remarkable varieties of peoples, whether they were considered as nations or races, whether they were best known by language or their religion, were all equally capable of the same achievements. Even if that had been conceded, there was no reason to suppose that they all entertained similar ambitions. The different nations of American Indians obviously differed not only from Euro-Americans but from one another in their skills and ways of life; much the same was true of the many peoples who migrated to American shores. Immigrants, like sects, had to struggle to establish their own claims to an equal place, supported by the remote clauses of an austere Constitution, but with very little assistance either from prevailing theory or from the evidence which presented itself to the sense of their contemporaries.

The Great Chain of Being, which held the whole of creation together in a fixed and permanent order, was compatible with the Biblical account of creation and offered a suggestive analogy with the orders of men, implicitly—though not necessarily—supporting notions of natural hierarchy. But the Bible, on the contrary, stood as an obstacle to the development of positive theories of human inequality. So long as the Old Testament remained the universal point of departure for knowledge about the human race, mankind was believed to be descended from a single pair, and all differences of colour, physiognomy, or aptitude must have been acquired subsequently during man's sojourn on earth. Some thoughtful souls were much troubled by these teachings. Thomas Jefferson was uneasy with the idea of equality among the races, and meditated on the possibility of innate differences from which, needless to add, the Negro did not appear to advantage.[6] Neither Jefferson's interest in

6. Thomas Jefferson, *Notes on the State of Virginia*, ed. Wm. Peden (Chapel Hill, 1954), pp. 142–3.

fossil remains nor the scientific researches of his time added much light to these problems. Theorists groping for a science of racial inequality encountered further obstacles from the limited span of time available for human development on earth. According to the best information, supplied by the computations of the seventeenth-century divine, Archbishop Ussher, the world had been created only in 4004 b.c. This did not give mankind a long period in which to have developed such marked differences.[7] If on the other hand it were possible to find some non-heretical way of circumventing the doctrine of single creation, it would be much easier to believe that the visibly different human types had possessed their differing characteristics from the beginning. The importance of finding such a solution was accentuated by information about Egyptian monuments depicting Negro as well as more European figures. If these marked differences had come about in the early years after the origin of man, it was strange that no comparable process had been observed to take place over much longer subsequent periods.

These problems were the subject of some speculation in eighteenth-century Europe. Lord Kames and Erasmus Darwin (Charles Darwin's grandfather) both proposed theories of human development, and notions of an evolutionary kind entered into popular thought and fancy in succeeding generations. But in Europe these were mainly matters for scientific or popular curiosity; even the writings of Count Gobineau, the first exponent of theories of racial distinction, had no immediate bearing on political policy, and did not modify European opposition to slavery or the slave trade.

In this respect, American political theory, with its particular emphasis on respect for equal rights and its implied obligation that all people be equally treated, gave the American racial problem its own peculiar character. In Britain a powerful emancipation movement could urge its cause in terms of both humanity and religion without appealing to anything so unattractive to the parliamentary classes as universal equality. This disclaimer was particularly important after the French Revolution had struck fear and horror into the hearts of the propertied classes. Thus, as David Brion Davis has ob-

7. See William Stanton, *The Leopard's Spots: Scientific Attitudes toward Race in America, 1815–1959* (Chicago, 1960), p. 50. There had been many disputes about Ussher's chronology but only over a few years more or less.

served, the British slave-trade abolitionists made a point of present-
ing themselves as "a force maintaining the existing political and
constitutional structure;" and in 1799 the abolitionist bishop of
Rochester replied to a charge of Jacobinism "that abolitionists had
never talked of equality or the imprescriptible rights of man; they
had strenuously upheld the existing gradations of society, objecting
only to a power which no good king would claim".[8] The British
system of political representation was itself gradually reformed
throughout the nineteenth and early twentieth centuries to absorb
the working people into what Gladstone once called "the pale of the
Constitution", on the basis of a series of subtle redefinitions of the
concept of the representation of interests and the cautious extension
of the idea of political responsibility. The latter process was extremely gradual, and could be turned to party advantage; but the
great Emancipation Act of 1833, which freed the slaves in the British
West Indies, did not confront the people of Britain with the problem
of defining the political or social status of a large domestic population
of freed blacks.

In the United States there were certainly many Abolitionists who
had no affection for Negroes nor any desire to incorporate them into
white society; the close connections between much early Abolitionism and the movement for colonization of the slaves to be freed
was enough to warn Negroes that they were not necessarily among
friends.[9] But Abolitionists who did believe not only in universal
equality of rights but in the equality of the Negro potential in terms
of American achievement faced a double burden of argument. The
point is made by the historian of the Abolitionist struggle for equal
rights, Professor James McPherson, when he tackles the problem
presented by the popular belief that Negroes were innately inferior,
which he describes as "one of the most formidable obstacles to the
abolition of slavery and the extension of equal rights to free Negroes . . .".[10] The two acts were linked by virtue of the fact that
American political theory had no room for inequality of rights;

8. Davis, The Problem of Slavery in the Age of Revolution 1770–1823 (Ithaca,
1975), pp. 436–7.
9. George M. Frederickson, The Black Image in the White Mind (New York,
1971), pp. 6–42.
10. James M. McPherson, The Struggle for Equality: Abolitionists and the
Negro in the Civil War and Reconstruction (Princeton, 1964), p. 134.

where abilities were believed to be determined by racial endowment, equal attainments were impossible; and it was not entirely
illogical for holders of these beliefs to conclude that a class of people
who inherited these genetic limitations could not be expected and
should not be allowed to share as equals in the political, social, and
economic life of the majority. Views of this character, however,
might easily slip over the edges of the strictly racial argument; if
heredity, intellectual ability or, for that matter, moral character
were to be considered in determining political rights, Negroes might
be the first but not the only victims—and by the time of the Reconstruction debates, educational tests were prominently urged as a
legitimate form of safeguard against unqualified voters. Whether or
not such qualifications were judged to be inherited, they could be
made the subject of individual tests; innumerable Southern poor
whites and foreign immigrants were at risk. Abolitionists might
therefore have comforted themselves that they were not entirely
alone in their dilemma. They had exposed a problem which constitutional theory would never again be free to ignore.

It was in the nature of their campaign that the Abolitionists were
to some extent responsible for stimulating a debate on the question
of racial abilities and consequently for the emergence of early formulations of the idea of Negro inferiority. A crop of books and pamphlets appeared to refute Abolitionist claims that American society
could absorb the Africans as it had absorbed other peoples, their
themes encapsulated in the title of J. H. Van Evrie's assertion of innate Negro inferiority: *Negroes and Negro "Slavery"; The First an
Inferior Race—the Latter its Normal Condition.*[11] These works drew
heavily on Biblical authority for slavery as an institution, on Aristotle for the view that some people are by nature slaves, on the record
of African heathenism for the blessings brought to Negroes by
Christianity, and on the history of Negro slavery for proof that Negroes were fitted to be slaves.[12] Their general tone was theological,
classical, and literary rather than scientific; they did not depend on
new observations but drew their emotive force very largely from
their ancient rhetoric. Yet ever since Jefferson's musings on the pos-

11. Quoted in ibid. (I have not been able to consult this work.)
12. Eric L. McKitrick, ed., *Slavery Defended* (Englewood Cliffs, N.J., 1963).

sibility of Negro separateness, an unfurnished story had existed in the edifice of American thought, ready to be filled by a more scientifically demonstrated theory of human inequality.

This peculiarly attractive vacancy was gradually filled during the first half of the nineteenth century by the appearance of an American school of anthropology.[13] The first substantial contribution was made in the 1820s and 1830s by Dr Samuel Morton of Philadelphia with his laborious work on the measurement of human skulls, of which he acquired a formidable collection. The measurable differences that he established between different human types could no longer be reconciled to those views that attributed observed differences to variations of climate and circumstance. Morton, a reticent man not much given to controversy, hesitated before the risks of heresy which his findings undoubtedly incurred. It was Dr Josiah Nott, a cheerful physician and horse breeder practising in Mobile, whose more blatant racial prejudices, blended with a breezy antipathy to the clergy, gave him the freedom to take the matter further and announce to the American public that racial differences were explained by the fact that the races of mankind had sprung from separate creations.[14]

Nott's compilation incorporated much of the work of Morton and of other investigators who had carried the search to the remains of ancient civilizations. Meanwhile, however, more dependable studies were in process of altering the entire perspective within which Nott and his contemporaries worked. The emergence of a science of geology, especially in the hands of Sir Charles Lyell, compelled people to contemplate the possibility that the earth's formation had been a continuous and not a sudden process. Then in 1858 Charles Darwin and Alfred Russell Wallace presented joint communications to the Linnean Society in London expounding the theory of the evolution of species through natural selection. When people had begun to take the full measure of this scientific revolution, the effect was to transform the whole time-span of human development; Nott's speculations were rendered irrelevant because there was no longer any need to find explanations within the short term of years that he and his predecessors had allotted to mankind since the creation.

The advance of the science of man had ironic consequences for the

13. Stanton, *Leopard's Spots*, pp. 25–53, 194–6.
14. Josiah Nott, *Types of Mankind* (Philadelphia, 1854).

more urgent problem of a science of human relations. It would eventually seem easier to account scientifically for the perceived differences among the earth's different peoples; the rigidities of older thought were gradually loosened in favour of general ideas of development, in which savage, primitive, or backward races could be conveniently arranged at remote stages in the line of a progress which placed the Europeans and Americans at the summit. Yet these teachings could not be rapidly absorbed or easily digested; for many Americans, spectators or partisans in the fearful struggles of the clergy against the new monster of science, Darwin was heresy. Louis Agassiz, a zoologist of considerable renown who left Switzerland for the United States in 1846 and settled as a professor at Harvard, made a much more acceptable contribution when he tried to contain his own assertion of separate racial origins within the precepts of formal religion. Among American scientists Agassiz had both a higher academic standing than most of his contemporaries and more influence on events. His position at Harvard threw him into personal relations with many of the politically active Boston intellectuals, with whom he exchanged ideas; one of these was Samuel Gridley Howe, who served in 1863–1864 as a member of the American Freedmen's Inquiry Commission, which supplied information and proposals to the Congressional Joint Committee planning for postwar conditions in the South. In reply to questions put to him by Howe, Agassiz— while welcoming emancipation—warned of the dangers in granting the newly freed blacks full equality of political and social rights. The history of the Negroes both in Africa and the West revealed them in Agassiz's opinion as "indolent, playful, sensual, imitative, subservient, good-natured, versatile, unsteady in their purpose, devoted and affectionate". But there was no evidence of qualifications for self-government. "I cannot think it just or safe", he observed, "to grant at once to the negro all the privileges which we ourselves have acquired by long struggles. . . . Let us beware of granting too much to the negro race in the beginning, lest it becomes necessary hereafter to deprive them of some of the privileges which they may use to their and our detriment".[15] While these expressions did not rule out all possibility that the Negroes might develop the characteristics re-

15. McPherson, *Struggle for Equality*, pp. 145–6.

quired for participation in self-government, they did rule out practically all possibility of establishing practical conditions in which such development would have any chance of taking place.

Ideals of equality helped to win the Civil War, but in much of the educated thought of the period and of the subsequent generation they were thrown increasingly onto the defensive. The views of Louis Agassiz, and of Darwin's own successors who adapted the idea of the struggle for survival into a national, racial, or economic process, made it increasingly easy to regard "primitive" peoples, who were becoming better known as a result of the European and American scramble for overseas territories, but less attractive since the decline of the romances of the noble savage, as having been arrested in the stages of childhood or adolescence. In this light it was temptingly easy to regard the Negro in America as a stranded representative of these apparently backward peoples, in need of care and protection but hopelessly incapable of aspiring to the heights of civilisation.

Lincoln himself had made it clear that Americans were not placed under any obligation to translate the Declaration of Independence into institutional terms. In the South, however, the Declaration's explicit language, in the sense of its generally understood universalist meaning, caused less sense of moral conflict. As slavery and the racial basis of Southern institutions were affirmed as positive benefits to black and white in their different roles in the development of the South's new civilisation, the Declaration lost its value for Southern thought, was rejected as a false doctrine devoid of either moral or constitutional force, and became a source of discord rather than harmony between the South and the rest of the nation. Southern spokesmen turned, moreover, from the defence of their own institutions to scathing and scornful attacks on the hypocricy of the capitalist North. John Taylor of Caroline had much earlier discerned something akin to slavery in the conditions of the industrial workers; but after the rise of Abolitionism in the North, John C. Calhoun and later George Fitzhugh turned the critique of Northern institutions and ideals into a systematic theme.

Calhoun's insistence on the importance of progress as a condition of civilisation was as positive as that of any Northern businessman; his arguments retained the essence of a commitment to equality of opportunity among whites; and he agreed that equality of citizens in the eyes of the law was essential to liberty in a popular government. But he denounced the doctrine that "liberty cannot be perfect without perfect equality" and argued that the highly unequal distribution of human abilities could only mean that liberty would in the normal course of events give rise to inequalities of condition. Inequality of condition, the natural result of liberty, was indispensable to progress. In these reflections, published posthumously in his *Disquisition of Government*, Calhoun faced with more candour than many of his contemporaries the conflicts arising from concomitant commitments to equality of opportunity and equality of condition. In 1838, some ten years before his death, he had offered the South a somewhat more attractive image of itself, and one which he neither abandoned nor fully reconciled to the idea of individualistic competition. Southern states, he said, were "an aggregate, in fact of communities, not of individuals. Every plantation is a little community, with the master at its head, who concentrates in himself the united interests of capital and labor, of which he is the common representative. The small communities aggregated make the State in all, whose action, labor, and capital is equally represented and perfectly harmonized".[16] It was an affecting picture, though it failed to provide room for competition even among members of the master race, which political and economic liberty were bound to permit. But whatever the inconsistencies of argument or imperfections in his evidence, Calhoun, with his picture of the harmony of the South, could claim to have presented an attractive alternative to the economic tyranny of the factory system and the disintegrative and abrasive individualism which ruled the social morality of the North.

George Fitzhugh, the first American to use the word *sociology* in the title of a book, was more informed statistically if considerably less systematic than Calhoun. Fitzhugh's most remarkable quality was his fearless pursuit of the consequences of his own reasoning. He accepted both the commonplace view that all high civilisations rested on some form and degree of exploitation of labour, and the historical interpretation which derived laisser-faire capitalism from the liberation of the individual at the Reformation, whence had followed the doctrines of human equality, the sovereignty of the individual,

16. McKitrick, ed., *Slavery Defended*, pp. 6–11.

and the right to private judgment, down to their logical consequences in the brutally acquisitive and competitive economy of the industrial era. Fitzhugh differed from his contemporaries by adopting opposite sentiments about these events. Apart from the Reformation, which he described as an act of society shaking off the evils of the past, he denounced instead of praising the entire process. He was equally scornful of the softness of Locke and the superficiality of Jefferson, while he attacked Adam Smith's individualist economics and Blackstone's insistence on individual liberty under English law. The American Revolution he regarded as the act of an adult society gaining its independence from another society, an event which had nothing to do with personal equality. In a powerful statement of protective paternalism he declared, "Liberty and equality throw the whole weight of society on its weakest members". The false doctrine of equality of rights begat "the greatest inequalities of condition", which in the modern age had led to cruel exploitation and starvation.[17] Although Fitzhugh believed that Negroes were best suited to slavery, he does not seem to have been animated by the common racial antipathies, and down to the Civil War, when he changed his mind, he regarded racial contempt as a bad reason for slavery because it led to debasement and abuse. He differed from Calhoun and from many of his contemporaries on both sides of the slavery issue in having a benign disposition, little real feeling of enmity for his ideological opponents, and a genuine compassion for the sufferings caused by the factory system. He drew much of his information about its worst abuses from the same British sources that Marx and Engels were soon to use and in which Fitzhugh saw close resemblances to the development of wage-slavery in the American North. In a tone strikingly similar to that of the Socialists and Communists of his time, he attacked the economic individualists for their irresponsible disregard for the consequences of their own doctrines and of their own pursuit of wealth. But for Fitzhugh, who believed that doctrines of equality rested on a lie about human nature, the answer lay in the direction of restoring the paternalistic form of responsibility in the extreme form of slavery. He was severe on the consequences of equality that he supposed had operated in Ireland,

17. McKitrick, ed., *Slavery Defended*, p. 38, quoting George Fitzhugh, *Sociology for the South* (Richmond, 1854), pp. 226–58.

asserting that the half-million who had died of hunger there in one year had died because "in the eye of the law they were equals, and liberty had made them enemies, of their landlords and employers. Had they been vassals or serfs," he added, presumably averting his gaze from contemporary Russia, "they would have been beloved, cherished and taken care of by those same landlords and employers. Slaves never die of hunger, scarcely ever feel want". The blacks, being incapable of higher attainments, were fittingly employed in laying the foundations for the South's superior civilisation.[18]

This school of thought was yet to receive its highest benediction. When Alexander H. Stephens of Georgia took his seat as vice-president of the Confederate States of America he took his stand against the expressed beliefs of Jefferson and the founders of the Republic. "Our new Government", he declared, "is founded upon exactly the opposite ideas; its foundations are laid, its corner stone rests upon the great truth that the negro is not equal to the white man; that slavery, subordination to the superior race, is his natural and normal condition. This, our new Government, is the first in the history of the world, based upon this great physical, philosophical and moral truth".[19] Four years later the Confederate edifice had collapsed. But after the rubble had been cleared away, the cornerstone appeared to have survived in remarkably good condition, and was soon afterwards used as the base for a piece of strikingly similar architecture. It did not follow that the whites need suffer from the same inequalities as those prescribed for the blacks, and in fact the system of white supremacy has been accredited with sustaining the morale of the white population, if not genuine equality among

18. Fitzhugh developed his views in *Cannibals All! Or Slaves without Masters* (Richmond, 1857; ed. C. Vann Woodward, Cambridge, Mass., 1960). See also Harvey Wish, *George Fitzhugh, Propagandist of the Old South* (Louisiana State University Press, 1934; repr. Gloucester, Mass., 1962). This line of argument had already made its appearance when the slave trade came under attack in the 1770s. David Brion Davis has noted that "as early as 1772 *The Scots' Magazine* reprinted ... an essay from a London paper comparing the condition of the West Indian slaves to that of English common laborers, who were 'more real slaves to necessity, than to Egyptian taskmasters'. In some respects the slaves were better cared for; and the freedom of English laborers was 'the liberty of changing their masters for the same wages'. But they would 'still remain slaves to the necessity of constant and hard labour' ". This essay gained the endorsement of Anthony Benezet as an indictment of English conditions. Davis, *Slavery in Age of Revolution*, p. 462.

19. Quoted by McPherson, *Struggle for Equality*, p. 61.

them.[20] But there were white sharecroppers as well as black ones in the generations after the Civil War, and Southern populists had their own enemies at home. Equality did not flourish in Southern soil.

The avowed enemies of any form of racial harmony other than that of complete white supremacy and black subordination were far from being the only persons who contributed during the middle and later years of the nineteenth century to the increasingly complex themes of the debate on racial character. When Negro-Americans convened to petition legislatures or present their case to the public, they usually rejected the inevitability of their subordinate status and frequently invoked the founding principles of the Republic.[21] For the most part they turned not only against the degrading concept of caste, but against the inevitability of any form of pluralism within the Constitution. But in 1852, Martin R. Delany, a black physician and editor of outstanding ability, gave expression to his despair of improvement in the United States by proposing a movement for voluntary Negro emigration. His first step was a book entitled *The Condition, Elevation, Emigration and Destiny of the Colored People of the United States Politically Considered.*[22] Two years later he followed this with a convention which was well attended despite the hostility of the Abolitionists and of Frederick Douglass, with whom Delany had previously worked in close collaboration.[23]

Douglass believed to the end of his life in the possibility of racial amalgamation—a faith that he consummated by his second marriage, to a white woman; Delany by the time of his book had come to regard this as an illusion. The sharp split between the two men symbolised the fundamental differences of what they regarded as practical hopes. Delany's defiant pronouncements contain some of the earliest declarations of intense black racial pride as well as national separatism, and in this they suggest the origins of a movement that could have looked towards some form of protective pluralism. But Delany did not believe any form of protection was to be had

20. C. Vann Woodward, *American Counterpoint: Slavery and Racism in the North-South Dialogue* (Boston, 1971), chap. 4.

21. See in general the documents collected in Herbert Aptheker, ed., *A Documentary History of the Negro People in the United States* (New York, 1968), I, 17–459.

22. Victor Ullman, *Martin R. Delany, the Beginnings of Black Nationalism* (Boston, 1971), pp. 140–50.

23. Ibid., pp. 153–60.

under the Constitution until the war, and Reconstruction, brought him back from his voluntary exile in Canada.

Delany dismissed those Abolitionists of both races who saw racial harmony within the Union as the only solution. To believe in harmony was not necessarily to be convinced of the basic similarity of the races, still less of the interchangeability of individuals. Yet it was one thing to observe obvious differences of appearance or aptitude; it was quite another to believe that they reflected either inherent differences that could never be affected by training or environment, or qualities that were in any case socially undesirable. White Abolitionists who genuinely befriended the blacks—rather than merely wanting to get rid of them—often found themselves trying to explain the differences they observed between the races. But these differences in the talents and it often seemed in the character of the two peoples did not invariably appear to the advantage of the Europeans. Theodore Tilton, who was a feminist as well as an Abolitionist, explained the nature of racial variety through a romantic racialism which exalted the Negro character as being akin to the best of feminine virtues. "In all the intellectual activities which take their strange quickening from the moral faculties—which we call instincts, intuitions—the negro is the superior to the white man, equal to the white woman", Tilton told a New York audience during the Civil War. He was also willing to lend himself to the view that the Negro was more peaceable than "either the Saxon or the Celt". What America needed was more of the Negro characteristics to modify those of the white population.[24] Moncure Daniel Conway, a Virginian turned Abolitionist, saw advantage in the differences of racial qualities. European superiority in intellect and energy was balanced by black superiority in goodliness, kindliness, and "affectionateness"; a mixture of the races could be expected to produce a better character than either possessed by itself.[25] Others not unnaturally remarked on the instinctive Negro feeling for music and the Negro understanding of religion.

These views in all their variety reflected the grappling of serious minds with perplexing problems which certainly presented the grav-

24. James M. McPherson, "A Brief for Equality: The Abolitionist Reply to the Racist Myth, 1860–65", in Martin Duberman, ed., *The Antislavery Vanguard* (Princeton, 1965), p. 163.
25. Ibid., pp. 165–6.

est of social issues. From the Negro point of view, however, even the opinions of their friends had an important disadvantage. They all tended to agree that blacks were defective in those hard, acquisitive, and competitive characteristics which undoubtedly dominated the world of European and American business. Few people really expected Negroes to prove themselves capable of competing with whites as equals; and still fewer felt that it was part of the government's responsibility to compensate Negroes or anyone else for the lack of qualities they did not appear to possess. The competition that Negroes faced both North and South in the business conditions of the era after the Civil War was enormously unequal for reasons which neither their training nor their political, economic, or practical position gave them much power to control. But an increasingly preoccupied and inattentive white world was easily able to reconcile itself to the difficulties experienced by American blacks in holding their own in the struggle; it was really only what one had expected.

Political Community Redefined

From the time of the Dred Scott decision of 1857 free Negroes were not citizens of the United States. This meant that American political society was so defined as to give legal sanction to a virtual caste system; a substantial portion of the population, who now stood within but not of the Republic, were declared to have no rights that a white man need respect. Even where Negroes did possess the rights of citizens, as in Massachusetts, a legal precedent had recently marked the outlines of a fundamental differentiation in rights. In 1849 Chief Justice Lemuel Shaw in the case of *Roberts* v. *The City of Boston* first announced the doctrine that the provision of separate facilities of equal quality did not impair the equal rights of citizens.[26] The Commonwealth of Massachusetts reversed this policy in 1855 when it introduced a law for common schools without racial segregation, though it may be doubted whether much educational integration followed. But on a national scale, the Civil War would have

26. 5 Cush. (Mass.) 198. Leonard W. Levy and Harlan B. Phillips, "The *Roberts* Case: The Source for the 'Separate but Equal' Doctrine", *American Historical Review*, LVI (1956), 510–18; David Donald, *Charles Sumner and the Coming of the Civil War* (New York, 1960), pp. 180–1.

been fought to little purpose if it had resulted in the hardening of a caste system sanctioned by the Constitution. Those who held these views found themselves confronted after Lincoln's death by a hostile president, a recalcitrant South, and an unstable majority; they therefore lost little time in passing a civil rights act in 1866 to confer citizenship on the freed slaves; under its provisions, citizens "of every race and color" were to enjoy equal status in all legal and civil transactions and equal protection for person and property.[27]

An act of Congress, however, was a frail protection for fundamental rights, which in principle ought to have constitutional status; the Republicans had good reason to fear that a future Democratic majority might reverse the gains of the war by repealing the statute. Citizenship had therefore to be written into the Constitution, and for very substantial political reasons the Southern states had to be induced to allow the blacks to vote. In democratic theory, the problem of raising the blacks—whether or not they had formerly been slaves—to the constitutional status of citizens with all its privileges and immunities was not dissimilar to that involved in extending the suffrage in earlier periods to wider classes of whites. The general theory of majority rule had by this time acquired acquiescence if not complete authority. But Negro suffrage encountered terrific resistance. To confer citizenship and the vote was to take them into the political community, and membership was not a mere formality. Taney himself had used the expression "political community" and had indicated a warmer aspect of its meaning when he had talked of "this new political family". The debates on the Fourteenth Amendment when it first came up in 1866 made very clear that much influential white sentiment was extremely hostile to the idea of sharing that community with the blacks on any terms. These resistances combined with a certain caution and lack of emphatic commitment among the Republicans help to explain why the Fourteenth Amendment was always intended as an act of persuasion rather than compulsion. Radicals were satisfied at this stage because they were convinced that the withdrawal of representatives from states which denied the suffrage to a given proportion of their citizens would produce the desired effect of Negro suffrage within five years.

27. 14 *Stat.* 27; W. R. Brock, *An American Crisis: Congress and Reconstruction, 1865–1867* (London and New York, 1963), pp. 111–15.

It was easy for opponents of the amendment, such as Senator Reverdy Johnson of Maryland, to point out that many Northern states still refused to give the Negroes the right to vote even after the Civil War. Johnson, an elderly Democrat of conservative but not intolerant views, was an honest example of the racial instinct which influenced the feelings of many of his countrymen of all parties. "The God of the white man and the God of the black man—I speak it with due reverence—is the Being who first made a distinction on account of color", he said in the Senate. "There is not a man within the sound of my voice—certainly I am not one—who has any feeling against the black race. There is nothing in the world that I am capable of doing that I would not do to elevate them. In a professional life of now more than fifty years' duration, I never failed to give them the benefit of my advice and services. But I feel with an instinct that nature has planted within us, and they perhaps feel it as strongly as we do, that nature has created the distinction, and there it must remain as long as white is white and black is black".[28] Hendricks of Indiana, though within the sound of Johnson's voice, did not seem to share his basic benevolence. "But, Mr. President", he asked, "do we want to make all the colored people vote? I am very free to say that I do not. I do not want to make any of them voters. I am not going to discuss the question of whether the colored man is the equal of the white man. I think there need be no discussion on a question like that. But . . . without reference to the question of equality, I say that we are not of the same race; we are so different that we ought not to compose one political community".[29] And he went on to deny assertions made previously by Daniel Clark[30] of New Hampshire that Negroes had fought gallantly in the war; supported by applause from the galleries, Hendricks repudiated claims that the black men had helped the North to win—it was won by white men, who ought not to be deprived of the credit. In his speech the phrase "political community" appeared once more, and again in the context in which membership of it, or credit for helping to defend it, was denied to the Negro.

Both sides clearly understood the issue; each knew what the other

28. *Congressional Globe*, 39 Cong., 1st sess. (1866), 766.
29. Ibid., 860.
30. Ibid., 833–5.

was contending for. The genuine racialists, whether apologetic like Johnson or outspoken like Hendricks, felt a deep repugnance at the idea of admitting Negroes into the circle whose circumference marked the limits of political participation, not because Negroes were ignorant or inexperienced (in which connection Clark observed sarcastically that he had "never found one of those persons who oppose negro suffrage upon the ground of ignorance willing to exclude the white man for the same reason. . . . If the negro should learn to read and write before he votes, let the white man do the same"), but because political participation was itself a form of social activity. Hendrick's more vituperative remarks were drawn out in reply to Clark's emotional speech two days earlier. The theoretical basis of Clark's views was a pure, though nonetheless respectable, form of American republicanism. He hotly denied the power of the Congress to confer the vote on the Negro as a gift or a boon: "The black man has just as much right to his vote as the white man has to his; and the white man has no more authority to confer or withhold it than the black man". The black man's rights had been equal from the beginning; the Declaration of Independence, which laid down that governments derived their just powers from the consent of the governed, implied that the governed could of right, not as a privilege, give or withhold that consent—which they did with their votes.

Clark was moving along the categories of equality. Equal political rights were the means by which the blacks could gain access to their other rights. "Man derives the right from his manhood and the quality of his manhood with his fellow-man", he explained; but this led him to the social question.

Does anyone say, Mr. President, that this is negro equality? So it is—political equality—no social. This last is not the creature of legislation, or political organisation, but of taste, propriety, and fitness. In some of the States the negro has now, and has for a long time had, the same political rights as the white man. The law makes no distinction for or against him, but he is left to acquire that position in society to which his abilities and behavior entitle him.

All this was included in the principle of political equality which lay at the foundations of American government. Political equality would give the Negro access, through his own efforts, to whatever social position he could fairly attain; but without political equality, there was no protection for property, no protection before the law. As for the restrictions that had been laid on the black man, they were "the miserable brood and spawn of slavery, and they should perish with it". Clark's views of political rights came back again and again to the common humanity of men; it was in that common humanity that they were to be considered equal. "Here is the difficulty", he declared; "the negro is a man! and however degraded, inferior, abject, or humble, it is our duty to elevate and improve him, and to give him the means of elevation or improvement; and the Senator from Kentucky may assert and prove that there are thirty-six, or fifty-six, or a hundred and six points of difference between him and the white man, but until he shows that he is not a man, the negro will be entitled to be treated by us as a man, and to remand and enjoy the same political privileges as other men." Henry Wilson of Massachusetts and Thaddeus Stevens of Pennsylvania, neither of whom had earlier regarded the suffrage as foremost among the issues demanding Congressional attention, expected the Fourteenth Amendment to produce the desired result within five years; they regarded the suffrage as an instrument to be used in pursuit of wider ends.[31] Clark's position, which was purer in its republicanism, implied that a government not based on universal suffrage was illegitimate, and by inference lacking in lawful authority over those who were not allowed to vote.

As finally passed, the Fourteenth Amendment established American citizenship for all persons born or naturalised in the United States, forbade any state to deny the citizens of the United States the privileges or immunities of citizenship, and extended to all persons, whether defined as citizens or not, the equal protection of the laws—an expression whose descent has been traced to Andrew Jackson. The complex suffrage provisions of the amendment were intended not to compel but to persuade, through the imposition of limitations on the representation of states which restricted suffrage. The persuasion failed, however, and the Fourteenth Amendment was duly followed by the Fifteenth, whose force was compulsive. The essence of his remodelling of the Constitution was that it withdrew from the states a portion of the power they had exercised over their

31. Ibid., 1254; H.R., 2459.

own electoral systems. But even the Fifteenth Amendment, which represented the outcome of much anguished debate and tortuous compromise, was both negative in form and limited in content. It said simply, "The right of citizens of the United States to vote shall not be denied or abridged by the United States, or by any State, on account of race, color, or previous condition of servitude". This simplicity concealed a wealth of meaning, most of it to the disadvantage of precisely those persons of "color, or previous condition of servitude", whom the amendment purported to protect. All attempts to include the right of nomination to public office, which at one time seemed to have a fair chance of adoption, had to be dropped in order to gain enough conservative support to pass the amendment;[32] and its negative form left the states free to impose other kinds of restriction. It was only in respect of the items enumerated that the states lost their internal control: another hundred years were to pass before the federal government took full possession of the field. As Oliver Morton of Indiana, who did as much as any member of the Senate to steer the amendment to its passage, remarked in exasperation near to despair: "This amendment leaves the whole power in the States just as it exists now, except that colored men shall not be disfranchised for the three reasons of race, color, or previous condition of slavery. They may be disfranchised for want of education or for want of intelligence. . . . They may, perhaps, require property or educational tests, and that would cut off the great majority of colored men from voting in those States, and thus this amendment would be practically defeated in all those States where the great body of the colored people live . . .".[33] By the early years of the twentieth century the former Confederate states had confirmed every detail of Morton's prognosis.

The debates on the Fifteenth Amendment cut deeper into the social context of constitutional problems than those on the Fourteenth, in which these things had already been near the surface. The radicals now tried to make the great occasion of constitutional amendment into an opportunity for a real advance—or redirection— of American society in the sense that lay nearer to their conception of its ideological basis. Morton thus argued that exclusion from the

32. Ibid., 40th Cong., 3rd sess. (1869), 1307, 1623, 1624.
33. Ibid., 863.

vote on grounds of property or of religion was a denial of democratic principles and republican sentiment, which he claimed was
"rife throughout the whole nation". Henry Wilson spoke with feeling about the human quality of the relationship that ought to subsist
among the people, white and black: "I recognize him not only as a
countryman, a fellow citizen", he said of the black man, "but as a
brother, given by his Creator the same rights that belong to me".
The amendment was not an end; it was a step, an instrument of a
greater programme. Equality, Wilson declared, was an unfinished
task: "If the black man in this country is made equal with the white
man—and I hope he wil be soon—I mean, by the blessing of God,
while I live to hope on and to work on to make every white man the
equal of every other white man. I believe in equality among citizens—equality in the broadest and most comprehensive democratic
sense. No man should have rights depending on the accidents of
life".[34]

These debates brought forward into the conscience of legislators
a moral perception which some of them gladly proclaimed while
others shrank from and rejected it. That perception was that where
rights were concerned, equality was indivisible. To give equality to
the black in political rights was an act, not a mere gesture; with that
political equality, blacks might do what they could, but no principle
in the moral law which sanctioned American democratic thought
could stand between equality in legal and political rights and the
full equality of individuals throughout society. With the discussion
taking this turn, there was no occasion for surprise that conservatives felt that much more was threatened than the structure of race
relations. There was less apparent danger of a racial upheaval than
of a new wave of labour unrest against the economic inequalities
which the war itself had done much to accentuate. All of the more
inclusive concepts which might have made the Fifteenth Amendment
into an instrument of radical politics were struck down in the debates. The form in which it emerged was the least positive, and the
least powerful it could have taken.

It should also be no matter for surprise that the rights of women
appeared in these debates. For some they were an instrument of mild

34. Ibid., 1326.

ridicule serving to illustrate the logical impossibility of the demands the radicals were making for Negro suffrage on grounds of general principle. "If you wrong the African", said James Dixon, a conservative Republican senator from Connecticut, "you wrong the woman. She has the same natural right to vote that the African has".[35] But Joseph Fowler of Tennessee and Willard Warner, an Ohio Republican now representing Alabama, fearlessly proceeded from the principle of equality as applied to individuals regardless of property or race to equality regardless of sex. Fowler, an advocate of equal suffrage, could not see why descendents of China or Africa or India should give laws to the women of America; the moral was that the women of America should have equal rights with the men. Warner believed that female suffrage was not attainable yet, but that they would get it when they united in action.[36]

The question of female suffrage was thus beginning to encroach on the definition of republicanism; women would soon take the cause to the point where they had forced men to redefine the political community. By the time the Fourteenth and Fifteenth Amendments had been proposed, debated, amended, and adopted, the problems of equality within the context of republican theory had been exposed to their most searching analysis at least since the days of Jackson. When conservatives argued in effect that equality was indivisible, they forced the radicals to face the consequences of their own theories. If majorities in Congress and state legislatures had fully believed that American blacks would climb to positions of social and economic equality through the instrument of political and legal rights, they might have declined to accept the risks; but the almost innate white assumption of the inferiority of Negro abilities had the ironical effect of facilitating the passage of the reforms by appearing to diminish the danger from their social consequences. People could believe with honest conviction that it was right that Negroes should have the powers that they and all other Americans needed to look after their own interests but that these powers would never enable Negroes to equal the whites in achievement or social status. Some reconciled themselves quite satisfactorily to Negro suffrage with the

35. Ibid., 860.
36. Ibid., 670, 862.

reflection that it was right in principle, and that once conceded, it would be little used.[37]

In the slow course of debates, the idea of equality itself advanced far beyond the heroic rhetoric of revolutionary times. If conservatives could sometimes trap their opponents into inconsistency, they themselves were not operating in total freedom from the theoretical constraints. They accepted an implicit right to egalitarian forms of political participation among whites, while differentiating between rights to vote and rights to office; and as between the races they rested on the assumption of white superiority, which they had reason to believe would reassert itself once the excitement had died down. On all sides it was recognised, as had not been the case during the Revolution, that an egalitarian rhetoric required the support of egalitarian theory.

37. William Gillette, *The Right to Vote: Politics and the Passing of the Fifteenth Amendment* (Baltimore and London, 1969), pp. 87–8.

Chapter Seven

More Separate than Equal

Between the Social and Political Orders

Justices of the Supreme Court were no strangers to problems of theory. In the Dred Scott case they had already made their attempt to define the limits of citizenship in the racial context of American life. The fact that egalitarian principles had now been written into the organic law was certain to draw the judiciary closer to the specific social situations in which those principles had to be applied and explained and thus to the continuing development of racial relationships than had formerly been required of it. Judges themselves were products of the social process, and were hardly less likely than their contemporaries to interpret constitutional questions in the light cast by the social thought of their time; but it is hardly less important to bear in mind the influence of judicial decisions on the thinking of legislators and on the conscience of the public. Law, especially when handed down by the highest court in the land, is an educator of opinion. In this sense even Mr Dooley might have admitted that the Supreme Court could anticipate the election returns.

Racial justice and egalitarian theory were not alone among the claimants to judicial attention. The courts had to consider the cases before them in the context of a long history, going back before the origins of the Constitution itself, in which the claims of states conflicted with those of federal authority as the determinants of individual liberty; republican principles in America were not yet ready—if they would ever be—to be separated from the liberties and privileges of the individual states. During the Civil War the Supreme Court gave fairly consistent support for the emergency extension of the needs of central government.[1] This policy did not represent a changed view of the Constitution's fundamental character, however, and within a few years the court began to recoil from the implications of extended federal power and to seek ways in which the states' earlier privileges could be restored as permanent and normal attributes of statehood.

What the Supreme Court seeks, it is apt to find. The first instance to have definitive consequences arose in a case that had nothing to do with the racial issues of Civil War or Reconstruction. The legislature of Louisiana had raised the ominous shadow of privileged monopoly by passing a law which gave to a particular corporation in New Orleans the exclusive right to slaughter livestock in that city. Rival butchers challenged the measure on the grounds that monopoly privileges deprived them of the privileges and immunities of citizens of the United States—a status which they could now claim as being superior to that of their state citizenship and subject to protection by the Fourteenth Amendment. The *Slaughter-House Cases* of 1873 thus constituted the first trial of the efficacy of the Fourteenth Amendment.

The court now contained five justices appointed by Lincoln— Chief Justice Chase and Justices Davis, Field, Miller, and Swayne— all of them opponents of slavery and its expansion and all, except Field, Republicans. Yet this court now engaged in a process of reasoning which restored to the states almost all the powers that the makers of the Fourteenth Amendment supposed they were handing to the federal government. The court's procedure was to distinguish between the rights of citizens of the United States as expressly protected by the Fourteenth Amendment against infringement by the states, and the rights of state citizens remaining wholly under state jurisdiction. The result, in a case where no blacks were involved, was a disaster for Negro rights. By way of apology for the restrictive line taken in matters not pertaining to the protection of the black

1. See in general Stanley I. Kutler, *Judicial Power and Reconstruction Politics* (Chicago, 1968).

race, the court observed, "We doubt very much whether any action of a State not directed by way of discrimination against the negroes as a class, or on account of their race, will ever be held to come within the purview of this provision. It is so clearly a provision for that race and that emergency, that a strong case would be necessary for its application to any other".[2]

To maintain this separation between Negro interests and others required a breach in the normal inferential processes of legal reasoning; the practical effect was to restrict the rights of citizens of the United States as against the powers of states, and the court's opinion not only proved to be a crashing error of judicial foresight, but left the Negro exposed to discriminatory action whenever it could be held that the discrimination in question applied to the characteristics of state rather than American citizenship. It was soon to emerge in the *Civil Rights Cases* that the decision exposed blacks to discrimination by private parties even in the exercise of public functions under license by the state; against such practice the state was not obliged to interpose any policy of equal protection of its own. The dissent of Mr Justice Field was noteworthy. The point of the amendment, as he declared, was that the privileges and immunities of United States citizens, already coextensive with the existence of the United States itself, were not henceforth to be abridged by any form of state legislation. If the amendment meant anything less than that—if it extended no further than the previously existing rights—"it was a vain and idle enactment, which accomplished nothing, and most unnecessarily excited Congress and the people on its passage". Not only had Congress enacted the Civil Rights Act of 1866 as an earnest of its determination to extend the rights of American citizens throughout every state in the Union, but after the passage of the Fourteenth Amendment it had passed that act again with some alterations in 1870, in the belief that any remaining doubts about its validity were removed by the amendment.[3]

Notwithstanding the assurance of the justices, the *Slaughter House Cases* provided ammunition for the Democratic opposition against the civil rights bill of 1874–1875. When enacted in 1875 this measure was the fullest assertion of the equality of civil rights yet

2. 83 Wall. 16 (1873), 81.
3. Ibid., 96–7.

placed on the statutes—and the last until 1957; civil rights were defined as including the equal enjoyment of the benefits of transport, entertainment, and accommodation in places of public amusement and hospitality.

This unusually sweeping measure was passed by a Republican majority which had just lost control of the House of Representatives in the mid-term elections of 1874. Some of the lame-duck legislators may have felt that at this stage they had little to lose and something to gain by placing on the statute book an act which would annoy and embarrass the incoming Democrats. Others were engaged in a last and very serious attempt to safeguard civil rights to the fullest extent of their powers before a Democratic majority could threaten to reduce them. Even so, the act as passed omitted provisions for mixed education, partly because of the strenuous opposition of the Peabody Fund, a charitable organisation which had undertaken much of the financing of educational enterprise in the South.[4]

The framers of the bill, warned by the restrictive tendencies already indicated by the Supreme Court, included a provision for the equal rights of citizens—therefore including Negroes—to sit on juries. Clearly they already feared that the Fourteenth Amendment might not be interpreted in that sense. Equality before the law was the oldest and clearest article in the American code of equality; by concentrating on the jury question the Democratic opposition made clear their determination to drive a permanent wedge between the races and to make the provisions of the law and the Constitution conform to that separation. Senator Thurman, Democrat of Ohio, argued that the Fourteenth Amendment did not confer the right and Senator Carpenter, Republican of Wisconsin, took the *Slaughter House Cases* to mean in advance that the jury provision would be held unconstitutional.[5] When Thurman interrupted George Boutwell of Massachusetts, who supported the bill, to observe that the Fourteenth Amendment made no mention of "race, color, or previous condition of servitude", Boutwell answered that equality was an individual attribute that had no connection with class or race;

4. Forrest G. Wood, *Black Scare: The Racist Response to Emancipation and Reconstruction* (Berkeley and Los Angeles, 1970), p. 139; Alfred H. Kelly, "The Congressional Controversy over School Segregation, 1865–75", *American Historical Review*, LXIV (1959), 553–4.

5. *Congressional Record*, 43rd Cong., 2nd sess. (1875), 1792, 1863.

the amendment extended the same rights to all—there could be no need to mention race or colour. Oliver Morton asked in turn whether the coloured man enjoyed the equal protection of the law when he was not allowed to sit on juries? In the circumstances of Southern life, it was obvious that he did not. In a state like South Carolina, where there was a black majority, whites would certainly claim their rights under the Fourteenth Amendment if a law were passed to prevent white men sitting on juries! The right to trial by one's peers, he pointed out, was a common law right. He presumably thought it superfluous to add that in existing circumstances whites and blacks were not each others' peers in Southern states.[6]

Thurman's attack was delivered with considerable acumen, however. He pointed out that property requirements, which Morton accepted, were also unequal. Morton answered this by saying that states could not impose property requirements on one race but not on another. But Thurman's argument attacked the reasoning of the Republicans along the line which consistency required them to hold: The bill, he said, forbade discrimination on grounds of race, while permitting it on other grounds.[7] A better answer to this attack might have been made by admitting its assumptions. Equality could not be divided into sections as happened to suit the demands of one or another class or interest group at any particular time, and laws should deal with principles that would hold firm when cases changed. Senator Edmunds of Vermont took firm grip of these principles when he replied to the Democrats late in the debate: A national Constitution created a national citizenship, and a citizen could not be deprived of whatever belonged to his character as a citizen; if laws could distinguish between black and white, why not between French and Germans, or between different religions? This argument, developed at intervals by opponents of racial discrimination, was never successfully answered. The truth was that those conservatives who wanted to maintain the line between black and white did not believe it necessary to deny that the principle of racial discrimination threatened other interests, because their social convictions marked the blacks out into a wholly different category from all others; for them the Constitution itself remained a white man's

6. Ibid., 1793–4.
7. Ibid., 1794, 1866.

constitution. This fundamental conviction controlled their constitutional reasoning.[8]

Edmunds gave a clue to the need for the civil rights bill when he warned the Congress that the Democrats intended to inaugurate a period of reaction. Reaction also threatened in the Southern states, in the form of laws to bind Negro labour. Under measures now pending, if a man broke his engagement, all the damages were to be a lien to all his future earnings, "a mortgage on that man forever". This was a renewal of involuntary servitude, another name for slavery.

The passage of the civil rights act in 1875 was to prove only a temporary failure for the Democrats in their struggle to prevent the legal codification of rules for the observation of social equality. Behind the constitutional reasoning of this opposition lay the deep anxiety involved in the assumption that whenever blacks gained access to judicial processes on an equal footing, whenever they entered into the trafficking of offers and services that formed the food and drink of everyday political life, the barriers of caste began to crumble. White supremacists in the North no less than in the South felt instinctively that the political life of the country was inseparable from its social life. This view was consistent with the policies pursued in the Southern states after the self-styled Redeemers of the white race had taken possession of their governments in 1876. The Negro vote in the South was exploited so long as it could be enlisted to serve Redeemer or Democratic party interests. But towards the end of the century, when changing political formations threatened to confront these parties with a new alliance of rebellious white Populists and Negro farmers, the old Southern rulers inflamed racial hatreds in the cause of political dominance. The Negroes could not count on constant allies among the Populists, whose followers had only a limited appetite for genuine racial alliance, and had often seen Negro masses enrolled to vote for their class enemies. Although conditions differed from state to state, there was a remarkable consistency in the manner in which Negroes were eventually driven out of political life.[9]

8. Ibid., 1870.
9. For this development, see E. Morgan Kousser, *The Shaping of Southern Politics* (New Haven and London, 1975).

The problem seemed less pressing in the North. Patterns of work and residence developed during the later nineteenth century in ways that made the blacks less conspicuous, less literally visible, than in the South; Northern whites increasingly perceived their black fellow-citizens only as the occupants of certain specified roles and places, and this development seems to have enabled them to practice a sort of psychological segregation almost as effective as that which whites achieved in the South, and hardly less oppressive. Negroes did participate more fully in politics and received a minor share of official consideration; but these practices could be continued without interference with the roles and patterns associated with the racial structure of Northern urban society.

Within a few years of the Civil Rights Act of 1875, the Supreme Court took over the fortifications which the Democrats in Congress had failed to hold. Contrary to the expectations expressed by the court in the *Slaughter House Cases*, the Fourteenth Amendment soon came to be applied as a matter of course to economic questions that had nothing to do with race; once it had been settled that corporations enjoyed the common law rights of persons, punitive or redistributionist forms of taxation and profit control were held to amount to unequal protection, and the amendment stood forth as the principal buttress. But the black minority received less considerate treatment. Beginning only three years after the passage of the act, a long series of cases deprived them of either the consolations of equality or the practice of protection.

Precisely because it failed to afford an effective means, the concept of equal protection failed to establish a new definition of the political community. The intellectual point of departure for the course which the court was to set appeared in the statement by Mr Justice Clifford, in the case of *Hall* v. *DuCuir*,[10] that "equality is not identity". The case arose from a dispute over a statute of the Reconstruction legislature of Louisiana passed in 1869 requiring carriers to provide similar accommodations for all travellers and expressly forbidding discrimination on grounds of colour. Mrs DuCuir, a passenger travelling upriver to visit her plantation, having been ejected from accommodations reserved for whites, sued the master

10. 95 U.S. 485, 503.

of the vessel on account of her "mental and physical suffering on that account". Although the plaintiff's voyage was begun and ended within the State of Louisiana the vessel continued its voyage across the river to Mississippi. This latter circumstance enabled the court to decide the case on an important principle of constitutional law descending from one of Chief Justice Marshall's most famous judgments. This ruling, given in *Gibbons* v. *Ogden* in 1824, had to do with the limits of state legislative competence in matters of interstate commerce, a field which the Constitution reserved to Congress. The essence of the ruling was that even if Congress had made no move to occupy the ground reserved to it, that ground remained wholly under federal authority, and was not open to occupation by the state legislature. This precedent offered the Supreme Court the opportunity to decide *Hall* v. *DuCuir* on grounds of interstate commerce rather than equal protection. But it was impossible to prevent the problem of racial antipathies from revealing itself in the thinking that controlled the line of judgment.

According to the court, Louisiana's antisegregation statute was an unwarranted interference with interstate commerce. In this field the Congress had so far remained silent; the court proceeded to state, "If the public good requires such legislation, it must come from the Congress and not from the State."[11] In the absence of such legislation, the court still had to deal with the conflict of laws between Louisiana, which prohibited racial segregation, and Mississippi, which required it. On this point, Clifford observed that carriers would be in an intolerable position if every state on an interstate route insisted on its own regulations. The silence of Congress left the ship's master free to adopt "reasonable rules and regulations for the disposition of passengers on his boat". This argument clearly presupposed that it was the law of Louisiana which imposed the carrier's difficulties, while that of Mississippi was acceptable. The court did not consider it relevant to its judgment of the case that Louisiana's policy conformed to that of the existing congressional civil rights policies while that of Mississippi did not. The difficulty, of course, was to find an alternative to the plain meaning of "equal protection". If one law had to be preferred to another in order to explain why the Louisiana statute was an interference with inter-

11. Ibid., 490.

state commerce but that of Mississippi was not, then a reason other than the intentions of Congress or the meaning of the Fourteenth Amendment had to be found for Mississippi and against Louisiana. The court's answer to this question appeared when Clifford upheld the lower court in finding that it "was not an unreasonable regulation to seat passengers so as to preserve order and decorum, and to prevent contacts and collisions arising from natural or well-known customary repugnances which are likely to breed disturbances, where white and colored persons are huddled together without their consent".

The court's reasoning thus took consideration of "natural or well-known customary repugnances". It was also well known, however, that these repugnances were more strongly entertained by whites against blacks than by blacks against whites. So it was to be inferred that white reasons were superior in law to black reasons. But was it still possible for these repugnances to express themselves in the form of separation while observing the stipulation of equal protection? It was here that Clifford answered by the dictum that equality was not identity, for which he looked back to *Roberts* v. *the City of Boston*. That case was decided in the free state of Massachusetts before the Civil War, before the abolition of slavery, and before the Fourteenth Amendment. As far as the relations between the races were concerned, in the opinion of the court these events had changed nothing. But Clifford also took his attack into enemy country by pointing to certain difficulties of a more general nature raised by the theory of equal protection. The "colored race" was not the only class of persons who might claim to be involved. It was not insisted, for example, that children of different sexes should as a matter of right be educated in the same schools; and Clifford raised the modernistic suggestion that if equal protection were rigidly enforced it might raise problems of equal opportunity for school children of differing intellectual abilities.

Even if no other considerations had entered into the case, the powerful precedent of *Gibbons* v. *Ogden* might have determined the outcome of *Hall* v. *DuCuir*. But a later case, also involving interstate commerce, threw revealing light on the social presumptions which influenced—perhaps it would not be too much to say they determined—the legal reasoning of the justices. In the *Louisiana*,

New Orleans and Texas Railroad Company v. *Mississippi*,[12] decided in 1890, the boot was on the other foot. The company was indicted for violating the state's segregation or Jim Crow law. As in the earlier case, of course, the state could enforce its rules only within its own borders, and the question which stood out was whether it had a right to enforce these rules, notwithstanding the Fourteenth Amendment, on a carrier whose traffic crossed state boundaries. "The question", the court held, "is limited to the power of the State to compel the railroad companies to provide, within the State, separate accommodations for the two races". Taking notice of *Hall* v. *DuCuir*, the Court observed that the Louisiana statute of 1869 had required interstate carriers to provide the same accommodations to members of the two races travelling between points inside the state —which was then held to be an unconstitutional regulation on an interstate voyage. The present case differed in that the Supreme Court of Mississippi (from which the company had appealed the case) had held that the Mississippi statute was wholly a regulation of commerce within the state. This reasoning drew a caustic comment from Mr Justice Harlan, whose dissenting opinion also took careful note of *Hall* v. *DuCuir*. "It seems to me that those observations are entirely pertinent to the case before us", he said.

In its application to vessels engaged in interstate commerce, the Louisiana enactment forbade the separation of the white and black races which such vessels were within the limits of that State. The Mississippi statute, in its application to passengers on railroad trains employed in interstate commerce, requires such separation of races, while those trains are within the State. I am unable to perceive how the former is a regulation of interstate commerce and the other is not. It is difficult to understand how a state enactment, requiring the separation of the white and black races on interstate carriers of passengers, is a regulation of commerce among the States, while a similar enactment forbidding such separation is not a regulation of that character.[13]

Before all this, however, the Supreme Court had risen to the defence of the only surviving meaning of equal protection under the Fourteenth Amendment. To deprive certain classes of citizens of the right to serve on juries was to deprive members of such classes of

12. 133 U.S. 587.
13. In this last sentence I think "among" must have been used to mean "within", as opposed to "between"; otherwise the sense is obscure. Ibid., 592–5.

equal treatment in the courts themselves. This was a matter that members of the legal profession understood; it was the point in *Strauder* v. *West Virginia*, decided in 1880. The similar case of *Ex-parte Virginia*, also in 1880, arose when a county court judge was held in custody on a federal indictment charging him with deliberately rejecting Negroes from jury service. The Supreme Court denied him the writ of habeas corpus for which he applied. The court here held that a state acted "by its legislative, its executive, and its judicial authorities. It can act in no other way. The Constitutional provision, therefore, must mean that no agency of a State, or of the officers or agents by whom its powers are exerted, shall deny to any person within its jurisdiction the equal protection of the law".[14] This line the court held wherever it was infringed, but not unanimously. Field and Clifford dissented strongly from *Ex parte Virginia*, arguing that it portended a grave threat to the independence of the states. In a sense it did, because it accepted the existence of a uniform national rule, and the application of a national rule, if seen in a slightly different light, would become comprehensive. That slightly different light was refracted from the yellow rather than the black races, as appeared in the cases of *Yick Wo* v. *Hopkins* and *Wo Lee* v. *Hopkins*, both in San Francisco and decided in 1886.[15]

These cases arose from the animosity felt on the West Coast against Orientals rather than blacks. The Chinese could claim special protection because in 1880 the United States concluded a treaty with China under which the emperor's subjects were to receive protection while living in the United States; in any case the Fourteenth Amendment extended equal protection to all persons, not merely to citizens. However, the San Francisco authorities had used an ordinance against wooden buildings for laundries, nominally a safety regulation, as a means of depriving a very large proportion of the Chinese launderers of their livelihood. About the nature of these proceedings the Supreme Court was very clear. The issue, in principle, was the use of arbitrary power, which could not be compatible with equal protection. The wording of the ordinance was impartial and unobjectionable; its intended victims were not mentioned by name or class; their identity came to light only when it was carried

14. 100 U.S. 303; 100 U.S. 339.
15. 118 U.S. 356.

into effect. That effect revealed the legislature's unmistakably true intentions. The court now rejected the contention that the state was the final judge of its own legislation and right-mindedly denounced "class" legislation. This decision did, however, leave open the question as to why the enforced separation of Negroes, who were actually mentioned as a "class" in the Jim Crow laws of the Southern states, was not considered objectionable on the same grounds. But the precedent did not escape the lawyers who presented the case against racial segregation in schools before the Supreme Court some seventy years later. At the time of the Chinese cases, segregation laws had not yet become widespread; but the segregationist impulse received distinct encouragement from the most important decision of the decade, in which the Supreme Court collected together and passed its judgment on the cases arising from the Civil Rights Act of 1875.

All of these cases arose from incidents in which facilities such as places of entertainment, hotel accommodations, or first-class railroad seats were denied to Negroes.[16] Although the facts cited in evidence were obvious manifestations of racial discrimination, the court did not rest its judgment on any explicit doctrine as to the rights of individuals irrespective of race. In a formal sense the judgment, which dealt with charges of violation arising under the Thirteenth as well as the Fourteenth Amendment, was confined to arguments about the constitutional powers of Congress. The court now held that the authority conferred on Congress was corrective but not direct. According to this thesis, the rights secured by the Fourteenth Amendment were secured by prohibitions on the states; no state was allowed to make laws or to take action which infringed the privileges and immunities of citizens of the United States, nor might any state deny equal protection. In the court's opinion, however, this meant only that each state was responsible for refraining from such acts, but that the power of Congress was nothing more than a power to intervene with corrective legislation when states did commit such infringements. It was merely corrective power, a power to remedy abuses.[17] In this connection the Tenth Amendment, which reserves to the states, or the people, all power not confided in the Congress, was employed to buttress an argument which showed signs of need-

16. 109 U.S. 3 (1883).
17. Ibid., 11.

ing external support. The court drew on its own record by referring back to the jury service issue, saying that the fourth section of the Civil Rights Act, dealing with this point, was indeed corrective and therefore permissible. But as to the clauses now under consideration, their effect "is not corrective legislation; it is primary and direct; it takes immediate and absolute possession of the subject of the right of admission to inns, public conveyance, and places of amusement. It supersedes and displaces State legislation and on the same subject, or only allows it permissive force".[18]

From the act under review the court was obliged to look back to the Civil Rights Act of 1866, repassed with modifications in 1870. About the constitutionality of these acts no question had been raised. But the court found adequate reasons in the opinion that the act of 1866 was "clearly corrective in its character, intended to counteract and furnish redress against state laws and proceedings, and customs having the force of law, which sanction the wrongful acts specified".[19] The aim of that earlier act had not been that of new, internal legislation; it was only "to declare and vindicate those fundamental rights which appertain to the essence of citizenship".[20] But Mr Justice Bradley's opinion included the parenthetical but significant statement that life, liberty, and property included "all the civil rights that men have".[21] Clearly then, in the Supreme Court's opinion, it had a duty to separate the "essence" from the appurtenances of citizenship and to draw a heavy line under the equal protection of the former. But which rights were of the essence? This, in a sense, was the central question in the whole subsequent history of the Fourteenth Amendment, which in the twentieth century became the crucial instrument through which ideas of equality were given such practical effect as they could attain. Meanwhile, the court had unwittingly disclosed the tenuousness of its reasoning when it declared that discriminatory "customs having the force of law" were illegal under the act of 1866, and remained so. In other hands this remarkable observation might have been a hinge on which to reverse the entire argument. These social customs certainly extended beyond the limited concept of "life, liberty, and property". It was of their essence that Negroes were treated as universal inferiors to whites;

18. Ibid., 19. 19. Ibid., 16.
20. Ibid., 22. 21. Ibid., 13.

[189]

and in the remark—if nowhere else in the judgment—the court came perilously close to admitting that unequal treatment conflicted with "the essence of citizenship".

The court had also to deal with the argument of counsel that racial discrimination was a relic of slavery and therefore a violation of the Thirteenth Amendment, but this problem did not long detain them. "It would be running the slavery argument into the ground", the judgment explained, "to make it apply to every private act of discrimination in which individuals might see fit to indulge".[22] This view makes interesting comparison with that put forward in court by the solicitor-general, Phillips, that private acts which tend to create an institution were fit subjects for public regulation—a view consistent with the court's ruling in *Munn* v. *Illinois*[23] that control of business "affected with public interest" did not lie beyond the states' constitutional powers. In language that spoke eloquently of the immense chasm between the white and the black experiences of life under laws made by white men, the court, through Mr Justice Bradley, opined that when a man had emerged from slavery a stage must be reached when "he ceases to be the special favorite of the laws, and when his rights as a citizen, or a man, are to be protected in the ordinary modes by which other men's rights are protected".[24] An even more revealing passage observed a moment later that, under slavery, many free Negroes were subjected to discrimination, "yet no one, at that time, thought it an invasion of his personal status as a freeman". This statement, in which Bradley did not explain how he came by his knowledge of free Negro feelings about discrimination, also left questions as to the "status as freemen" of victims of discrimination belonging to other minorities. They were equally without redress, equally without any grievances known as such to the Constitution.

The judgment drew only one dissent.

Mr Justice Harlan, in taking it upon himself to expose the fallacies in his brethren's reasoning, pointed out that a great deal of constitutional history provided the required precedent for the federal powers required by the civil rights act and its enforcement. In *Prigg*

22. Ibid., 24.
23. 94 U.S. 133 (1877).
24. 109 U.S. 3, 25.

v. *Pennsylvania*, decided in 1842, the court had shown that Congress possessed powers enough to implement the intentions of the Constitution with regard to the recapture of fugitive slaves; and he argued that the Supreme Court, so far from finding reservations with which to check the operation of such protections, had uniformly held that the national government possessed the power whether it was expressly given or not to secure and protect rights conferred or granted by the Constitution itself. The decisive passage was a quotation from Mr Justice Story: "The fundamental principle, applicable to all cases of this sort, would seem to be that when the end is required the means are given, and when the duty is enjoined the ability to perform it is contemplated to exist on the part of the functionary to whom it is entrusted".[25] Harlan even rejected the majority's reasoning on the Thirteenth Amendment, abolishing slavery. The peculiar character of American Negro slavery was that it rested wholly on racial inferiority, which meant in his opinion that the amendment did entail freedom and immunity from racial discrimination.[26] He also drew the Comity Clause into evidence for the uniformity of treatment to which all citizens were entitled—an argument which at least showed that the conventionally negative and limited view of the rights to be respected under that clause was not shared by all justices at all times.[27]

The central statement in Harlan's long opinion was reached when he declared that freedom from racial discrimination was "a new constitutional right, secured by the grant of State citizenship to colored citizens of the United States"—a right which the United States had the power to enforce by its own direct legislation.[28] This view was virtually submerged during and long after Harlan's lifetime; but it was the answer to the view that national legislation was permissible only when it dealt with "the essence of citizenship" and defined the essence in a narrow sense. Harlan's assertion in fact represented a crucial insight into the meaning of the Fourteenth Amendment, and it was the light of this perception that was to illuminate the subject with increasing intensity during the twentieth century. He went on to sweep aside any restriction introduced by the court in the *Slaughter House Cases*: The states themselves had never had any power to

25. Ibid., 28, 29, 30. 26. Ibid., 36–7.
27. Ibid., 47–8. 28. Ibid., 50.

abridge the privileges and immunities of citizens of the United States; consequently the Fourteenth Amendment's prohibition on state laws was an express limitation on the power of the state, but was never intended to diminish the nation's authority in protecting rights secured by the Constitution.[29]

Harlan was able to show that the court had recently agreed, as in *Ex parte Virginia*, that any denial by a state of equality of civil rights was indeed a denial of the equal protection of the laws. But he struck his most devastating blow with a weapon from the court's own armoury, for *Hall* v. *DuCuir* had found the court arguing (as we have seen) that if in the context of interstate commerce the public good required such legislation, "it must come from Congress, and not from the States". It was from Congress that it had now come; and drawing upon the long history of Congressional and Supreme Court actions to uphold the rights of slaveowners, all of which furnished decisive evidence of the adequacy of the existing constitutional powers to execute public policies, Harlan observed pointedly that "with all respect for the opinions of others, I insist that the national legislature may, without transcending the limits of the Constitution, do for human liberty, what it did, with the sanction of this Court, for the protection of slavery and the rights of masters of fugitive slaves".[30] Harlan identified race discrimination as a form of class tyranny and added a warning that if this kind of policy were accepted, Negroes might not be the only victims.

This opinion constituted one of the earliest distinct indications—and probably the first to have emerged from the Supreme Court—that the Fourteenth Amendment might in the future be held not only to limit the power of government to protect individual equality, but to sustain alternative possible social structures. The United States had always consisted of a variety of regions, societies, and even of social orders, held together by a limited number of shared beliefs, ideals, and laws; the Civil War and the subsequent amendments had drawn these together. But now they seemed to be gaining constitutional sanction for pulling apart once more, and if this trend continued until the separate structures were harder, more difficult to penetrate, and more independent of each other, then Americans

29. Ibid., 54–5.
30. Ibid., 53.

of the future would have to adapt themselves to recognised limits on their mobility—limits set by designations of race and colour, religion and nation of origin, and possibly even by region or class. Such considerations as these were extremely remote and speculative at the time of the *Civil Rights Cases*; they were contained, however, within the logical order of possibilities mentioned in Harlan's warning, and they were to evolve into much more concrete forms during the next generation.

The judgment in the *Civil Rights Cases* reduced the legally objectionable forms of racial discrimination to those which were actually sanctioned or enforced by state governments so as to deprive any individual of protection, privilege, or immunity in circumstances affecting his civil or legal liberties. There did remain therefore an area in which discrimination constituted a grievance which the law must redress. The effect of this position was untenably contradictory. The Fourteenth Amendment was still held to deny the illegal consequences of social prejudices while permitting the practices which were the normal and consistent expression of those prejudices. The court in other words accepted the existing sociology of race relations and attempted to apply the Fourteenth Amendment as a brake only when that sociology actually invaded the courts and did such things as executing black men where white men were set free. Yet the Supreme Court would hardly have risked greater charges of logical inconsistency if it had found an unconstitutional denial of equal protection in social practices which inevitably produced unconstitutional consequences. It was no doubt an intractable problem; white racial prejudice was profound and resilient, as the history of Reconstruction shows. The court chose to settle it not in accordance with its authority under the Fourteenth Amendment to maximise the protection of those privileges which were threatened, but in accordance with the actual distribution of social and political power in Southern states. By checking the patently illegal consequences of discrimination (which in *Strauder* v. *West Virginia* and *Ex parte Virginia* it did over strong dissenting voices), the Supreme Court left open a residual possibility that its successors might trace back the line it had dropped—leading back from these consequences to the practices behind them—particularly where they were established rather than merely tolerated by law. In the opinion of Harlan, who caustically described his colleagues' course as "a subtle and ingenious verbal reasoning", the plain meaning and intent of the Fourteenth Amendment was being defeated and the court was denying to government the power to perform its protective duty. Yet discriminatory legislation by class remained illegitimate; an area of ambiguity remained unresolved. Where the court recognised the government had a duty to protect, it refused the means to implement protection. A gap had been disclosed—or created—between the government's implied obligations and its lawful powers.

Even that position was perhaps unwittingly undermined by the court in the same year as the *Civil Rights Cases*. White people seldom seemed free to think clearly in matters involving sex, and numerous state laws prohibited both sexual intercourse and marriage between members of the white and black races. *Pace* v. *Alabama* came up to the court in 1883 on appeal against a conviction for felony where a Negro man and a white woman had been found guilty of fornication, which was treated as a case of intermarriage, presumably because they were living together. The law had been applied equally to a member of each race. The Supreme Court therefore held that neither race could complain of unequal discrimination and the requirements of equal protection had not been infringed. It is perhaps evidence of the power of sex to derange the normal sequence of a reasonable mind that even Harlan concurred in this reasoning. Yet the Fourteenth Amendment does not refer to races; it refers to citizens and to persons—in other words, to individuals. The question to be decided could therefore have been defined as whether the individual man and the individual woman in this case were receiving equal protection from a law which denied them the freedom, normally experienced by all other individuals in such matters, of making their own emotional choices. The judgment of the Court recognised "Negroes" as a subject available for legislative action just as women, children, aliens, and citizens were already distinguished in law. Negroes were not the only subjects of "class" legislation, but in their case such legislation was aimed entirely to their disadvantage. The leading decisions of the period made clear that the justices shared with other whites a fundamental perception of Negroes as different in ways that required and justified treatment which no classes of whites would have been expected to tolerate.

Pace v. *Alabama* suggested that the anomalous gap between obligation and enforcement would one day be closed with the court's consent; Clifford's dictum that "equality is not identity" indicated the way it would come. In 1896 the ambiguities were resolved when in *Plessy* v. *Ferguson* the Supreme Court announced the doctrine of "separate but equal".[31]

This doctrine, traceable to the pre-Civil War case of *Roberts* v. *The City of Boston*, had acquired federal status from a similar ruling by the recently formed Interstate Commerce Commission. Plessy's case, like that of DuCuir, came up from Louisiana, where a law imposing segregation in public transport had been passed in 1890. It did not arise by chance. The Negro and anti-Jim Crow interests had watched the advance of segregation laws in Southern states with increasing alarm and had concluded that if they were not to become the permanent, settled custom of the South, sanctioned by the passage of time, a constitutional challenge was necessary. Albion Tourgee, a former Northerner who spent several years as a Reconstruction judge in North Carolina and also wrote a popular novel, *A Fool's Errand*, was engaged as counsel. As Tourgee fully and anxious appreciated, much was at stake, for the timing of the case did not seem propitious and a defeat would have lasting and profound effects.[32]

Adolph Plessy was chosen for the test in part because, being seven eighths "Caucasian", he claimed the rights and privileges of a white man. Though Tourgee did not press this aspect very hard, the case rested in part on the claim that classification as a Negro deprived him of the reputation of being white, which was a form of property. This aspect of the strategy did not please a number of blacks, who suspected that a judgment on these lines might benefit light-skinned persons of Negro descent while relegating more visible blacks to constitutional darkness. The court was in any case not impressed by the claims, which however drew from it a revealing comment.

As for the issues arising from the Thirteenth Amendment, the

31. 163 U.S. 537 (1896).
32. Jack Greenberg, *Litigation for Social Change: Methods, Limits and Role in Democracy*, Benjamin N. Cardozo lecture before the Association of the Bar of the City of New York (New York, 1974), pp. 12–15.

court dismissed them out of hand. That segregation could no longer be considered as a mark of slavery was "too clear for argument". If this claim had been upheld, Negroes would in fact have had a sort of double protection—though this point did not concern the court; but there are certainly some forms of discrimination which, while being racial in bias, are not derivatives of slavery; anti-semitism is presumably not traced exclusively to the period of Egyptian servitude. The question of the Thirteenth Amendment raised the complicated problem of whether white prejudice against blacks was derived exclusively from the relationship established by slavery or whether it had other sources which would have had similar effects even if slavery had not existed. Mr Justice Harlan still held that discrimination on grounds of colour was a badge of slavery and fell under the ban of the antislavery amendment; his colleagues had no time for such thoughts. In 1883 this question was considered worthy of serious discussion; by 1896 it was dismissed as trivial. Yet in the interval the real position of the black race in the South had gravely deteriorated, a fact which the court did not choose to observe.

The court's opinion, given by Mr Justice Brown, distinguished between two kinds of equality, social and legal. "The object of the Amendment"—the Fourteenth, that is—"was undoubtedly to enforce the absolute equality of the two races before the law", he declared, "but in the nature of things it could not have intended to abolish distinctions based on colour, or to enforce social, as distinct from political equality, or a commingling of the two races on terms unsatisfactory to either".[33] In this as in all other such cases, it was the white race to whom the commingling was "unsatisfactory"; yet this obvious fact did not deter Mr Justice Brown from remarking a little later that the underlying fallacy of the plaintiff's argument consisted "in the assumption that the enforced separation of the two races stamps the colored race with a badge of inferiority". In language that could only have been supposed to have been deliberately satirical if it had proceeded from any other source, he went on, "If this be so, it is not by reason of anything found in the act, but solely because the colored race chooses to put that construction upon it".[34]

33. 163 U.S. 537, 544.
34. Ibid., 551.

Yet the court did recognise that a claim might be entertained for "the reputation of belonging to the dominant race".[35] Their point was that Plessy did not have a right to this reputation; but the remark revealed their recognition of the fact that one race was "dominant"; and when one race is dominant, the other must be inferior. The coloured race's "choice of construction" appeared to correspond closely with the court's view of the actual state of affairs. Nothing in Brown's opinion suggests that it occurred to the court to raise the question of whether the accommodations available to Negroes were actually equal to those reserved for whites.

It is permissible to doubt whether the Supreme Court has ever exposed the fundamentally racialist assumptions behind its reasoning with quite such incontinence, and it is also permissible to hope that it has never committed itself through such inferior reasoning. Brown proclaimed that a legal distinction between the two races, imposed by the master race, had "no tendency to destroy the legal equality of two races". This distinction he found "in the color of the two races . . . which must always exist so long as white men are distinguished from the other race by color". The admitted dominance of one race over the other did not constitute a social grievance; according to the court's sociology, it lay "in the nature of things". Consequently there was no remedy at law. The government was, indeed, required to secure "to each of its citizens equal opportunities for improvement and progress".[36] That, apparently, it had done. As to the argument put by counsel, that the same reasoning could lead to the state legislature requiring all sorts of other distinctions between white and coloured people or between people of different nationalities, or hair colours, the answer was that the exercise by the state of its police power must be "reasonable".[37] Within a very few years the white Southern conception of reasonableness had imposed just such differentiations and separation on the minutiae of daily life, with the result that whites and blacks sat in different waiting rooms, bought their tickets at different booths, used different entrances to the same buildings, and settled to a pattern of segregation more profound and rigid than anything since the end of slavery. In 1935 a distinguished

35. Ibid., 549.   36. Ibid., 551.
37. Ibid., 549–50.

constitutional historian could conclude—not without relief—that "for the main purpose in the minds of its originators, the [Fourteenth] Amendment has been a complete failure". He was satisfied, however, that the essentials of civil liberty were not interfered with by state enactments.[38] That satisfaction was not shared at the time by Mr Justice Harlan.

Harlan's dissent has become one of the most celebrated of American constitutional documents. It was not entirely free from logical imperfections, however. Harlan recognised that a sociology of race must underlie any public policy on the subject, at least to the extent that he said that "the destinies of the two races, in this country, are indissolubly linked together", and dismissed the irrational fears of the whites by remarking that 60 millions of them were in no danger from 8 million blacks.[39] This remark may have been intended to alleviate white hysteria, but in many Southern districts blacks were a majority; these proportions in no way affected the constitutional position, which, of course, would have been quite unaltered even if there had been a black majority throughout the nation. That, indeed, was central to Harlan's argument. The Constitution, as he eloquently said, "is color blind. There is no caste here".[40] The Constitution literally did not know, and could in no way sanction, distinctions of class or colour, and therefore could not permit public officials to enforce distinctions based on them.[41] Harlan was keenly aware of the damage the decision would do in the South. It could only encourage whites to pass legislation hostile to citizens of the United States and intended to humiliate them, which, according to the court's decision, would be held to be consistent with the Constitution. He correctly anticipated the advent of new forms of segregation. As for the arguments to which the majority of his bretheren subscribed, he was not deficient in the candour which their reasoning seemed to invite: "The thin disguise of 'equal' accommodations for passengers in railroad coaches will not mislead anyone, nor atone for the wrong this day done".[42]

38. Andrew C. McLaughlin, *A Constitutional History of the United States* (New York, 1935), p. 727.
39. 163 U.S. 537, 560.   40. Ibid., 559.
41. Ibid., 554.
42. Ibid., 562–3. An excoriating critique of Brown's opinion will be found in Robert J. Harris's *The Quest for Equality* (Baton Rouge, 1960), p. 101, which

With *Plessy* v. *Ferguson* a caste system had been legitimised under American constitutional law. Two years later a test of the Fifteenth Amendment brought more bad news for the Negro. Mississippi had moved to exclude Negroes from the suffrage rolls by enacting a literacy test, and in *Williams* v. *Mississippi* the Supreme Court agreed that the state had a right to impose such tests as did not specifically exclude citizens on grounds of "race, color, or previous condition of servitude". This development, as we have seen, had been very precisely anticipated during the debates on the Fifteenth Amendment. It was only on their face that Mississippi's laws did not enact racial discrimination; the court admitted that "evil" in their administration might make them an instrument of discrimination, in which case they would presumably have fallen under the amendment—as Oklahoma's "grandfather clause" was to fall in 1915—but at this period the court did not make a practice of enquiring how a statute was actually being applied. It left such matters to the good faith of the states, with Mississippi in voting, with Louisiana in the provision of "equal" accommodations on the railroads.

The reasoning of successive justices of the Supreme Court in this long series of cases tended towards a conclusion that became explicit in *Plessy* v. *Ferguson*. That conclusion was a regression to the ancient principle that equality before the law could stand alone as an isolated but indestructible principle, unblemished by gross inequalities in every other walk of life. Mr Justice Brown's attempt to argue that the law could provide "equal opportunities for improvement and progress" could survive only so long as the court refused to make any enquiry into the actual state of affairs; but it was the actual state of affairs which had produced the laws of segregation. If members of the two races had really been equals, in "opportunities for improvement and progress", in political rights, and above all in respect for one another as individuals, it is scarcely conceivable that segregation laws would have come into existence or the court have had any problem to resolve. It was also inherently unlikely (though not perhaps technically impossible) that Negroes would receive equal protection from laws which in other ways treated them as inferiors. The court's reasoning no doubt satisfied the vast mass of

describes it as "a compound of bad logic, bad history, bad sociology, and bad constitutional law".

whites; but its incongruities demonstrated the intellectual as well as the practical difficulties of maintaining a division between some of the different categories of equality.

The Southern states by this time were already in the process of redesigning their constitutions to erect impossible—though technically neutral—barriers against Negro participation in political life. The development, which began in Mississippi in 1890, was gradual, complicated, and piecemeal, each state taking its own time and giving its own reasons. In retrospect the results were uniform, if somewhat rough around the edges. But it was not the blacks only who were swept so unceremoniously into political oblivion; restrictions based on poll taxes, literacy, and the complexity of the operation of voting tended to disfranchise the poor and the uneducated, a result which made elections somewhat safer and easier for the prevailing party managers. The process was accompanied by a very frank reaction in political theory. Speakers and writers in several Southern states reverted to the views of earlier periods when they attacked the modern democratic ideas and urged that political power should be restored to competent and socially responsible hands.[43] At a level of abstraction which could not have been expected to appeal to these speakers, these arguments against political and economic equality had the perverse effect of illustrating the implicit unity of egalitarian theory. Sixty years later that unity might show fragmentary tendencies on gaining some degree of success, but its outlines were more clearly revealed in face of defeat.

The Economics of Fitness and Survival

Harlan's dissent in *Plessy* v. *Ferguson* took up a significant point from Plessy's counsel—which, as a matter of fact, Harlan himself had made as early as the *Civil Rights Cases*—that the principle being introduced could be extended to other minorities and to other social or religious differences. Catholics and Protestants, aliens and native Americans might find themselves arranged by law in separate stations. But the true social significance of this argument was soon to appear not in its intended sense but in the silence which received

43. Kousser, *Shaping of Southern Politics*, pp. 144, 151, 160, 164, 169.

it. Other American minorities did not rise up in outrage at the wrong
that day done to blacks, nor did they take up the fight as an advance
line of self-defence. Nothing could have more cruelly portrayed the
isolation into which the Negro interest had been thrust by the dominant, competitive forces of the surrounding society.

The truth was that these judicial opinions did not stand alone in
their time. Negroes in America were only some among a heterogeneous assortment of racial religious and economic groups with
overlapping memberships but dissimilar interests, disunited by their
common interest in economic survival. From the early days of Reconstruction, economic issues dominated the aims of many of these
interests, especially those of the newly organising forces of labour,
while political equality was defended as the most practical means of
giving strength to demands for equality, or at least competence, in
the defence of economic interests.

During Reconstruction radical leaders such as Charles Sumner in
the Senate and Thaddeus Stevens in the House, who fought whole-
heartedly to give meaning to racial equality in America, could differ
widely over economic issues; and the policies of government on
economic matters would inevitably affect prospects for other—and
to many people more urgent—aspects of equality. Sumner was a
firm adherent of the principles of unregulated competition taught
by Manchester economics.[44] Government in his view could not assume responsibility for the economic aims of society; it existed to
serve them, not to control or define them, and its duty was to leave
them alone—with the strict proviso that it should leave them fairly
alone. These attitudes divided Sumner from Thaddeus Stevens, who
combined his passionate belief in racial equality with a potent brand
of economic nationalism.[45] Both, however, could recognise the need
for the confiscation of the estates of former Southern rebels; the
class whose greed and intransigeance they blamed for both slavery
and the war was thus to be prevented from repossessing itself of
power over the South—or in the counsels of the Union. Their lands
were to go to the Negroes, as earned compensation for their past

44. Kenneth M. Stampp, *The Era of Reconstruction* (London, 1965), p. 106.
45. Ibid.; David H. Montgomery, *Beyond Equality: Labor and the Radical
Republicans, 1862–1872* (New York, 1967), chap. 2 and pp. 84–5.

labours and as the minimum requirement of their economic and political liberty in the future. Congressional majorities, however, never followed the Radicals to these revolutionary extremes.

The Southern problem aside, the egalitarian in Sumner was satisfied with the economics of fair competition; and he was fully consistent with these principles in denouncing the effects of racial oppression. His aim was to use whatever government action was required to set the victims in a position of equality with other competitors. This system raised no impediment or moral objection to the larger differences of wealth which rapidly grew from the conditions of American capitalist competition—the full consequences of which Sumner, who died in 1874, did not live to contemplate. Stevens had died six years earlier, but his brand of utilitarian nationalism could ultimately have proved a more effective instrument for holding the disparate ingredients of egalitarian principle together in a single spectrum. Stevens had much more confidence in government as the proper agency for shaping the character of the Republic and was ready to use it for economic policy as well as for racial justice. The failure of the Radical plan to distribute land to the freedmen, however, placed a heavy burden on the efficacy of the political weapon that did remain in Negro hands after the Fifteenth Amendment. The right of suffrage satisfied the demands of other Republicans who stood on the principle of political individualism without looking too closely into the social context in which it had to be exercised. Most of the freedmen's political allies, in fact, were quite satisfied that the suffrage alone would bring their other needs within reach. Even such a determined antislavery campaigner as Wendell Phillips could take a remarkable degree of satisfaction in the efficacy of the suffrage. "A man with a ballot in his hand", he said in supporting the Fifteenth Amendment, "is the master of the situation. He defines all his other rights. What is not already given to him, he takes. . . . The Ballot is opportunity, education, fair play, right to office, and elbow room".[46]

The ballot had not yet resolved labour's problems in its struggle with capital. Neither did Northern states show any particular relish

46. In the *National Anti-Slavery Standard*, 20 March 1869, quoted by William Gillette, *The Right to Vote: Politics and the Passing of the Fifteenth Amendment* (Baltimore and London, 1969), p. 87.

for genuinely universal suffrage until the Fifteenth Amendment forced it on them as it did on the South. Moreover, labour in its organised capacities shared this distaste for full Negro participation in the institutions of civic life. It is true that the first post-war labour convention, held in 1866, adopted an unusually broad declaration of racial and religious solidarity concluding with the words, "If these principles be correct, we must seek the co-operation of the African race in America".[47] But this language proved too strong within a year, and in 1867 the new National Labor Union, meeting in congress in Chicago, decided to lay the whole Negro question over until the following year on the grounds that "While we feel the importance of the subject, and realise the danger in the future competition in mechanical negro labor, yet we find the subject involved in so much mystery, and upon it so wide a diversity of opinion among our members, we believe it is inexpedient to take any action on the subject in this National Labor Congress".[48]

A spirited debate followed the introduction of this resolution. One member, who asked whether any union could be induced to admit "colored men", pointed out that "respectable colored mechanics" were persistently excluded. Another member, on the other hand, was sorry to see the words "colored" and "white" being used; labour owed a duty to the coloured worker in common brotherhood, and coloured men were proving themselves industrious, and susceptible of improvement and advancement. One member understood that the intention was "to legislate for the good of the entire laboring community of the United States", but went on to argue that the blacks would combine together on their own part, without assistance from the whites, who ought not to try to carry them on their shoulders. "God speed them", he blandly remarked, without clearly indicating the direction in which he hoped they would proceed. To these and similar remarks, William H. Sylvis, America's first great labour leader, replied. In the South, he said, the question had already arisen, the whites striking against the blacks, and creating an antagonism which would kill off the trades unions unless the two were consolidated. "There is no concealing the fact", he pointed out, "that

47. John R. Commons and Associates, *A Documentary History of American Industrial Society*, 10 vols. (Cleveland, 1910), IX, 158–9.
48. Ibid., IX, 185.

the time will come when the negro will take possession of the shops if we have not taken possession of the negro. If the working men of the white race do not conciliate the blacks, the black vote will be cast against them".[49] Sylvis's contemporaries were unprepared to face the consequences of this reasoning, and took refuge in the view that the interests of all labour could be equally well served by sepa- rate organisations. In times of hardship, when employers brought in black labour to undercut white strikers, this reasoning was to be disproved, though it is to be doubted that their views were reversed.

The unions were more sympathetic to the claims of women. From the constitutional standpoint, white women, who did not enjoy the benefit of the suffrage, were more decisively excluded from the po- litical process than black men, many of whom did enjoy it. The de- mands of women—exclusively white ones, it is to be presumed— caused a heated debate at the labor convention of 1868, where the members refused to commit themselves on the broader political ques- tion of suffrage, but willingly supported the principle of equal treat- ment for women as fellow-workers. Similar motions were adopted in 1869.[50]

The blacks understood the situation only too well; they had the advantage of experience. In 1869 they held a National Colored Labor Convention in Washington where the resolutions adopted made an addition to the known list of natural rights—that of labouring in the field of one's abilities. This represented a refinement of the idea of equality of opportunity which was to have particular importance when egalitarian theory turned a century later to the problem of education. The convention adopted a "harmony of interests" view of the relations between capital and labour, thus firmly rejecting the socialist doctrine of class antagonism, deplored intemperance, and advocated a universal free school system to be instituted "without regard to race, creed, or sex". The standpoint of the black labouring classes gave an unobstructed perspective of those aspects in which equality might be considered indivisible. The resolution most poi- gnantly expressing their feelings declared that the country was the common property of the whole people and bitterly denounced the white trade union practice of excluding blacks. The convention also

49. Ibid., IX, 185–8.   50. Ibid., IX, 198, 233.

favoured the development of co-operative workshops and building and loan associations.[51]

By this time, when organised labour was obliged by its own interest to confront the problem of race, it was clear that republican theory was not in control of the situation. Northern workers were heavily engaged in defining their class interests in terms of certain specific issues, the greatest being the struggle for the eight-hour day; when labour congresses rallied in this cause and committed themselves on such issues as banking, currency, and equitable distribution of the public lands, they did move out onto the broader ground of general republican principles.

When they adopted this outlook the representatives of the new labour movement at their most articulate were close to the social and economic aspirations and policies of the Radical Republicans, at least as far as their brightest hopes were dreamed of by Thaddeus Stevens. He had always believed it possible that the abolition of slavery might break up the foundations of national institutions, giving "the intelligent, pure and just men of this Republic" an opportunity to remodel it in such ways as to free them from "every vestige of human oppression, of inequality of rights, of the recognized degradation of the poor, and the superior caste of the rich". What Stevens believed in, and still believed possible, given the appropriate crisis in American public life, was a remaking of the Republic on its true moral foundations, so that "no distinction would be tolerated in this purified Republic but what arose from merit and conduct".

By this time the economic structure of the country had so altered from that of Jeffersonian dreams that two-thirds of all productively engaged Americans were now employees. The revolution to which Stevens aspired could not look to the past; any hope it might have from the future must arise with the growing organised power of labour. This power soon made itself felt. But liberal ideologists of the older school did not necessarily welcome labour's new drive for equality of condition, which threw that liberal intellectual E. L. Godkin into a distinctly illiberal fright. Taking note of the concessions that Massachusetts Republicans made to labour demands in the elec-

51. Ibid., IX, 243–52.

tions of 1872, Godkin commented that the labour question "contains the disease from which this Christian civilization of ours is to perish". Why? Because of the very pursuit of "equality of conditions on which the multitude seems now entering, and the elevation of equality of conditions into the rank of the highest political good"— a process which would "prove fatal to art, to science, to literature, and to law . . .". Although Godkin was himself an immigrant, his abilities and standpoint soon made him a strongly representative and influential spokesman of those interests which he had described as being at risk, and such he was to remain through a long editorial career. A very great distance had been travelled since another European had observed equality of conditions as the very foundation of American social life and the end to which not only American but in the long run European society was tending. The point of view had now changed. Godkin was assuredly right in observing that equality of conditions did not then exist. His sense of the foundations of social stability and his fears for the future of American social order were expressed when he asserted that the gathering movement he detected in the direction of equality of conditions would be nothing short of disastrous to the intellectual and moral fibre of the Republic.

Labour and agrarian reformers, including the group known as Sentimental Reformers—who were moved by the ideas of Susan B. Anthony's Woman Suffrage Association—did not regard that direction as leading to disaster, and all continued to employ the language of equality. Farmers' conventions in the 1870s invoked the ideals of equal justice and equal division of the profits arising from work.[52] When the Knights of Labor declared their aims they reverted to a theme that recalled the class consciousness of labour's earlier struggle for identity. "We mean to uphold the dignity of labor, to affirm the nobility of all who live in accordance with the ordinance of God, 'in the sweat of thy brow shalt thou eat bread' ", they declared, but concluded by advocating the harmony of the interests of capital and labour.[53]

The historically venerable idea of American equality affected the thinking of labour leaders. The reformist analysis was often restrained in the face of the exemplary successes of capitalist enterprise

52. Ibid., X, 47–8, 61.
53. Ibid., X, 24.

and the academically reputable doctrines of free competition which provided the system with a highly articulate theory. Again and again, labour's public pronouncements harped on the mutual interests of capital and labour in language surprisingly redolent of the more unctuous statements of that theme from the capitalist side. American workers were an extremely heterogeneous body, incorporating a high proportion of immigrants of more or less recent standing in the country. Such people could not lightly discard the commitments, emotional as well as economic, that they had made on emigration to America, and immigrant attitudes could be easily reconciled to uses of equality now adopted to serve the purpose of the industrial order.

The situation caught the attention of the central committee of the North American Federation of the International Workingmen's Association—the First International—when it addressed a message to the General Council in London in August 1871. This statement was unusual in its critique of the uses of American values. The workers, particularly the immigrants, were dupes of an ideology which hired them into a captivity that they celebrated as freedom. "We are sorry", the American committee observed,

to state that the workingmen in general, even in spite of the industrial development—are quite unconscious of their own position towards capital and slow to show battle against their oppressors for the following reason:

I. The great majority of the workingmen in the Northern States are immigrants from Ireland, Germany, England, etc. (in California, coolies imported under contract), having left their native countries for the purpose of seeking here that wealth they could not obtain at home. This delusion transforms itself into a sort of creed, and employers and capitalists, parvenus having gained their wealth in the former period, take great care in preserving this self-deception among their employees.

The capitalists rendered the goal ever more impossible to realise. Yet the trades unions, founded in the vision of that idea—wealth through capitalist enterprise—now found it to be the stumbling block over which they fell and perished. The address continued with a scathing denunciation of the "so-called Reform Parties" which were growing up and disappearing overnight, advocating "glittering educational measures, benevolent and homestead societies", and other schemes. Wrong guidance within the labour movement itself was also chosen for criticism; labour activities were directed to reforms that ended by taking their abode "in one of the political parties of the ruling class, the bourgeois".[54] These passages are notably free of references to the Republic's founding ideals, to the harmonising of the interests of capital and labour, or of rhetorical invocations of the ideal of equality. From this standpoint, at least, that ideal had proved a snare and a delusion, misleading workers into believing that they had a share, or a prospect of a share, in a social system whose whole tendency in reality was to deprive them of the fruits of their toil. It is significant of the extent to which the prevalent ideology permeated their thoughts that labour spokesmen generally subscribed to the nomenclature in which the economic system under which they worked was called not a "capitalist" system, but one of "free labour".[55]

Ideas of equality had no part in the vocabulary of Social Darwinism, which in the later nineteenth and early twentieth centuries did much to cast the discussion of social relations in an evolutionary light. The massive accumulations of corporate but private property which marked American economic growth after the Civil War created the most conspicuous inequalities in the country's history. So much, if not self-evident, was certainly evident to the senses, and received detailed documentation in the writings of social critics such as Ida Tarbell, Henry Demarest Lloyd, and other forerunners of the Progressive movement. Public enquiries such as the Senate investigation of the Sugar Trust were themselves products of public concern about these new concentrations of economic power. The problems raised by these vast accumulations, and the power they wielded throughout the nation, were recognised as a challenge to old republican principles. But one at least of the new giants, Andrew Carnegie, soon equipped his class with a new theory, gained by the social applications of Darwinism. The ethics of the theory associated with the survival of the fittest through adaption to natural environment did not seem to have much in common with earlier doctrines about natural rights; but its leading beneficiaries demonstrated a remarkable facility not so much in adapting themselves to their environment as in adapting the environment to their own interests. This at least was not an uncharitable interpretation to place on the way in

54. Ibid., IX, 361–6.
55. Montgomery, *Beyond Equality*, p. 14.

which the Fourteenth Amendment was taken over by constitutional lawyers and judges in the defence of gigantic but legally vulnerable business corporations.

The unfit did not accept defeat gracefully. Out of the conditions of rapid population growth, of an increasingly competitive and mechanised agriculture, of rapid but unplanned urban development, of massive immigration from mainly non-English speaking countries, there sprang the grievances and resentments which followed the experience of failure and disappointed hope. When the Populist party raised its colours in 1892 it returned once more, and not merely in passing, to the displaced theme of equality. Populists believed "that the forces of reform this day organised will never cease to move forward until every wrong is remedied, with equal rights and equal privileges securely established for all the men and women of this country". They sought "to restore the government of the Republic to the hands of 'the plain people', with whose class it originated". And they asserted that their purposes were identical with those proclaimed in the national Constitution. Among the specific economic and political policies they set forth, the graduated income tax was one whose ultimate effect would have had the most power to restore the equality of goods that was thought to have been lost. This statement depended on a folk-belief of great importance to the emotional stability of people who felt themselves to be victims of the new industrial and financial tyranny. The Populists believed that the American Revolution had been made by the "plain people"—the yeomen of America who came from the same stock and had similar moral qualities to the yeomen of England. This belief was associated with another historical concept, that the Revolution was made by a people among whom the country's resources had been more or less equally distributed.

This belief was particularly important in the political thinking of Henry George, who advanced his own specific remedies for the country's ills in *Progress and Poverty*, published in 1879. George was impelled by the need to secure, in the existing more complex state of society, "the same equality of rights that in a ruder state was secured by equal partition of the soil, and by giving the use of the land to whoever could procure the most from it".[56] Whether or not

56. Henry George, *Progress and Poverty* (1879; London, 1931), p. 286.

this "equal partition of the soil" had ever actually existed would have made little difference to the moral basis for George's proposals for the confiscation by the state of all rents from land; but the conviction that Americans had at one time lived under a different, more equitable order undoubtedly made the plan seem more legitimate. It was thus more consistent with American traditions, and it tended to rectify an injustice that had come about since the Revolution. But since George believed that land was the only true basis of wealth—a view consistent with John Taylor's—he would presumably have held that if it had in fact been wrongly distributed in earlier times, that wrong distribution could have been corrected without injustice to the owners of excessive property. George's book is transfused with the language of equal rights, but he did not confuse equality of rights with similarity of attainments. George also believed that progress was kindled by cooperative action, which he called "association"; inequality perverted it into "retrogression". He called "association of equality" the "law of progress"—but then, in a significant parenthesis, defined equality almost out of existence by offering as equivalents "justice or freedom, for the terms here signify the same things, the recognition of the moral law".[57] This casual remark warns us not to take too seriously Henry George's concept of equality as the moral basis of the state. Whatever view one may hold about the categories of equality or of their relationship to such concepts as liberty or justice, they are certainly not interchangeable, and to treat them as such diminishes the value of equality itself as a social aim.

George's single tax was the sovereign remedy intended to recover for the benefit of the people all the profits accruing from the rise of land values. His notion that land had been evenly distributed at the time of the Revolution, and that all the distortions that now needed correction had crept into the system as a result of subsequent capitalist development, was shared by nearly all reformers of the later nineteenth century, including Edward Bellamy. Bellamy had spent years reflecting on the perplexing injustices of modern society and had filled notebooks with moral and political reflections before he published his most famous novel *Looking Backward* in 1888. At some date apparently a few years after the Civil War, he rejected the ethics of competition with the comment, "What difference does

57. Ibid., p. 359.

it make if you or your oppressor is a self-made man risen from the ranks? His rod is even heavier than the born rich man's".[58] This was Bellamy's reply to the attempts of so many contemporary reformers to come to terms with the existing system of demanding merely that equal opportunities should be restored. But an agrarian order of society was not going to dominate the future, and Bellamy instead conceived of a society that was to be mechanised to a degree one day to become known as "automation". In a manner closely akin to the somewhat later method of H. G. Wells, Bellamy used the novel to combine science fiction with political science. When his sleeping protagonist awakes in the year 2000, he finds himself in a world of refined and deliberately depersonalised technology. Private accumulation still figures in the incentives of the workers of *Looking Backward*, because Bellamy was realistically aware of the importance of personal ambition in stimulating individual contributions even to a fully collective social system; but by this time the country is run by a small group of nobler citizens who are liberated from the profit motive and respond to an inner directive. The universal free education which forms an important element of his society consists mainly in training in industrial and professional skills. Since all the fundamental problems of society have been resolved by agreement, there is no further need to make laws; government has become the most routine form of management.

Looking Backward was not merely a romance, it was a manifesto, expressing Bellamy's decision, taken after several years of doubt, to set forth a programme of national reform.[59] It did not trouble him that the system was not fully cooperative and that the need for a central group of managers, moved by morally finer sentiments than the masses, had about it a strong flavour of the kind of moral hierarchy that had once characterised the Puritan magistrates; a later generation would call it "elitism". This aspect failed to deter his admirers. *Looking Backward* sold some 60,000 copies in its first year of publication, rising to 100,000 the next year, with editions in Britain, France, and Germany. In America Bellamy proceeded to found the "Nationalist" movement which was to lead without social

58. John L. Thomas, Introduction to Edward Bellamy, *Looking Backward* (Cambridge, Mass., 1967), p. 19.
59. Ibid., p. 50.

upheaval to the promised age. In a series of articles and in his editorials for his movement's paper, *The New Nation,* he explained that Nationalism—an expression that referred to the national scale and purpose of the organisation, without implying the competition with other nations which it came to have later—was a purely American programme rooted in the political egalitarianism of the American Revolution. It is clear that for him, no less than for others, this claim of consistency with American traditions was of the utmost importance. Bellamy asserted that his party were the true conservatives, seeking to maintain and conserve the original purposes of the Republic.[60] In restoring the nation to its own true ideals, an aim which for him had an almost religious meaning, equality was a moral imperative. Then, for two years, Bellamy threw himself into the Populist movement, which at first seemed capable of achieving his aims, or at least of taking steps towards them. Politics failed him, however, and in 1897 he turned back to publication with his last book, *Equality.* Bellamy had spent much of his time in religious musings, and now made it his purpose to bring the American egalitarian tradition into union with the country's potent capacity for religious revivals; Christian evangelism would continue the tradition begun by the Declaration of Independence.[61]

Bellamy's Nationalist movement faded rather quickly into obscurity. Its Western elements were absorbed into the more politically promising Populist movement; in the East it lost its force.[62] Nationalist clubs had sprung up on every side and no doubt contributed some political awareness, some spring of vitality, to other movements with greater prospects of getting things done in local or national politics, but they had never been co-ordinated into a political force, and Bellamy was not the man to give them leadership. He did offer Americans a unified vision of their society, and that vision was inspired by the ethics of equality. It may well have been the last of its kind. Bellamy did not break equality into categories or try to draw a line between equality before the law and other varieties; he saw no need for such distinctions, which indeed would have spoiled the purity of his theme. Deviations there might be, but

60. Ibid., p. 76.
61. Ibid., pp. 82–3.
62. Robert H. Wiebe, *The Search for Order 1877–1920* (New York, 1967), pp. 70–1.

they would have to justify themselves as deviations from the dominant ethic. Other views, more practical policies, were later to incorporate and revive the egalitarian categories that American history had already brought to light. In them the unity of vision had gone: Its disappearance, however, was a precondition of practical success.

To incorporate Bellamy's vision under the auspices of the Fourteenth Amendment would have required unusual ingenuity—though great ingenuity was indeed being exercised in other, more practical, causes. Perhaps it remains the most significant fact about his dream and its widespread popularity that it was a dream, which bore no relation to American reality or to the American Constitution.

Chapter Eight

Opportunity, Race and the
Concept of Pluralism

The Threat to Economic Democracy

Practical success for the readoption of the individualist core of American egalitarian principles might well have seemed more remote at the beginning of the twentieth century than at any previous period. A disinterested observer of the rise and consolidation of the trusts and great business corporations, and at the same time of the increasing imposition of rigid racial segregation, together with the deepening divisions affecting other minorities, might reasonably have predicted that ideas of equality would soon die of neglect. Such a prognosis would have expected defeat not in open battle but from attrition. Inequalities of wealth, inequalities of power, and associated inequalities of opportunity seemed to dominate all possible patterns for the future. The language of equality would not be wrested from its place in the Constitution; through the agency of the Supreme Court, the victorious powers had already begun to adapt it to their own uses.

The most intelligent contemporary observers, however, were far from being disinterested, and equally far from giving up the struggle. The successive waves of crisis which afflicted the closing decade of the old century produced one distinctive effect in political style; the state of the Republic became a matter of the most active moral and intellectual concern, and many of the ablest minds of the period, particularly among the younger generation of journalists, politicians, and other publicists, felt impelled to give their best efforts to diagnosing the complaints of their generation.

These publicists, often loosely designated as "Progressives", differed from one another both in the subjects of their concern and in the remedies they proposed. They all appreciated, however, that equality was not merely a technical rule of law but a fundamental and threatened value in American life.[1] Equality was at stake in two fundamental respects. In the economic sphere, corporate business was not only making its own rules, but was restricting the very notion of individual opportunity. Meanwhile the American population was changing in ethnic composition and character on a scale never previously contemplated, giving rise to the question of how much diversity the American system could sustain.

The concept of equality was broad and flexible enough to contain differing and even divergent points of view. But William Graham Sumner, who dominated the teaching of sociology at Yale, and whose doctrines have continued to represent the most forthright statement of satisfaction with the consequences of virtually unlimited competition in the struggle for economic survival, had no time for such sentiments. Observing that the best men of the seventeenth century believed that witches ought to be burnt, which he saw as the culmination rather than a contradiction of faiths and doctrines then popular, he compared these beliefs with "the dogma that all men are equal and that one ought to have as much power in the state as another"—in turn the culmination of nineteenth-century political dogmas and social philosophy.[2] It was the expression rather than the fundamental character of these views that made Sumner seem idiosyncratic. Reformers who were much less comfortable with the consequences of the economic struggle found it difficult to agree about the exact requirements of the doctrine of equality of opportunity and still more difficult to translate that doctrine into social policy.

Yet some of the dominant trends of recent years were clearly alarming. American agriculture, as Frederic C. Howe pointed out, had witnessed a great increase in the two related phenomena of tenancy

1. I am indebted to John Thompson and Marcus Cunliffe for guiding me to several of the publications considered in this section.
2. William Graham Sumner, *Folkways* (1906; repr. New York, 1940) p. 66.

and the size of the larger farms. By 1900, one-fourth of all farms under cultivation were of over 1,000 acres, and 25 percent of farm acreage was owned by 0.006 percent of the people, giving rise to a hierarchy of owners and labourers, landlords and tenants. In a truly Jeffersonian vein he argued that from 10 to 20 million persons might have been housed in this area on farms of fifty acres each. Howe's strictures were not confined to agriculture, however. He also noted the still greater rise of tenancy in the cities, where the homeowner was rapidly disappearing; only 29 percent of homes were owned free of encumbrances. Howe feared that America would soon be comparable with Ireland.[3]

Although many Progressives were concerned with the social consequences of economic inequalities, Howe was unusual in his insistence that the unequal distribution of wealth, accompanied by the growth of steep hierarchies of power, themselves required public attention. "We know practically nothing of the distribution of wealth", he remarked; the universities were silent on the subject, and it was neglected by political science.[4] The difficulty in formulating anything like a political policy was to reconcile this kind of anxiety with the aspirations for self-advancement which led Howe's contemporary, Charles Horton Cooley, to comment on the "almost inevitable dualism which makes it natural that a man should strive to aggrandize himself, his family and his class even though he truly wishes for a greater equality of privilege". This notion of "equality of privilege" was revealing; privilege is by definition a form of inequality. He defended the sentiment of class against imputations of aristocracy, maintaining that in America class did not mean hereditary caste—which indeed would be uncongenial to commerce. The main aim was freedom of opportunity.[5]

This generation of Progressives, whose roots tapped the wellsprings of economic and social protest dating from the rise of the trusts in the 1880s, and whose activities flowed into the political movements that led both Theodore Roosevelt and Woodrow Wilson

3. Frederic C. Howe, *Privilege and Democracy in America* (New York, 1910), pp. 75–87.
4. Ibid., p. 185.
5. Charles Horton Cooley, *Social Organization* (1909; repr. New York, 1962), pp. 265–7.

to commit themselves to reform by the time they contested the presidency in 1912, faced certain problems and formed certain attitudes which may be distantly likened to those of the *philosophes* of the French enlightenment. The condition observed in America around 1900, so far from being Tocqueville's "equality of conditions", was one in which immense consolidations of corporate wealth were able to dictate their terms to the nation's other institutions, and in which popular legislatures hurried to attract the favour of the corporations while courts of justice, if not actually bought and sold, showed a marked disposition to favour their causes. The owners of these mountains of wealth were very naturally likened to feudal barons and often seemed to behave as though they possessed the feudal kinds of privilege and exemption. Even the president of the United States sometimes found himself in a position rather resembling that of those feudal kings who were expected "to live of their own" and were obliged to contend for authority among their barons. The regime of eighteenth-century France was postfeudal, but the privileges of nobility and church had feudal roots; privilege had become a form of injustice, and inequality its most distinguishing characteristic. These injustices, which had aroused the indignation of the French *philosophes*, could not be righted by appealing to those very orders of nobility who were the beneficiaries of privilege; equality before the law, the cardinal unifying principle of Enlightenment ideas of justice, was the antithesis of privilege. It was this state of affairs that turned philosophic minds towards the monarchy itself as the one institution that might have the power to unify the nation in the interests of a more equal idea of social justice.

In a somewhat similar fashion, the American Progressives, whatever the character of their convictions or hopes, could turn only to the power of national institutions to dominate that of the great private corporations. It is a notable fact that men as varied in their views as Herbert Croly, whose *Promise of American Life* promoted him to an influential position in the counsels of Theodore Roosevelt, his contemporary Walter Weyl, John Spargo, the socialist who became famous as the author of *The Bitter Cry of the Children*, and the young Walter Lippmann, all recognised the necessity for national power. At that point, however, the comparison fails. The *philosophes* faced the formidable task of establishing equality as a principle of justice and of convincing the monarchy of its own duty to the nation; the American Progressives, on the contrary, had behind them a Constitution which incorporated certain clearly stated egalitarian principles, a strong national faith in vaguely defined equal rights, and national institutions which were at least in theory accountable to a wide electorate. It may therefore seem an irony that any comparison with the French *ancien régime* should spring to mind; but it was an irony that need not have disturbed the equanimity of the great J. Pierpont Morgan, or of Andrew Carnegie, who acquired the Castle of Skibo in Scotland, from which in 1892 he declined to return to his own industrial base in Pittsburgh to attend to the crisis of the Homestead strike.

For the reformers, again as for their French philosophic predecessors, equality was not a concrete aim but a mode of protest. This comparison should help to explain why the idea of equality, though pervasively accepted in some form or other, was so limited an instrument of substantive policy. Early twentieth-century Progressives had little interest in reviving the kind of popular egalitarian formula that had appealed to past generations. Croly recognised that "all Americans, whether they are professional politicians or reformers, 'predatory' millionaires or common people, political philosophers or schoolboys, accept the principle of 'equal rights for all and special privileges for none' as an absolutely sufficient rule for an American democratic political system. The platforms of both parties testify on its behalf".[6] In keeping with this ideology, Theodore Roosevelt was able to declare without fear of contradiction, when he accepted his party's nomination for the presidency in 1904, that "this government is based on the fundamental idea that each man, no matter what his occupation, his race, or his religious belief, is entitled to be treated on his worth as a man, and neither favored nor discriminated against because of any accident in his position".[7]

As had happened before, the successful candidate felt that from a political point of view the system worked satisfactorily. Before leav-

---

6. Herbert Croly, *The Promise of American Life* (New York, 1909), pp. 183–5.
7. A. B. Hart and H. R. Ferleger, eds., *Theodore Roosevelt Cyclopedia* (New York, 1914), p. 167.

ing the presidency, Roosevelt observed, "Politically we can be said to have worked out our democratic ideals, and the same is true, thanks to the common schools, in educational matters".[8] But the concept of equality was extremely popular, especially among the discontented, and could not easily be confined to politics. Political power indeed would have had little point if it could not be used to alter economic policies.

It was at this link in the argument that Herbert Croly turned from party politics to develop a remarkably scathing attack on the damage done by the popular addiction to the prevalent idea of equality; and in Croly's treatment it becomes a little difficult to distinguish the faults due to popular misconceptions from those to be attributed to the principle itself. The weakness of the equal rights principle, according to Croly, was that it concealed a contradiction—the elementary contradiction between rights to an equal start and rights to equal degrees of fulfilment. The contradiction, he observed, was concealed so long as the economic opportunities of the country had not been developed or appropriated, but "continued loyalty to a contradictory principle is destructive of a wholesome public sentiment and opinion". The principle itself, not merely imperfectly considered belief in it, was to blame. "The principle of equal rights encourages mutual suspicion and disloyalty. It tends to attribute individual and social ills, for which general moral, economic and social causes are usually in large measure responsible, to individual wrong-doing; and in this way it arouses and intensifies that personal and class hatred, which never in any society lies far below the surface".[9]

Yet Croly strongly affirmed his American faith in social equality, and in terms not altogether consistent with the foregoing critique, he attributed "the fluid and elastic substance of American life" and the accessibility of economic opportunities to the "democratic dislike of any suggestion of authentic social inferiority". If the flexibility of American institutions had permitted the present concentrations of wealth in the hands "of a few irresponsible men", the task for the future was to gather up into national institutions the power to con-

8. Ibid., pp. 167–8.
9. Croly, *Promise of American Life*, pp. 183–5.

front them, and the responsibility "for a morally and socially desirable distribution of wealth". And in this programme he discerned the beginnings of a revolution.[10]

John Spargo, in two books, first on the principles and then on the applications of socialism, was concerned to disavow primitive notions of human equality. "Not human equality, but equality of opportunity to prevent the creation of artificial inequalities by privilege is the essence of Socialism",[11] he explained. This would hardly have been considered the *essence* of socialism by the movement's European founders, and helps to show how far even an American socialist was permeated with the ethos of equal opportunity. In a later book, Spargo made clear that he recognised inequalities of talent and denied that socialism meant equality of remuneration; equality should not be confused with uniformity. He quoted with approval Lester Frank Ward's assertion that "all men are intellectually equal in the sense that, in persons taken at random from different social classes the chances for talent or ability are the same for each class". Spargo objected to the present social system because its unequal opportunities repressed much talent and latent ability; the removal of these inequalities would result in much greater equality of intellectual equipment than actually existed.[12] Spargo's ideals might have seemed to have little in common with Croly's, yet both in their different ways wanted to return to the individual some of the control over his own life, some of the power of self-realisation, that had been lost to the corporations; and both recognised the state as the agency for the process. The more Jeffersonian Gifford Pinchot, leader in the first major American struggle for the conservation of natural resources and amenities, shared this basic commitment to the old idea of equality of opportunity, declaring that it was "the real object of our laws and institutions". It was also their moral justification; by turning away from equality of opportunity, the economic order inflicted "a bitter moral wrong".[13] Walter Weyl, also a campaigner for con-

10. Ibid., pp. 14, 23–4.

11. John Spargo, Socialism (New York, 1906), p. 236.

12. John Spargo, Applied Socialism (London and New York, 1912), pp. 171–4. The title of this book recalled Lester Frank Ward's Applied Sociology. Spargo was an English immigrant, concerned to represent socialism as compatible with American ideals.

13. Gifford Pinchot, The Fight for Conservation (New York, 1910), pp. 24, 69.

servation, which he extended to the general principles of social organisation, saw some grounds for hope in the "socialization of con-
sumption". Weyl was willing to reduce the comparative rewards of
the successful in the cause of raising the status of the lowest; much
like Spargo, he held that "What a socialised democracy demands is
an equalization, not of men, but of opportunities . . .".[14]

Like Herbert Croly, Walter Lippmann—writing later, under
Woodrow Wilson's administration—wanted to establish mastery
over the drift of the times. Like his contemporaries, he assumed a
general right to something resembling equality of opportunity,
though he was too shrewd to define it. He had before him, however,
the example of a muddled administration with incoherent social
aims. "I am for big business", Lippmann quoted Wilson as saying,
"and I am against the trusts". "That", Lippmann continued, "is a
very subtle distinction, so subtle, I suspect, that no human legislation will ever be able to make it. The distinction is this: big business
is a business that has survived competition; a trust is an arrangement
to do away with competition".[15] Wilson's desire to restore the conditions of a much freer competition, among businesses that had not
yet become giants and had not eaten up their competitors, seemed
rather to recall Andrew Jackson than to anticipate the modern state;
however his policies might have developed under the conflicting
pressures of American politics, they were interrupted by American
entry into the Great War.

The war led the federal government to assume powers for economic mobilisation which it might eventually have been obliged to
acquire for purposes of social legislation. From the point of view of
all those who, at least until that moment, had been primarily concerned to adapt the powers of government to the control of domestic
developments and for the reform of economic institutions, it was a
bitter irony that an overseas war could produce unity of purpose
and effectiveness of action greater than those called forth by the
unresolved crisis at home. Since, from this position, the war was the
wrong crisis, it could not be surprising that it led to the wrong consequences, under which almost all ideas of equality were virtually
buried for another generation, and another war.

14. Walter Weyl, *The New Democracy* (New York, 1912), p. 353.
15. Walter Lippmann, *Drift and Mastery* (New York, 1917), pp. 138–9.

Immigration and the Concept of Race

The preoccupation of most Progressive reformers with the problems of corporate capital and social class constituted a natural and
legitimate concern for any heir to the traditions of American democracy. It had, however, the concealed value of deflecting attention
from the gravest, and morally the most intolerable—if apparently
the most insoluble—of the country's problems. With attitudes ranging from helpless anxiety to virtual complicity, the reformers acceded
to the suppression of the Negro vote by the white South and the
establishment of the "color line" throughout the social institutions
of the South. Wilson, the first president of Southern upbringing since
Zachary Taylor, did nothing to disturb this settlement, and his interest in reopening opportunities for owners of small businesses did
not extend to the reassertion of a comparable obligation to the most
persecuted of American racial minorities. The attitude was general.
As Walter Weyl observed, "Even the Socialist party, which is a de-
fender of desperate causes, seems to avoid the problem".[16] But Weyl
did not think the problem would sit still, and solemnly warned his
fellow-countrymen of the dangers of indefinitely suppressing the
black race in such ways as to outrage its self-respect.[17] Inequalities
of right when defined by race were implicitly reinforced by the nation's most authoritative opinion. The Supreme Court condoned the
dual standards now increasingly practised by state governments, incidentally depriving individuals of the personal opportunity to challenge such standards by personally practising racial equality. *Plessy
v. Ferguson*,[18] while affirming in theory that governments had a duty
to ensure equal opportunities to both blacks and whites, actually left
the rights of blacks in a state of tolerated neglect. Given this doctrine
and these conditions, blacks had been offered no prospect of remedy
or hope of recovery. In the *Williams* case,[19] the Supreme Court condoned voting restrictions where the intention to exclude blacks from
the electoral system, though not acknowledged, was the whole reason
for the presence of the restrictions in the statutes. Here the court
hedged by recognising that an intent to discriminate would be in-

16. Weyl, *New Democracy*, p. 343.
17. Ibid., pp. 343–5.
18. 163 U.S. 537 (1896).
19. Williams v. Mississippi, 170 U.S. 213 (1898).

admissible; but it permitted the practice. The court lent its power to assist in the suppression of equality in education in the strikingly illustrative case of Berea College, an institution that practised racially neutral admissions and was prosecuted by the State of Kentucky. The Supreme Court avoided the constitutional question of equal rights but found it possible to agree with the state that a corporation was subject to state control. The college argued in vain that it was entitled to corporate status comparable to that on which business corporations had succeeded in defending themselves against state intervention.[20] It would take both the blacks as a group and the white egalitarians who wanted to define liberty on an individual rather than a group basis many years to regroup their forces against these shattering blows from the combined powers of racial prejudice, custom, and law; and meanwhile it was by no means certain that their position would be improved by the other aspect of the great racial and national problem posed since the late nineteenth century by mass immigration.

The responses of native white Americans, and of immigrant Americans already well settled, to the new scale of mass immigration were more varied and confused than their general prejudice against the blacks. The distinction between white and black was the clearest case of what people meant by differences of race. In popular parlance, as John Higham has observed, race meant colour.[21] The only other races of which the mass of Americans had any clear notion were the American Indians and the Orientals, and both these were special cases, local to particular geographical areas. Gradually, however, as immigrants who seemed to most Americans to be indistinguishable from one another in the 1880s began to step forward from the huddled masses to identify themselves by distinctions of appearance, language, and custom, new concepts of race began to harden in the minds of uneasy nativists. In these perceptions only the broadest outlines were clear; the more subtle personal details about immigrant character and ability remained blurred and obscure, the necessary facts being filled in by rumour and explained by preconceived ideas.

20. Morroe Berger, *Equality by Statute: The Revolution in Civil Rights* (New York, 1968), p. 84.
21. John Higham, *Send These to Me: Jews and Other Immigrants in Urban America* (New York, 1975), p. 45.

It would be quite misleading to characterise American reactions to mass immigration and the further mixture of populations as one of undiluted dismay and rising hostility. On the contrary, it was the nativists, working for restrictions, who felt that the tide was against them. Labour and its political allies exerted enough power as early as 1884 to secure the passage of a law banning contract labour—the practice by prospective employers of paying the passage of immigrant labourers to take up contracted jobs on their arrival—but after this mild success, which in any case dealt with only a small portion of the problem, union leaders in their continued fight for restrictions faced not only much inertia in the public but the positive opposition of the more politically powerful employing classes. American public opinion, as expressed for it by most of those who concerned themselves with the practical consequences of immigration, continued for many years to face Europe with a fluctuating but recurrent form of nationalistic optimism. Americans would have been required to repudiate an immense tract of their past, in which a large proportion of them were more or less distantly involved, if they were to accept the gloomy thesis that American society was incapable of absorbing foreign peoples. Even such a pro-restrictionist newspaper as The Press of Philadelphia had observed in 1888 that "The strong stomach of American civilization may, and doubtless will, digest and assimilate this unsavoury and repellent throng. . . . In time they catch the spirit of the country and form an element of decided worth".[22] The newspaper's ambiguity of feeling was highly significant because it symbolised the tension between personal sentiment and political hope; it helps to explain the prolonged nature of the difficulties in obtaining politically unified action to restrict unlimited immigration.

The "repellent throng" consisted of aliens of stocks still largely unfamiliar in the United States. Yet until the middle of the 1890s some 80 percent of all immigrants continued to come from the more traditional sources in Northwest Europe.[23] It was only for a period of some nine years beginning in 1899 that the notion of the "new immigration" corresponded with the statistical facts. During that

22. John Higham, *Strangers in the Land: Patterns of American Nativism* (New Brunswick, N.J., 1953), pp. 62–3.
23. Ibid., p. 88.

period a staggering rise in the intake from Eastern Europe and Russia's European provinces, from the Balkans, Italy, and Sicily, altered all the old perspectives of the problem. But impressions had long preceded facts, and the effect of these crowded years was to quicken older anxieties about the problem of assimilation.[24]

These anxieties were made the more acute and disturbing during the last decade of the old century because they coincided with and became part of a series of shocks to America's older and more confident nationalism. The formal information that the frontier of settlement had ceased to exist, as reported by the commissioner of the census for 1890, had an impact less significant demographically than psychologically; it removed an imagined "open" frontier of development and served as a sharp reminder that the United States must accommodate itself to the same kinds of geographical limitations as other countries. The idea that America would one day lose its unique separateness was far from new. Violent labour troubles had recently shown that the struggle between capital and labour could not be confined to the Old World merely by defining the American form of capitalism as a "free labour system". In 1882 a writer in the *Atlantic Monthly* observed that "every year brings the conditions of American labor into closer likeness to those of the Old World"— adding pessimistically that a form of American socialism was inevitable.[25] Native anxieties about the economic consequences of unrestricted immigration which began to affect organised labour early in the 1880s spread rapidly to include more general considerations of civic life and politics, and in the process became just as prominent in the minds of people dedicated to political reform as in those of self-proclaimed social or racial purists. As early as 1883 no less a reformer than Henry George perceived a dangerous connection between the closing of free land and the continuation of immigration: "Will it make our difficulty any the less that our human garbage can vote?" he asked. Five years later the American Economic Association, whose patrons were associated with measures for economic reform, offered a prize for an essay on "The Evil Effects of Unrestricted Immigration". In 1891 Samuel Gompers requested the con-

24. Ibid., pp. 158–9.
25. Higham, *Strangers*, p. 35.

vention of the newly formed American Federation of Labor to place the issue of immigration on its agenda.[26] These apprehensions were violently jolted by the panic of 1893 and the depression that followed. It now looked as though the American economy might have come to the end of its ability to process immigrant labour into the massive force that had helped its recent expansion. Owners of capital, formerly willing to draw on an unlimited pool, lost some of their confidence; a mood of restriction attained a new strength in the anxious and stricken areas of the South and West.[27]

It was idle to deny that the problem had assumed unprecedented proportions. The fact that certain people who were genuinely concerned about the future of American democracy with special reference to class structure and economic power should have been among the most anxious about the consequences of unlimited immigration does not prove that their reformism was shallow or hypocritical or that their humanity was flawed. It rather reveals the existence of a deep assumption that American civilisation had been built on foundations of a distinct, pervasive, and continuous homogeneity of national character.

This conviction, which was based on the history of the founding of the Republic, was clearly revealed in the opinions of the dominant political rivals, Theodore Roosevelt and Woodrow Wilson, who both believed that the character of American nationality was fixed in the period from 1776 to 1789. All subsequent mingling was a process of continued assimilation into the original type; the numbers might be enlarged, and the type in some respects might be enriched; but it retained its characteristic qualities in law, education, religion, in the sense of political obligation and in certain aspects of social and personal style.[28] Views of this kind were shared by the Progressive publicists. John R. Commons, a Progressive of the Wisconsin school and a historian of the labour movement, explained the problem by reference to the overwhelming importance of the fact that Americans had always possessed a common language, an instrument at hand "for conscious improvement through education and social environment". It was not physical amalgamation but mental community that

26. Ibid., pp. 35–43; 71.
27. Ibid., pp. 73–4.
28. I have elaborated this comment from a statement by Milton M. Gordon, *Assimilation in American Life* (New York, 1964), p. 122.

united mankind: "To be great a nation need not be of one blood, it must be of one mind", he declared. Commons emphasised that everyone should have "equal opportunity to make the most of himself, to come forward and achieve high standing in any calling to which he is inclined"—a fair assertion of the standard doctrine of equality of opportunity. It had its corollary: It was equally important not only that laws and institutions should generate these opportunities, but that all should be capable of participating, especially in making and enforcing the laws.[29]

The obvious question, then, which no one seriously concerned about the scale of the recent development could avoid, was whether the traditional institutions of American political, economic, and cultural life could receive the new immigrant masses without being altered in form or indeed dwarfed by sheer numbers. Both seemed to be happening in the Eastern cities. But implicit in this question was another, which, once perceived, took logical precedence, and this was whether alien candidates for admission to the status of Americans could or should be identified by specific reference to their assimilability. It was in this atmosphere and with regard to these questions that American concepts of race began to assume political forms. Proceeding from the primitive statement that Americans defined race by colour—which held true whether the users of the term were white or black, or for that matter Indian or Oriental—it would hardly go too far to say that Americans came to think of race in terms of assimilability. It followed that the higher the number of a certain race already present in the United States, the greater the likelihood that outside members of that group would find means of assimilation, and would eventually lose their racial dissimilarity.

But assimilation was not a self-defining process. To some, both immigrants and residents, it meant absorption into a more or less separate social and economic structure already formed by their racial, national, or religious predecessors; and this process was of the highest value to those who most desired to retain and preserve the customs and sometimes the religion of their group. But to others, and particularly to those who watched the process with gathering anxiety from the traditionally American standpoint, assimilation meant

29. John R. Commons, *Races and Immigrants in America* (New York, 1907), p. 20.

—or ought to mean—a loss of the earlier national identity in a course of merging into the America they already knew and wished to preserve.

After the patrician nativists, led by Henry Cabot Lodge and Charles Warren, both of Massachusetts—the former a politician who had written a life of Alexander Hamilton, and the latter a founder of the historical study of American constitutional law—had begun about 1905 to found a systematic ideology on the distinction between the "new" and the "old" immigration, it became increasingly clear that two concepts of assimilation were under discussion. The first of these was cultural and political. Foreigners could be said to be assimilated when they adopted and governed themselves by prescribed American rules of procedure, style, and manners, without subjecting those things to violent distortion. The adaptation could not be expected to be sudden; but conservative patricians shared with Progressive reformers the conviction that it had happened continuously throughout the American past, and that the safety of the Republic required that this concept should determine the extent and character of all future immigration. The second concept was racial or genetic. The racial problem logically preceded the cultural, however, because it presupposed some doubt as to whether certain physical or genetic types were inherently capable of adapting themselves in the manner prescribed.

All parties to these debates drew on certain assumptions of physical anthropology, which worked with the very loosely defined distinctions among the larger races of the world—the Caucasian, the Mongoloid, and the Negroid—but which did nothing to disabuse the popular mind of the tendency to ascribe to their racial characteristics the types of civilisation they had produced.

In the interests of intellectual clarity it should be noted that at this stage the physiological argument lost its direction. More and more minute measurements of the anatomy of physical types revealed such a plethora of variations that no strict inferences could be rationally drawn from the examples found by research. The problem that Samuel Morton had faced in an earlier generation in constructing an explanatory system on the basis of minute variations in crania, many of which were probably contained within single tribes, was appearing again in a different form. The variations that Morton found were too minute to be explained by differences in environment: Modern investigations were similarly discovering physiological varieties which undermined the supposition of a physical basis for variations in national character. Moreover, even a cursory investigation into demographic history revealed as common knowledge that the peoples of Europe and Asia had been in the process of almost continuous movement and intermixture for thousands of years; no credible explanation of history, or usable prediction of behaviour, could be based on such iconographical specimens as past or present maps of the distribution of population.

Whatever side American social analysts took, however, they were on familiar ground when they addressed themselves to the connections between physical type and cultural achievement. To nineteenth-century scientific thought there was nothing novel or surprising in the knowledge that different civilisations, some crude and undeveloped, others of high moral and technological orders—and some a mixture of each—had existed in the past, or that high civilisations had crumbled to dust. In very broad terms it was a commonplace that such civilisations could be identified by the appearance and character of their peoples. Neither was there anything especially new in the idea that evolutionary processes could be social as well as biological. During the formative years of the American Republic, European social evolutionists generally assumed that all people had innate abilities that would enable them eventually to ascend to the heights attained by Europeans and Euro-Americans—and it was with reference to this proposition that Jefferson harboured doubts as to the abilities of the Negro race.

Evolutionary beliefs actually declined in the early nineteenth century in face of a marked revival of the polygenist theory that different races had sprung from different origins—a view which early American anthropologists were slow to adopt, primarily it seems out of biblical piety rather than scientific conscience. Darwin himself assumed a monogenist origin for mankind, but his biological hypothesis owed a great deal to previous theories of social evolution, and did nothing to promote any suggestion of an idea that the past achievements or present distribution of races reflected an equality of abilities. On the contrary, in his popular work he seemed willing to adopt the view that the successes of the Anglo-Saxon peoples were attributable to racial superiority.[30] The idea that inequalities of observed achievement between the industrial and the seemingly more backward peoples had a racial basis was greatly fortified by the reception of the "biogenetic law" propounded in Germany by Ernst Haeckel, a populariser of Darwin and a considerable influence in German biological circles. Haeckel argued that each human being passed during his growth in the womb through the evolutionary phases experienced by the human race, but that certain races had been arrested or had only reached an early phase. They were thus literally "primitive" in being physiologically and psychologically closer to man's beginnings.[31] Although this theory later ceased to have any scientific standing, its influence survived much longer, and continued to be revealed in the common use of the word "primitive".

Physical anthropology amplified these views with additional information about the human body, with special emphasis on brain size and head forms. And since intellectual ability, in turn emphasising powers of abstract thought and synthesis, seemed to be inseparably associated with Western supremacy, it was not unnatural that the weighing and measuring of brains played a large part in the process. The ideas of E. B. Tyler, the English anthropologist who originated the anthropological study of culture, provide an interesting example of the set of assumptions from within which the idea of cultural anthropology was drawn. Tyler regarded European brains as more fully developed organisms than African ones; but he seems also to have thought that primitive stages of development remained like older deposits in an advanced civilisation, and he compared savages and barbarians to "what our ancestors were and our peasants still are".[32]

It was an important corollary to these prevalent views that American Progressives in general—and the same incidentally was true of their European counterparts—were decidedly not cultural relativists in the modern sense. They fully accepted the definitiveness of the evidence that Western history had established the cultural superiority

30. Charles Darwin, The Descent of Man (London, 1871), I, 179.
31. International Encyclopedia of the Social Sciences, ed. David L. Sills (New York, 1968), IV, 12; Richard Hofstadter, Social Darwinism in American Thought, 1860–1915 (Philadelphia, 1945), p. 166.
32. George Stocking, Race, Culture and Evolution (New York, 1971), p. 116 and chap. 10.

of Western man.[33] It was Western man who was now engaged in studying his neighbours in or from other continents by the concurrent techniques of physical and, increasingly, cultural anthropology. These views were easily adapted to the belief that physical type explained historical behaviour and provided predictive clues for social policy, which reflected the persistence among social scientists of the Lamarckian principle that characteristics acquired during encounters with the environment could be transmitted through the genes to succeeding generations. It was assumed that races had in fact acquired their dominant characteristics in these ways, and it seemed to follow that such characteristics might change in the future, in which case racial type was not immutably fixed, and improvement might be hoped for. But this process was so glacially gradual, the time-span of human development was now (correctly!) understood to have been so immense, that makers of American policy could hardly be expected to wait until foreign races had adapted their genes to the requirements of republican forms of government.

In the very period when these questions were opening to the explorations of the idea of the comparability of cultures, the advance of physical anthropology took a form which produced a curiously paradoxical setback for the advocates of open social policies based on the cultural adaptiveness of different ethnic groups. During the twenty years after 1890, the forgotten laws of heredity propounded in 1865 by the Austrian monk Gregor Mendel were rediscovered by new geneticists seeking confirmation of the results they had recently obtained. These publications, beginning about 1900, rapidly superseded the views of Lamarck.[34] It now appears that genetic characteristics followed interior laws of transmission that owed nothing

33. Ibid., pp. 129–30. Stocking makes this remark about Reform Darwinists, that is, social reformers who accepted Darwinian views of society but believed in working to change men's social environment for the better. It applied to political Progressives more generally, whether or not they concerned themselves with the social adaptations of Darwinian theory. In this connection, see Commons's distinction between "superior" and "inferior" races, where he believed that the Chinese, whom he regarded as superior in innate abilities, were in a backward state of civilisation. Commons, *Races and Immigrants*, p. 211.

34. Though not universally. Soviet Russian official biology under Stalin sponsored Lamarckian ideas in Lysenko's researches on cereals, and ruthlessly persecuted geneticists who rejected official doctrine. In the West scientists gradually came to reject the theory of acquired characteristics—which, however, has recently exhibited signs of renewed life. Sigmund Freud, incidentally, all his life remained a convinced Lamarckian. Review by Joseph Frank in *The*

to the organism's experience in the external world. This discovery would not affect the results of obviously complex racial mixtures, but did tend to harden the idea that physical characteristics were immutable, and provided encouragement to the development of the concept of eugenics.

The eugenics movement had about it an attractive air of benign reformism. Its sponsors had the advantage of representing precisely that level of genetically endowed and historically authorised Anglo-Saxon superiority that gave them a presumptive right to pass judgment of the qualities of other races; and if they wanted to breed out the poorer stocks and raise the population to their own standards they seemed at the worst to be combining science with self-esteem. The weakness of the movement, which in any case could hardly be expected to appeal to the representatives of ethnic inferiority, lay in its failure to supply any credible racial typology; but it did supply a core of doctrine around which racial purists could gather, and a platform from which they could address the public. As a specific programme, eugenics had no prospect of success, but as the basis for a popularised notion of white and Nordic superiority its effects multiplied long after the more scientific bases for racial selectivity had begun to crumble.[35]

Led by Charles B. Davenport and supported by the amateur zoologist Madison Grant, the eugenicists formed the Galton Society in New York in 1918 for the study of "racial anthropology" and confined the membership to native Americans who were to be anthropologically, socially, and politically "sound".[36] Since the movement was based on the assumption that racial type determined individual quality, and that some races already present in the United States were inferior to others, the implication was certainly that their rights ought to be adjusted to these differences. Whatever the law might say about equality, society must not repeat the mistake. These and related views acquired a considerable vogue after the Great War, and were represented by genetics in the persons of Lothrop Stod-

---

Times Literary Supplement, 18 July 1975. *International Encyclopedia*, ed. Sills, XIV, 403.
35. Higham, *Strangers*, pp. 149–52.
36. Stocking, *Race, Culture*, p. 289.

dard and Harry Laughlin, along with academic or amateur anthropologists and sociologists.[37]

Among these, Madison Grant attained a leading place in the literature of militant racial nostalgia with his book, *The Passing of the Great Race*, which attracted little attention when it appeared in 1916 but received much wider notice in the 1920s, when the *Saturday Evening Post* began to popularise his ideas.[38] It is significant that Grant used the rediscovered laws of Mendel to affirm the immutability of racial characteristics, and argued that, although environmental advantages could enable a race which had lived under adverse conditions to achieve its own maximum, that maximum was fixed forever by heredity and not environment. Grant was trying to rewrite world history in terms of race as others had written it in terms of religion or economics, but he seemed unaware of the problems of historical explanation and failed to establish any material connections between racial typology and historical events. For these intellectual deficiencies he compensated by very strong racial feelings, warning his fellow-countrymen against the decline of the Nordic American race in face of the swarming invasions from Eastern Europe. A mixture between a superior and an inferior, he said, always resulted in degeneration: "The cross between a white man and an Indian is an Indian; the cross between a white man and a negro is a negro; and the cross between any of the three races of Europe and a Jew is a Jew".[39] He concluded by warning Americans that altruistic ideals and maudlin sentimentalism, which had made America "an asylum for the oppressed" and which had earlier prevented the fixing of a definite American type in the middle of the nineteenth century, "are sweeping the nation toward a racial abyss".[40]

The belief that race determined character and therefore set the limits of possible attainment was encouraged by the relatively new science of applied psychology. The war gave psychologists the opportunity to apply recently invented intelligence tests to American

37. Oscar Handlin, *Race and Nationality in American Life* (Boston, 1957), pp. 176–7.
38. Higham, *Strangers*, pp. 201, 265.
39. Madison Grant, *The Passing of the Great Race* (London, 1917), XV, 11–12, 15–16.
40. Ibid., pp. 77, 228.

soldiers on a large scale. The tests continued after the war, accompanied by widely publicised findings which, despite certain refinements of technique, reported that the newer immigrants were of inferior intellectual quality to the older American stocks. William McDougall, one of the leading applied psychologists of the period, went so far as to advance a racial interpretation of history based on the results of "intelligence quotient" tests, and Carl C. Brigham, who had been engaged in arranging the evidence gathered from wartime investigations, concluded with satisfaction that "the intellectual superiority of our Nordic group over the Alpine, Mediterranean and negro groups has been demonstrated".[41] This was a view which might not have wholly pleased Madison Grant, who entertained an understandable suspicion of intellectual ability, and seemed to share with the readers of popular novels an affection for tall, fairheaded but rather obtuse heroes who were usually opposed by small, dark villains of high intelligence.[42]

The effects of the army intelligence tests were particularly damaging to Negro Americans, who through the whole history of economic, nutritional, and educational deprivation and of what may be called the deprivation of legitimate hopes, were the least equipped to meet the challenge. But this only confirmed the suspicions that so many white Americans already entertained—the suspicions first expressed by Jefferson of innate Negro disability. Yet John R. Commons showed in his own book on the racial aspects of immigration that these doubts could survive alongside more pragmatic hopes for improvement under better conditions. He showed himself thoroughly a child of the era of Reconstruction historiography dominated by the school of white supremacy when he remarked that "other races have been civilized—the negro has only been domesticated". But he did not attribute the Negro's failings to hereditary deficiencies, and readily acknowledged that "qualities of intelligence and manliness which are essential in a democracy were systematically expunged from the negro race by two hundred years of slavery". Commons believed the Negroes capable of elevation to the levels required for democratic life, but did not believe they should vote until they had proved themselves capable of the democratic qualities. He did not

41. Higham, Strangers, pp. 275–6; Stocking, Race, Culture, p. 267.
42. Grant, The Passing, p. 199.

explain how people were to prove themselves capable without taking part in political life; but he sharply reproved the Southern states for depriving them of educational opportunities, pointing out that they spent $2.21 for every Negro child where they spent $4.92 for every white child.[43]

Events springing from American development seemed to be conspiring with the outside world to maim the Negro image in the esteem of the white world. Early theories of biological evolution assumed struggles for survival against backgrounds of varying environments, but they gave no particular comfort to ideas of human equality, or of the potential for equal achievement. The explorations of Australia, Tasmania, and of the African interior, as reports reached Europe and America, had the damaging effect of connecting the Negro American with recent origins in primitive life and barbaric customs. It is no exaggeration to say, in more general terms, that the rise of industrial civilisation in Europe and North America had the conspicuous effect of widening the gap between Western civilisation and those of aboriginal peoples who were for the most part illiterate, who supplied their needs by ancestral methods, whose lives repeated themselves, and who had not yet thought of the Idea of Progress.

Then in 1898 the United States joined the imperial powers in overseas adventures. Even though the Senate soon developed a bad conscience over Cuba, the Spanish-American war gave a vital stimulus to the relatively new phenomenon of racial nationalism,[44] which entered public opinion and was quickly translated into an explanation of the situation of the Negro in America. In the light cast by all these events and developments, ideas of equality, or of equipotentiality, failed to provide either evolutionary scientists or social reformers with a plausible working hypothesis.

There was in principle no obvious reason why concepts of natural inequality should be confined to the differences between races of European and African origin. If the formative forces in national character were racial, then the direction of research must be to discover the history of the races. When American social thinkers addressed themselves to these problems they had first to confront the con-

43. Commons, *Races and Immigrants*, pp. 44–5. Commons emphasised environmental hostility as a cause of Negro backwardness. Ibid., pp. 39–62.
44. Higham, *Send These to Me*, p. 44.

siderable existing body of European writing, which claimed to have established the three dominant European races—the Nordic, the Alpine, and the Mediterranean.

William Z. Ripley, the American sociologist and economist, after combing masses of the evidence already collected, confirmed these findings for Americans in a book called *The Races of Europe*. Much of the literature that Ripley used assumed that racial type accounted for character, behaviour, and history, a view that was freely and uncritically reflected a few years later in the writings of amateurs like Madison Grant. But Ripley was not impressed by the evidence for these conclusions. His scepticism was aroused by the immense and inextricable racial mixtures that had taken place, by the utter uncertainty and inconclusiveness of the historical records when applied to the concept of race, and by the absence of any precise correlations between physical type and social behaviour on which the conventional inferences rested. After discussing matters as diverse as tendencies to divorce, artistic genius, and the proclivity to commit suicide (said to be high among Teutons), he concluded, "It is not race but physical and social environment that must be taken into account".[45]

It is a mistake to suppose that social scientists such as Ripley, Commons, or Edward A. Ross, who concerned themselves with the long-term implications of immigration, were trapped in a narrow-minded racialist determinism. The orientation of their views was cultural rather than racial, but in their firm conviction of the superiority of the values that America had maintained throughout its history, through the agencies of education and the Constitution, they saw no grounds for doubting that their own duty lay in finding means to maintain those values for the indefinite future. In their opinion that duty did not lead in the direction of making America into a replica of the racial, religious, and social complexities of the rest of the world.

Ross, another member of the contentious school of Wisconsin Progressives and an outspoken opponent of big business, put the whole question into a phrase when, after observing the continuance of population pressures in the countries from which immigration was originating, he challenged "the equal right of all races to American

45. William Z. Ripley, *The Races of Europe* (New York, 1899), p. 527.

opportunities".[46] Ross used racial designations to sustain his objections to unlimited immigration but his argument was political and cultural, not racial. Race was at the most a weak descriptive designation for groups who were difficult to define in terms of strict nationality. Although Ross can easily be quoted as making remarks which sound distinctly anti-Semitic, an attentive reading shows quite clearly that his hostility to the recent waves of Russian-Jewish immigrants was based on economic methods and social attitudes which, in common with many others, Ross disliked.[47] Ross believed that the Jews included both the finest and the worst among foreign contributions to American culture; the first wave of Russian-Jewish migrants of the 1880s he placed with "our British, Scandinavian, Teutonic . . . naturalized citizens who have benefited American politics".[48] So far was Ross from wanting to be racially exclusive that he described America as "probably the strongest solvent Jewish separatism has ever encountered" and welcomed mixed marriages as ending the distinct ethnic strain and absorbing the Jewish qualities for the benefit of the community.[49] He was much more concerned about the inability of the Irish to adapt themselves to the American idea of law. "What is the Constitution between friends?" was not an attitude that he found compatible with popular government, and he condemned the "principles of the Celtic clan" which were responsible for heavy casualties from bad water, bad housing, poor sanitation, and rampant vice in the running of American municipalities.[50] Among Slavs he found evidence of ill-treatment of women, and among a variety of immigrants he reported evidence of weak educational attainments.[51] Whatever may have been the truth of these assertions, the problem of assimilation continued to present itself as a problem of the consequences, not merely for the immigrants, but for the complexion of American culture. After two world wars, the sociologist Henry Pratt Fairchild could still in 1947, with the Ives-Quinn anti-discrimination law now on the New York statute book, ask whether democracy extended to people with widely different so-

46. Edward A. Ross, *The Old World in the New* (New York, 1914), p. 227.
47. Compare also the view of W. E. B. Du Bois, who observed that Russian Jews had seized much land on which Negroes had worked all their lives. W. E. B. Du Bois, *The Souls of Black Folk* (Chicago, 1903), pp. 126–33.
48. Ross, *Old World*, p. 263.   49. Ibid., p. 166.
50. Ibid., pp. 260–3.   51. Ibid., pp. 138–9, 267.

cial habits, customs and ideals, standards and values? These remarks, which were directed against the Jews, were once more conceived of by their author as social, not racial in the genetic sense, but on the other hand he did distinguish the Negro problem as based on racial identification.[52]

From the point of view of physical identification, many of these objections were in a sense aesthetic. When Lincoln had said that the Negro was not the "equal" of the white in colour, he meant that he liked white better than black. Ross, his attention turned to recent immigrants, was repelled by types who in his view "belonged in skins, in wattled huts at the close of the great Ice-Age. These ox-like men", he added, "are the descendants of those who *always stayed behind*".[53] Even this was a statement not about the race they represented, but the residual segment of it which had got left at the bottom. At some level, everyone believed that appearance was a guide to character. The inference that followed was that type of appearance and type of physiognomy stood for type of character.

Americans were in general not expected to doubt that the Anglo-American type was not only the best for Europe and North America, but was the standard of excellence by which all the rest of the world would be judged. Yet an alternative to this way of looking at the world had begun to develop around 1870 from the work of Edward Tyler, leading gradually to the isolation of a virtually new concept—that of "culture" in its modern anthropological sense. Tyler wrote of "Primitive Culture", a highly novel and original use of language. Franz Boas, the immigrant German Jew who settled in the United States in 1882 and who through his intellectual power and dominant if abrasive personality came to influence successive generations of anthropologists, appears to have been the first scholar before 1900 to have used the word "culture" in the plural.[54] In Boas's hands, the study of cultures became the study of each ethnologically separable group in its entirety and in its integrity; his approach assumed a fundamental respect for the values of other cultures and a profound recognition of the truth that each ethnological group possesses tech-

52. Henry Pratt Fairchild, *Race and Nationality* (New York, 1947), pp. 148–9, 162.
53. Ross, *Old World*, p. 286.
54. Stocking, *Race, Culture*, p. 69.

niques, beliefs, and language reflecting its own perceptions and experience.

Boas set forth his basic position in 1894 when he delivered an address as vice-chairman of the American Association for the Advancement of Science, and chairman of its section on anthropology. These views received much fuller statement with the appearance in 1911 of his most influential book, *The Mind of Primitive Man*, and remained the principal theme of his teaching despite various revisions. "There is no fundamental difference in the ways of thinking between primitive and civilized men", Boas argued. "A close connection between race and personality has not been established. The concept of racial type as commonly used even in scientific literature is misleading and requires a logical as well as a biological definition".[55] In 1910 Boas contributed a large section to the Report of the Congressional Committee on Immigration, known as the Dillingham Commission, in which he applied biometrics to the study of man and demonstrated the plasticity of the human organism. In tracing the physiognomical development of persons of immigrant stock, Boas found surprisingly recent changes in head forms[56] and argued that his findings suggested the emergence of an "American type" with a uniformly "American" face.

This view, which presumably offered reassurance to those who feared the disappearance of the earlier homogeneity of type, countered the prevailing idea that head form was one of the most stable indices of race.[57] It aroused immediate discussion and caused obvious consternation among racial purists. Madison Grant alluded to the theory with contempt but refrained from mentioning Boas by name.[58] But while Boas was educating the public away from ideas of racial fixity and determinism, his methods did not contribute much towards liberating the popular mind from the notion that head forms and physical structure really did matter and had something to do with what was inside. Boas's contribution was of immense impor-

---

55. Franz Boas, *The Mind of Primitive Man* (1911; rev. ed. New York, 1963), p. 8.

56. I confess, as a layman, to sharing the surprise, and cannot dismiss the possibility that this was another case of a scientific researcher finding what he was looking for.

57. Higham, *Strangers*, p. 125.   58. Grant, *The Passing*, p. 15.

tance. But he was educated in a generation dominated by ideas of physical determinism, and in contributing to the creation of the new concept of cultural anthropology he drew on materials which owed their authority to the old methods that he was trying to supersede. It was possible to attack Boas's work with arguments based on his own continued respect for measurements of the cephallic index.[59]

The educational task before the cultural anthropologists was fraught with immense political significance, for it was nothing less than that of dispelling the popular belief that the different races and peoples of the world owed positions they occupied, their technological attainments and intellectual systems, whether more or less "advanced", to inherited natural endowments, that these were unalterable, and that properly informed policies should follow directly from the knowledge of these principles. Since a surprisingly large proportion of the world's races was now represented in the United States, it was certain that domestic attitudes would be affected by the opinions that Americans held about their fellow men and women—in fact about each other. Yet there was an alternative American tradition on which to draw. American individualism, and American rejection of ideas of class and caste ran back to the ideological origins of the Republic, and provided a basis on which to confront the evolutionary doctrines that seemed to dictate policies of separatism and exclusion.

Lester Frank Ward, the extraordinary, largely self-taught social anthropologist who from the 1880s gradually compelled the academic world to listen with respect to his views, who was one of the first social thinkers to deny the social implications of evolutionary doctrines, brought to his arguments a strand of American experience that was missing from the arguments of Boas. Ward, like Boas, rejected the idea that the great differences observable among individuals and classes arose from differences of race, or class, or colour, or nationality; like Boas he maintained that there were no inborn inequalities of any kind that could of themselves prevent the equalisation of opportunity.[60] The existing inequalities between men—and between men and women—were due to circumstance, not to class or race or blood. "There is no better or nobler blood", he said; "there

59. Fairchild, *Race and Nationality*, pp. 97–103.
60. Lester Frank Ward, *Applied Sociology* (Boston, 1906), p. 95.

are no inferior peoples, only undeveloped or stunted ones. The same is true of individuals". Ward thus brought the strongest of American ideological convictions to the belief that equalisation of opportunity would bring about equalisation of intelligence.[61] Boas in his turn developed the same theme in relation to the most stubborn of domestic problems when he argued that whatever differences bodily build might tend to give to the direction of Negro activities—a somewhat uncertain question—there was no obstacle to Negro participation in American social organisation, and no evidence of racial inferiority. "We do not know of any demand made on the human body or mind in modern life", he said, "that anatomical or ethnological evidence would prove to be beyond his powers". In keeping with the spirit of comparative cultural thinking, he added that the traits of the American Negro were adequately explained on the basis of history and social status.[62]

When Ward died, in 1913, Boas had not yet reached the height of his influence, and it was far from certain that the arguments against physical and racial determinism would prevail. Boas lived to see that battle substantially won, at least in university departments of anthropology throughout the country, where by the 1920s and 1930s his pupils occupied many of the leading positions. But it would have been a flight of improbable optimism to have equated university departments with public opinion.

Among the public and in Congress the racial restrictionists after the close of the war in 1919 mounted a new and finally successful campaign against unlimited immigration. The passage of laws to control immigration should not in itself be a matter for surprise; no country is likely to continue for an indefinite period to admit all who seek access to its soil and resources. It was not immigration restriction but the population preferences incorporated into the laws that reflected the national and racial preferences that controlled political power.

By the end of the war, organised labour had been fighting for restrictions on immigration for some thirty years, opposed by em-

61. Samuel Chugerman, *Lester Frank Ward, the American Aristotle* (Durham, N.C., 1939), pp. 431, 433, 436–8.
62. Boas, *Primitive Man*, p. 240.

ployers who wanted cheap labour, by Progressives who believed in the nation's assimilative powers, and by presidents who were not prepared to commit the nation to a denial of its past. In earlier years a literacy test was intended as the instrument of exclusion, but by 1921 the revived forces of restriction were able to secure an act based on quotas of population. The act took the census of 1910 as a guide to the population structure of the country, operating on the principle that future immigration was to correspond to the proportions found in that census. The use of the census of 1910 did in fact bear witness to the surviving idea that no national group ought to be placed at an invidious disadvantage. Since that year had marked the highest tide of the "new" immigration, the restrictionists were dissatisfied with the results, and proceeded to press for far more radical revision.

After much debate in Congress, the racial restrictionists turned the critical corner by arguing that the use of the census of 1910 actually discriminated against the older American stock, giving an unfair—and unequal—advantage in favour of the new. In the Immigration Act of 1924 the principle adopted was that of the supposed national origins of the American people as they stood in the year 1890. This principle did not yield significantly different results from the use of the census of the same year; but it did take into account the long history of American immigration, and it could be defended on grounds of equity to all ingredients of the population without positively discriminating against any minority. It was with these soothing explanations that Congress passed the measure whose effects gave an immense advantage to Northwest Europe—which had still been sending a majority of immigrants in 1890. The full application of the act was not felt until 1929, but the issue rapidly subsided from its prominent place in public debate.[63]

One area in which Americans felt no need to hesitate or apologise for openly racialist feelings lay on the West Coast, America's face towards the Far East. The violent clamour against Chinese immigration, to which the federal government yielded by passing the Chinese Exclusion Act as early as 1882, had no original connection with other

63. Higham, *Stangers*, pp. 317–24; Maldwyn A. Jones, *American Immigration* (Chicago, 1960), pp. 247–77.

aspects of nativism; it was presented as a defence of white civilisation against an alien and inferior form. In 1904 the Chinese were completely excluded, a ban that was not repealed until 1943.[64] Early in the twentieth century the West Coast discovered another enemy in the Japanese, who soon made matters worse by their success as farmers. The Japanese were the chief victims of the limited Immigration Act of 1907, but a new frenzy rose against them after the Great War. Restrictionists on the European side had long felt that the "new" immigration represented types that could not assimilate into American life, and which would presumably remain as undigested lumps. But the anti-Japanese Americans, who began to make their feelings seriously known in the East and South after the war, regarded the Japanese as representing something far worse—an alternative civilisation, wholly un-American rather than merely unassimilable. This violent antipathy was reflected in the total exclusion built into the act of 1924, which clearly marked the Japanese with the Chinese as belonging to a different category from the restricted, but not excluded, Europeans. The Orientals in America experienced no refreshment from new intakes of their own kind, which in turn weakened their political position by contrast to those of European descent. The hostility continued to afflict race relations on the West Coast, growing more ominous with the rise of the Japanese military empire in the 1930s. In one sense anti-Japanese sentiment was to subject American doctrines of constitutional equality to their most severe test when the United States found itself at war with Japan in 1941.

Restrictionists of all sorts had been forced to fight hard to get their views translated into law; the struggle, they might reflect by the end of the 1920s, had taken nearly half a century. They knew very well that they had to contend not only with the fact that Henry George's "human garbage" was armed with the ballot, but with the stealthy advance of an alternative sociology. While the children of recent immigrants gained political power and economic advancement, and while the new school of cultural anthropologists took possession of the centres of learning, the fight to instruct public opinion in the refinements of racial prejudice resembled the move-

64. R. M. MacIver, *The More Perfect Union* (New York, 1948), p. 34.

ments of an army whose infantry are spreading out over the land while its intelligence services, observation posts, and communications are being stealthily taken over by the enemy's agents.

Racial egalitarians, whether they worked in politics, in the arts, or in academic departments, had to struggle to plant in the public mind the basic principle that peoples of the different races and religions present in the United States—and by a necessary extension, throughout the rest of the world—were by nature interchangeable. That was the conviction that Lester Frank Ward had expressed. It was expressed with particular confidence by the sociologist A. L. Kroeber when he affirmed in 1915 that cultural anthropology must assume the "absolute equality and identity of all races and all strains".[65] It was the conviction that gave hope and self-respect to the immigrants and their children. To win the argument it was necessary to supplant the belief that race was expressed in physical type and that physical type determined, if not the details, then certainly the limits of character and potential.

But to win this argument did not resolve the problem or satisfy the requirements of equality as interchangeability. The argument about race had always been vague; in the hands of sophisticated analysts such as Commons or Ross it was little more than a convenient short-hand. And the difficulty remained that when specific groups—the Jews, the Irish, the South Italians were prominent examples cited in most discussions—adhered among themselves through strong cohesive forces which continued to dominate their language, their economic behaviour, their religious observances, and their relations to other Americans, nativists could still object that their group characteristics made them unsuitable for assimilation into American life. The argument was not really, in the last analysis, about natural abilities; it was about group psychology and its effects on group behaviour.

As immigration and its consequences formed settled patterns in the distribution of the American population, the demographic, economic, linguistic, religious, and social realities that followed showed

65. Though Kroeber's confidence was shaken soon afterwards by the results of the army intelligence tests and his own collaboration with Lewis Terman in trying to develop a culture-free intelligence test at Stanford. Stocking, *Race, Culture*, p. 298.

very little sign of conforming to ideas of individual interchange-ability. They settled instead into complex patterns of structural and cultural pluralism.

The Pluralist Alternative

At a time when the professed enemies of human equality were so numerous among the population at large and were actually gaining ground in so many of the nation's social and intellectual centres, it might have seemed a little gratuitous that their efforts should be sup-plemented by ammunition from the other side. The Anglo-Saxonist racialists left no one in any doubt that they regarded assimilation in any form as degenerative in terms of inheritance and undesirable on grounds of social consciousness. But they did not belong to the only group to hold somewhat exclusive views of its racial inheritance.

The school of cultural anthropology that had grown to authority in comparatively recent years had a corollary in the development of cultural pluralism. Its chief early exponent was the Jewish social philosopher and early Zionist Horace Kallen, who began to expound his views on assimilation in *The Nation* in 1915. Kallen, who was as anxious to preserve the integrity of Jewish culture from the corrosive influences of the American environment as Madison Grant was to preserve the American environment from Jewish influence, had clearly been alarmed by the popularity of Israel Zangwill's famous play *The Melting Pot*.

Zangwill—who dedicated his play to Theodore Roosevelt—used the drama to expound a fusionist theory of the American social fu-ture. The idea was as old as Crèvecoeur's, but it had not played so prominent a part in American social philosophy since his day. The implications were naturally destructive to strong group identities. In opposition, Kallen held that the special duty of government in a free society, dedicated to the emancipation of human capacities, was to permit free development of the ethnic group, for the individual's happiness was "implied in ancestral endowment". Kallen's feelings were deeply affected by his sense of ancestry. "Men may change their clothes, their politics, their wives, their philosophies to a greater or lesser extent", he observed, adding with an unmistakeable air of having closed an argument, "They cannot change their grandfathers".[66]

Kallen shared with the Anglo-Saxon racialists the conviction that the influence of race was central to the individual's character and to any development of which he was capable. It is clear, moreover, that he used the concept in the more strict and physiological rather than the more loosely ethnical sense. The basic difference between those who held Kallen's views of Jewish identity and the racial anti-Semites was that they belonged to and preferred different races. Kallen collected his essays into a book which he published, apparently without receiving wide attention, in 1924;[67] but already by that time another Jewish writer had subjected his views to a searching critique.

Isaac B. Berkson argued from a standpoint which, without departing from its deep roots in Jewish consciousness and tradition, placed much fuller emphasis on individual choice. Equality of opportunity, he emphasised, must include a multiplicity of actual choices for the individual. Society must recognise the uniqueness of the individual; it must open multiple choices; and individuals must recognise their interdependence: These were the criteria for democracy. He went on to examine four possible theories of the process of assimilation into American society. The first was "Americanisation"—a total assimilation to the previously existing norm of the Anglo-Saxon "core"; the second was the melting pot. Both of these were objectionable on the ground that they called for a destruction of previous identity. He then came to Kallen's "Federation of Nationalities". This view, because it made ethnic groups basic and permanent, offended Berkson's sense of individual freedom of choice. He dismissed Kallen's assertion that men cannot change their grandfathers as a mere sophism: Grandfathers were psychological, he re-

66. Quoted by Isaac B. Berkson, *Theories of Americanization, A Critical Study with Special Reference to the Jewish Group* (New York, 1920), p. 79. See also Higham, *Send These to Me*, pp. 198–208. I have not been able to see the original articles in *The Nation*, nor have I found a copy of Kallen's *Culture and Democracy in the United States* (New York, 1924), and I rely here on the discussion and quotations in Berkson and Higham.

67. Higham, *Send These to Me*, p. 213. Higham also traces the development of pluralist values from the philosophy of William James and the "revolt against formalism", with its qualitative value on variety—an addition to Madison's political concept of multiplicity.

plied, not physical, people's memories and attitudes to their forebears could change, and in any case, by marrying outside his group,
a man could change the ancestry of his children. Berkson preferred
a fourth concept, that of community, which gave people a kind of
prior interest in their own groups, and gave these groups a limited
social and educational interest in individuals born into them, without
claims to racial or moral determinism. He regarded it as a duty of
democratic government to provide favourable conditions for the continued existence of groups with different cultural heritages and
contributions to offer to the American community.[68]

By the time Kallen's views on pluralism were collected into a symposium some forty years after his original publications, very little
remained of the early structure, although he retained his intense interest in the preservation of Jewish cultural and religious identity.[69]
By that time other studies had added more realistic information as to
the meaning of economic and educational "pluralism" as they actually affected freedom of choice in the United States. Professor R. M.
MacIver, writing shortly after the Second World War, remarked
of the consequences of anti-Semitism that the economic and educational concentrations to be found were evidence not so much of
aptitudes and interests characteristic of the Jewish group as of "the
deep fissure line that separates the group from the community". He
proceeded to analyse the effects of poverty and permanent exclusion
from opportunities of economic advancement on the Chinese, the
Mexicans, and the Negroes, described the advance of the restrictive
covenant in closing large areas of desirable land and property against
residence by undesired minorities, and suggested that the recent
trend was towards an increase in segregation, which had accentuated group tensions and disturbances. The only redeeming feature of
this ominous situation was a growing concern over racial prejudice
and an increasing resistance to it by the victimised minorities.[70]

Nevertheless, the pluralist position had two important sources of
strength. First, whether one liked it or not, it gave at the least one
intelligible account of the material facts, if not of their most desirable
implications. According to MacIver, various forms of exclusion

68. Berkson, *Americanization*, pp. 32–9, 54–5, 73–9, 88.
69. Horace M. Kallen, *Cultural Pluralism and the American Idea* (Philadelphia, 1956).
70. MacIver, *More Perfect Union*, pp. 33–5, 41–2, 43.

placed some 40 to 50 million Americans where they might feel that they were not wholly incorporated into the community.[71] When Daniel Patrick Moynihan and Nathan Glazer analysed the social structure of New York City some fifteen years later, they found a society of well-formed and clearly identified groups, known by national origin, religion, and ethnic designation. "Conceivably the fact that one's origins can become only a memory suggests the general direction of ethnic groups in the United States", they remarked. "Yet it is hard to see in the New York of the 1960s how this comes about. Time alone does not dissolve groups if they are not close to the Anglo-Saxon center".[72]

Assimilation still seemed to be defined as a disappearance of differences that divided the minorities from the Anglo-Saxon centre, and it would follow that equality in America would be measured by the success of these minorities in absorbing in their own beings the aims and characteristics of that ancient but vital core. It should be worth considering the alternative likelihood that all these different minority groups might influence one another in ways that bore little relation to the older norms. Whether that was happening in any considerable degree, it remained important to distinguish between two conditions, both of which were loosely described by these studies. The first was little short of oppression. The large numbers of various minorities mentioned by MacIver were victims of economic and educational deprivations over which they had little or no control. But under a condition of acceptable pluralism, parallel columns might rise to considerable heights without mutual interference and with a minimum of mutual exchange. In this situation, persons belonging to one or another group could reasonably expect to have opportunities within the business, educational, professional, and social structures maintained by that group.

It is this form of pluralism, structural rather than genuinely cultural, in which the main aspirations and values of American society and its political life are reflected separately in each of a variety of major vertical columns, that emerged as the dominant motif of the deeply divided American social order after the Second World War.

71. Ibid., p. 26.
72. Daniel Patrick Moynihan and Nathan Glazer, *Beyond the Melting Pot* (Cambridge, Mass., 1963), p. 20.

The Negro upper and middle classes in many respects resembled the corresponding classes of white Protestants; it was at the lower levels that cultural differences remained more acute. While Jewish society preserved its basic religious observances and certain identifying affinities, its major institutions became increasingly indistinguishable from those of other sectors of the American population. Under the aegis of the concept of America's three leading faiths, intermarriage tended to occur only between different subgroups or sects within each religious order. Shifts brought about by professional promotions and geographical movements conferring new choices on individuals have composed a picture in process of incessant alteration; yesterday's information no longer describes today's people, and if the outlines hold it is only because they are vaguely defined. There has been evidence, moreover, of the development of a comparatively new, independent class of the intellectuals and artists—a category of marginal men and women consciously emancipated from the constraints of ethnic background.[73]

It is clear that the more rigorous concept of pluralism would be hopelessly at odds with the shifting shapes to which this description is appropriate. Instead of one melting pot at least three appear to have emerged. They are defined as Protestant, Catholic, and Jewish. But many of their members are secular in opinion and almost interchangeable in style, not to mention personal appearance. The pluralism that may survive as a sociological fact in these conditions could not claim the protection of constitutional law.

Yet that was precisely the second source of strength for the older version of pluralist doctrine. Under the principles laid down by the Supreme Court in *Plessy* v. *Ferguson*, it was legitimate to conceive of equality upheld within the separate vertical structures, each of which could in theory give to every one of its members both the equal protection of the laws common to all Americans, and equal opportunity for personal advancement. Even in the case to which *Plessy* actually applied, the status of the blacks, it was quite possible to imagine that the doctrine of "separate but equal" might be converted into reality. That in fact became the official aim of many Southern states under white domination when, soon after the

73. Milton M. Gordon, *Assimilation in American Life* (New York, 1964), 67; 80–81; 105–14; 141–49 (on Kallen); 157–59; 172–73; 194–216.

end of the Second World War, they caught the scent of equality that came down on the breezes from Washington.

When President Harry Truman's Commission on Civil Rights published its report in 1947 it declared that separateness was incompatible with equality. But that pronouncement did not end the possibility of a sophisticated pluralist alternative. The report laid the large share of its emphasis on the existing inequalities of condition, listing the massive differences of tax money spent by Southern states on white and Negro education and the gross inequity of material provisions of every sort. The obvious fact was that the doctrine of separate but equal had never been carried into effect, and that conclusion alone was enough to demonstrate the true meaning of the historical doctrine. But its history was not conclusive evidence as to its constitutional logic: Harlan had warned the court that they were opening the possibility of new forms of unexpected but legally sanctioned separateness, and many such forms had been sustained and had grown in their penetration of American life for more than half a century. It is at least arguable that constitutional law could have been adapted to those circumstances. The cases through which the Supreme Court turned the Constitution against restrictive covenants and eventually against racial segregation in every form represented a profound change of policy, indicated by a handful of preceding decisions, but in no sense growing naturally or by inevitable logic from the rationale of precedent. Cultural and structural pluralism, with a pattern of officially sanctioned separate but equal institutions, was a genuine alternative; and until at least the Second World War, and in some respects for several years after, it could claim as much right to the Supreme Court's authority under the Fourteenth Amendment as could any doctrine of interchangeable individual rights.

As late as 1951, four years after the publication of the Truman Commission's influential report, To Secure These Rights, after the establishment of Truman's Fair Employment Practices Commission in 1948, and after the Democratic party had committed itself as the party of civil rights notwithstanding the entrenched opposition of its own Southern wing, the Congress included in a bill for the support of education of federal establishments a provision to respect the laws of the states in which those establishments were sited. This meant simply that federal installations in the South would operate racially segregated schools. President Truman, whose convictions on racial equality had shown some signs of following rather than preceding his party's policies and his own pronouncements, stopped the bill with a veto in which he twice linked "equal rights" with "opportunity". The direction of federal policy, at least while the Democrats remained in the executive, had by this time been firmly set. But it was not yet possible to foresee what course the Republicans might take. A Republican Congress had given signs of encouragement to segregationists, and it had to be recognised that some long-term policy along the lines suggested by the doctrine of separate but equal remained an open possibility for the American future.

For racial or ethnic separationists or, where they survived, for cultural pluralists, the problem posed by this situation was to demonstrate that the doctrine could operate without violating the meaning of equal protection. The tide of the times might be running against them, but they still had the advantages of constitutional law on their side. They had also the advantage that so much of the actual structure of American life reflected their preferences and embodied their prejudices that an unusual combination of forces would be required to bring fundamental change.

The opposite problem faced the individualist egalitarians. They had not yet demonstrated to the satisfaction of the courts or to public opinion throughout the Union the truth of their conviction that all forms of arbitrary exclusion by group identity rather than by individual qualification was a violation of the very definition of equal protection. The concept of "arbitrary" exclusion was here pinned to the practice or designating individuals by race, religion, or ethnic group; at this stage of the proceedings it seemed a rather simpler matter than it was later to appear. The search for "neutral" principles of public policy, where fairness to individuals was defined by fairness to groups, was to emerge as one of the major issues of future contention.[74]

Under the prevalent version of constitutional law, equal protection had in effect reverted to its narrower legal bounds. As Professor MacIver insisted, in two powerful works of analysis and advocacy written in the immediate post-war period, what was needed was to

74. Herbert Wechsler, "Toward Neutral Principles of Constitutional Law", *Harvard Law Review* (1959).

expand the outlook of public policy beyond merely legal equality towards equality of opportunity. Ethnic discrimination was a denial of equal access to what he called "public opportunity", meaning opportunity in those affairs and callings which it was in the province of public policy to protect. The Progressives of what now seemed a distant generation had never doubted that America was committed to equality of opportunity. This conviction had old roots in American ideology, but rather less standing as an object of constitutional law. Yet even before the Fourteenth Amendment, Mr Justice Field had taken the occasion of a test oath (which was intended to prevent ex-Confederates from entering certain professions) to give a strikingly firm statement that constitutional theory protected equality of opportunity: "The theory upon which our political institutions rests is, that all men have certain undeniable rights—that among these are life, liberty and the pursuit of happiness; and that in the pursuit of happiness all avocations, all honors, all positions are alike open to everyone, and that in the protection of these rights all are equal before the law".[75] The question after two world wars, both fought ostensibly for democracy and individual rights, was whether equality of opportunity could again be defined as one of those rights that fell within the equal protection of the laws. An answer to this vital question had been developing, with some encouragement from all branches of government, over a period of some twenty years, yet there was no point during Truman's presidency when the outcome could have been predicted with certainty.

75. Cummings v. Missouri, 4 Wall. 277, quoted by Thomas R. Adam, "Isotes, or Equality Before the Law" in Lyman Bryson et al, eds., Aspects of Human Equality (New York, 1956), 172.

Chapter Nine

Remaking the
Constitutional Environment

The Social Geology of Change

Strategy for the restoration of egalitarian principles to positions where they could exercise renewed influence on American social thought and constitutional law, whether those principles were ultimately to take the individualist or the pluralist course, was realistic to the extent that it accepted the inevitability of gradualism. But as Ralph Bunche once remarked, for those who are suffering from the deprivation of inalienable rights, gradualism can never be a sufficient remedy, because inalienable rights cannot be enjoyed posthumously.[1] And those who pursue gradualist methods are likely to lose the fruits of their patience if they fail to recognise, and seize, sudden opportunities. By the time of the Second World War, minority leaders had a generation or more of patient effort to look back on, but their future success would depend vitally on timing.

The changes which made this timing possible, although slow and intermittent, were cumulative and profound in their effects. Since the close of the nineteenth century the shifts in the structure and distribution of the components of the American population had assumed an almost geological scale and definitiveness. At that time, when the Supreme Court sanctioned racial segregation and permitted Southern states to exclude blacks from the polls, 90 percent of

1. In a lecture at Princeton University attended by the author in 1952.

[253]

American blacks lived in the South. Two great developments in national affairs effected a decisive shift from this disposition. American entry in 1917 into the Great War, though taking place when the conflict was nearly three years old, called for a wholly new mobilisation of resources; not since the Civil War had any such concentration been required, and never had the whole nation been committed to a modern war whose outcome would depend in large part not only on man and woman power but on the depth and efficiency of industrial capacity. Immigration largely came to a stop for military, not for ideological reasons; and Southern blacks began on a much larger scale than ever before their movement to the cities of the border states, the Midwest, and the Northeast where work existed for mass unskilled labour—much as it had in the recent past for the unskilled labour of European peasants. Soon after the war, the immigration laws closed the gates of American opportunity on the European masses. The continued growth of domestic industry, stimulated by the frenetic prosperity of the 1920s, could now be promoted only by further migrations of the nation's great unused pool of resources in its Southern black population. The process was to be interrupted by the Depression, to be renewed with the renewal of prosperity, and spurred on by the industrial demands of the Second World War. Over the whole span of half a century, the effect was overwhelming; by 1960 more Negroes lived in the State of New York than in any other state of the Union. Illinois's black population outnumbered those of all but four Southern states, while Pennsylvania and California each had a larger population of blacks than either South Carolina or Virginia.[2] While one incidental consequence of the migrations was to leave Southern whites in larger majorities at home, a deeper significance attached to the fact that the black presence had become a national presence, and the problem presented by race relations—usually described by whites as "the Negro problem"—had become national in its dimensions.

The problems of the economic system had become national at a somewhat earlier period. When the old capitalist system collapsed in 1929, its basic inequalities were brutally exposed; and the only equality the country knew for the next ten years or more was the

2. Alan P. Grimes, *Equality in America: Religion, Race and the Urban Majority* (New York, 1964), p. 67.

[254]

equality of misery. The historian of American immigration, Marcus Lee Hansen, commented in 1942 the New Deal would have been more difficult to achieve had it not been for the reception of Frederick Jackson Turner's theory of the American frontier, for the frontier philosophy, which Turner had helped to inculcate, reconciled many Americans to the belief that the measures taken to aid the underprivileged would restore by law an equality which had formerly been granted by the conditions of American life.[3] Yet equality was never an explicit aim of the New Deal, and Franklin Roosevelt, despite a well-known if somewhat equivocal denunciation of "economic royalists", was decidedly sparing of egalitarian rhetoric. The Depression was generally recognised as an emergency rather than an opportunity. It is a striking fact of American history that this extreme economic crisis produced so little by way of egalitarian social thought or political planning for a more egalitarian society. Despite the popularity of Marxism and the hopeful expectations of Soviet communism that many intellectuals embraced for a few years, there was more articulate concern to restore conditions of equality during the earlier Progressive era than during the New Deal. Beyond the economic recovery that it falteringly engineered, the New Deal's achievement was to introduce government as a permanent instrument of domestic policy on a national scale. The increasing commitment of Roosevelt's administration to the interests of the weak, the underprivileged, and the ethnic and economic minorities made it more likely that the power of government would one day be available as an instrument of egalitarian as well as economic recovery. But never during Roosevelt's lifetime could it be regarded as certain that even if the Democrats remained in power the federal government would become the patron of an individualist interpretation of equal rights.

When the United States entered the world war in 1917 it heard President Wilson call for a national effort that would be justified by the cause of making the world "safe for democracy". The outcome did not satisfy the claim, nor did the claim carry universal conviction. During the 1930s the world again became increasingly unsafe for democracy or for any form of individual freedom. When the na-

3. Marcus Lee Hansen, *The Immigrant in American History* (Cambridge, Mass., 1942), p. 59.

tion once again went to war in the cause of democracy in 1941, it did so after several years of education which gave it greater unity than in 1917, and with a more widely diffused certainty that the issues at stake touched intimately on American ideals.

The fundamental change in the domestic situation brought about by the Second World War was that aggrieved minorities, who had long perceived themselves as having unfulfilled claims on the moral sense of the whole nation, could now exert an unusual degree of purchase on that moral sense and make it bear on the processes of law and law-making. In this sense the war achieved more for the moral and ideological identification of American society than the New Deal had been able to do. The nation's enemies might almost be said to have done as much as its leaders to emphasise the commitments of American ideology. Racial and religious hatred, tyranny over the spiritual, intellectual, and physical liberties of all individuals and associations that failed to conform to the state's prescriptions, were fairly clear opposites to anything that Americans were willing to claim as their own inheritance. It was to be admitted that neither Nazi doctrines nor even the Allies' general objectives could lay down the details for American domestic policy, but both were potent influences in causing Americans to re-examine their own society. Victimised minorities were provoked to a newly urgent sense of the need and opportunity for remedy. In every direction the grievances calling for correction took the visible form of inequalities; in both politics and constitutional law the ground was being prepared for the reassertion of equality as practical policy. What form that reassertion took, how fully it would reach towards the establishment of equal rights as rights individually defined but public in application, and how far these would be pressed beyond the formal outlines of equality before the law, would depend on strategy, on leadership, and on timing. The possibilities inherent in the new configuration of forces and the new climate of sentiment rendered a more comprehensive definition probable; but they did not determine the outcome nor the forms that such a redefinition would take.

The wartime upsurge of egalitarian sentiment was forcefully stirred by minority interests, notably by the Jews and the blacks, the latter of whom had well-grounded reasons to be sceptical of their country's war aims. Those Negroes who regarded the whole conflict as a white man's war were among the most committed isolationists. Negroes were quick, however, to appreciate the tactical openings that the war created for them. "This is no fight merely to wear a uniform", declared *The Crisis*, a leading organ of militant Negro opinion, in December 1940. "This is a struggle for status, a struggle to take democracy off parchment and give it life".[4] Yet when America entered the war a year later the armed services maintained the same kinds of discrimination to which the blacks were drearily accustomed in civil life; but at home they were now in a better position than at any time since Reconstruction to exert their own leverage on the springs of political power. War created a different kind of crisis and a different kind of commitment than the economic disaster had done a few years earlier. Acting just in time to avert a Negro march on Washington, Roosevelt in January 1941 announced his first order establishing a Fair Employment Practices Commission. The commission's life was terminated after the war by the Eightieth Congress, elected in 1946—for which reason Truman's habit of calling it "the do-nothing Eightieth" may perhaps be considered to have been unduly flattering.

Before this time, however, and well before the end of the war, minority interests had already seized a carefully planned initiative. The promoters of this move were on stronger ground than the old Progressives after 1918; and nothing could have been more significant of the currents now stirring in American history than the difference between the prospects of domestic reform after the First World War and at the close of the Second. Reformers now had a history of gradual but cumulative constitutional cases to sustain their confidence; moreover, they represented an alliance of minority interests whose abilities, resources, and voting power were more impressive than ever before.

Equality of Opportunity: An Object of Law

Inequality was spread over the whole face of American life, but the incidents of local policy sometimes suggested specific areas where the concentration of effort might produce significant general results.

4. Richard M. Dalfiume, "The 'Forgotten Years' of the Negro Revolution", *Journal of American History*, 1968, p. 22.

One of the first to emerge in this way was that of segregated residence, and the possibilities that a national rather than purely local
set of principles might come under the cover of constitutional law
did in fact date from the earlier period, for it had been suggested as
early as 1917. In pursuit of the ultimate logic of white supremacy,
Southern states in the early twentieth century applied their powers
of domestic regulation to enforce a separation more rigorous and
more detailed than had probably ever been practised before. Such
regulations necessarily curtailed individual freedom in the use and
disposition of property. The population movements that had taken
place throughout Southern history, and especially in recent years,
had not deposited the races in clearly marked areas of residence, but
it became a purpose of segregationist policy to establish such separation by law. The issue came to a head in Louisville, Kentucky,
where an association was formed to secure a city ordinance for the
segregation of Negro housing. It was significant that the alarm now
spread beyond the immediately intended victims. Harlan had observed twenty years earlier that if whites and blacks could be lawfully separated, so too could other classes; and it is not altogether
surprising that Jews began to suspect the longer term repercussions
of the precedents being established. In 1916 the chief of the Louisville residential association went to the trouble of assuring local
Jewish leaders that no extension against their people was contemplated;[5] But if the principle were accepted it is hard to see how Jews
or any other minority could have maintained a constitutional defence of their rights. It was the blacks—the immediate victims—
who fought the issue through to the Supreme Court, which found
the problem significantly easy to decide under the Fourteenth
Amendment. Of particular interest was the court's view that the
amendment was intended to embody the rights protected by the
Civil Rights Act of 1866, an interpretation which might be expected
to extend rather than to contract the constitutional cover to which
individuals were entitled. The city ordinance clearly deprived persons affected of the power to acquire, use, and dispose freely of
property, a violation of the rights both of property and of equal pro-

5. Winston L. McIntosh, "The American Negro Faces European Immigration, 1830–1924", Cambridge University Ph.D. thesis (1970), pp. 199–200, citing
The Crisis, April 1916, May 1916.

tection which could not be defended as a legitimate exercise of police power. Mr Justice Day, in giving the opinion, emphasised the connection between group classification and individual rights with a significant quotation from an earlier case involving segregation in trains: "This argument with respect to volume of traffic" (held by the defence not to warrant the outlay required by equal accommodations) "seems to us to be without merit. It makes the constitutional right depend on the number of persons who may be discriminated against, whereas the essence of constitutional right is that it is a personal one".[6]

Campaigns were not won as easily as this. After the Supreme Court's failure to offer protection to what counsel for Louisville called "the purity of the race", lawyers and land agents devised the restrictive covenant, by which property purchasers undertook a contractual obligation not to dispose of the property to persons of certain designated classes. The apprehension of the Jewish community of Louisville proved to have been well founded, for restrictive covenants frequently operated to reserve whole neighbourhoods not only for whites but for "Caucasians". For a full generation the courts upheld these covenants and permitted them to be administered by the machinery of the state; but when the state afforded the protection of the laws to arrangements which discriminated unequally between specified classes, in ways to which the specification bore no necessary functional relationship, could it be said that all these persons enjoyed the equal protection of the laws? This was a problem of some complexity. Contracts after all are normally private arrangements, and the law which upholds their administration may be neutral as to their content; the machinery of law, for example, was technically involved in the administration of wills, through which it was normally held that private persons had an almost sacred right to make their own dispositions, and in such cases the law might be called on to protect the most idiosyncratic prejudice. But it was soon after the Second World War, with its transforming effects on attitudes to racial prejudice, that the Supreme Court looked again at the constitutional implications of restrictive private covenants. The arguments on either side were not new, and the court itself could look back to a federal precedent, for in 1892 a federal trial judge had

6. Buchanan v. Warley, 245 U.S. 50 (1917).

held that a racially restrictive covenant denied the equal protection of law to its victims. But the position taken by the Supreme Court ever since 1873 was that the Fourteenth Amendment had no power to reach beyond the state government; individuals remained free to exercise their own prejudices even when their actions required some form of official sanction—a view firmly upheld in the *Civil Rights Cases*. In the new case of *Shelley* v. *Kraemer*,[7] however, the justices looked at the problem from an alternative angle of approach. As the state itself lacked any power to limit land tenure or the occupancy of property by race, or by other inadmissible criteria, it consequently lacked the power to enforce a racial covenant that caused the legal action. It was thus established that criteria such as the desirability of keeping different races apart in the interests of peace and order, which had often been used in the past, constituted no grounds for state action under the police power. When people exercised their constitutional freedom to live where they would, it became the duty of the state to maintain order and afford equal protection to citizens to buy and sell their own property and make their own choices.

Where aggrieved minorities could collect and concentrate their forces, legislation offered the attraction of quicker and more positive results than the courts. It was in New York in 1944 that spokesmen and political sympathisers with minority interests first seized the legislative initiative. The strong bill prepared that summer proved, however, too indigestible to the legislature and had to be watered down, giving way to the Ives-Quinn Bill of 1945. This measure, which was to be famous in the annals of civil rights, provided for the establishment for the first time of a permanent state commission to maintain and enforce fair employment which, in the context of the time, meant the elimination of racial and religious discrimination in hiring, promotion, and job allocation throughout the business sector of the state's life. The bill had an exciting passage, often competing with the Allied invasion of continental Europe for space in the newspapers. It was opposed by a dignified array of public bodies, including the New York Chamber of Commerce, the West Side Association of Commerce, the Railroad Brotherhoods, and the City Park Commissioner Robert Moses. Yet nothing could have more forcibly demonstrated the profound shifts that had taken place in the social

7. 334 U.S. 1 (1948).

composition of the state, or the new configurations of political power which these shifts had brought into being, than the news that Republican strategists had begun to perceive a need to support the bill in order to regain the lost favour of minority groups. This process culminated in the intervention of the Republican governor, Thomas E. Dewey. It may be surmised that majorities of both parties in the Assembly would have liked to see the bill's teeth extracted; opposition senators went so far as to support an amendment to include the sale and rent of property under the activities covered by the bill in the hope of arousing enough opposition to get the whole measure thrown out; but Republican leaders recognised the political dangers of resisting the combination which had formed in the bill's support. The Congress of Industrial Organisations had almost made the bill its own; representatives of the Protestants, Catholics, and Jews and leaders of organised labour and of the Negroes all gave evidence at a hearing in Albany, planned by the bill's opponents, which backfired against them and virtually ensured its triumph. Eventually *The New York Times* reported, in an expression charged with profound social significance, that opposition had "crumbled today under the weight of one of the most formidable political combinations ever to appear in support of a single legislative proposal". The Assembly read the signs and passed it by the convincing majority of 109 to 32, the Senate by 49 to 6.[8]

In striving to rally public opinion through the press, the bill's supporters laid emphasis on the fundamentally American character of the right to make one's own living. References to equal justice and the Declaration of Independence made formal appearances, but the argument struck home on employment and earnings. Senator Irving M. Ives himself presided over a commission which proposed the measure in a report warning the legislature that "Social injustice always balances its books with red ink".[9] But the debates make clear that supporters, who were far from sure of success, deeply feared that if the impetus given by the war were to be lost without effective action, and if an expected post-war recession caused large-scale unemployment, the aggrieved minorities would have lost in the strug-

8. *New York Times*, February 7, 8, 12, 13, 14, 15, 16, 17, 18, 19, 21, 22, 28; March 1, 5, 1945.
9. *New York Times*, January 29, 1945.

gle and would be in a weakened position for the future. It was this danger that made the matter of timing so crucially important. But the bill's success, once achieved, was much more than a local legislative victory and more than a signal to other minority interests to press their specific claims through legislative channels. It introduced the principle that the old but neglected doctrine of equality of opportunity was a legitimate object of legislative protection.

The new commission's objectives were relatively modest. Beginning with an authority to establish procedures for the elimination of racial and religious discrimination in employment, the commission's scope and powers were periodically increased by further acts in later years. Its changes of name, from the Commission Against Discrimination to the Human Rights Commission, reflected these advancing aspirations. In the next twenty years the commission realised few of its enemies' worst fears but at the cost of failing to realise all of its sponsors' higher hopes; it chose to rely less on continuous or energetic intervention than on its own marked preference for conciliation, and fought very few cases through the courts or through the use of its own ultimate powers of enforcement. Yet after twenty years, its considerable achievements in altering the patterns of employment and housing could fairly be measured against the profound rigidity of earlier years—a rigidity whose details were largely brought to light by the commission's own reports.[10] The commission was not the only agency in the field, since city and state governments sponsored racially balanced housing and contracts. Yet a less tangible rule of measurement remained in the more subtle discriminatory practices of which minorities still complained, and most distinctly in the persistence of racial concentrations in residence. Some clearly felt that the roots of prejudice had not been unduly disturbed.

The New York commission formed a prototype for similar agencies which other states brought into existence during the next few years. As in New York, the range of duties with which they were charged was steadily extended. The processes required by the in-

10. Morroe Berger, *Equality by Statute* (New York, 1968), pp. 169–215; New York State Executive Department *Annual Report of the State Commission Against Discrimination* (1956); Jay Anders Higbee, *Development and Administration of the New York State Law against Discrimination* (University, Alabama, 1966).

vestigation of complaints, in the rectifying of grievances by persuasion or by legally binding orders, and in the keeping of records to verify patterns of employment, were inherently complex; but they also involved problems of principle, for they brought into the purview of governmental action a class of decisions which had formerly and generally been thought of as private, or at least as falling within the province of business management. The argument for the exercise of the new powers did have recourse to well-authenticated precedents, however; it was not difficult to justify the powers of the commissioners of human rights by analogy with such older agencies as those of factory inspection, and of the protection offered to members of minority groups as comparable to the kind earlier afforded to women and children in factories. The extensions of state power, which progressively involved agencies of government in responsibility for maintaining equality of access not only to employment and economic opportunity but to housing, public accommodation, and entertainment, brought about a corresponding transformation in the American concept of the obligation owed by society to its members. It was an old doctrine that government had an obligation to maintain equality of access and opportunity—not even the Supreme Court of *Plessy* v. *Ferguson* had formally renounced that view; but it was a new discovery, amounting to a new principle, that this duty imposed on government a continuous responsibility for intervention, supervision, and enforcement. Formerly the rights of aggrieved individuals had to be sought in the courts, but the establishment of permanent agencies institutionalised the new parameters of political obligation.

One ironic certainty in the situation was that state governments would never voluntarily take responsibility for all these duties. To the extent that the Constitution itself was now held to mean that all individuals were to be equally protected in an active sense, requiring government intervention to make individual rights secure, it could also be argued that another constitutional principle stood as a defensive barrier against such intervention by the federal government. This barrier was of course the federal principle itself. It was only after the Supreme Court had announced a general principle of equality in education as fundamental to constitutional law, and had followed this by a series of extensions to the other areas already covered by many Northern state laws, that federal government began to move back into the field. Tentative steps were begun under President Eisenhower's aegis. The pace quickened, not because of any government initiatives, but because of the rising expectations and the awakened consciousness of Southern blacks. The rapid rise of a new civil rights movement in the early 1960s created a tense state of insistence on one hand countered by resistance on the other. With the murder of three young civil rights workers in the State of Mississippi in the summer of 1963, these attitudes flared up into a mood of emergency that spread throughout the nation. A new civil rights bill was introduced into the House of Representatives on 20 November 1963; the Kennedy administration had begun to respond to the movement of protest. But two days later President John Kennedy was assassinated.

The young president's death produced a mood of national horror and contrition which conduced to the exceptionally rapid passage of a bill that might otherwise have encountered more formidable obstacles; there can be no doubt about the importance of the newly inaugurated President Lyndon Johnson's leadership in aiding its congressional passage. The bill became law on 2 July 1964, and brought the federal government back into the field of individual rights on a scale not seen since 1875. Its effect was to make a national responsibility of those areas of access and opportunity which many Northern state governments had in recent years built into the fabric of their policies.[11] Yet the legislative impetus was hard to sustain. Two years later a bill to add a provision for open housing to the range of federal responsibilities proved too indigestible for the Senate, the recently successful coalition of Northern Democrats and Northern Republicans dissolved, and it seemed that the impulse of the almost revolutionary movement of the previous generation had already begun to fade.[12]

It would have been much too early to say that it had begun to fade from the aspirations of the underprivileged minorities, many of whom seemed only to be beginning to catch the idea that they had

11. HR 7152. *Congressional Quarterly Almanac,* 1964, p. 338.
12. *Congressional Quarterly Almanac,* 1966, pp. 450–1.

positive claims to make from society. Certainly the chequered history of domestic policy during the ensuing few years gave faltering and uncertain hope for the full implementation of federal policies of civil rights, and hope in any case became confused by the development of conflicting opinions about the correct meaning of equality of rights—an issue that soon proved to be of serious proportions and genuine complexity. But these difficulties followed upon an advance whose scale in turn should be recognised. What had happened through executive initiatives—dating as far back as Franklin Roosevelt's executive order of 1941—and through federal legislation was a fundamental extension of responsibility for the categories of equality. The American doctrine of equality of opportunity had once belonged to the free play of economic forces, leaving to government the limited and residual role of an umpire or caretaker to ensure that the play was fair as well as free. All that had now profoundly changed. Equality of opportunity, at least in principle, was now held to be an objective of national policy, and a charge laid upon its government by the nation.

These executive policies and legislative programmes, which can be traced from the war years, did not stand alone. In the American constitutional setting such policies could hardly have survived without judicial approval. Ever since the late nineteenth century, when private businesses went to court as a means of defeating various forms of legislative regulation, and more particularly since the American Liberty League and its National Lawyers Committee took to the courts to oppose New Deal and civil rights measures, the judicial campaign had played a part in American public life quite unlike that to be found in the politics of any other country. Even when these activities are unsuccessful, court actions are sometimes regarded as a useful exercise in public education; but when they miscarry—from whichever point of view—the results can be extremely far-reaching, a point not missed by civil rights advocates who had to find some means of overturning *Plessy* v. *Ferguson*.[13]

The specific policy planning of the National Association for the

13. Jack Greenberg, *Litigation for Social Change: Methods, Limits and Role in Democracy*, Benjamin N. Cardozo lecture before the Association of the Bar of the City of New York (New York, 1974), pp. 9–11.

Advancement of Colored People dated from 1929, when a foundation called the American Fund for Public Service gave the association a grant with a view to testing in court the unequal allocation of school funds between the different races. The initial policy memorandum on which this strategy was based assumed that the doctrine of separate but equal would remain as the guiding rule for the interpretation of the Fourteenth Amendment and that the aim of the NAACP should therefore be to force the Southern states to bring their black schools up to the standards provided for the whites.[14] Thus at this stage a basic if unwilling pluralism entered into the controlling assumptions of the group who were most deeply at odds with the racial structure of American society. A long-term pursuit of this analysis might have had constitutionally different results.

Early in the 1930s, however, a group of lawyers for the NAACP, after making an exhaustive analysis of the problem, brought about a change of policy. Equality in their view could never be maintained under a system of separation, if only because school administrators could not be depended on to enforce equality in the allocation of resources. Nathan Margold, who wrote the group's report, further argued that segregation itself was "the very heart of the evils in education against which our campaign should be directed". Margold's argument was based on constitutional cases which showed that segregation had always been a synonym for inequality. The reasoning of the Supreme Court in 1886, where Chinese launderers and not Southern blacks had been the victims, provided a satisfactory precedent for Margold's strategy. Shortly afterwards, three leading NAACP lawyers brought about another shift in direction.[15] Charles Houston, William Hastie, and Thurgood Marshall decided to strike at their enemies' weakest point by challenging racial discrimination in Southern law schools—the institutions closest to the experience and interests of the justices themselves, and institutions in which the denial of equal admissions or equal facilities most obviously represented a basic denial of equal treatment for persons of similar qualifications.

14. Ibid., p. 17.
15. Ibid., pp. 17–18. For the Chinese case, Yick Wo v. Hopkins, 118 U.S. 356 (1886).

The State of Missouri provided the required target by refusing to admit a qualified Negro, Lloyd Gaines, to its law school, while offering to pay for his maintenance at the law school of another state. Gaines rejected this offer on the grounds that his own state, in refusing him admission, was depriving him of equality in the facilities offered to its citizens and thus failing to provide him equal protection. As the NAACP lawyers had anticipated, the Supreme Court had no difficulty in perceiving the character of the deprivation as a clear violation of the Fourteenth Amendment. Over the dissent of two justices, who saw clearly enough the direction that events were taking and the more distant consequences to be expected, the court handed down a strongly worded opinion by Chief Justice Hughes. The central point was that the right to a law school education was a personal right, which was quite unaffected by the fact—asserted by the state—that only a few of Gaines' race had so far sought to claim it.[16] This case was settled in 1938, and no doubt influenced other Southern states to build and equip alternative facilities; Texas tried to anticipate the trouble by founding a law school for Negroes, which the state courts held to be equal in quality to the one available for whites. This argument reached the Supreme Court in the case of *Sweatt* v. *Painter* decided in 1950.[17] The issue was more complex and its implications more subtle than in Gaines's case. The court had to establish for itself a meaning for the concept of equality in education; and later judgments were foreshadowed when, at this date, Chief Justice Vinson could already speak for a unanimous court in holding that the Negro law school was in fact inferior in its faculty, in the variety of courses offered, and further "in those qualities which are incapable of objective measurement but which make for the greatness of a law school". The justices knew whereof they spoke; such qualities included intangibles such as the reputation of the faculty, the tradition and prestige of the school itself, and the influence of its alumni. The fact of separateness was itself emerging as a substantive issue in identifying inferiority. Yet the fact of separateness was not a random effect: It was the result of one group's decision taken without consulting the wishes of the other, and this

16. Missouri ex rel. Gaines v. Canada, 305 U.S. 337 (1938).
17. 339 U.S. 629 (1950).

aspect of the case was a crucial element in the nature and effects of the decision itself. Having taken these steps the court could hardly fail to explore their deeper implications.

The judgment in *Sweatt* v. *Painter* did not fully develop its own inner implications, however. Presumably, for example, a new law school, however well equipped, would be likely to suffer some similar disadvantages compared with an old and famous one; yet suppose that some superior students were assigned to a new school on the ground that it needed this element among its intake in order to ensure high standards and make it equally attractive in the future. Such students would not be likely to succeed in the claim that they had been denied the equal protection of the law. The underlying and not fully disclosed meaning of the decision was the court's objection to the assignment of students to one school or another on inadmissible grounds—grounds of race rather than academic criteria; it was thus not only the quality of the school that counted for constitutional purposes, but the grounds of the assignment.

On the same day as the *Sweatt* decision, the Supreme Court made the direction of its thinking clear in a case of more decisive implications when it ordered the cessation of discriminatory treatment against a Negro student, McLaurin, who had already been admitted. McLaurin had testified that enforced separation within the school interfered with his studies although the education he was receiving was the same in content to that of the white students. In this case it was the effect of segregation that proved an unconstitutional denial of equal treatment.[18] The justices' collective thinking now seemed unlikely to be deflected from the course indicated, yet critical questions remained. The court had treated these cases on the merits of the evidence presented, but it had refused to go behind the fundamental doctrine of separate but equal. While *Plessy* v. *Ferguson* stood, the possibility remained that conditions which somehow satisfied the formal requirements of that judgment would be upheld. Southern states had poured their resources into building bright, new, and well-equipped black schools: and if the resources offered were effectively equal in all tangible points, if by the criteria of books, laboratories, buildings, gymnasia, and the training and abili-

18. McLaurin v. Oklahoma State Regents, 339 U.S. 637 (1950); Greenberg, *Litigation*, pp. 18–19.

ties of teachers the separate schools appeared to be equal, would the fact of separation alone constitute an unconstitutional failure of equal protection? Might not the doctrine of equality of opportunity still be maintained within a structure of pluralist institutions?

This question was at the heart of the celebrated decision of 17 May 1954 known as *Brown* v. *Board of Education*[19] or more widely as the *School Segregation Cases*. In pursuing this group of cases, which had begun five years earlier in South Carolina, the NAACP followed a continuous line of principle from the law schools to the public school system. After one round of hearings the justices sent counsel on both sides away to prepare arguments on the intentions of the framers of the Fourteenth Amendment—which in due course the court held to have been too uncertain to enter into their conclusions. Counsel for the plaintiffs, led by Thurgood Marshall, brought forward a variety of types of testimony. The facilities were shown to be tangibly unequal in certain instances, and expert evidence showed that segregated facilities were unequal in their effects and psychologically damaging; it was also argued that racial classification followed no rule of reason. But as the case advanced, the emphasis fell on the argument that segregation was unlawful because it was in the very nature of the case a manifestation of inequality. Eventually, after the appointment of Chief Justice Earl Warren—who promptly joined in the judgment and wrote the court's opinion—the court, having reviewed the course of historical events since 1896 and having taken notice of arguments based on recent research, concluded that "in the field of public education the doctrine of 'separate but equal' has no place. Separate facilities are inherently unequal".

This judgment aroused a storm of most bitter protest throughout the South. Its consequences were to prove tortuous and obscure but nonetheless profound. Long before the "deliberate speed" called for in the court's own orders had advanced the Southern schools far along a road to integration, a revival of black separatism had raised at least in some quarters the question as to whether separateness must in all circumstances be regarded as a reflection of inequality. The logical status of the word "inherently" was one of the more vulnerable points in the opinion. The characteristic of separate facilities is that of being separate, but non-identical entities are capable of

19. 347 U.S. 483 (1954).

being in other respects equal. Why, then, was this not true in the field of public education? The answer lay not in logic but in experience, which Oliver Wendell Holmes once called "the life of the law".[20] One may speculate that if mutual consultation in an atmosphere of mutual esteem had produced a plan for separate educational facilities, and if such facilities had actually been of approximately equal value, then the fact of separateness might have been regarded as one possible variation of arrangements permitted by the Fourteenth Amendment. It seems likely for practical reasons that if all these implausible circumstances had existed they would have been tolerated by the Supreme Court. But that does not make it any less important to note that such a view could survive only if classification by race were to be regarded as a permissible reason for school assignment—or for other kinds of legislative action.

Criticism of the court's opinion in *Brown* was not confined to embittered opponents of racial equality in the South. Subsequent investigations of the Southern school systems, carried out with a view to implementing the *Brown* principles, suggested an important distinction. On the one hand, the justices examined the effects of school segregation and took account of the psychological consequences of segregation; on the other, they adopted the legal premise—already implicit in earlier decisions—that race itself was an improper criterion on which to determine school assignments. Both of these premises were involved in the chief justice's reasoning without being clearly distinguished. The court was impressed by evidence, notably from Dr Kenneth Clark, that segregation had detrimental effects on the mind of the black child, and adduced these researches as grounds for reinterpreting the Constitution: "Whatever may have been the extent of psychological knowledge at the time of *Plessy* v. *Ferguson*, this finding is amply supported by modern authority. Any language in *Plessy* v. *Ferguson* contrary to this finding is rejected". The obvious inference was that race was an improper ground for separation because separation on racial grounds damaged individual members of the socially inferior race. It was undoubtedly important to establish that constitutional protection could not be extended to arrangements which resulted in systematic damage to a class of unconsenting victims, and no amount of criticism of the chief justice's

20. Oliver Wendell Holmes, Jr., *The Common Law* (Boston, 1881), p. 1.

style of reasoning should obscure that fundamental point; but in principle it is almost equally important to bear in mind that if such damage had not been proved, if for example—as argued with some force by counsel for the board of education, with some of Dr Clark's own publications in his hands—Negro children in Southern schools showed more stability than Negro children in the North, or if a representative Negro majority actually agreed to separation, in such circumstances there would still have been grounds for very grave doubt under the equal protection clause of the Fourteenth Amendment. Race has in truth become a symbol of social fortune and can in some instances be an indication of special privilege or special needs; but it cannot in itself be a criterion of an individual's educational needs—as poverty, deprivation, or for that matter exceptional abilities can, for example—and it therefore remains a constitutionally objectionable criterion for assignment.

The judgment in these cases was limited to public education. There quickly followed a series of cases in which the Supreme Court passed judgment *per curiam*, and therefore without being required to give its reasons, in which the antisegregationist principles of the *School Segregation Cases* were extended to virtually the whole range of places involving public access.[21] Reasoning which extends from public education to golf courses, bathing beaches, hotels, buses, and amusement parks could not be based exclusively on the consequences of the educational process. Chief Justice Warren had given a clue, perhaps, in writing of the damage done to children by the experience of forced separation; and the logic that controls the extension beyond school and beyond childhood is equally close to the central principles of the Fourteenth Amendment in protecting the rights of individuals against painful and humiliating treatment inflicted by virtue of an invidious classification. Once again the impropriety of the grounds of separation or exclusion became the matter of constitutional substance.

By a quirk of the Constitution, the court was obliged to look else-

---

21. Baltimore v. Dawson, 350 U.S. 877 (1955); Holmes v. Atlanta, 350 U.S. 879 (1955); Gayle v. Browder, 352 U.S. 903 U.S. 903 (1956); New Orleans Park Association v. Delige, 358 U.S. 54 (1958). Herbert Wechsler, "Towards Neutral Principles of Constitutional Law", *Harvard Law Review*, 1959; Louis H. Pollack, "Racial Discrimination and Judicial Integrity: A Reply to Professor Wechsler", *University of Pennsylvania Law Review*, CIII (1959/60), 24.

where for similar principles in the District of Columbia, to which the language of the Fourteenth Amendment does not apply. (It refers only to the states.) This oddity gave the court an opportunity for a slightly fuller statement of its own underlying principles. The chief justice declared in this case that segregation was not directed to any legitimate governmental objective but deprived Negro children of their liberties without due process of law. The court therefore despatched the case under the Fifth Amendment as a deprivation of due process—almost incidentally recognising that the benefits of equality as protected by the Fourteenth Amendment were to be experienced in the equal exercise of individual liberty.[22] The necessity imposed by this attribute of the Constitution, which made the District of Columbia subject to different jurisdiction from that of the states, thus usefully revealed a convergence between the constitutional doctrines on equality and liberty.

Once the lock of educational equality was sprung, the issue could not be confined; as Archibald Cox later remarked, "The idea of equality, once loosed, could not easily be cabined".[23] Education itself remained within the jurisdiction of the courts because the courts had in many cases to decide whether one or another plan submitted by school boards or other authorities was a legitimate application of equal protection. But the clear lines of the early decisions gave way to new complexities both of fact and principle. Twenty years after *Brown*, a largely reconstituted Supreme Court seemed through its majority to be anxious to check the further spread of constitutionally decreed egalitarianism.

A particularly contentious case arose in the city of Detroit, whose demographic history was a striking example of the major trends of recent years. Since about 1920, when the population had been largely white and largely young, the most conspicuous changes were an increase in the average age of those who lived within the city boundaries, a marked increase in the proportion of blacks, and a decrease in wealth. Among this newly black population, however, a high proportion were of child-bearing age, so that, as the younger whites moved into the suburbs and the older and poorer whites remained,

22. Bolling v. Sharpe, 347 U.S. 497 (1954).
23. Archibald Cox, "Constitutional Adjudication and the Promotion of Human Rights", *Harvard Law Review*, LXXX (1966/67), 91.

the prospects were of an increasingly heavy proportion of blacks in the inner city.

During the late 1950s the school board had attempted to separate Jewish from gentile children as well as accepting the consequences of the residential separation that tended to concentrate whites and blacks in different schools. These so-called "optional" areas were phased out in the early 1960s, though not before they had brought about noticeable results, and the attempt is worth recording as further evidence of the survival of pluralist concepts for defining individuals and prescribing their rights. The form of pluralism that survived was the simple dichotomy between everything defined as white and everything defined as black. After a generation of the population drift of blacks into the city and whites out of it, the very large proportion of black children who found themselves in all-black schools might not appear to have been victims of deliberate segregation. But the federal district judge who took the case at the local level found that the school board had provided bus transport to carry black pupils past and away from closer white schools, while with one exception the board had never transported white children into predominantly black schools. He concluded that the board's policy amounted to a deliberate creation and perpetuation of school segregation.

Judge Roth considered that these results were detrimental to Negro children and therefore amounted to an unconstitutional denial of equal protection. School districts should be drawn with the intention of avoiding, not creating, racially identifiable schools. And although he found much to praise in the board's use of advanced integrationist concepts in teaching materials, and in staff and administrative appointments, the shaping of school attendance zones on the north-to-south rather than an east-to-west orientation reflected an acceptance of the dividing lines formed by racially dominated zones of residence, which also violated the Fourteenth Amendment.

Some of these problems lay outside the city's control. Its own political boundaries no longer gave it authority over a large number of the people who lived in the suburbs but used the city. The judge did not believe that this development should be used as an instrument of unlawful policies, and held that the responsibility devolved upon the state. He therefore designed a new school district map which integrated the suburban and country schools with those of the city and achieved a racial mixture which reversed the results of the previous generation's demographic drifts, accentuated as they had been by public authorities. The judge did not intend to design new school zones as a punishment for past faults but did regard racial segregation in public schools as an evil to be corrected where possible by constitutional means.[24] But the Supreme Court rejected the view that the Constitution ordained a reversal of historical processes, declined to accept the district judge's concept of a broader base for the school system than that provided by the city boundaries, and overruled his decision.[25] While the criteria of admissible and inadmissible reasons for assignment were not interfered with, it began to emerge at least that racial mixture was not now regarded as an end in itself; separate facilities were perhaps no longer "inherently unequal". It could depend on how they came to be separate.

Race was not the only object of unequal treatment. In San Antonio, Texas, a state-sponsored school finance system gave great advantages to the rich Alamo Heights district while depriving the poor Edgehill neighbourhood of any possibility of comparable attainment. The district court held that the system amounted to discrimination on the basis of wealth, an inadmissible denial of equal protection; wealth was declared to be a constitutionally suspect ground for classification, the state having failed to show a reasonable basis for its system. The implications of this question were portentous; if unequal systems of school finance were to be held unconstitutional, reorganisations of vast scale and complexity might be expected to follow. The Supreme Court did not sustain this threat to the supremacy of the suburban classes.[26] Mr Justice Powell, for the majority, took carefully chosen narrow ground in holding that the system did not operate against any class "fairly definable as indigent or with incomes below the poverty level". The Texas system did not operate to the disadvantage of any "suspect" class—meaning a constitutionally invalid classification. Neither could he find that education constituted a "fundamental" right in a sense calling for constitutional provision and therefore equal protection. A deprivation

24. Milliken v. Bradley, 338 F. Supp. 583 (1971).
25. 418 U.S. 717 (1974).
26. San Antonio Independent School District v. Rodriguez, 411 U.S. 1 (1973).

of equal education, even if proved (which was not admitted), would therefore presumably not amount to a constitutionally inadmissible deprivation unless the denial were itself on inadmissible grounds such as race. It appeared that social or economic class was a tolerable ground for unequal allocations.

To all this Mr Justice Marshall, one of four dissenting justices, replied that the court was now engaged in a retreat from "our historic commitment to equal educational opportunity". The equal protection clause was addressed not to the question of whether the state supplied a minimal sufficiency but to the unjustifiable inequalities of state action. "It mandates nothing less than that 'all persons similarly circumstanced shall be treated alike'". And he added that it was inequality—not some notion of gross inadequacy, as the majority seemed to think—that raised the question of denial of equal protection of the law. Mr Justice White, also dissenting, observed that the Texas system provided a meaningfull option for the rich district but almost none to Edgewood and those districts with a low basis of real estate taxes for each pupil; where the property raised no funds, no real choice of spending was possible, so that the scheme of local participation, desirable in principle, worked exclusively to the advantage of those who could afford it. At all events the majority now took the view that the problem was political. The people of Texas could presumably change the system through their representatives—a course which Marshall regarded as too unlikely for serious contemplation. The court seemed, however, to be contracting the sensitive and extended boundaries of the Constitution. Frankfurter, who recognised that political decisions could be wrong without being unconstitutional, would probably have approved the retreat from the affirmative commitments of the court at the time of his death.

The Right to Vote: An Equality of Impotence

The right to vote is the ordinary citizen's most direct means of sharing in the exercise of political power. It is a paradox of formal democracy that every increase in the size of the electorate reduces the weight of each individual voter, and that universal suffrage represents the point at which the individual vote counts for the least. Nor does the vote reflect the maximum leverage that individuals may be able to exert; and the low significance of the single ballot constitutes an additional incentive to those numerous forms of group organisation and special access to centres of political decision which in fact form the rich undergrowth of practical politics.

Republican theory has not always considered the right to vote as a specific identifying mark of citizenship. Qualifications of property, age, sex, residence, have been normal attributes of the suffrage, and American states until the transforming events of the 1960s always depended for the legitimation of political consent on the implicit assumption of a considerable measure of the repudiated doctrine of virtual representation. These questions arose for discussion at intervals of social change. They were debated in the making of state and federal constitutions during and after the Revolution, and debated again whenever state constitutions had to be revised in new conventions. The Reconstruction debates reopened the whole question of the meaning of citizenship and revealed that men in highly responsible and representative positions differed widely on the question whether the right to vote was a right implicit in the very structure of politics, or whether it was a privilege conferred by the system on persons of suitable quality. These debates within a space of two years produced both the Fourteenth and the Fifteenth Amendments; the Fifteenth was intended to complete the work of enfranchising the black people, which the Fourteenth had failed to bring about; both were to prove of vital importance in establishing the principles of political equality through voting rights in the twentieth century. The Fifteenth Amendment, with its simple prohibition on voting restrictions imposed on account of race, colour, or previous condition of servitude, was a far less refined weapon than the Fourteenth with its affirmation of the right to equal protection—an indefinitely expansible concept. Since, however, the various sophistries by which Southern states denied the suffrage to Negroes were obviously intended as race barriers, the Fifteenth Amendment provided the ammunition in the opening rounds of the NAACP's long campaign.

The State of Oklahoma, which had established one of the "grandfather" clause methods of exclusion, was the first to feel the ground shake. Under an amendment to the state constitution, voters were required to show that they could read or write any section of that constitution; but loopholes were provided for those who, though failing the test of literacy, had been entitled to vote on or before 1 January 1866, or who had lived in a foreign country before that date, or were lineal descendants of such persons. All members of these subtly designated classes, of course, were whites; all those likely to be excluded were Negroes. It rested with the election officers to decide whether an applicant to vote had proved his literacy. The case reached the Supreme Court in 1915, and the court still agreed, as it had in 1898, that a state was competent to require a literacy test for voting; but the exclusive provisions were so clearly directed against Negroes that the court declared it a violation of the Fifteenth Amendment without seeing any need to look into the question of equal protection.[27]

The South had emerged from the years of counter-Reconstruction as a series of one-party states. One consequence of this situation was that since no contest occurred at the formal elections all choices were effectively made in the primaries of the Democratic party. By excluding Negroes from membership of the party, or from voting in the primaries, Southern politicians could therefore easily maintain a system of racially exclusive politics unaffected by the blow that had fallen in Oklahoma. The next step therefore was to test the constitutionality of the all-white primary. The issue was raised in Texas, where in 1927 the Supreme Court declared that this exclusion by class of a designated group of citizens constituted a violation of the equal protection clause of the Fourteenth Amendment;[28] when the state legislature attempted to continue the scheme by confiding power to determine party membership to the executive committee of the party, the court at once cut through the subterfuge. Mr Justice Cardozo in giving the judgment offered the legislature a line of escape when he observed that the power to run the party lay not in the executive committee but in the state party convention. Only three weeks later the state convention of the Texas Democrats voted to exclude nonwhites from party membership, a policy which the Supreme Court sustained three years later in *Grovey* v. *Townsend*.[29]

This decision appeared to block the lines of advance on the Southern citadels. Its defect lay hidden in the fact that it concentrated the

27. Quinn v. U.S., 238 U.S. 347 (1915).
28. Nixon v. Herndon, 273 U.S. 536 (1927).
29. Grovey v. Townsend, 295 U.S. 45 (1935).

test of constitutionality in procedure without examining the question of intention. The actual disfranchisement of a large section of the citizenry was an obviously unsatisfactory state of affairs; nor could it be reasonably claimed that the Democratic party was a strictly private club. All avenues to political position led to its doors, and it controlled the public life of the state. The court was bound sooner or later to face the question whether a primary election was a form of political closed shop. The question arose, six years after *Grovey* v. *Townsend*, in 1941—the year in which the United States entered the Second World War. *U.S.* v. *Classic*,[30] as it happened, arose from an election fraud and did not involve Negroes. The Supreme Court did at last recognise that to deprive would-be voters of the free exercise of the suffrage at a primary was to deprive them of all power to cast an effective vote; and the conclusion that this amounted to a denial of equal protection was of course of vital importance to the case the NAACP was fighting to establish. The court had disclosed a new interest in the intentions behind the law; it was no longer satisfied with arguments to the effect that the state had complied with the forms of the Constitution. The principle that emerged was that a constitutionally objectionable result could no longer be tolerated as the intended outcome of a technically permissible procedure. The NAACP read the lesson and promptly proceeded to challenge the exclusion of Negroes from primary elections; the issue reached the Supreme Court in *Smith* v. *Allwright*.[31]

Mr Justice Reed gave for the court an opinion that descended from the earlier Texas cases, and had been interrupted rather than concluded by *Grovey* v. *Townsend*. The court addressed itself firmly to the issue in that case; where the consequences of a procedure were totally at variance with constitutional principles, the consequences must be held to invalidate the procedure. It was observed that primary elections were conducted by the party under state statutory authority, and no name could appear on the ballot without having been certified by the party committee or the state convention. The opinion then adverted to fundamentals: "The United States is a constitutional democracy. Its organic law grants to all citizens the right to participate in the choice of elected officials without restric-

30. U.S. v. Classic, 313 U.S. 299 (1941).
31. 321 U.S. 649 (1944).

tion by any state because of race. . . . Constitutional rights would have little value if they could be thus indirectly denied". The appeal to past determinations was blocked: "*Grovey* v. *Townsend* is overruled". This judgment deprived the white supremacists of important legal powers, but did not provide the means of opening the Southern political system to black participation. With a determination which even the counsels of self-interest might have put to better use, even after the *Brown* decision on schools Southern legislatures persisted in devising obstacles to the participation of their black communities in the political life of their societies, with effects that could have been anticipated. The federal government was drawn back into the field of direct protection of the rights of citizens who could not obtain relief from their states.

Under the Eisenhower administration Congress took the first steps since the years of Reconstruction to make itself responsible for the right to vote. The Civil Rights Act of 1957 established a federal Civil Rights Commission, entrusted with limited powers of investigation and intervention, but produced disappointing results; a further stiffening was injected by an act of 1960 which empowered the federal government to enjoin a state, and established a federal voting referee to whom aggrieved persons might appeal.[32] Continued Southern resistance was not blunted by the arrival of a new Democratic administration, and in turn produced a sort of crisis of conscience throughout the rest of the nation which came to a climax with the dramatic march on Selma, Alabama, in the summer of 1964. President Johnson was determined not to let the initiative slip, and his leadership helped to secure the new Voting Rights Act of 1965.[33] This act did not abolish literacy tests or similar methods of selection, but it did establish machinery for placing in the attorney general's hands the power to determine whether such tests were being used as a means of racial discrimination, and to ensure that when this happened federal examiners were appointed to supervise the elections. Every phase of the electoral system was included. The new federal examiners, appointed by the Civil Service Commission, were empowered to determine an individual's qualifications to vote not only

32. Berger, *Equality by Statute*, pp. 34, 103–5; Noel T. Dowling and Gerald T. Gunther, *Cases and Materials on Constitutional Law* (Brooklyn, 1965), pp. 436, 472–8.
33. Senate 1564; HR 6400, *Congressional Quarterly Almanac*, L 1965, p. 533.

in federal, state, and local elections, but for delegates to party caucuses and state political conventions.

The whole procedure was duly tested in the courts through the objections of South Carolina.[34] When the Supreme Court, in this case and in other kindred cases held in the same term, validated the powers of Congress it cleared the way for Congressional intervention wherever the states themselves failed to afford equal protection to the rights of United States citizens. The process amounted to a reversal of the *Civil Rights Cases* of 1883, which had curtailed the powers of Congress in its attempt to provide uniform rules for the rights of citizens. Events of less portentous significance have often been given the name of revolution.

Yet these developments were far from being the culmination of the re-establishment of equal rights. Even in the crucial matter of voting, it was only by the middle of the 1960s that constitutional lawyers were grasping the fact that equality itself had emerged as the guiding principle in the dominant areas of public interest. At the same time that the voting rights issue was coming to a head with specific references to the black vote in the South, the Supreme Court was called on to consider the right to vote within the broader context of political representation.

There appears to be an elemental common sense to the assumption that when a person casts a vote in a free election he or she casts one vote: not five votes, not one-fifth or one-third of a vote. This assumption, however, has seldom corresponded to the facts as established by the actual numerical relation of voters to their elected representatives. When Thomas Jefferson wrote his *Notes on the State of Virginia* he complained of the unequal representation of counties, which gave the Tidewater an unearned superiority of voting power in the Assembly;[35] but no Virginian assembly took serious notice of this grievance for nearly another fifty years. James Wilson, an influential member of the Constitutional Convention and a justice of the Supreme Court, took advantage of his lectures at the University of Pennsylvania Law School in 1792 to explain the egalitarian basis of the principles of representation as established in

34. South Carolina v. Katzenbach, 383 U.S. 301 (1966).
35. Thomas Jefferson, *Notes on the State of Virginia*. "Query VIII: Constitution", ed. Wm. Peden (Chapel Hill, 1954), pp. 119–29.

the United States. Two things were "essentially necessary" to the "legitimate energy and weight of true representation". The first was that representatives should express the same opinions that their constituents would hold if possessed of equal information; the second was that the sentiments of representatives "should have the same weight and influence as the sentiments of the constituents would have if expressed personally". It followed that all elections ought to be equal, which Wilson explained in very clear language: "Elections are equal when a given number of citizens, in one part of the state, choose as many representatives, as are chosen by the same number of citizens, in any other part of the state. In this manner, the proportion of representatives and of the constituents will remain invariably the same".[36] The Constitution itself provided in its original form that there should be not more than thirty thousand electors to each representative in Congress, but to avoid the nonrepresentation of any thinly populated state it was also provided that each state should have at least one representative. This provision gave rise to a strong inference that electoral districts were intended to be equal in numbers, though not necessarily in other factors such as area, wealth, or tax payments. To these principles, supported by Wilson's explicit words, the Supreme Court was able to revert when confronted with the issue more than one hundred and seventy years later.

The first question to confront the court, which it grasped firmly in the leading case of *Baker* v. *Carr*,[37] was that of justiciability. Electoral districting, now coming to be called apportionment, had always been a legislative responsibility which legislators, having an interest in the outcome, had always been willing to keep in their own hands. Two of the Supreme Court justices felt deeply that the issues involved were essentially and crucially political, and lay outside the competence of the judiciary. In the view of Justices Frankfurter and Harlan—the latter a descendant of the famous dissenter of earlier years—the courts could judge the rectitude of apportionment only at the risk of entering into the details of political arrangements which ought to represent the balancing of those divergent interests whose

36. *Works of James Wilson,* ed. R. G. McCloskey (Cambridge, Mass., 1967), I, 405–6.
37. 369 U.S. 186 (1962).

very existence was the essence of political life. These were "political thickets" which the judiciary should avoid; it would be easy to enter, but not to emerge, and the court would necessarily find itself entangled in the mesh of conflicting interests and local circumstances, a party rather than a judge in the political process. Both justices took their reasoning further than this, however. Frankfurter's long and learned opinion included a disquisition of the unrepresentative character of the House of Commons in the nineteenth century, which could have fitted just as well into the opposite argument; he was on stronger ground when referring to the British Boundary Commission, which held itself free to preserve certain local peculiarities which a completely uniform system would eclipse. He also attacked the view that the principle of "equal protection" entered into the definition of American forms of representative government, pointing out that the concept itself would involve "an enquiry into the theoretic basis of government in an acceptably republican state"; this in turn would require a determination of the meaning of the Guarantee Clause of a "republican form of government"—which the Supreme Court had declined to do as long ago as 1849 in the case of *Luther* v. *Borden*. Whatever forms republican government might take, Frankfurter denied that they depended on representation "proportioned to the geographic spread of population", and the proposition that this principle established a link between the American system and "the standard of equality between man and man . . . preserved by the Fourteenth Amendment" he described as "bluntly, not true".

Mr Justice Harlan's dissent testified to the survival of a style of Whig thought that had been prominent during the Revolution, and which could have claimed almost as legitimate a place in the republican tradition as that of straight majority rule. It occurred to him that "the location within a county of some major industry may be thought to call for dilution of voting strength". Thought by whom? Not presumably by the workers whose votes were to be diluted. Yet James Madison, who had made a similar point about the voting strength of prospective cities,[38] might well have agreed with Harlan.

In America as in Britain representation grew not from a precon-

38. "Observations on Jefferson's Draft for a Constitution of Virginia", in Gaillard Hunt, ed., *Writings of Madison* (New York, 1910), V, 284–9.

ceived plan of mathematical precision but from the actual places where people lived and worked and owned property. Frankfurter and Harlan were conscious that representativeness implies a sense of affinity with the people represented, and this affinity is often achieved when local characteristics and interests cling to the local representatives, even at the cost of a certain logical clarity. The difficulty of defending this historically derived cluster of connections through a series of judicial actions lay in the unmistakable fact that the makers of electoral systems had consistently abused their authority for purposes of racial, economic, or party domination. American republican government in the mid twentieth century tolerated anomalies too gross to ignore, but which legislatures had repeatedly refused to correct. The constitution of Tennessee, whence *Baker* v. *Carr* arose, had laid down in 1910 that districts were to be recast according to the information in each decennial census; yet in fifty years this had never once been done and the people of Nashville, headed by their mayor, were grossly under-represented in a legislature dominated by more thinly populated rural areas. Comparable distortions appeared all over the political map of the United States, affecting both state and congressional representation. Granting Frankfurter's conviction that the whole issue was political by nature, and that remedy was the duty of legislatures, it would have to be conceded that few legislatures would indulge in voluntary acts of self-correction at the expense of their members' personal interests or the group interests of the areas which gained advantage from the system.

Harlan made a remark in *Baker* v. *Carr* which, whether deliberately or not, assimilated the principles of constitutional judgment on voting to those in which the courts had to decide on the legitimacy of the various forms of legislation which discriminated between social groups. "It is not the inequality alone that calls for a holding of unconstitutionality", he observed; "only if the inequality is based on an impermissible standard may this Court condemn it". Departures from strict equality in voting, and departures from strict forms of equal protection, could then be tolerated when the criteria were "permissible"; and it fell to the court to judge this question. Although Harlan and Frankfurter were outvoted, and their dissenting opinions represented the last major statement of the intellectual objections to the court's new majoritarianism, the justices were to find within surprisingly few years that there was truth in these reflections which could not be ignored.

The immediate reply, however, was simply that the standards were indeed impermissible. In the trenchant language of Chief Justice Warren, speaking for the court about inequalities in the electoral districts of Alabama,[39] they were "so obviously discriminatory, arbitrary and irrational" that a detailed test of specific factors under the federal Constitution became simply unnecessary. The chief justice's opinion in this case had at least some of the merits of a simplicity which John Marshall in his day might have appreciated. "Legislators represent people, not trees or acres", he declared. "Legislators are elected by voters, not farms or cities or economic interests. . .". And to the argument that certain interests deserved to be given additional weight, he replied that it was "inconceivable that a State law to the effect that, in counting votes for legislators, the votes for citizens in one part of the State would be multiplied by two, or five, or 10, while the votes of other persons in another area would be counted only at face value, could be constitutionally sustainable". The Constitution forbade "sophisticated as well as simple-minded modes of discrimination". He confronted the impressive body of arguments against getting involved in "political thickets and mathematical quagmires" with similarly straight speech: "Our answer is this: a denial of a constitutionally protected right requires judicial protection".

Through a series of cases involving both state government and congressional districting the court moved with great firmness of purpose to establish the principle of one person, one vote. The clear simplicity of the rule had much to commend it; it was not subject to perplexing local exceptions and variations, conferred no privileges, had no favourites. The other side to this coin was the specific weakness of the position defended by Frankfurter and Harlan: No uniform rule could be adduced in defence of the numerous cases of imbalance in the forms of representative districting historically arrived at. Malapportionment was not the result of a series of unhappy historical accidents; it reflected decisions over matters for which legislators were responsible. They should hardly have been surprised

39. Reynolds v. Sims, 377 U.S. 533 (1964).

when the judiciary at last took the whole matter out of their hands. In a sense the extremely low potential of the individual vote rendered the whole issue fictitious; in exercising the power to vote along with countless millions of others, the citizen exercised almost no power at all. That consideration, however, did not even begin to establish a case in favour of unequal voting power. A better answer might have been found to lie in such devices as the multiple transferable vote, under which voters could express their preferences, while the progressive elimination of the least popular candidates could produce a form of consensus.[40]

The strict application of the equality principle, however, did nothing to settle specific boundaries. Frankfurter had been right in his warning that the court would be drawn deeper into the details of the political process, and within a few years it was beginning to vary the principles that applied to Congress from those that determined the representation in state assemblies. It seemed that United States citizens must be more equal than state citizens;[41] congressional districts, observed Mr Justice White, were not so freighted with local interests as state ones, and where "minimal" deviations from the norm of equality occurred they did not require state justification; the burden was on the plaintiff to show that the deviation was invidious. The court now seemed willing to tolerate a variation of 10 percent between one district and another. When congressional districts were drawn so as to exclude or minimise the voting power of special minority interests, as happened in Texas, such interests could claim special protection. The interests in question were those of Negroes and Mexican-Americans, which were impaired by the device of multi-member electoral districts whose effect was to dilute the minority voting strength for the legislature. It appeared at the same time that where single-member districts were concerned, a much wider margin of tolerable error was acceptable—a move away from the mathematical purities of some important leading cases of very recent years. Three justices, Powell, Rehnquist, and Chief Justice Burger, observed that legitimate state interests could actually be violated by the use of mathematical precision. They did not, how-

40. See in general for this discussion the essays in Nelson W. Polsby, ed., *Reapportionment in the 1970s* (Berkeley, 1971).
41. Abate v. Mundt, 403 U.S. 182 (1971); White v. Regester, 412 U.S. 755 (1964).

ever, choose to depart from recent precedents, though their observations clearly indicated that the rule of mathematical equality might come up for future reconsideration.

The decisions which had most firmly applied the law of precision[42] gave no indication as to the standards by which districts might be fairly drawn. This disclosed a new and deeply disturbing if not altogether surprising paradox, for these cases were widely interpreted as a license to party managers to gerrymander the districts. The opportunity was plain: With no rule to guide or restrain them other than that of equal districts, the managers were free to resume the form of craftsmanship which had often cordoned off special groups so as to give them minimal representation, or had divided them so as to give none. The politicians of Connecticut took the view that the political parties themselves were interests entitled to representation, and in order to allow the public a fair opportunity to change its preferences, a certain number of "swing" districts were provided for in their plan. In the ensuing case of *Gaffney* v. *Cummings*,[43] in 1973, the Supreme Court reversed the District Court, which had held these arrangements to be a denial of equal protection. The superior body could not see the "political fairness" principle as a "gigantic gerrymander". Citing precedents, they repeated that a districting statute that was otherwise acceptable could be invalid if it fenced out a racial group so as to deprive them of a previously existing municipal vote; but they were disenchanted with ideas of complete political neutrality. There was in the majority opinion no such thing as politically neutral districting, because all districting was bound to produce certain groupings, whose effects must inevitably be political. "The reality", declared the court, "is that districting inevitably has and is intended to have substantial political consequences". A sharp disagreement now existed on the bench as to the possibility or desirability of neutral districting. Mr Justice Marshall, dissenting in the related case of *White* v. *Regester*, maintained that the judicial remedial process in reapportionment must be "a fastidiously neutral and objective one, free of all political considerations, and guided only by the controlling constitutional requirement of strict accuracy

42. Wells v. Rockefeller, 376 U.S. 52 (1964), Kirkpatrick v. Preisler, 394 U.S. 526 (1969).
43. 412 U.S. 735 (1973).

in representative apportionment". The majority, in *Gaffney*, regarded the concept of political neutral districting as "politically mindless".

Neutrality was one way of approaching strict political equality. Yet it was a way that put the initiative firmly in the hands of managers who knew the lie of their own political land and how to produce desired results without violating the equality of districts. To check this kind of abuse, it was necessary to depend on local knowledge—which meant the identity of the interests affected—but the use of that knowledge could not be a "neutral" act. The court would never be free from the problem of determining the actual content of permissible standards. Those standards, however, would always have to take the assumed equality of individuals as political units as a starting point, and the burden of explanation would fall on whoever chose to depart—or depart more than a few percentage points—in the direction of numerical inequality.

Equality as Neutrality: More and Less

Equality is a synonym for uniformity—not among people, but in the rights guaranteed to them by the state. In the new civil rights era the national legislature assumed the power to determine and to enforce uniform national standards. The Supreme Court anticipated legislative action by redefining the Constitution to lay down the basic principles of uniformity, but it was appropriate that Congress should make itself the agency for working out the methods and applications of what was essentially a political process. When it did so, in civil rights and voting rights measures, the court gave it the necessary blessing and confirmed that the branches of national government were in effective harmony as to the right ends of government and the appropriateness of the means employed to those ends.

It is not surprising that observers discerned a threat to the federal character of the system.[44] It was not necessary to conclude, however, that the judiciary was also arrogating excessive powers to itself; what it did, where not determining that certain types of discrimina-

44. Philip B. Kurland, "Foreword: Equal in Origin and Equal in Title to the Legislative and Executive Branches of the Government", *Harvard Law Review*, 78 (1964–65), 143–76.

tory practice were themselves unconstitutional, was to restore to the legislature the powers intended for it by those clauses of the Fourteenth and Fifteenth Amendments which specifically enabled the Congress to pass such legislation as was required to enforce them. The Constitution is neutral as to persons. It bears on individuals without distinguishing between classes; the defenders of individual equality in civil rights could reasonably contend that the constitutional prohibition against titles of ennoblement and laws of attainder created a strong presumption against any form of policy based on differences between classes of citizen or—still more—on preferences for one class over another. On the other hand legislation in its nature constantly distinguishes between different groups, frequently doing so in order to respond selectively to special needs. When women and children were made the objects of protective legislation against oppressive industrial conditions, or when Indians were provided with special geographical reserves, or when farmers, impoverished one-parent families, or oil operators became the objects of legislative solicitude, selective treatment in each case was conferred on specially designated groups. The characteristic drive of the era was towards elimination of discriminatory inequalities resulting from racial and religious prejudice—which are states of mind—and from poverty or social disadvantage. The latter may or may not be an individual's personal fault, but clearly do not alter his constitutionally given rights.

Poverty could affect the quality of justice itself. A case early in the Warren era revealed that state laws required convicted prisoners to pay for trial transcripts needed for their appeals. Being unable to pay, a prisoner in Illinois was denied right to appeal. This, said the Supreme Court,[45] violated both due process of law and equal protection. Mr Justice Douglas quoted Leviticus: "Ye shall do no unrighteousness in judgment: thou salt not respect the person of the poor, nor honour the person of the mighty: but in righteousness shalt thou judge thy neighbour". And he reached a little less further back to Magna Carta, in which the king avowed, "To no one will we sell, to no one will we refuse, or delay, right or justice". Notwithstanding these formidable precedents, Mr Justice Frankfurter, while concurring, rather deflatingly insisted that the court was establishing a new

45. Griffin v. Illinois, 351 U.S. 12 (1955).

rule of law for the United States. A few years later another case revealed that in Florida only defendants charged with capital offences
were entitled to free counsel. The Supreme Court held[46] that the
Sixth Amendment—which does guarantee the right to counsel
in all criminal prosecutions—was obligatory on the states through
the Fourteenth Amendment. These cases went some way to redeem
the promise carved over the entrance to the Supreme Court building,
EQUAL JUSTICE UNDER LAW, and to give practical meaning to
the ancient concept of equality before the law, a fundamental premise of the American Revolution.

It was more difficult to determine rules for cases arising from
social prejudices because these prejudices were so often present in
the mental habits, the education, and the economic structure of the
community. Yet once the Supreme Court had perceived the general
objective of an unprejudiced, nondiscriminatory society, it tended
to sweep details aside and to strike down whatever local attitudes
supported prejudice, whenever—as often happened—those attitudes
had the support of law or the least connection with local authorities.
Some justices went further, for when black students were ejected
from a restaurant in Baltimore in which they had staged a sit-in,
Chief Justice Warren and Mr Justice Goldberg stated that the federal
Constitution guaranteed to all Americans the right to be treated as
equal members of the community with respect to public accommodation; they thought the State of Maryland had failed to protect the
petitioners' constitutional right and had prosecuted them for attempt-
ing to exercise it. Since Maryland had lately passed an equal accommodation law, the case was returned to the State Supreme Court.[47]

The Bill of Rights was changing in character. In all its previous
history it had been a negative, defensive instrument, protecting the
individual against the encroachments by the powers of government;
but now it had become an instrument of action, commanding governments to intervene against the institutional forms taken by private
or social prejudice. It now became the state's duty to eliminate inequalities even where the state had not imposed them.

Yet in another connection the Warren Court inflicted a startling
defeat on the general character of its own policies. The laws of Vir-

46. Gideon v. Wainwright, 372 U.S. 335 (1963).
47. Bell v. Maryland, 378 U.S. 226 (1964).

ginia forbade certain classes of inter-racial marriage. In 1956—perhaps because the justices felt excessively defensive about the storm they had already aroused in the South—the Court upheld this rule by dismissing an appeal from the Virginia courts.[48] This decision can only be considered an aberration from the court's own central line of judgment. It was no more true in 1956 than in 1883 to argue that members of different races were treated equally when a prohibition affected them both alike; individuals, not races, were the proper subjects of constitutional protection, and when individuals were so defined because of their race as to be prevented from exercising a free personal choice, those particular individuals were not equally treated. The problem was to discover permissible standards of legislative categorisation and to strike down the use of irrational or arbitrary standards. The court was not generally inclined during this era to recognise race as a permissible standard except in such cases as required special help to correct the effects of past wrongs, and reversed itself a few years later when it invalidated Virginia's anti-miscegenation law as a violation of equal protection and due process; the right to be married was now held to be a basic civil right.[49]

The Supreme Court, however, had not clearly passed the most severe test of the principle of constitutional neutrality. For the United States, the Second World War began in the Pacific with Japan's attack on Pearl Harbor. The large Japanese-American population on the West Coast, long the object of bitter economic rivalry and racial resentment, was at once suspected of disloyalty; and the commanding officer of the region, General DeWitt, issued orders to exclude them from certain sensitive areas. These orders excluded a Mr Korematsu from living in his own home, and after declining to comply with them, he was arrested; he took his case as far as the Supreme Court.[50] It should be noted that as a United States citizen he could not be classified as an enemy alien. Mr Justice Black began the court's opinion with a firm tone covering an ambiguous opinion: "Pressing public necessity may sometimes justify such restrictions; racial antagonism never can". Real military dangers were discerned, and the

48. Naim v. Ham Say Naim, 197 Va. 80; 350 U.S. 985 (1956).
49. Loring v. Virginia, 388 U.S. 1 (1967).
50. Korematsu v. U.S., 323 U.S. 214 (1944).

majority had no doubt of the general's right to take whatever steps he deemed necessary to protect the territorial integrity of the country. The difficulty, however, was that the "pressing public necessity" was perceived in the light cast by "racial antagonism". General De-Witt's own final report on the evacuation from the Pacific Coast spoke of the Japanese as an "enemy race" and of all persons of Japanese descent as "subversive". No reliable evidence was cited to support these views, but much light was thrown on local attitudes by Austin E. Anson, managing secretary of the Salinas Vegetable Grower-Shipper Association: "We're charged with wanting to get rid of the Japs for selfish reasons", he said. "We do. It's a question of whether the white man lives on the Pacific Coast or the brown man. They came into this valley to work, and they have stayed to take over. . . . They undersell the white man in the markets. . . . We don't want them back when the war ends, either".[51] The dissent of Justices Roberts, Murphy, and Jackson made quite clear that military necessity was not the only principle which the court's constitutional duties required it to consider. Roberts, admitting that he might have agreed if the facts required it, denied that an emergency had existed and observed that the government record distorted the facts disclosed, which were among others that Korematsu had been required to leave his home. Murphy perceived an obvious case of racial discrimination and quoted the evidence just mentioned. Jackson drew attention to the constitutional rule against attainder of treason working "corruption of blood, or forfeiture except during the life of the person attainted". Korematsu had not been attainted, except in plainly unconstitutional sense that his ancestry aroused in white Americans an unfounded suspicion of disloyalty. It was nevertheless an uncomfortable fact that in a previous case the Supreme Court had permitted a curfew on racial grounds, which in principle was certainly an act of racial discrimination, even if its effects were comparatively light. If however they had stood their ground at that point, the subsequent more serious case would have been much clearer. The outcome was that in the definitive case of its kind the United States was left with a ruling that did not, in all possible circumstances, eliminate race as a "permissible" subject of discriminatory action.

War certainly makes hard cases. The reasoning of the court ma-

51. These remarks are quoted in the court record, ibid., 236, 239.

jority in the Japanese-American cases was more consistent with those emergency circumstances in which the rule of law is temporarily laid aside, to be resumed and injustices redressed after the emergency has passed, than with the obvious requirements of equal protection. That might have been a wiser judicial course than to uphold the dubious pretense that everything known of the behaviour of the Japanese-Americans caused legitimate fears of treason. The court in any case rejected the notion that racial prejudice could be a legitimate cause of discriminatory action in itself and chose the view that the restrictions rested on other grounds.

The treatment of the Japanese-Americans was out of character with the surrounding and ensuing cases that involved other American minorities. Once the idea of equality was out of its box again, it multiplied and divided like the sorcerer's apprentice's broom. The period that followed the close of the Second World War was marked by a succession of epoch-making events—the Ives-Quinn Act in New York and its successors there and elsewhere; the *School Segregation Cases*; federal legislation on civil rights and voting; the Supreme Court's decisions on representation. These were not isolated events. They were elements in a great and increasingly unified historical process. But the process was made by the efforts of men and women and the unity itself was an artifact, not an affair of the spirit. Each of these events gave rise to new problems and in many cases to new divisions of purpose and opinion in both practice and interpretation. The pursuit of equality was the pursuit of an illusion, because equality was a complex concept and not a simple or single goal. The mere fact of occupying new and higher ground in the pursuit changed the perspective of the viewer. The concept of equality, once unfolded, was a source of intense gratification, challenge, and excitement, but it was found also to be full of variations, or proliferating rewards and deceits.

Chapter Ten

Sex: Where Equality Is Not Identity

The Discovery of Woman

The advance of equality as a principle of constitutional law has been based in the United States as in other Western countries on the precept of legal and moral individualism. The individual, being of full age and sound mind, is held to be accountable and responsible for his, or her own conduct, and it is each individual who is entitled to claim the full and unalienable rights of man. The individualist principle dissociates people from the context of family, religion, class, or race and when linked with the idea of equality in the most affirmative sense—a sense widely accepted throughout a large part of American history—it assumes the co-ordinate principle of interchangeability.

The interchangeability principle in turn means simply that, if the requisite training and experience were given—which for reasons of social history, oppression, and privilege has not usually been the case—a white and a black, a Protestant and a Roman Catholic, a Jew and a gentile, as well as a peasant and a nobleman, could take each others' places in work, in sport, in intellectual discourse, and in the respect their personal bearing could command from others. To state the idea in its own most emphatic form is to risk reducing it to ridicule. A member of the landed nobility who was really interchangeable with a peasant would presumably not wear his robes with the as-

surance appropriate to his rank, while members of profoundly differing religions are the recipients of training and indoctrination that
really control many of their convictions and attitudes. The moral
choices confronting medical practitioners of the Roman Catholic
faith under liberal abortion laws, and the question whether doctors
who are conscientiously bound to refuse abortions should hold appointments which give them the power to do so, are painful but real
and recent cases of the difficulty of applying the interchangeability
principle in a society of mixed views. Such dilemmas are not resolved merely by the exercise of tolerance or respect for the views
of others: Each side feels bound by moral imperatives, and the imperatives are sometimes opposites.

Yet it is something very close to the interchangeability principle
that has inspired generations of Americans to hold faith with their
society and their country. Ideas of the permanent and definitive character of social class were rejected earlier in America than elsewhere;
but it was only after social class and inherited rank had been repudiated as criteria of merit or as qualifications for advancement that
Americans began to discover the existence of other socially defining
categories—though in some cases the occupants of these categories
had already expressed their dissatisfaction a little earlier.

Race and religion were the broadest and most familiar of these
social determinants. The fact that a man was of a certain race or
religion did not determine his inherent abilities, but it was often
enough to determine the attitudes he would encounter or the opportunities he would enjoy. The founders of the Republic were aware
that some of these distinctions raised problems of principle, though
they were divided in their opinions as to what should be done; many
of their successors regarded them as matters of momentous gravity.
Yet these early generations were almost entirely oblivious to the idea
that sexual equality might deserve similar consideration. Even after
early feminists had begun to stir the question, male reformers generally refused to assimilate sexual equality into the other categories
that occupied their attention, and this refusal proved to be particularly stubborn and enduring.

After the more extensive versions of egalitarian doctrine had been
translated into public policy, and the right to pursue happiness
had been generally conceded to all individuals of either sex—a

development which cannot be dated before the mid twentieth century—the actual equality of the sexes still tended to elude the kind
of classification required by the principle of interchangeability. The
reasons for this persistence, though rooted in biology, were reflected
in the mirror of social custom. The claim to interchangeability was
not one that men of any colour or religion would in all respects wish
to make about women, or women about men. There is nothing in the
biological nature of masculinity that distinguishes its possessors as
capable of tasks that lie beyond the powers of women. The sexes
indeed are not biological opposites; it is a commonplace of physiology that all the intermediate stages occur on the spectrum between
male and female. But experience and experiment were required to
demonstrate that when women were properly trained, socially encouraged, and acting from choice, they could in fact operate inter-
changeably with men in all those walks of life to which men had
traditionally been called.

It would be absurd to suppose that the existence of these subtle
gradations between the sexes diminishes the importance of the obvious differences. As American society has moved, irregularly and
at intervals, towards equality of opportunity and of choice, the emotional and symbolic significance of these differences has greatly ex-
aggerated their biological reality, and the movement has exposed the
acute and not fully resolved tension between demands for accommodation to the biological differences between the sexes on the one
hand, and the insistence of more radical feminists that sexual differences are entirely without physiological or practical significance.

The vulnerable and often reiterated case against female equality
rested on assumptions which in turn were derived from analogies
with other forms of inequality. As with racial inequality, the sexual
form had a biological basis; and again as with certain forms of racial
inequality, it was supported by a record of contrasting types of
achievement. Nothing was more familiar in the rhetoric of white
supremacy than the argument that Africans, in Africa, had not produced the Mediterranean or European types of civilisation and had
not reduced language to written forms. Races or similar genetic types
much less strongly contrasted than Africans and Europeans, such as
the Nordic and the Mediterranean, or the Jews and the gentiles—
examples can be multiplied—were also commonly held to owe not

only their different appearances but their different achievements to genetic distinctions. Beliefs of this kind grew more pronounced and more widely diffused in the middle and later nineteenth century with the development of the early stages of a racial anthropology. American investigators had become interested in the American aborigines perhaps before they began to think systematically about Africans, and in the cases of American Indians, Africans, and Australian aborigines, white investigators extrapolated from measurements of heads, jawbones, and skeletons to the moral and intellectual powers of the persons who possessed these attributes. And it was true, though not in any significant sense for the genetic reasons to which they attributed them, that white investigators could also observe and build their theories on sharply contrasting records of historical performance.

The case of women, though seldom expounded in explicit detail, was based on analogous connections of assumption and achievement, and in both instances, biological structure, genetics, and the chemistry of the body were held to yield definitive explanations of the differences. White and almost invariably male authorities, including theologians, law-makers, moralists, and psychoanalysts satisfied themselves with the aid of almost no investigation that the elemental differences between male and female established precisely that superiority on which their own authority was based. For whatever reasons, such authorities could point to a contrasting record of achievement, and it was not until the twentieth century that more than the merest handful of sceptics or malcontents declined to draw what seemed the commonsense conclusions from the fact that there were female saints, but no female theologians, that there was female intuition, but no female philosopher, female musicians but few female composers, no female Rembrandt but innumerable nineteenth-century lady colourists. Men—and women—who extrapolated from the biological facts of child-bearing, lactation, comparative size and strength, and related characteristics to the entire range of abilities and qualities attributed or denied to the female sex were thus using a method that was strikingly analagous to that employed in making biological race distinctions. The physiological comparison was false, since women and men of similar genetic types derive their genes from the same pool, while it is differences in genetic pools that remain the only viable basis for the notion of race; but the supposed types of inferiority were closely comparable.

In their struggle to establish equality of potential achievement, women actually stood at a disadvantage when compared with members of the non-European races. According to Genesis, all men and women were descended from a single pair, and from the point of view of a geographically Eurocentric theology it remained necessary to conceive of dark-skinned peoples as deviants from the original norm, not as descendants from a separate and perhaps inferior creation. But it was also according to Genesis that God created Man in his own likeness, afterwards creating Woman as Man's companion and helpmeet. Scriptural language even suggested that the female sex had no place in the original of God's plan, but occurred to him only as an afterthought—a possibility that raised problems about Man's having been originally provided with equipment for procreation. However that might be, records written by men reflected the laws made and customs perpetuated by them, through all of which women were relegated to inferior positions, inferior education, inferior expectations, inferior rights, and unequal esteem. Milton, a contemporary of the early generations of Puritan settlers in America, made matters quite clear in *Paradise Lost* when he assigned the relative theological standing of Adam and Eve:

Hee for God only, shee for God in him.[1]

Ancient Greeks of the male sex had discussed the question whether women had souls, which Christians later did resolve in their favour; that neither men nor women had souls was a form of equalisation

---

1. *Paradise Lost*, IV, 299. Milton was keenly aware of the psychological dimension of equality of esteem. See Eve, as quoted on the fly-leaf of this book (*Paradise Lost*, IX, 816–25). Mr John Hollander has pointed out to me that this is the first appearance in English of the phrase "more equal". Milton was also aware of the importance of equality of esteem as a force in revolutionary politics:

Is this the Region, this the Soil, the Clime,
Said then the lost Arch Angel, this the seat
That we must change for Heav'n, this mournful gloom
For that celestial light? Be it so, since hee
Who now is Sovran can dispose and bid
What shall be right: fardest from him is best
Whom reason hath equald, force hath made supream
Above his equals.
Paradise Lost, I, 242–49.

[297]

arrived at by still later and more secular thinkers. Throughout the ages of subordination, men occasionally showed glimpses of awareness that women were not wholly satisfied with the humble positions and moderate talents ascribed to them by the prevalent, male-dominated social order. A knight who, if we are to believe the record, risked his life to win a princess's hand at King Arthur's court by telling what women really wanted, revealed the underlying masculine fear that equality would be only the first stage of the women's movement. Speaking (as later transpired) under female instruction, he asserted,

> Women desiren to have sovereinetee
> As well over hir housbond as hir love,
> And for to be in maistrie him above.[2]

He thus won the hand of an old hag who, being given the last word, promptly transformed herself into a beautiful princess and—moreover—promised to be faithful.

The aims, laws, and customs that accompanied English colonisation of North America contained nothing that could be expected to upset the established superiority of men in civic and political life. It was only among the Quakers, who had faith in the intimate and direct relationship between God and the individual soul, that women were regarded as equal to men. When the Awakening shook established society in and after 1740, the new-light sects also recognised the immediacy of this relationship and women took active parts in their congregations; but even they did not admit women to the ministry. American circumstances of settlement, farming, and domestic economy naturally resulted in a more sharing of labour than in an older, more stable—and a more prosperous—economic system, and women revealed themselves as capable managers and sometimes as businesswomen during the long processes of colonial development. At one period shortly before the Revolution, the *Virginia Gazette*, the Old Dominion's only newspaper, was owned and printed by a woman, Clementina Rind. But in those years, William Blackstone's *Commentaries on the Laws of England*, first published in 1765, began to make its way into American libraries, through which it reached the courts, and was to have a profound and prolonged effect on

2. Chaucer, *The Wife of Bath's Tale.*

American practice. The colonies made no claim to depart from English common law principles, and were not allowed to pass laws repugnant to those of England, so it would be speculative to suggest that they might have developed on lines that recognised a greater degree of female autonomy; but Blackstone's great work gave them a massive, authoritative, and comprehensive codification of the common law, which was to survive American independence and become the most basic of American legal textbooks for at least a further lifetime. Under the common law, an unmarried woman had great independence and complete control of her own property; but the key to the law of marriage was conveyed in one phrase—that "husband and wife are as one, and that one is the husband".[3] A married woman surrendered all her property to her husband, to whom she became in almost every sense a complete legal subordinate.

The code had the virtue of a certain symmetry. The husband, having assumed legal control, also undertook the burden of providing for his wife and children; the sexually differentiated roles that followed from this structure implied a moderately clear and intelligible division of labour and an economically efficient distribution of responsibilities. To say this is not to imply that these distributions between work and home corresponded to everyone's real abilities or gave men and women equal opportunities for self-expression. It seems probable that early American agricultural life demanded a wide sharing of labour and that sex roles were far less distinctly drawn than they came to be when the economic system parcelled its labour force into specialised or merely mechanical operations. Women never seem to have been admitted to such professions as law, the ministry, or politics. As a result of a drafting peculiarity of the constitution adopted in New Jersey in 1776, in which the suffrage clause referred to "persons" but not to "men", it was held that women had the right to vote in that state. They exercised the right at intervals, and particularly at moments of political excitement, until a bitterly contested election over the location of the Essex County courthouse in 1807. After numerous votes by women, children, nonresidents,

3. Sir William Blackstone, *Commentaries on the Laws of England* (London, 1765), I, 430–3 (in which Blackstone comments that the female sex are the favourites of the laws of England, and II, 433: "Husband and wife are one in law, so that the very being and existence of the woman is suspended during the coverture, or entirely merged and incorporated in that of the husband").

Negroes, and transvestites had carried the election, masculine guardians of the political proprieties then decided that the joke had gone too far, and passed a law which in effect amended the constitution by excluding women from the polls.[4] The fact that women took advantage of the loophole over some thirty years strongly suggests that Abigail Adams, who in a famous letter in 1776 asked her husband John to make sure that the Continental Congress did something to relieve her sex from the tyranny of his,[5] was not the only American woman of her generation to be conscious of a claim to equality of rights.

With the exception of prominent but rare individuals such as Margaret Fuller and Frances Wright, women played no appreciable part in American public life outside the Abolitionist movement which arose in the 1830s. Abolitionism had a dramatic and transforming series of effects on the political aims and consciousness of American women. When women became abolitionists they inevitably entered into the world of man-made politics. The laws and institutions they challenged were made and maintained primarily by men, and in turn the attack on those laws was led by men. When Sarah and Angelina Grimké, daughters of a South Carolina slaveholder, left their home to move North and speak in public against slavery, they found to their dismay that the anger of a male-dominated society turned against them as women. The Council of the General Association of Orthodox Churches of Massachusetts—the Congregationalists—declared in a pastoral letter in 1837 that the New Testament had clearly defined the duties of woman, and that "The power of woman is her dependence, flowing from consciousness of that weakness which God has given her for her protection. . . . When she assumes the place and tone of man as a public reformer . . . she yields the power which God has given her . . . and her character becomes unnatural".[6] Denunciation and ridicule of women abolitionists were sometimes followed by physical assault. The women who insisted on

---

4. Richard P. McCormick, *The History of Voting in New Jersey* (New Brunswick, 1953), pp. 98–100. *Centinel of Freedom*, 15 September 1807; *New Jersey Journal*, 15, 24 February, 3 March 1807; *Journal of the Legislative Council of N.J.*, 1807, p. 623.

5. Page Smith, *John Adams*, 2 vols. (New York, 1962), I, 225–6.

6. Elizabeth Cady Stanton, Susan B. Anthony, and Matilda Joslyn Gage, eds., *History of Woman Suffrage* (New York, 1881), I, 81–2.

being heard soon had their attention turned to the disagreeable connection between Negro slavery and their own relationship to the male world. So many anti-slavery societies excluded women from membership that they began to form their own; and in 1837 Sarah Grimké wrote the president of the Boston Female Anti-Slavery Society a letter addressed directly to the question of women's status. "All history", she maintained, "attests that man has subjugated woman to his will, used her as a means to promote his selfish gratification, to minister to his sensual pleasure, to be instrumental in promoting his comfort; but never has he desired to promote her to the rank she was created to fill. He has done all he could to debase and enslave her mind; and now he looks triumphantly on the ruin he has wrought, and says, the being he has thus deeply injured is his inferior. . .".[7] Only slight alterations would have been necessary to translate this indictment into an explanation of the white sense of superiority to the black. In women's writings there began to emerge an analysis of the social and psychological processes of the moral as well as the physical aspects of subjugation. Women were better placed than men to perceive the connection.

This unwelcome advantage received sharp confirmation at the World Anti-Slavery Convention held in London in 1840. The presence of women in the American delegation caused a storm of indignation among the men, some of whom obviously feared that their presence would damage the convention's reputation, with the result that the women were relegated to the galleries and denied any right to participate in the proceedings. Lucretia Mott and Elizabeth Cady Stanton, making their way home after the meeting, determined to embark on a campaign for women's education as the first step towards a political programme of women's rights. It was not until 1848, however, that they succeeded in organising the first Woman's Rights Convention, which met in the New York town of Seneca Falls and approved a Declaration of Sentiments that followed to model of the Declaration of Independence.

Holding it "self-evident that all men and women are created equal," the declaration alleged a series of "injuries and usurpations on the part of man toward women, having in direct object the estab-

7. Judith Hole and Ellen Levine, *Rebirth of Feminism* (New York, 1972), pp. 3–4.

lishment of an absolute tyranny over her". Facts were then duly "submitted to a candid world". The parallel was remarkable, for men had certainly compelled women to submit to laws in the formation of which they had no voice; had made them "if married, in the eye of the law, civilly dead"; had monopolized profitable employments, had allowed them but a subordinate position in Church or State, and had "created a false sentiment by giving to the world a different code of morals for men and for women". The drafters of this declaration had already grasped the vital significance of the question of self-esteem: "He has endeavoured, in every way that he could, to destroy her confidence in her own powers, to lessen her self-respect, and to make her willing to lead a dependent and abject life".[8] Like Negroes, like the working classes, like racial and religious minorities from abroad, women would measure their social progress in terms of equality of esteem.

The Seneca Falls convention was considered by the founders of the women's movement as the formal beginning of the organised and continuous campaign for women's rights. The founders maintained that three immediate causes could be ascribed to the demand for equal political rights for women. The first was the recent discussions in state legislatures of the property rights of married women. In this way, as they observed, "all phases of the question were touched upon, involving the relations of the sexes, and gradually widening to all human interests—political, civil, religious and social". The second was the general educational work of recent years, and notably that of Frances Wright and Ernestine Rose. Third, "And above all other causes of the 'Woman Suffrage Movement' was the Anti-Slavery struggle in this country". As the editors of the *History of Woman Suffrage* pointedly remarked, Sarah and Angelina Grimké and Abby Kelly "in advocating liberty for the black race, were early compelled to defend the right of free speech for themselves. They had a double battle to fight against the tyranny of sex and color at the same time".[9]

These feminist reformers were making an intellectual discovery

8. Stanton et al., *Woman Suffrage*, I, 69–71; Hole and Levine, *Feminism*, pp. 5–7.
9. Stanton et al., *Woman Suffrage*, I, 53.

that was to be repeated many times in the future, and was bound to recur whenever the movement for equality broke the surface of political life. It was the discovery that in many practical instances, the different elements or categories of equality were united. Yet women and their male supporters were very far from agreement on the order of priority in their demands for enfranchisement from the world of male domination. Many members of the Seneca Falls convention would have been satisfied with a campaign directed to securing property rights for married women. In face of serious disagreement, Stanton and the Abolitionist leader Frederick Douglass—whose paper, *The North Star*, consistently defended the cause of women's rights—insisted that these aims could be secured only by means of the suffrage. The opposition to them feared that so outlandish a demand would expose the whole movement to ridicule and damage the chances of legal reform; a resolution demanding female suffrage was eventually carried by a small majority after strenuous debate.[10]

The perception of an analogy between Negro slavery and the female condition was not inherently likely to prove attractive to most white women. It was open primarily to women—and for that matter to men—of strong will and independent mind whose moral vision swept away any psychological need to bolster their self-esteem with synthetic supports. One such woman—assisted by independent circumstances—was the English visitor Barbara Leigh Smith Bodichon, who spent about a year in the United States in 1857–1858 and lived much of that time in New Orleans. Mrs Bodichon, who later used her private fortune in helping to found Girton College, Cambridge, was quick to recognise the analogous forms of slavery. Her own first concern was naturally for the rights of women in England, but her observations could as well have been applied to American women. In both cases she perceived the corrupting influence on people otherwise well-disposed of living, as she said, "in the belief of a vital falsehood" which "poisons all the springs of life". The deformity of judgment could not be confined to one issue;

10. Ibid., I, 53–62; Judith Hole and Ellen Levine, "The First Feminists", in Anne Koedt, Ellen Levine, and Anita Rapone, eds., *Radical Feminism* (New York, 1973), p. 8.

men and women who "hold false opinions concerning one half of the human race" were in her view incapable of judging rightly on other matters. She felt that Negro slavery was a greater injustice, but she added that "it is allied to the injustice to women so closely that I cannot see one without thinking of the other and feeling how soon slavery would be destroyed if right opinions were entertained on the other question".[11] This last remark disclosed an unwarranted optimism. There was little room to believe that emancipated white women would be disposed to proceed with a programme of emancipation based on the analogy between their former condition and that of the blacks.

American women did, however, subordinate their cause to that of emancipation during the Civil War—only to find their demands for political recognition ignored or treated with derision. During the course of debates on civil rights and Negro suffrage throughout the Reconstruction era, opponents of suffrage extension periodically used the example of female suffrage as evidence on their side of the argument. The essence of their position was that the right to vote was a privilege conferred by society on certain classes of persons possessing the requisite qualifications: It was in no sense an absolute right derived from nature or from membership of a particular political society. Women, children, convicts, the insane did not vote—yet they all enjoyed such rights of citizenship as were appropriate to their position in society. The state, as Senator James Dixon of Connecticut observed in the debates on the Fifteenth Amendment, had the right to make the distinction.[12]

In these arguments it was the debating role of the conservatives to invoke the abstract claim that equality was in principle indivisible: If it was to be extended to blacks, then no logical ground remained on which to resist its extension to women or to other groups who had remained below the line of political visibility. In 1869 Senator Willard Saulsbury of Delaware raised merriment in the Senate by offering an amendment to abolish all distinctions of colour or sex.[13] When similar tactics were used in the debate on the civil rights bill

11. Barbara Leigh Smith Bodichon, *An American Diary 1857–8*, ed. Joseph W. Reed, Jr. (London, 1972), pp. 62–3. I am indebted to Betty Wood for drawing my attention to this book.
12. *Congressional Globe*, 40th Cong., 3rd sess., pp. 858–61.
13. Ibid., p. 1310.

of 1875 Oliver Morton, a Republican supporter of the bill, accused his opponents of "getting behind the ladies".[14] But in the debates on the Fifteenth Amendment and later on the civil rights bill, most radical Republicans were anxious to avoid entangling their cause with that of female suffrage or women's rights, which had no practical prospect of success, but could impair their immediate object. Republicans were divided on women's claims, which was itself a tactical reason for avoiding the issue, but did not mean that they viewed them with contempt. The Republican Senator Willard Warner of Alabama expressed his sympathy, and while he declined to incorporate women's interests into the movement for Negro civil rights he assured the women that they would get the suffrage as soon as they acted with unanimity.[15]

In this same year the Supreme Court expressed the generally held masculine view of the issue by deciding in a test case that the protection afforded by the Fourteenth Amendment did not give women the right to vote, which a state government therefore had power to deny.[16] This decision changed nothing, but it did effectively draw the line of distinction between the rights of male citizens and those of females. Men could still be denied the vote for a considerable variety of reasons, such as nonpayment of minor taxes, illiteracy, or nonresidence—the full richness of such obstructions had at this period yet to be discovered—but women who fulfilled all these requirements would still be denied the vote for no other reason than that they were women. This situation accentuated the political significance of Warner's remark in the Senate: Women must concentrate their attention on obtaining a constitutional amendment, a need that had already begun to emerge from the split between the interests of women and Negroes over the Fifteenth Amendment.

Sharp differences of opinion emerged from this period of disappointment. Elizabeth Cady Stanton and Susan B. Anthony believed that women should challenge male oppression on every front; perceiving the complex character of the network of sexual domination, they founded a radically feminist weekly paper, The Revolution, with the motto, "Men, their rights and nothing more; women, their rights

14. Congressional Record, 42nd Cong., 1st sess. (1875), p. 1795.
15. Congressional Globe, 40th Cong., 3rd sess., p. 862.
16. Minor v. Happerset, 21 Wallace 162 (1875).

and nothing less". Stanton and Anthony used this medium, which exerted greater influence in arousing women's social consciousness than its modest circulation or brief lifespan might have suggested, to examine the whole range of institutions by which women were adversely affected and unfairly judged. They thus made women aware that many customary practices and institutions were implicit denials of equal or fair treatment. The dominance of men in the property laws of marriage, the difficulties besetting women who were ill-treated by their husbands, the conventionally accepted double standard of sexual morality, all came under their scrutiny. Stanton soon became particularly conscious of the antagonism of organised religion to any change in the sexual structure of social or political relationships; the clergy seemed especially susceptible to the fear that women who assumed masculine roles would exert a disruptive influence on their own authority, or that which divine providence transmitted through their agency. Anthony, with the assistance of a group of twenty-three women (three of them ministers of religion) attacked this clerical influence by producing a volume called *The Women's Bible*, which exposed the Bible itself to a searching feminist critique. The story of Eve's creation was dismissed as "a petty surgical operation", and the subjugation of women was traced to the story of the temptation propounded in Genesis. Stanton, first president of the National American Woman Suffrage Association, which she and Anthony had founded, became increasingly preoccupied with the need to combat the influence of organised religion, but these activities had dubious repercussions in public opinion and *The Women's Bible*, widely considered as sacrilegious, threatened to bring the movement into some disrepute. The more strictly political wing of the movement was represented by Lucy Stone, who founded the American Woman Suffrage Association about the time, soon after the Civil War, that Stanton and Anthony launched their own organisation. Stone's purpose was to win the suffrage by confining attention to clearly respectable and political issues and avoiding the wider problems—which by implication could be tackled when women had won the voting power to influence events through the processes of political life. The two organisations ran their parallel courses for some twenty years; but it was only in the twentieth century that the

NAWSA, under a new generation's leadership, gathered the wider body of women's resources into a dominant movement.[17]

These associations were representative of an emerging social self-consciousness among women, who as individuals were consequently less threatened than in the past by the total individual isolation of the injured wife or exploited, dependent female. The leadership, however, was entirely composed of women of substantial middle-class background or expectations, and even the poorest of them, Frances Perkins Gilman, who sometimes had to struggle to make ends meet, had been brought up to expect middle-class standards. Gilman, exerting intellectual gifts of the sort then usually attributed to males, became an influential critic of economic institutions. Florence Kelley, whom Governor John Peter Altgeld appointed chief factory inspector of Illinois, perceived the general character of the connections between the industrial system and the social morals which it generated, and drew a further lesson from the moral heritage of slavery: "Our industrial epoch [she wrote] has corroded our morals and hardened our hearts as surely as slavery injured its contemporaries, and far more subtly. There is grave reason to fear that it may have unfitted us for the oncoming state of civilisation, as slave-owning unfitted the white race for freedom and democracy, while it left its blight of race hatred from which the Republic still suffers".[18] Far from gaining in personal freedom, women were increasingly the victims of the factories and workshops; competition no doubt drove their employers to exploit their defenceless position on the labour market just as the need for subsistance, the absence of special qualifications, and the lack of alternatives drove innumerable young women into the factories and garment-making shops. In 1909 a great strike of New York women garment workers under the authority of the New York Women's Trade Union League dramatised the power that organised labour could exert; it did more, for middle-class women identified themselves to a previously unknown degree with their working-class sisters, joined their pickets and demonstrations, and spread

17. Hole and Levine, "First Feminists", pp. 9–13.
18. Florence Kelley, Modern Industry in Relation to the Family, Health Education, Morality (New York, 1914), p. 122, quoted by William L. O'Neill, Everyone Was Brave: The Rise and Fall of Feminism in America (Chicago, 1969), p. 149.

the message of their cause in circles where it would not ordinarily have been heard.[19]

Some manifestations of feminine consciousness were more socially exclusive; the Daughters of the American Revolution, founded in 1890, emphasized for women the same kind of inherited claims to social distinction that had often been claimed by men. Self-proclaimed women aristocrats could reasonably argue to their patriarchs that any demands they might make for political participation posed no threat to the established order. The women's suffrage movement was not based on any revolutionary critique of the economic system or of the social relationships which upheld it; in 1902 the aged Elizabeth Cady Stanton expressed herself as willing to accept more general restrictions on the suffrage itself, and was prepared to suppress the votes of the ignorant among both men and women, provided that appropriately educated women were allowed to vote.[20] This position was strikingly similar to the "impartial" suffrage that Booker T. Washington favoured for Negroes qualified by education or property along with similarly qualified whites; in both cases, those without sufficient qualifications would be disqualified from participation in the political process.[21]

White women, however, had more effective and intimate means of access than black men to the white men who voted and made laws. Perhaps the most significant example of their influence was their very prominent part in the temperance movement. From earlier beginnings among the reform movements of the Jacksonian era, temperance became a major cause in the later nineteenth century, and from being rural or merely local, it acquired a special focus in the cities. The appalling nightmares of working women whose husbands habitually came home drunk and frequently violent from the taverns and saloons that dominated the social life of many working-class areas helped to make the temperance movement into a kind of test of society's interest in the protection of its women. No other general social cause was so distinctively associated with women's interests. In conjunction with the clergy, women exerted persistent and ef-

19. O'Neill, *Everyone Was Brave*, pp. 130–33, 141.
20. Andrew Sinclair, *The Better Half* (London, 1965), p. 299.
21. Louis R. Harlan, *Booker T. Washington, The Making of a Black Leader, 1856–1901* (New York, 1972), pp. 302–3.

fective pressures for the passage of numerous local laws restricting the sale of liquor; but in the process, the temperance movement incurred hostility from the powerful brewing interests against the broader demand for female suffrage. It is remarkable that the Eighteenth Amendment, which empowered Congress to forbid the sale of liquor and led immediately to Prohibition, was adopted in 1918— a triumph for women's influence in American public life occurring two years before the adoption of the Nineteenth Amendment, which gave them the federal suffrage.[22]

A new and more militant leadership steered the women's movement to this culminating achievement. Carrie Chapman Catt had injected new life into the National American Woman Suffrage Association after the older leadership had passed from the scene; soon afterwards Alice Paul founded the small but more intense and dynamic Congressional Union—later the Woman's Party—to concentrate all attention on the ultimate objective of a constitutional amendment. These moves made considerable headway among individual states over a long period in the later nineteenth and early twentieth centuries. But it was as a direct result of American participation in World War I that women were able to make their greatest contribution to their own cause. As had happened in the Civil War, women released men for military service, now filling still more tasks, technical as well as unskilled, formerly reserved for men. The argument for their indispensability merged with that of indebtedness to them for their contribution to the war effort; and there was now no prior cause such as Negro suffrage to stand in their way. In the United States as in Great Britain the adoption of women's suffrage at the national level—in the American case through constitutional amendment, in Britain by an act of Parliament—took place soon after the Great War and as a direct consequence.

The sequel showed how little there had been to fear. The newly politically liberated womanhood of America made no move to disturb the social order; they arranged themselves instead along lines already marked out by the structure and economic interests of a society dominated by men. What was more surprising, and disappointing to those who had hoped for real alterations among the roles

22. Hole and Levine, *Rebirth*, p. 11.

in American society, was the limping and limited manner in which women attempted to move into positions occupied by men throughout industry or the professions. Leaders of the suffrage movement did not see their duty now as that of inspiring a diffused and dispersed multitude of followers to seize the strongholds of business and education. Carrie Chapman Catt, perhaps the most prominent of them, turned her energies to the peace movement, and may have felt that her efforts had been eventually rewarded in 1929 when the United States signed the Kellogg-Briand Pact, whose signatories renounced the use of war to settle international disputes. The failure of women to build educational, economic, and political strength on the foundations of the suffrage bore a remote but curious comparability with the earlier failure of Negroes to make similar gains, during the thirty years after the Civil War.

Old Ribs in New Skins

Unlike other minority or deprived groups, American women were slow to convert the Second World War into a hinge for their own advancement. Undoubtedly women had occupied many indespensable positions and had once again proved themselves capable of assuming responsibilities customarily reserved for men; and while one woman, Frances Perkins, had served during the New Deal as Secretary of Labor in Roosevelt's administration, another had exercised a continuous and profound influence on the development of the president's social policies. No record is ever likely to reveal the full extent to which Americans are indebted to Eleanor Roosevelt for the infusing of attitudes of moral responsibility towards minorities, and particularly to blacks, into her husband's policies; no informed student is ever likely to doubt that this is the greatest individual debt of all. Despite all this, the achievements of women and their contributions to national life tended to be regarded as emergency measures which did not need to be continued after life had returned to normal. Women remained remarkably rare in Congress, almost unknown on the bench or at the bar, absent from the stock exchanges, and exceptions in business management, while male-dominated university departments seldom offered them senior or even permanent appointments. Even in the 1960s, only 7 percent of the nation's doctors, 3 percent of its lawyers, and 1 percent of its engineers were women; there was evidence of an actual decline after the Second World War.[23]

These numerous areas might well have constituted the objectives of a drive for reassertion taking its origins in the American ideological involvement in the war itself. Some new feminist writings could be traced to that period; only after the basic antidiscrimination laws had been passed, however, did a new wave of feminist reformers begin to demand the addition of clauses on sex to the laws against discrimination. The prosperity which bathed much of the country in the postwar era swept people upward to the enjoyment of more glittering and attractive consumer goods, but perhaps for that very reason it seemed to diminish the urgency of social change. Women were very clearly the material beneficiaries of these advances in production and distribution; they acquired their own cars—even if mainly for running around town—and mechanical assistance in the home which largely replaced the always disappearing class of domestic servants. They were not encouraged, however, to aspire towards achievements outside their homes or to aims that looked far beyond the upbringing of their children. Exponents of the child and adult psychology generally advised them to treat these as the normal areas for their highest ambitions and deepest fulfilment. Women who developed signs of hysteria through inability to maintain this circumscribed role were counselled or treated in ways designed to return them, satisfied and undamaged, to the protective comforts of domesticity. There was a marked difference between the official medical attitude to men who showed signs of strain under the stress of business and women who showed similar signs under the stress of their homes. Women were more frequently assigned to mental institutions and certified insane. Yet these problems were private rather than public; the experts, marriage counsellors, and psychiatrists to whom women in distress were obliged to turn were usually men, and in these situations women had little opportunity to be aware that

23. Martha Weinman Lear, "The Second Feminist Wave", in June Sochen, ed., *The New Feminism of the Twentieth Century* (Lexington, Mass., 1971), pp. 163–4.

their difficulties had a more general, socially induced character and were common to many of their sex, not the product of abnormal natures.[24]

While its aims were thus diffused, and its own natural membership remained inchoate and undefined to the point of being unaware of its own existence, a new women's movement was bound to experience a difficult and slow birth. Among many specific inequalities, however, a diminishing number were still defined by law. Legal reform in matters of divorce and property had a respectable history: The founders of the Woman Suffrage Movement gave New York the credit for being the first state to emancipate wives from the old common law of England by securing equality of property rights to them in 1848[25] —overlooking the claims of Mississippi, which had done so in 1839 —and during the later nineteenth and twentieth centuries women acquired independent status in matters of contract, in control of property, in responsibility for children, and in a widening range of grounds for divorce. By the 1960s there was little to differentiate single women from men in legal rights; but married women were hedged in by a multitude of restraints, some great and some small, some formal and others informal but effective.[26] Yet the struggle to establish female independence, to make every woman a free and equal agent in the American market, encountered obstructions raised by earlier successes in legislation passed by the Progressives. This ironical turn of events came down from the leading case of *Muller* v. *Oregon*, decided by the Supreme Court in 1908; in that case Muller, an employer, challenged the validity of a state law limiting the work of female factory employees to ten hours a day. If the court had followed its own recent judgment in *Lochner* v. *New York*, it would have been obliged to hold that this law represented an unwarranted interference with freedom of contract, adversely affecting the rights of both employer and worker; but the fact that the object was to protect women altered the character of the case. In upholding the act, the court through Mr Justice Brewer defined

24. Naomi Weisstein, "Psychology Constructs the Female", in Koedt et al., *Radical Feminism*, pp. 178–97; Phyllis Chesler, *Women and Madness* (New York, 1972).
25. Stanton et al., *Woman Suffrage*, I, p. 63.
26. Leo Kanowitz, *Women and the Law: the Unfinished Revolution* (Albuquerque, 1969), p. 197.

the issue in terms that applied different standards to the female sex. "The two sexes differ in structure of body, in the functions to be performed by each, in the amount of physical strength, in the capacity for long-continued labour, particularly when done standing, the influence of vigorous health upon the future well-being of the race, the self-reliance which enables one to assert full rights, and [a Darwinian touch] in the capacity to maintain the struggle for subsistence. This difference justifies a difference in legislation, and upholds that which is designed to compensate for some of the burdens which rest upon her". While this decision was clearly designed to afford constitutional protection to women against industrial exploitation, and was in that sense more benign that the court's views on the rights of the male sex, the language just as clearly envisaged the dependence and basic inferiority of women as the permanent and natural condition which alone could justify a departure from constitutional precedent; the court was also influenced by the need to protect women as bearers of healthy children. After describing women's condition and admitting that personal and contractual disabilities might be removed by legislation, Mr Justice Brewer went on to say, "Differentiated by these matters from the other sex, she is properly placed in a class by herself, and legislation designed for her protection may be sustained, even when like legislation is not necessary for men, and could not be sustained".[27]

Allowing for the fact that the *Muller* decision helped to protect women from exploitation, the principle of difference was not inconsistent with a much less friendly decision rendered during an earlier phase of women's demands for public recognition. A woman citizen of Illinois had been denied the right to practice law, although in all respects properly qualified. The Supreme Court decided the case on grounds set by the precedent of the *Slaughter House Cases,* just decided in the same term; although the plaintiff was a citizen of the United States, the question at issue was held to pertain to state citizenship only, and the Fourteenth Amendment would not come between the state and its citizens. In a separate concurrence, Mr Justice Bradley—later to speak for the court in the *Civil Rights Cases*— went further, perhaps disclosing the social assumptions which the majority were concerned to protect. "The constitution of the family

27. Muller v. Oregon, 208 U.S. 412 (1908).

organization, which is founded in the divine ordinance, as well as in the nature of things, indicates the domestic sphere as that which properly belongs to the nature and function of womanhood. The harmony, not to say identity, of interests and views, which belong, or should belong, to the family institutions is repugnant to the idea of a woman adopting a distinct and independent career from that of her husband", he explained.[28] Quite apart from the consideration that women do not always have husbands—although this plaintiff did—the court clearly shared Bradley's susceptibility to a formalistic conception of the natural order which controlled the interpretation of constitutional rights; the expression "in the nature of things" would reappear in Mr Justice Brown's opinion in *Plessy* v. *Ferguson*. Not for the moment only, but for what might be an indefinite period, sex was ruled as analogous to race as a legitimate ground for discriminatory legislation.

Industrial conditions gave rise to new laws to protect women. These protections assumed that women were weaker and more vulnerable than men, a type of assumption which was later found to militate against the autonomy and independence asserted by women's movements. The intentions behind factory legislation were initially benign, but certain forms of protection, by confining women to limited tasks, also served to protect the jobs of men. It became common, for example, to forbid firms to allow women to lift weights, sometimes no heavier than that of an average eighteen-month-old child.[29] Women were also frequently protected from serving in bars at night, although no law saved them from working the same hours as cleaners or, for that matter, as entertainers. It was against these accumulations of law and prejudice, partly well intentioned, partly the issue of generations of man-made conventional wisdom, and most of them deeply encrusted in the minds not only of male workers, male employers, and male legislators but of the vast majority of their own sex, that the new wave of women's liberationists began their struggle in the years following the New Deal, the Second World War, and the initial successes of the movement for antidiscrimination laws. Their early progress was slow. Then during the adminis-

28. Bradwell v. Illinois, 83 U.S. 130 (1872).
29. Kanowitz, *Women and the Law*, pp. 100–31; Pauli Murray and Mary Eastwood, "Jane Crow and the Law", in Koedt et al., *Radical Feminism*, pp. 165–77.

trations of Kennedy, Johnson, and Nixon more striking advances were made in both law and the public imagination than the posture or public repute of the movement might earlier have led one to expect.

Women held a small number of moderately prominent positions in various walks of public and professional life, and perhaps exerted a particular kind of political influence because of their activity in electoral campaigns. Yet on the whole the progress of the women's movement represented a remarkable example of political persuasion. Women did not follow blacks into sit-ins, civil disobedience, or dramatic acts defying existing conventions. They rarely initiated or exposed themselves to physical violence. They exerted their influence through a combination of publications, whose messages were addressed as much to the consciousness of women themselves as to the consciences of men, and persistent, well-directed political pressure. In 1963 President John Kennedy recognised the claims of this pressure on the conscience of his own administration by appointing a Commission on the Status of Women.

The commission worked through a series of study groups, each of which examined conditions in a specific field and produced its own report. These studies brought to light a mass of evidence about the disadvantages of being a woman in the United States. Despite progress made over more than a century of agitation, many state laws still discriminated against women, especially when married, in matters of control over conjugal property, contractual rights, and the jobs women were allowed to do, all affecting a woman's basic independence as an economic, social, and moral being. Women were worse educated and more poorly paid and their status and expectations were generally lower than those of men in comparable situations. The report of the full commission was more temperate than the findings of some of its study groups might have seemed to suggest, and posed no immediate threat to male control; it did propose an executive order on equal opportunity in employment, but did not think it would be expedient to add "sex" to existing proposals for equal opportunities in matters of race. The commission favoured a view of marriage by which "each spouse makes a different but equally important contribution". This statement has attracted criticism from feminists who object to the implicit assignment of spheres proper to husbands and wives; as to the question of an Equal Rights Amendment for women, the commission was unimpressed, but its only strongly feminist member, the lawyer Margaret Rawalt, succeeded in modifying their negative recommendation on this point at least to the extent of adding the word "now" so that the commission only concluded that "a constitutional amendment need not now be sought".[30]

President Kennedy's political obligations to women, many of whom had worked effectively in his election campaign, were met in part by the commission and in part by the Equal Pay Act of 1963—the only federal legislation dealing exclusively with sexual equality. The exceptions to this act's provisions, which included executive, professional, and administrative employees, were so extensive as to render it ineffective in many of the cases where women's contributions were likely to be most distinctive. Pressure brought by women's groups effected an extension of its provisions in 1966; complaints under the act's administration meanwhile revealed that technically and professionally qualified women were habitually paid anything from 3 to 10 percent less than men for the same work. The next step was clearly to establish the principle that sex should rank with race, economic status, and religion as an impermissible ground for discrimination. Events began to move rapidly in the era of civil rights, and the opportunity for further action arose with the Civil Rights Act of 1964. By a remarkable legislative *tour de force*, sex was added to race, colour, religion, and national origin as prohibited ground for discrimination, making equality of opportunity between the sexes into official national policy. There are reasons for believing that women's interests owed this success to the blundering tactics of Representative Howard Smith of Virginia, an opponent of the whole measure, who moved the sex clause as an amendment with implausible professions of sincerity but the apparent object of making the bill objectionable to a majority of members. Once adopted, the amendment was incorporated into the full bill as passed by both houses of Congress in July 1964.

The powers conferred on the Equal Employment Opportunity Commission by Title VII, the operative article, were not impressive. In effect the measure was likely to be more important as a proclama-

30. Hole and Levine, Rebirth, pp. 17–28.

tion of national aims than as a method of detailed enforcement. Title VII left a certain latitude for discretion in a class known as "bona fide occupational qualifications", which included such categories as attendants for women's lavatories, models for women's clothes, and—a touch that would have surprised Shakespeare's contemporaries—actresses. While room may exist for some latitude in the definition of these occupations, there would have been little hope for a law that did not recognise their existence. The commission hesitated to define its views or even to enforce its authority, and for the next few years it preferred to leave the states to work out the details, provided only that such measures as differentiated between the sexes could be seen to protect women rather than denying them opportunity. When the Southern Bell Telephone Company in Georgia refused to promote a woman because a state law limited the weight that women were allowed to lift, it was clear that protection was cutting both ways. The state simplified matters by repealing the law, but the federal court took occasion for a ruling that placed upon the employer the burden of proving that he had factual basis for believing that "all or substantially all women would be unable to perform safely and efficiently the duties of the job involved". In a further dictum, the court explicitly rejected "romantic paternalism" and laid down that in matters of remuneration for "strenuous, dangerous, obnoxious, boring, or unromantic tasks . . . the promise of Title VII is that women are now on an equal footing".[31]

The assertion of a principle does not enforce its practice. The principle itself could fluctuate according to differing notions of what constituted "bona fide" tasks appropriate to one sex only; sexual discrimination is implicit in advertisements listed under "Jobs for Women" as distinct from men, and vice versa, and the women's movement proceeded to mount a campaign to eliminate these distinctions from the newspapers. The ultimate ramifications would leave almost nothing untouched, and Title VII itself offered a path that could lead most of the way.[32]

Proponents of the now recently revived Equal Rights Amendment sought to disarm opponents and allow for real physiological

31. Ibid., pp. 28–37.
32. Anna Hobson, pseud., *The Equal Rights Amendment: How Do I Love It, Let Me Count the Ways* (Pittsburgh, Pa., 1976).

necessities by the doctrine of "unique physical characteristics". Childbearing would thus attract special recognition; child-rearing, in which both parents might wish to engage equally, would not claim the same legal protection. Successively more stringent constructions of the meaning of "bona fide occupational qualifications" meanwhile made the legal tests for that subject similar to those proposed under the heading of unique physical characteristics, and this convergence of attitudes was further assured when women gained recognition of equal rights to higher education in a class action against the University of Virginia.[33]

The Equal Employment Opportunity Commission moved a little uneasily towards stronger lines of policy, in August 1969 revising its guidelines to announce that "state laws and regulations, although originally promulgated for the purpose of protecting females, have ceased to be relevant to our technology or to the expanding role of the female worker in our economy".[34] In principle it followed that state laws protecting women against burdens they were willing to undertake could no longer establish "bona fide" exceptions and were in conflict with the official reading of Title VII. Firm and continuous pressure had converted that article from a declaration of intent into an instrument of searching and detailed policy. Women were in fact not always even the nominal beneficiaries of laws ostensibly designed to save them from unpleasantness. Although jury service is not a popular activity, it had long ago been held essential to the maintenance of equal protection for Negroes; yet Alabama excluded women from jury service in a law held invalid by a federal district court in 1966. "Jury service is a form of participation in the process of government", declared the court, "a responsibility and a right that should be shared by all citizens, regardless of sex".[35] Several states in their penal laws unwittingly revealed how women might be deprived of equal protection by manmade legislation. Men were perhaps more shocked when the weaker sex committed crimes of violence, and in certain cases they mandated severer sentences for

33. Ibid., p. 8. Kirstein et al. v. Rectors and Visitors of University of Virginia, E.D. Va., Richmond Div. civil no. 220-69-R.
34. Hole and Levine, *Rebirth*, p. 35.
35. Kanowitz, *Women and the Law*, pp. 231–7; White v. Crook F. Supp. 401 (1966).

the same offences. Such a law in Pennsylvania was overturned by the Supreme Court of that state in 1967—in the process undermining the more general principle that sex might be regarded for any reason as a valid basis for classification. A year later a federal district court in Connecticut held that a law allowing longer sentences for women than for men was a violation of equal protection.[36]

In 1923, when Alice Paul—already a veteran of the successful suffrage campaign—first formulated the Equal Rights Amendment, women still suffered a range of legal disabilities. The comprehensive simplicity of the amendment appeared to leave no room for evasion or for the ingenious alternatives which had been found in the Reconstruction amendments: "Equality of rights under the law shall not be denied or abridged by the United States or by any state on account of sex". The intention was that such exceptions as could be permitted would fall under the classification of physiology, but no women would be forced into formerly masculine roles against their will. The amendment experienced an active revival when in 1972 it was passed by Congress, at which point Alice Paul, now over eighty, began a campaign for ratification by state legislatures. The first wave of enthusiasm carried more than thirty-four states, after which the impulse began to fade, and some legislatures rescinded their acts of ratification.[37] Whether the passage of the amendment would amount to anything more than a rhetorical victory was a matter of some dispute. A convincing case could be made, based on common law and constitutional principles of legal reasoning, that the Fifth and Fourteenth Amendments could do for sexual equality as much as they had been made to do for racial equality and that the struggle for the Equal Rights Amendment was a diversion of energy from specific issues on which definitive constitutional victories could be won.[38] On the other hand, when the Supreme Court hesitated over the precise application of equal protection on the grounds that the issue was currently open for political decision, it implied that the Constitution was unclear[39]—which in turn strengthened the case for a new amendment. It was not to be overlooked, however, that women's

36. Kanowitz, *Women and the Law*, pp. 167–70.
37. Hobson, *Equal Rights Amendment*.
38. See the discussion in Kanowitz, *Women and the Law*, pp. 192–6.
39. Frontiero v. Richardson, 411 U.S. 677 (1973).

gains in the post-war era had been wrung from institutions generally dominated by men, and largely by the force of argument and insistent moral pressure. Women had the advantage in this struggle of being continuously close to men in a way that blacks were not continuously close to whites. An important part of the truth, moreover, was that by the time legislative victories were being won, the main dialectical corners had already been turned. The case for unequal opportunity could be defended only by resort to dark biblical rumblings and invocations of the order of nature[40] or by examples and theories that were in continuous process of being disproved. The history of the advance of women's rights suggested that the men who so largely made and interpreted the laws were not wholly impervious to the force of the evidence.

The evidence, however, has been subject to differing views among women as well as men. Women's movements at various periods would have found their task much easier if women experienced their relationship to men in identical ways. In the cruelly corrosive world of unlimited business competition which has frequently restricted the interests, exhausted the energies, and shortened the lives of men, it is only true to say that women have often enjoyed a very real measure of protection, a greater diversity of interests, and longer lives than their husbands. Women, moreover, have often accepted masculine assumptions about sex roles, which have become so deeply embedded in feminine psychology that the efforts of women's liberationists have had to be directed primarily at arousing an independent feminine consciousness. There need be no doubt that the acceptance of masculine assumptions and the consequent obsequious curtailment of many of the more vigorous and independent kinds of activities both intellectual and physical have resulted in distortions of women's personalities. The damage done to victimised social or religious minorities has been closely comparable. At each stage of its revival, the women's movement has invariably had to encounter the resistance and resentment of women who objected to the disturbance which threatened a social order under which they had learnt to live. Earlier in the twentieth century, when individual states were anticipating the federal government, female resistance to the suffrage movement is credited with having delayed the adoption of women's

40. Senator Sam Ervin was a particularly volcanic source of these.

suffrage in several states.[41] In the later surge of feminism that followed the Second World War, an enormous variety of women's groups debated divergent female attitudes and rival philosophies as well as mere differences of opinion about tactics. This splintering diversity must be held to have reflected differences of personal experience and to have embodied very real differences of opinion as to the kind of social order that should be made to emerge from the revolution in women's rights.[42]

The women's movement has taken different views of history from those of the resurgent black movements. Blacks have insisted, as women have insisted, on concepts of history that emphasise their own experience; but the theme on which black history tended to concentrate was the search for positive black contributions to the making of an undeniably male-dominated society. It was the neglected Negro contribution to the building of American prosperity, to the growth of Southern agriculture, to the heroism of Union armies in the Civil War, to the development of a distinctive American culture, that seemed to guide the purposes of "Black History". Women appear to have felt less comparable need to assert the fact of their achievements. Feminists on the other hand have availed themselves of the counter-argument that the world would be a very different—and by implication a better—place if women had historically participated in making the laws and running the institutions which have shaped society. Yet this is a fruitless exercise in counterfactual analysis, and the historical researches which have informed the writings of the women's movement have on the whole had two central purposes. One has been to seek out and claim attention for the struggles of women for social, legal, and political equality; the other, to emphasise, more perhaps for the understanding of their own sex than for that of men, that women's experience had indeed been an experience of oppression. That this point comes across so intensely in the work of Barbara Bodichon, Susan Anthony, or Elizabeth Cady Stanton in one generation or in that of Alice Paul and then later Betty Friedan or Kate Millett in others, is no evidence that the mass

41. Carl Degler, *Is There a History of Women?* An Inaugural Lecture (Oxford, 1975), p. 23.
42. See in general the essays in June Sochen, ed., *The New Feminism in Twentieth-Century America* (Lexington, Mass., 1971) and Koedt et al., *Radical Feminism.*

of American women had generally appreciated or thought there was any hope of altering the special and separated character of their position in society and in laws derived from centuries of subordination.

The problem of equality of esteem, which lay at the centre of this need for identification, was complicated for women as it was for other minorities by the history and consequences of psychological domination. Even under conditions of controlled tests, women revealed a very marked tendency to place a higher value on the works of men than of women. A characteristic example resulting from a study published in 1969 concerned a set of six academic articles presented to two separate groups of women students. One group was given these articles under the names of male authors, the other under the names of female authors; both groups were asked to evaluate the articles for value, persuasiveness, and profundity, and to rate the authors for style and competence. Regardless of their subject matter, the articles under men's names fared uniformly better than the same articles under women's names.[43] The smallness of this sample renders the conclusion questionable—but not incompatible with everyday experience. Until women could achieve real equality of esteem in matters of professional competence among their own sex, they would be engaged in an unequal struggle. The need for equal protection in the more formalistic sense established an obvious case for equality in law, in political power, and in religious conscience. But at this point the familiar categories began to lose their certainty. Women had to convince other women that they wanted, or ought to want, equality of opportunity in all aims open to men, and had to persuade them to accept the risks that might seem to follow from the withdrawal of certain traditional protections.

It was in keeping with this new consciousness that the American women's movement tried to reach behind the enemy's entrenchments by an assault on the language itself. At the cost of neologisms which ranged from inoffensiveness to positive inelegance, certain conventional masculine designations began to fall into a sort of sexual no-person's-land. Some of these changes were intended to challenge what feminists held to be an assumption in the roots of the English

43. Jo Freeman, "The Building of the Gilded Cage" in Koedt et al., *Radical Feminism*, p. 142.

language, in which the noun *man* means the human race as well as the male sex;[44] but it was wholly in keeping with this mood that black power revivalists also insisted on certain modifications to usages which they found racially offensive. Changes in consciousness involved changes in the language which mediated that consciousness. The campaign to alter the habits of sexual association had equally potent visual objectives. Children's books and their illustrations were written or rewritten to exemplify the principle of interchangeability in the kitchen, the garage, and the workshop. The very fact that the concept of "sex roles" became a commonplace of popular social science was evidence of a new scale of awareness that these things were results of custom and convention, not inevitable manifestations of a natural order.

Differences between female and male experiences suggested strongly that women had historically held points of view, sensibilities, and aspirations which the conventional records as written by male historians had ignored or treated as trivial. Popes might be elected by male cardinals, ecclesiastical policy determined by male bishops and synods, wars declared by male politicians and fought by male soldiers, but the commands of religious doctrine bore differently on men and women; the experience of victory in war and the experience of defeat might be deeply different for the two sexes. Medical history also suggested that female physiology alone might constitute a differentiated experience.[45] None of these differences, however, detracted from the grounds on which the women's movement argued for equality of opportunity, which must to a large extent depend on removing the barriers to women's own capacity for self-realisation.

Sex might mean difference of experience, without turning difference into inequality. There was no inequality in protecting women in childbirth and its immediate aftermath, which pertained strictly to womanhood. But the Equal Employment Opportunity Commis-

44. In Anglo-Saxon the word "man" seems to have applied to both sexes. Before the tenth century the word *wifman* (literally, wife-man) emerged to define the female sex; but Anglo-Saxon *wif* did not mean "wife": it meant "woman", being one of the variants of the general noun, "man". See Walter W. Skeat, *Etymological Dictionary of the English Language* (Oxford, 1882, repr. 1972).
45. Degler, *Is There a History of Women?*

sion, in drawing up its guidelines for maternity benefits, separated childbearing from child-rearing, which can be undertaken by either sex. Either mothers or fathers could qualify for leave, though unpaid, just as either sex could receive unpaid leave for further education. But while the potent influences of convention—if not those of sexual chemistry and psychology, which remains uncertain—moulded the great remaining majority of women to choose early child-rearing if only because they expected it of themselves, it would remain true that the female experience of home life would be significantly different from men's. In certain circumstances equal rights might justify differential policies. If women could claim a right to have these choices protected by law, then here was a new turn to the argument that equality was not identity, for these distinctions of treatment were required not to impair but to maintain equality of rights. It was by their fitness or proportion to specific needs that the justice of such arrangements could best be ascertained. This was a conclusion that Aristotle would have been bound to approve; that it should have been demonstrated with special application to the rights of women would have caused him considerable surprise, but that need not surprise his latter-day followers.

Chapter Eleven

An Incomplete Revolution

The Transformation of Consciousness

Revolutions by the nature of the historical process are always incomplete. Apart from the truism that a change of rulers does not necessarily produce an improvement in the lives of the people, it seems also to be a necessity of the case that when a successful movement depends on a significant level of popular support it will raise—even create—expectations which it cannot satisfy. To describe historical transformations as revolutions when they not only remain half finished but leave their followers doubtful and divided as to what course to follow next, may risk provoking charges of superficiality or cynicism. Yet the risk must be taken. When the American situation as it was in the years of McKinley and Theodore Roosevelt, or even as late as the accession of Truman in 1945, is compared with that of 1974, and when the standpoint from which the Supreme Court was obliged to view the requirements of equal protection and of governmental neutrality in matters of religion and conscience, and the measurements of equality between man and man, or between man and woman, and when the principles of fairness which even the more conservative judges now regarded as constitutionally normal are compared with those of any earlier generation, the difference to be observed amounts to a far greater transformation both in the distribution of opportunity and the obligations of government than in any period that had occurred since the American Revolution.

For the first time in American history, equality became a major object of government policy; and also for the first time, with perhaps the exception of the Freedmen's Bureau of the Reconstruction period, governments not only made laws but constituted themselves instruments of egalitarian policy. The very fact that government agencies, and above all the courts, have been obliged to examine constitutional principles in the light of egalitarian pressures has in turn opened up hardly foreseen complexities that had lain buried in the doctrine of equality. The courts have been forced to scrutinise a variety of choices while the society for which they had to answer was issuing forth a proliferation of demands. What was coming about, in short, was a transformation of consciousness which tinged with sensations of injustice and exploitation many inequalities that in the past seemed almost to have been part of the order of nature. The categories of equality can thus in a sense be seen to correspond to levels of awareness. Perhaps not all inequalities can ever be rectified; and it is certain that some can be rectified only by creating new inequalities and new grievances. It is this that has made and will continue to make the judiciary the fulcrum of such continuous tension, for it is the judiciary and above all the Supreme Court which has the duty of mediating these conflicting demands back to American society through the prism of constitutional interpretation.

The courts, however, deal with the problems that society presents. Levels of awareness and corresponding senses of grievance have arisen at different times for particular historical reasons, often tending to differentiate among the categories of equality rather than unifying them. Inequalities of class, race, religion, and sex have presented themselves at different periods as primary grievances; but the remarkable aspect of the period during which Chief Justice Earl Warren presided over the Supreme Court was the unprecedented convergence of these issues, which made almost the whole intelligence of the country conscious of the demand for equality and the moral obligations arising from—but neither defined nor satisfied by—the nation's founding principles. Despite the many and often bitter disagreements as to methods and aims, this nationalisation of consciousness had no precedent in American history.

The concept of a unified national consciousness implied the possibility of a unified national interest, which had historically been extremely alien to American political life and thought. It was first raised by the Civil War—and the fact that four years of war were required to establish the supremacy of the nation over the states might alone have seemed sufficient proof of the alien character of the concept. Still more to the point, however, was the remarkable complacency with which even a Supreme Court containing a majority of justices appointed by Lincoln slid back into the distributionist and away from the centralist position so soon after the Civil War, and thereafter, with considerable consistency, made the integrity of the states rather than the obligations of the federal government the primary test of the legitimacy of egalitarian legislation.

Yet the spectre of that unified concept of national interest remained as an example and a warning of all that was alien to the decentralised, unconcentrated, and morally pluralistic principles of the federal system which long-standing traditions—primarily associated in politics with the Democrats—formally regarded as the highest possible level of desirable unity in American politics. Late in the nineteenth century the shadow of a national principle reappeared over distant horizons, for reasons far removed from those of racial equality, when the federal government decided to raise a national income tax—a move that was frustrated by the Supreme Court in 1895. By contrast with all other great nations, the United States appeared to live by a Constitution which made it virtually impossible for the government to govern, not in the sense of exercising arbitrary power over individuals, but in the ordinary sense of deciding what questions required prior national attention, and what means were appropriate to achieving the required objects. It is an extraordinary fact of comparative history that William Pitt had first raised a national income tax in Great Britain in 1797!

In the United States, as in Britain, the exigencies of war brought these matters home in harsher light than the needs of the people in time of peace. When the United States overcame its own constitutional conscience by passing the Sixteenth Amendment the year was 1916 and the war in Europe was soon to claim American participation. Not until the New Deal did the federal government assume responsibility for the economic survival of American citizens. But this was not equal economic protection; its greater significance lay rather in the recognition that the people as individuals had claims on their government. Beyond this—and far beyond the New Deal— it provided a base for more effective action towards the satisfaction of the claims of the underprivileged than had ever previously existed if only because their voting power was not more effectively organised than ever before.

The convergence of interests that flowed into the national consciousness in the post-war era did not have the power to alter fundamental economic structures. The distribution of American wealth remained profoundly unequal. In round figures, while Lyndon Johnson was president of the United States, it was still true that the wealthiest fifth of the nation received 46 percent of its income and owned 77 percent of its wealth, and at the top one-twentieth of the population owned 20 percent of the national income and 53 percent of its wealth. By contrast, 3 percent of the national income, and less than half of 1 percent of its wealth, were spread among the lowest paid sector, also amounting to approximately one-fifth of the people. Comparable inequalities dominated the distribution of income and ownership of corporate assets in the business world, among whose total of almost 2 million corporations, 55 percent of the corporate assets were controlled by one-tenth of 1 percent.[1] These inequalities might or might not be considered inequities, depending on services performed and the comparability of the distribution of public burdens through taxation; but the Internal Revenue Code of the United States systematically extracted higher proportions from the poor than from the rich. Although welfare programmes which disbursed public money among the needy attracted much attention and no little criticism, it could in the circumstances be no great flight of fancy to describe the preferences and exemptions granted to the recipients of high incomes, and holders of public securities and the owners—or purchasers—of property, as "a welfare program that reverses the usual pattern and gives huge welfare payments to the super-rich but only pennies to the poor".[2] The rediscovery of the ex-

1. Herbert J. Gans, *More Equality* (New York, 1974), pp. 13–14.
2. Philip Stern, *The Rape of the Taxpayer* (New York, 1973), quoted by Gans, *More Equality*, p. 15.

istence of the poor came to America as a humiliating shock at a period of generally self-satisfied affluence with the publication of Michael Harrington's book *The Other America*, which gave the country the disturbing information that the poor had indeed always been with them; they had not disappeared from existence, only from view. Between 40 and 50 million Americans, about the one-fifth of the population mentioned as receiving 3 percent of the income, lived in poverty and hunger; the American economy had failed to feed, clothe, house, or minister to them but it did succeed in concealing them from sight.[3]

These revelations, which received very wide publicity and attention, particularly during President Johnson's administration, led directly to a series of legislative and administrative policies aimed at relieving poverty and the terrible condition of material undernourishment in which it was perpetuated. Not until George McGovern became a presidential candidate, however, was the question of income redistribution placed on any party's agenda for serious political consideration,[4] and it seems to have been enough to convince many voters that the Democratic candidate's ideas were dangerously radical. The increasing economic depression of the late 1960s and 1970s did not seem a propitious time for the kind of government spending that would have been required by effective programmes that looked beyond relief to a reordering of the entire scale of government subsidies and supports. In any case, the structure of political power made such programmes unlikely. The poor may, though many of them do not, vote at elections, but they never finance candidates or maintain continuous or organised pressure on congressional committees. Such pressure as the poor were able to exert on the political process sprang much more directly from the power of race than from the condition of poverty. Many of the urban poor were blacks, most of the urban blacks were among the poor. Consciousness of racial inequality stimulated the demonstrations of the period, and it was to this consciousness—uneasily shared by increasing numbers of whites—that American society responded, rather than to the stimu-

3. Michael Harrington, *The Other America* (New York, 1962; Harmondsworth, 1963), p. 19.
4. Gans, *More Equality*, p. 53.

lus to conscience arising from distinctions of economic class and unbearable frustrations of economic opportunity.[5] Meanwhile, not altogether fortuitously, the Supreme Court registered its own intimations of the theme that equal protection was a principle with economic dimensions. After remaining unmoved through generations of contention, it declared in 1966 that the venerable Southern system of using the poll tax as a qualification for the suffrage was a violation of the Fourteenth Amendment.[6] The federal government had already used the Voting Rights Act of 1965 to prohibit the use of the poll tax in federal elections. Four years later the Supreme Court upheld a federal district court ban on a literacy test for the suffrage in North Carolina on the ground that, although progress had been made recently toward equalising and integrating the schools in that state, the history of educational discrimination had placed adult Negroes at an educational disadvantage, and the test therefore conflicted with equal protection.[7] The court did not address itself to literacy or educational tests as a general principle involving the question as to whether such tests deprived illiterate people of equal protection.

Even in education, traditionally a matter for local attention, the drift of national politics was reflected in a gradual equalisation of opportunity. If years of school attendance, without reference to what takes place in schools, may be regarded as one index of educational opportunity, then a striking increase was registered at the elementary level between the beginning of the New Deal and the end of the Nixon administration, in which period inequality in years of schooling decreased by no less than 45 percent.[8] Among persons born around 1900, the fifth part enjoying the largest share of school education had spent an average of 14 years in school while the least

5. This and a number of the remarks in this section are admittedly impressionistic. Others must simply compare their impressions. See, however, the bibliography in Gans, *More Equality*, in which it is significant that a great majority of the works cited are recent, most of them from the late 1960s and 1970s; Edward C. Budd, ed., *Inequality and Poverty* (New York, 1967); William L. Taylor, *Hanging Together: Equality in an Urban Nation* (New York, 1971).
   6. 383 U.S. 663 (1966).
   7. Gaston County, N.C. v. United States, 395 U.S. 285 (1969).
   8. Christopher Jencks et al., *Inequality: A Reassessment of the Effects of Family and Schooling in America* (New York, 1972), p. 20. Also essays in Review Symposium in the *American Journal of Sociology*, LXXVIII, no. 6 (May 1973).

formally educated received only 3.7 years; of those born during the Second World War, the most educated fifth still had the advantage of twice as much time in school as the least educated fifth—no doubt a difference of decisive importance for their respective futures, but nevertheless representing a great and increasing change in the direction of equality of school time. As Professor James Meade had observed, the expansion of the early stages of education has been financed by taxation that must have fallen "at least somewhat more heavily on the rich than on the poor", has been spent without direct charge to the poor, and "has been an equalizing factor of the greatest importance". American evidence, moreover, has shown that returns on education have been very high when assessing the effects for equalisation of economic performance.[9]

The considerable redistribution of wealth and resources implicit in these changes must be measured in relation to other changes of which they were only a part. American society placed constantly more emphasis on primary and secondary education, and especially after the Second World War it offered important advantages to the beneficiaries of the expanding field of higher education. The lesser educated made their gains not against a static position held by their superiors but in a constantly expanding field in which the better educated were also gaining in length of training, in the importance attached to accreditation in seeking well-paid and prestigious employment, and moreover in many cases in the quality of the content of higher education. The difficulties in measuring the gains and losses in this immensely complex flux, not only in education but at the humbler level of maintenance, health, and welfare, were still further accentuated by massive regional differences—in some cases as great as between the richer and poorer nations of Europe—and the large-scale movements of population from poorer to more prosperous districts. The flow of people from the poverty-stricken rural South into the welfare-stocked cities of the Northeast, the Midwest, and increasingly of the old border states created stresses which the resources of those states and cities had not been equipped to deal with, and intensified the complex of racial and economic deprivation.

9. J. E. Meade, *Efficiency, Equality and the Ownership of Property* (London, 1964), pp. 32–3; Theodore W. Schultz, *The Economic Value of Education* (New York and London, 1963), p. 65.

In the long run these people might discover the power of the vote. Voting power had assuredly lain behind many changes in the respect shown by politicians to deprived areas in earlier but not too recent years. But the long run had not arrived by the late 1960s when Johnson's war on poverty seemed already to have exhausted its impetus. The short run, on the other hand, had long shown a distinct propensity for continued existence, and what it revealed was that masses of these uneducated, ill-fed, and ill-housed people were too poor to vote—too poor, that is, to have any sense of the possibility of political effectiveness, any sense of their own ability to exert the slightest control over their environment. One important convergence which might have been expected to follow from the implicit unity of egalitarian theory had not taken place. The reorganisation of electoral boundaries ordered by the Supreme Court in accordance with the principle of one person, one vote had far more effect on the racial structure of politics in the South than in the North, placed black mayors and councils in office in some Southern towns, and also gave blacks in certain Northern cities an enhanced degree of access to the central political process. But this increase in power resulting specifically from the application of the principle of political equality did not prove the instrument of any clearly corresponding advance in the field of economic equality or equality of opportunity. Comparable advances had very little effect among the lower classes.[10] The lesson appeared to be that in order to benefit through the workings of the political system it was preferable to belong to a group whose membership already overlapped into the higher levels or was able through concentration of forces or political skill to exert specific leverage on the centres of power. Even a poor member of a labour union or of a strategically poised racial or religious minority had certain characteristics in common with wealthier or more influential members, and at certain moments the benefits could be reflected in such things as the distribution of civic funds or contracts; but the leverage was exerted by virtue of a palpable social identity, whether racial, religious, or political, rather than by the condition created by sheer economic distress. The poor who were only poor had only their poverty.

10. See footnote 5.

Social Esteem and Personal Identity

Americans wanted a society run on egalitarian principles without wanting a society of equals. It was therefore not only much easier, but in closer conformity with the preferences of a wide range of otherwise differentiated people, to respond to critical needs with welfare and social security policies than to envisage an egalitarian society. Between the crash of 1929 and the Republican administrations of Dwight Eisenhower popular economic thinking effected a large-scale transition from ideas of dynamic opportunities to ideas of security. Just as the corporation had proved itself better insulated against economic shocks than the private firm, the individual became increasingly identified with corporate aims and with the security offered by great institutions. Some of these were business institutions, others were the functions of local or federal government. In neither case did an independent ideal of equality play any significant part. Security and a fair return were as much as most people wished for. Moreover, the continued idealisation of success as confirmed by wealth, the residual glow from the diminishing fires of individual enrichment, continued to exercise a sort of dull enchantment. Particularly among the working classes the idea of equality imposed on individuals a burden of responsibility which few of them wanted to bear. When the attitudes of American skilled workers were investigated around 1960 by Professor Robert E. Lane, they did not express their aims either for themselves or for society in egalitarian rhetoric. Opportunity remained important, and an individual worker's skill, energy, and ambition were seen to create a legitimate claim on society's capacity to maintain opportunities. But opportunity for the fulfilment of earned aspirations was not all. Skilled workers tended to feel that a man should be allowed to keep the goods of fortune, and that one who had made a million dollars had deserved his reward; they were perhaps reluctant to exclude all thought of such possibilities from their own hopes, or from their hopes for their children, however illusory such aspirations might be. No evidence or sign appeared of any general vision of a different social order, nor any clear picture of how a more equally ordered society would distribute its goods.

The series of carefully constructed interviews with which Professor Lane drew out these observations reflected certain assumptions together with their corresponding aspirations and anxieties, and the fact that many of these were contradictory or ambivalent in no way detracted from their human authenticity—and neither did it mark them as products of particularly class-bound limitations. One of the most important and prevalent assumptions was that American society was basically sound. Whatever grievances might emerge about special privileges, or threats of relative deprivation, no one seems to have thought of such disparities as reflecting a wrongly constructed social order. As a corollary, it was also assumed that in spite of the obvious class differences in educational opportunity—clearly perceived as being of importance—enough economic opportunity existed to give each man some chance to prove himself in the admittedly competitive struggle for self-advancement. This helps to explain why no one was really prepared to admit that his failure to occupy a higher economic and social status was a fault of the system; blame tended to be attributed to one's own past mistakes, missed opportunities, or to bad luck. Even partially disappointed men could take some satisfaction in their superiority to those below them, itself an indication that a differential system could show some sense of rightness in the distribution of rewards. What people overwhelmingly wanted was recognition and reward within a social group to which they felt a sense of belonging and which in return offered them a sense of respect and recognition. As with comparable observations on social status among working-class people in Britain, it was the local group that mattered, and it was status within close and personally measurable horizons that did most to determine the individual's sense either of satisfaction or of relative deprivation. Neither the rewards and consolations nor the grievances under this set of arrangements deprived the persons involved of their sense of justice; but where things had gone wrong, it did not seem to require a new social system to set them right. One of the workers interviewed, a machine operator and part-time janitor, after expressing a slightly inauthentic sounding sense of satisfaction with his station in life, significantly added, "I hope to God my children will do better than their father did".[11] Some ten years later, further investigations revealed little

11. Robert E. Lane, *Political Ideology: Why the American Man Believes*

dissatisfaction with the way in which the American economy distributed its rewards for different types of work; people chosen at random gave an interviewer their own ideas of wage differentials which almost exactly corresponded to those that actually prevailed in 1970.[12]

A slightly defensive and vulnerable sense of self-respect constituted one consistent keynote through these discussions, as it has done through so much of this history of social relations. American labour unions no longer made spacious pronouncements about the social order as they had done in the 1830s; by the mid twentieth century, an appeal by the American Federation of Labour for the implementation of the ideals of the Declaration of Independence accompanied by a detailed programme of appropriate action would have been decidedly out of character. Self-respect, which would always be crucial to the balance and integrity of the human personality, could be maintained by reference to social groups limited to occupational or local points of reference, provided always that those groups were not specifically deprived of respect by the rest of society.

The claims for equality that Americans made for their society, and towards one another, from the earliest days of the Republic, were always tinged with a strong and sometimes acid consciousness of this most emotive category which I have characterised as "equality of esteem". It therefore seems fitting to ask whether American society had historically been as successful as its friends and advocates constantly proclaimed in vindicating the claim that older societies were said to have denied, the claim that each individual was valued and respected on his—and eventually on her—own worth, not on a basis previously determined by birth, rank, or fortune. This unfortunately is a kind of enquiry that remains susceptible to impressionistic rather than precise answers. Yet the impressions of perceptive observers may sometimes convey as much as the findings of more exact methods of analysis, and a remarkable consistency of opinion runs through the observations of some of the most intelligent Europeans to have visited the United States over a period of more than a century from the beginnings of the Republic. When the new Repub-

---

What He Does (New York and London, 1962), pp. 57–81; W. G. Runciman, *Relative Deprivation and Social Justice* (Harmondsworth, 1972).

12. Jencks et al., *Inequality*, p. 232.

lic was only some twenty years old, one of those intellectually enquiring, upper-class Frenchmen whose observations have added
periodically to the world's knowledge of the United States, was
struck by a certain simplicity in the way people in Massachusetts
talked to each other. "The rich man shakes hands with the worker
and talks with him", wrote the duc de la Rochefoucauld-Liancourt,
"not as elsewhere in order to honour him, but as one who may need
his help one day—and further, without calculation, by habit, by
education". The contrast between honest informality and artificial
good manners was obviously a contrast with France, where citizenship had lately come into vogue; but the sense of a certain wholesome
straightforwardness between people as individuals struck him as
something new in social relations, and he found this spectacle, which
arose not from superiority but from homage paid to the quality of
men, "very satisfying to the free soul".[13] Many comparable remarks
could be found until, forty years later, Tocqueville made equality
the central theme of his own book.[14] The "equality of conditions"
which he described as the leading characteristic of American social
and economic relationships was an imperfect measurement of the
structure of education, wealth, and status, but it stood for Tocqueville in sharp contrast to Europe, and would have been inconceivable
without a distinctively American informality in personal relationships. Europeans were commonly struck by the accessibility of men
in public office, by a characteristic lack of ceremony, and by a certain
straightness in the way people talked to each other. Indeed it seems
likely in retrospect that Tocqueville may have been led by these
things into overestimating the amount of effective equality in economic opportunity, education, and class relations. The very fact of
possessing the vote, of being an object of attention to parties and
candidates, gave ordinary people an assurance that they visibly
lacked in Europe. Barbara Bodichon was impressed twenty years later
by the pride in being American that she observed in the Germans and
French. "It makes them feel at home, gives them an importance which
probably they never had before, makes them respect themselves,
and gives them a standing which creates a new motive for self-

13. La Rochefoucauld-Liancourt, *Voyage dans les Etats-Unis, fait en 1795,
1796 et 1797*, 5 vols. (Paris, L'An VII de la République), pp. 253–6.
14. Alexis de Tocqueville, *De la démocratie en Amérique* (1840), ed. J.-P.
Meyer (Paris, 1961).

improvement", she observed, all of which threw her back once again to painful reflections on home: "What an incredible amount of humbug there is in England never struck me before. They talk Christianity—all men equal before God—but it is only in the Free States of America that that idea of Christ's about equality is beginning to be understood".[15]

Since Mrs Bodichon was under no illusions about slavery or about the status of women, these remarks—which were not intended for publication—give a telling indication of the attitudes she discovered among immigrants. Some thirty years later a far more famous Briton, James Bryce, devoted a section to "Equality" in his book *The American Commonwealth*.[16] Bryce's definition of the subject included "estimation", which he clearly discerned as essential to the popular sense in which equality was understood. Bryce was not favourably impressed by Tocqueville's abstractions and wanted to set the observation of the United States on a much firmer footing;[17] he was bound also to observe that great changes had taken place. Inequality of wealth had grown greatly in the previous sixty years and would continue to grow; he saw no prospect of a return to primitive simplicities, and American ideals accepted these developments because the gifts and attainments of men who had won great wealth by the display of remarkable talents—men such as manufacturers and railroad kings—were felt to be a credit to the nation. Bryce was too observant to miss the grades and distinctions in society which, though they found no tangible expression, were as sharply drawn as in Europe; the exclusiveness of the "best sets" was spreading from the East into the Western cities. Yet there remained for him a profound impression that seemed to outweigh these refinements, an "equality of estimation" based on the simple fact that "in America men hold others to be at bottom exactly the same as themselves". He obviously liked the special kind of earthy realism with which Americans looked on men of high achievement. "Respect for attainment excites interest, even reverence", he observed, but it did not

15. Barbara Leigh Smith Bodichon, *An American Diary 1857-8*, ed. Joseph W. Reed, Jr. (London, 1972), pp. 72–3.

16. James Bryce, *The American Commonwealth*, 2 vols. (American ed. Chicago, 1891), II, 615–27.

17. Hugh Tulloch, "The Anglo-American Background of James Bryce's *American Commonwealth*", Ph.D. thesis, Cambridge University, 1974.

lead a man to treat the object of this respect "as if he were made of porcelain and you only of earthenware".[18] The attitude was to be noticed even among servants. He also remarked that on the West Coast coloured people often sat down to table with whites, although he noted the ill-treatment of the Chinese there. On the whole Bryce averted his attention from the more serious aspects of race relations; the American commonwealth that formed the subject of his observations, especially in his earlier editions, was an almost entirely white commonwealth.

Even in Tocqueville's day, an observer as systematic and scrupulous as Bryce would have noted more of the inequalities of condition and opportunity than Tocqueville did, though such differences might not then have affected the central theme of the argument; Bryce himself, while emphatic about egalitarian manners and the egalitarian assumptions on which individual appraisals were based, left little doubt that differential developments would grow more extreme. He certainly did not claim to have observed an equality in political or economic power, and saw no way of arresting the growing accumulations of wealth with corresponding status and influence. The characteristic that remained and that he picked out so clearly was a social style rather than the distinguishing marks of a social structure. American contemporaries of his, more concerned with reforming the massive inequities which dominated the structure itself, took little comfort from the brash informalities of the political barbecue or its social and industrial counterparts.

Other American contemporaries had still less reason for comfort. The Reverend Alexander Crummell, an Episcopalian clergyman, had spent the middle years of the century in Liberia; he had originally left the United States to take a degree at Cambridge because of the humiliating conditions of training offered him, as a Negro, by his bishop in Philadelphia. When he returned to his own land in the early 1870s, he found to his sorrow that the emancipation of his people had given them much less than the liberty expected by other Americans. The observations he made in a sermon calling for racial consciousness and solidarity threw into sharp relief the demoralising consequences of racial inequality: "We are living in this country, a part of its population", he told his parishioners,

18. Bryce, *American Commonwealth*, II, 622.

and yet, in diverse respects, we are as far from its inhabitants as though we were living in the Sandwich Islands. It is our actual separation from the real life of the nation, which constitutes us as a "nation within a nation". Thrown very considerably upon ourselves for many of the largest interests of life, and for nearly all our social and religious advantages; as a consequence on this state of things, all the stimulants of ambition and self-love should lead this people to united effort for personal superiority and the uplifting of the race; but instead thereof, overshadowed by a more powerful race of people; wanting the cohesion which comes from racial enthusiasm; lacking in the confidence which is the root of a people's stability; disintegration, doubt and distrust almost universally prevail, and distract all their business and politics.[19]

These psychological consequences were not at all difficult to observe; it depended not on the quality of the observer's vision but on the point of view he was willing to adopt. Crummell's painful observations were confirmed in clearly perceived detail by the white Virginian merchant Lewis Harvey Blair, one of the very few who tried in post-Reconstruction years to draw the attention of fellow-Southerners to the harm done to both races by segregation. Blair boldly advocated mixed schools, arguing that separate schools poisoned the sources of education. "At the fountain of education", he said,

the doctrine of caste . . . is enshrined in fresh vigor and authority, and it seizes with its rigid, icy grasp the impressionable minds of the children, and taints them; and the blind superiority thereby inculcated fosters sentiments of false pride, disregard of the rights of others, and unfeeling haughtiness to all, regardless of color, whom they deem their inferiors; and the inferiority thereby taught the blacks cultivates feelings of abasement and of servile fear of all whom they consider superior—sentiments totally destructive of manliness, courage and self-respect, the noblest jewels in the character of man.[20]

Blair, who saw clearly enough that separate schools tended "to keep the whole Negro population in a degraded condition", would have agreed with Dr Kenneth Clark, who testified more than sixty years later to the Supreme Court that segregation damaged the moral character of whites as well as the psychology of blacks. Blair's ob-

19. Alexander Crummell, "The Social Principle among a People", in *The Greatness of Christ and Other Sermons* (New York, 1882), pp. 290–1.
20. Lewis Harvey Blair, *A Southern Prophecy: The Prosperity of the South Dependent on the Elevation of the Negro* (1889), ed. C. Vann Woodward (Boston, 1964), pp. 148–8.

servations on the consequences of segregation, which remained almost unheard of until they were republished in 1964, anticipated all the essential points of the NAACP case before the Supreme Court in the hearings of *Brown* v. *Board of Education.*[21]

The problem of Negroes gaining recognition from a society which preferred to ignore them caused successive waves of revulsion, colliding with the more hopeful aspirations of Negro leaders and spokesmen. As Southern oppression increased, Crummell's theme of racial consciousness gained popularity. In 1883 the Bethel Literary and Historical Association in Washington held a lively debate on racial pride and unity. The trouble with making it a policy to stress individual rather than racial achievements, as one speaker pointed out, was that "the white people will not let you get rid of the idea of race". As the debate continued in the pages of the Negro press— notably in the *African Methodist Episcopal Review*—contributors urged the importance to Negro self-advancement of the theme that the race must supply its own models and standards of behaviour. The Kansas lawyer and editor C. J. H. Taylor pointed out that Negroes were weakened by their own habit of self-depreciation. "We have no reason to complain until we take more pride in our own", he observed, a state of affairs which was not improved while Negroes hated themselves, despised their own folk-songs, bleached their skins, and straightened their hair.[22] This essential spirit of self-esteem, and of the need to inculcate it where it proved weak and debilitated, was never absent from the motive force of Negro protest. It emerged in moments of great crisis and endurance such as bus boycotts and the struggles for admission to schools from the early years of the twentieth century to the famous Montgomery boycott of 1957; just as surely and no less significantly it was present in a miniscule matter of etiquette that found its way to the Supreme Court in 1964. The Alabama state prosecutor insisted on addressing a black woman, Mary Hamilton, as "Mary". She refused to answer his questions unless he addressed her as "Miss Hamilton". The state supreme court, finding the name Mary "an acceptable appellation", upheld her conviction for contempt of court; but the appeal was carried to the

21. See Brown v. Board of Education, 347 U.S. 483 (1954); Kenneth B. Clark, *Pathos of Power* (New York, 1974), especially pp. 92–119.

22. August Meier, *Negro Thought in America, 1880–1915* (Ann Arbor, Michigan, 1968), pp. 50–1.

Supreme Court of the United States which held that it was the prosecutor, not Miss Hamilton, who was in contempt of the proprieties
of judicial procedure.[23] This miniscule episode encapsulated a charge
of enormous moral significance. On a seemingly trivial question of
forms of address there turned the fundamental issue of equality of
esteem.

Personal Needs, Public Aims

It was relatively easy to determine that persons of different races
should be accorded the same formalities in courts of law; similarity
of address was akin to other similarities of procedure, already provided for by due process. In this sense the agencies of government
had it in their power to enforce equal standards of manners between
different groups. Government could not perhaps force them to like
each other but it could ensure that equal opportunities were actually
kept open in employment, promotion, and even to some extent in
housing. The best hope that followed from this was that the experience of closer contact in ordinary life would engender better understanding, good humour, respect, and ultimately friendship between
individual members of different groups. The guiding principle in
these policies was that practices arising from disrepect for another
race—or any other form of designated group—and practices whose
pursuit would in turn engender disrespect of the same kind were
illegitimate and not to be tolerated. The principle was clear; but the
constitutional difficulty was to find grounds for the necessary distinction between illegitimate forms of discrimination and those which
public policy could fairly approve. Measures intended to aid disadvantaged groups would also have to depend on certain forms of
group classification, a procedure which was in any case part of the
normal methods and objectives of legislation. It was when the
grounds of discrimination were seen to be arbitrary, irrational, and
damaging to members of the group designated that they were bound
to be disqualified as illegitimate. But many harmless opinions are arbitrary, and no doubt some harmful ones must be tolerated in a relatively free society; by "arbitrary" in this connection the judges and

23. Morroe Berger, *Equality by Statute, The Revolution in Civil Rights* (Garden City, N.Y., 1968), pp. 116-7.

lawmakers came to mean a detrimental opinion held without reasons that could be substantiated in objective or "neutral" criteria. This position in turn implied a comparatively optimistic view of human nature. It assumed that persons born and brought up as victims of historical prejudices and social disadvantages, often of the most crippling kind, could normally overcome these obstacles when they were given equal opportunities in schools and jobs. That these hopes would be easily fulfilled was less likely than at first seemed to be imagined. The result was that government and private agencies were drawn deeper and deeper into the study of the social and psychological as well as the economic consequences of prejudice, where they discovered situations of appalling complexity. No simple or systematic remedy suggested itself for the problems of welfare, housing, alienation, apathy, truancy, and the struggle for order, let alone education, in inner-city schools. Constitutional formulae about equality were incapable of exact application in this environment; what was required, as had once been said in a larger but no less critical context, was bold and persistent experimentation.

Constitutional rules about equality could not dictate specific policies, but they did increasingly call for intervention rather than mere restraint on the part of the government. By 1967 Archibald Cox, reviewing the cases decided during the previous term by the Supreme Court, had no difficulty in pronouncing equality as their principal theme.[24] It was highly important that in the case of *Katzenbach* v. *Morgan*[25]—dealing with the application of the Voting Rights Act in South Carolina—the court had deferred to Congress's opinion in over-ruling a state; Congress was now able to decide within broad limits how the equal protection clause was to apply to local conditions. The case, as Professor Cox said, "cleared the way for a vast expansion of congressional legislation on human rights", yet it was "soundly rooted in constitutional principles". The general consequence of these decisions was that Congress resumed the power it had taken in 1875 to deal with "the whole domain of rights appertaining to life, liberty and property, defining them and providing for their vindication". When Mr Justice Bradley spoke for the Su-

24. Archibald Cox, "Foreword: Constitutional Adjudication and the Promotion of Human Rights", *Harvard Law Review*, LXXX (1966/67), 91–272.
25. 384 U.S. 641 (1966).

preme Court on the Civil Rights Act of 1875 he checked the encroachments of Congress into the domain of state legislatures; now, more than eighty years later, the fundamental principles underlying that act were reaffirmed. Professor Cox concluded that the Warren court had overturned the judgment in the *Civil Rights Cases* of 1883.[26]

The cumulative direction of these cases established that when either legislatures or other agencies such as public or private corporations exercised forms of choice and discrimination it must be done on grounds that were relevant to their proper function; neither the caprice of personal taste nor the protection of vested interests could stand as reasons for restricting the opportunities of any appropriately qualified person. This view was advanced an important step further when in 1971 the Supreme Court held that the use of test scores and other credentials to select employees was a violation of Title VII of the Civil Rights Act of 1964 when, first, the process of selection resulted in the under-representation of minorities, and, second, the employer could show no relationship between test scores or similar criteria and the qualities required for performing the job.[27] All of this amounted to something doctrinally more solid than the removal of an earlier generation's objections to congressional invasion of the suzerainty reserved to state governments. In his lonely dissenting opinion of 1883, Mr Justice Harlan[28] had concluded that freedom from discrimination was a new constitutional right; he drew this conclusion not only from the civil rights laws, but from the inner logic of the Reconstruction amendments, which authorised appropriate legislation. His views ran completely counter to the thinking of the contemporary white majority both in matters of political sovereignty and—though this was less frankly admitted—in matters of racial equality. There was nothing inevitable about the ultimate

26. Cox, "Foreword", pp. 106–7, 118.

27. Griggs v. Duke Power Company, 91 U.S. 849 (1971). But more recently the Supreme Court has held that a general, not specifically job-related test, although it produces racially unequal recruitment, does not necessarily deny equal protection if there was no *intention* to discriminate racially. "Respondents, as Negroes, could no more successfully claim that the test denied them equal protection than could white applicants who failed". Mr. Justice Brennan, dissenting, held that "today's decision has the potential of significantly weakening statutory safeguards against discrimination in employment". Washington v. Davis, 109 U.S. 6 (1976) 11 EPD, no. 10,958.

28. Civil Rights Cases, 109 U.S. 3 (1883).

vindication of Harlan's views: Change is a law of history, progress in any particular direction is not. But when they were ultimately vindicated they could be seen to contain a firm internal consistency whose logic exposed dangerous flaws in the structure of thought that sustained the old regime.

As Alexander Crummell and many other minority leaders knew only too well, social attitudes have a shaping effect on the self-image, which in turn means the self-respect, of the people affected. Racial and religious discrimination were far from being the only social attitudes to shape—or distort—the individual's view of himself; they could even be thought in certain instances to have compensations when they drove the persons affected to discover sources of strength in the identity of the group to which society ascribed them. But the more important fact was that these compensations obviously did not satisfy the needs and aspirations of many of the persons so affected, and that damage to self-respect was reflected in impaired achievement and limited prospects. Yet self-respect is itself a more complex concept than the discussion of these questions seems often to have implied. One possibility arising from the intensified phase which these debates entered during the 1960s was that of a significant refinement of the concept of self-respect.

When Congress passed the Civil Rights Act of 1964 it commissioned an enquiry into inequality of educational opportunity "by reason of race, color, religion or national origin in public education institutions at all levels". The commission, under the direction of James S. Coleman, produced a report[29] which has dominated the debate on educational equality—in schools rather than in higher education—and has opened many of the paths leading to more philosophical reflections on the validity of the concept of equality. The Coleman Report is famous for having discovered that the schools available in predominantly black or white districts were far closer to being equal in quality than had been supposed and, still more important, that differences in the quality of schools contributed in only comparatively low degree to the differences in children's measured educational attainments. These findings have been reduced at times to the conclusion that schools make virtually no difference at all,

29. James S. Coleman et al., *Equality of Educational Opportunity* (G.P.O., Washington, D.C., 1966), listed as the *Coleman Report*.

a simplification that distorts some of the report's statements about minorities—notably that even though the differences may be small, the achievement of minority pupils are more closely related to the quality of the schools they attend than the achievement of pupils belonging to majorities in the population.[30] The commission reasonably expected to find connections between achievement and self-esteem, but discovered that black parents showed if anything greater interest than whites in their children's school performances and that black self-esteem was equally high. The refinement that occurred at this point in the enquiry turned on the more subtle question of whether the children expected to be able to exert any control over the environment in which they were to live. Here Coleman found that not only Negroes but other minorities—including Puerto Ricans, for whom it was lowest of all—had much less sense of control of the environment than whites. Among blacks the sense of control was lowest outside metropolitan areas.[31]

This discovery received much less attention than the more sensational findings about the effects of schooling. The report amplified it by reference to an enquiry into the risk-taking propensities of Negro and white adults which showed blacks as significantly more inclined to leave events to chance than to depend on their own actions.[32] It is easy to translate these attitudes into a general lack of belief in the efficacy of political action and cynical apathy towards such idealised concepts as that of equality in political power through the exercise of the suffrage, however conscientiously the right of suffrage might have been distributed on the principle of one person, one vote. It seems reasonable to argue, consistently with the general nature of the commitments undertaken by governments to individual citizens as members of minorities, that society had some obligation to intervene through legislation to prevent this kind of demoralisation and to reform it where it occurred. It is one thing for elements in the population to choose not to participate in its public life, but another thing for them to feel incapable of participation.

The problem of self-esteem had other ramifications. After all,

30. Ibid., p. 22.
31. Ibid., pp. 288–9.
32. The study here cited is Herbert M. Lefcourt, "Risk-Taking among Negro and White Adults", *Journal of Personality and Social Psychology*, II (1965), 765–70.

racial and other designated groups consist of individuals. It is the individual members of deprived groups who experience diminished prospects, not only of employment but of the full development of their personal potentialities, as a result of the existence of inequality of opportunity. It is as individuals that persons must appeal to the Constitution for protection against unjust deprivation. Yet few individuals are as free from the webs of their socially defined identity as they might have appeared to be in the pure light of constitutional law. Long-maintained policies in admissions to law schools and medical schools, the mere translation into professional policy of the received attitudes of previous generations, have ensured that many of America's ethnic minorities have remained heavily under-represented in professional resources. In 1965 only 1.5 percent of the country's law students were black; and California, with a Chicano population of more than 2 million, had as late as 1969 only three Chicano graduates from the state's law schools. At the same time the universities of Arizona, New Mexico, and Utah, states with large Indian populations, had never graduated an Indian.[33] Facts of this scale and import stood behind the policies known under the title of "affirmative action", through which federal and state governments moved to increase the admissions of minority members to all levels of professional and higher educational opportunity. The pressure emanating from the Department of Health, Education and Welfare for increased admissions and employment opportunities for women were part of the same policy, supported by exactly the same principles. Indeed, since women were not a numerical minority in the American population, the word itself came to be redefined to refer to people who suffered a minority status with respect to their rights.

Social justice might demand, and political interests might make expedient, a policy of correction in favour of individual members of minority communities. But at this point the principle or individual equality of opportunity lost its direction. Affirmative action played off not only one individual of one group against another of another group, but the present against the past. In the past many privileged

33. Nina Totenberg, "Discriminating to End Discrimination", *New York Times Magazine*, April 14, 1974. Between 1969 and 1974 the total number of Blacks, Mexican-Americans, and mainland Puerto Ricans enrolled in medical schools was 8 per cent. Bakke v. Regents of the University of California, SF 23311, 1976. Super Ct. No. 31287, p. 27.

persons of mediocre ability had benefitted from the indulgence of a system that was unquestioningly biased in favour of whites, of Protestants, and also of the urban middle classes; but the egalitarian critique of the manifest inequities of the past provided no obvious answer to the grievance that arose when individual members of socially advantaged groups were displaced in favour of others of more doubtful ability. This was the problem raised by the case of Marco DeFunis, and it was if anything made more poignant by the fact that the plaintiff, being Jewish, himself belonged to a minority which had suffered bitter disabilities in the recent past. In 1971 DeFunis was rejected by the University of Washington Law School despite the fact that thirty-six applicants from other minorities—blacks, Chicanos, and Indians—with lower college grades and school aptitude test scores were admitted. On a judicial injunction the law school admitted him while the case passed through the courts. By the time it reached the Supreme Court his legal education was nearly complete and he was about to qualify, on which ground, when the time for the decision arrived in April 1974,[34] his case was held to be moot, requiring no formal judgment. The issue, however, had raised acute and often bitter dispute. Those who had fought a long fight for university admissions on the sole principle of individual merit discerned the renewed threat of quota systems, which within recent memory had been used as a legitimating instrument to restrict the admission of specific and otherwise qualified minorities—Jews being perhaps the most conspicuous victims. Law schools and government departments were deeply divided over the principles at stake. Affirmative action programmes were developing all over the country, but time was required to reveal their effects; a negative decision by the Supreme Court might well have called the whole concept into question. If it was true that the situation called for further experiment, further trial and error based on observation and correction, then the policies involved were in a critical sense political rather than con-

---

34. DeFunis v. Odegaard, 416 U.S. 312 (1974). Ronald Dworkin, "The DeFunis Case: The Right to Go to Law School", *New York Review of Books*, February 5, 1976. Nothing in the case of Allan Bakke, who sued the Regents of the University of California on similar grounds after being rejected in favour of minority applicants with lower test scores by the Davis Medical School, tends to alter my comment on the principles under consideration. Bakke v. Regents of the University of California.

stitutional; in their exercise of judicious restraint, the five judges of the court majority may therefore have been well advised as well as self-considerate. It could no longer be ignored that opinions were by now sharply divided as to the actual meaning of equality under existing constitutional rules.

By this time, therefore, the great public concentration of mind and energy of the previous twenty years had begun to produce paradoxical results. From one point of view, which did not lack influential theorists, it could even be held that the primary problems had been solved, and that those that remained had arisen in large part from the success of that enterprise; but the paradox arose precisely from the fact that the direction of effort, itself reflecting a virtual revolution in public policy, had uncovered new problems and had set differing ideas of equality against one another. The deeper implications of a fundamental public commitment to ideas of equality were examined in the most important work of moral philosophy of the period, Professor John Rawls's *A Theory of Justice*. Rawls, whose formulations had developed from their beginnings in a critique of utilitarianism, plainly accepted the generally egalitarian outlines of American political philosophy. The justice of any political structure would have in large measure to be based on the recognition of the principle that self-respect on the part of each individual member of the community was "perhaps the most important primary good".[35] Self-respect was defined as an ability, within one's own powers, to fulfil one's intentions—a definition that is in tune with Coleman's concept of ability to control one's environment.[36]

Respect was also identified as a vital category by the more politically orientated work of Christopher Jencks and his associates, who reviewed a vast bulk of evidence about schooling and family under the challenge of the simple title, *Inequality*.[37] In place of self-

35. John Rawls, *A Theory of Justice* (Oxford 1972), pp. 433, 440.
36. There is no internal evidence, however, that Rawls was influenced in this by the Coleman Report, which is not mentioned in Rawls's book. This view appears to be consistent with that of Bernard Williams, who defines self-respect as "a certain human desire to be identified with what one is doing, to be able to realise purposes of one's own, and not to be the instrument of another's will unless one has voluntarily accepted such a role". "The Idea of Equality" in Bernard Williams, *Problems of the Self* (Cambridge, 1973), pp. 233–4.
37. Jencks et al., *Inequality*.

respect they used the concept of "prestige", and had no difficulty in discerning that American society was committed by its professed values to attaching different measures of prestige to different occupations. Although they saw no prospect of equalising occupational prestige, it is significant of the American ethos—and of a part of it which Jencks would presumably not wish to renounce—that the type of respect he speaks of is related to what people do rather than what they are by birth and inheritance, a point of view which would have met the approval of that prince of entrepreneurs, Benjamin Franklin.[38] Jencks argued, in agreement with Coleman, that as the effects of schooling were socially trivial, nothing short of socialism would produce an adequate measure of the equality to which Americans were in theory committed by their own avowals of principle. Anything less was a mockery of the name. Jencks was in direct dialogue with Coleman and the sociologists; his dialogue with the moral philosopher Rawls, who had no such politically polemical purpose, was oblique. Yet Rawls's system, which in important respects seemed permeated with characteristically American assumptions about the normative character of such things as "an approximately free market economy", is also basically egalitarian. This assertion follows from his fundamental vision, which achieves social fairness by placing all people in an "original position" before the formation of society, where they are behind a "veil of ignorance" as to the positions they can expect to occupy when the social system begins to work. The just society that results is supposed to reflect a series of rational individual choices in which no one will risk choosing a position of worthlessness or subjugation. It is clear that all the persons in the "original position" must be in a state of primary equality; and the argument as it develops makes clear that subsequent departures from equality may be permitted if they are also to everyone's advantage.[39] From the moral consequences of the "original position" Rawls develops the view, advanced for somewhat other reasons by earlier philosophers, that all persons ought to treat one another with the respect due to their human character, an attitude which assumes a basic belief in the equality of persons as moral characters. This fundamental requirement of mutual respect is the

38. Ibid., pp. 10–11.
39. Rawls, *Theory of Justice*, pp. 19, 60–2.

basis of the Kantian command, discussed by Rawls in some detail, that people are always to be treated as ends in themselves, never merely as instruments of the purposes of others.

Rawls's moral person is assumed to have a conception of his own good, and is also assumed to have a sense of justice. Moral personality may not always be fully present, but in normal persons it exists as a potentiality capable of realisation. This statement seems to express a principle of fundamental moral importance, but nevertheless of somewhat limited application. The statement that people owe each other *equal* esteem in their capacity as moral beings had earlier been criticised on the ground that it is respect alone that does the required work: The idea of equality adds nothing to it. What is required of people is simply that they treat each other as complete humans, each of whom is, for himself, an end and not a means.[40] Egalitarian theory would impose an impossible burden on human judgment if it required each person to ask whether the respect that all are held to owe to each other, simply because they are people, was to be all the respect they owed to each other for any reason at all. Stated like this, the demand for equality of respect becomes untenable. Societies live by meeting the needs of their members, and the existence of forms of social organisation is always justified by the claim that individuals undertake to discharge responsibilities for which their qualities and qualifications are appropriate. If these desiderata could always be clearly and rightly related to each other, it would be wrong to withhold from persons of proven experience, or skill, or any ability related to function, the respect due to the exercise of that function— due to it in order that it should be properly exercised. It need not follow that such persons should be accorded more respect than was due to them for those specific reasons; as soon as the duty was over and the tools laid down, the basic level of shared and equal respect would be restored to view. Societies do not work with this degree of rational simplicity, and perhaps an excess of rationality tends to dehumanise human relations. Yet this does seem to be the kind of order that can be dimly discerned behind the vigorous, corrective thinking of some of those radical egalitarians who, throughout the

40. Stanley I. Benn, "Egalitarianism and the Equal Consideration of Interests", in J. R. Pennock and J. W. Chapman, eds., *Nomos IX: Equality* (New York, 1967), pp. 66–7.

history of the American Republic, have periodically called it back to the principles which they believed to be its moral foundations.

How many Americans have ever desired such a republic, how seriously they have meditated on its meaning, and with what degree of commitment they have sought for more radical forms of equality are all questions thrown up by successive attempts to give a precise formulation of the meaning of equality itself. A crucial contradiction that has emerged from the attempt to unify the concepts of equality is that equality of opportunity is not wholly compatible with equality of esteem. This weakness lay in the divided nature of American ideology itself. A stable system of economic equality was not inconceivable, but attempts, such as Thomas Skidmore's, to map it in detail could only show how unlikely it was ever to be achieved. This unlikelihood arose not only from the obvious opposition of powerful and numerous interests in the existing structure. It arose also from the fact that a genuinely egalitarian ideology would conflict with the American system of incentives, which was just as important to the public conscience and probably more popular. The incentive system of American political economy may have rested lightly on half-considered notions of equality of opportunity, but it never held equality in view as an aim or a resting place. The tension between egalitarian principles and anti-egalitarian incentives is crucial to an understanding of the bearing of constitutional principles on social and economic policy. The Supreme Court, as the authoritative interpreter of constitutional law, has reflected this tension because it is charged with the obligation of ensuring equal treatment between economically and socially unequal persons, while being obliged to defend many of the conditions which have made people unequal.

These conditions have historically produced conspicuously unequal results. One intellectually important consequence of the Coleman enquiry into educational inequalities was that concepts of equality began to polarise around two dominant principles: one was the old traditional value of equality of opportunity, but the other was the newly appreciated—if not newly conceived—idea of equality of results.[41] It was the results of the educational process that Coleman and his team actually measured, while clearly recognising that

41. James S. Coleman, "Inequality, Sociology and Moral Philosophy", *American Journal of Sociology*, LXXX, no. 3 (November, 1974), p. 741.

equality of opportunity remained the dominant ideal. The analytical problems began at this stage to uncover the ambiguity and confusion in the aims of many people who made equality their watchword. In the first place, as Coleman clearly perceived, when equal results were achieved in academic records it did not follow as a matter of course that they sprang from equality of conditions in the schools. Beyond this difficulty, the somewhat crude results thrown up by test scores and other school records could too easily be transmuted from methods of measurement into educational aims. When the aim of the schools was to achieve an equality of recorded measurements the system might be in working order, but some doubt would arise as to whether it was a system of education. Educational specialists would find nothing to surprise them in this problem. Its most acute form had long afflicted America's more gifted children, frequently held back from anything like their full potentialities by the stubborn pace of satisfied mediocrity. When equality meant equal opportunity for each child to develop fully his or her own potential, it could not be easily reconciled with that view of equality which aimed to produce a steady stream of similar products and failed to offer the incentives, the equipment, or the intelligence needed by children of innately superior abilities.

The problem discovered through investigations into school education could be generalised. The political structure answered to an electorate whose members possessed one vote each. But this power to cast a single vote gave no account of special needs, exceptional abilities, usual or unusual occupations; democracy at bottom proved to be a method of counting, and it was only through refinements of processes available within the republican system that the interests of people with special claims or needs could be advanced. In all these cases the response of legislators represented a political judgment. The strongest statement of egalitarian consensus that could be rationally extracted from the tangle of American commitments was that, in cases where the meaning of equality was agreed, or easily ascertained by objective rules, whenever any interest demanded a departure from equality that departure would have to be justified by reference to the prevailing principle. As Rawls had observed, the burden of proof was on the person who argued for any form of inequality.

But to reach this point was only to define the problem, not to solve it, for the tortuous passages of public policy had already shown the difficulties of reaching agreement on the meaning of equality, and of formulating objective tests that satisfied the moral as well as the purely formal criteria demanded by interested parties rather than philosophers. If, for the purpose of standardising objective rules, persons were regarded as irreducible units, it was not because individuals were to be regarded as uniform in their needs—or even invariably consistent with themselves—but for two reasons, one practical and one philosophical. The practical one was that individuals can be counted. Refinements of private emphasis or interest that resist this form of statement are difficult to measure accurately, and always remain open to speculation. On the philosophical side, republican theory regards individuals as having independent moral responsibility for their acts. In this way the principle of equality of political power formed a morally consistent unity with equality of conscience.

The educational enquiry had exposed the more intractable difficulties of the philosophical problem.[42] Certain aspects of the concept of equality held together; others were revealed as divisible into mutually inconsistent and even incompatible parts. As the enquiry gained ground from year to year, so the objective receded, and below—perhaps only just below—each day's horizon lay the bright illusion of a future that cast its glow into the sky. Society might cherish, and must pursue, an ideal of equality, but it would have to determine its own meaning for the concept, and that choice would always be political. Such criteria as the psychological and social satisfaction of individuals, or democracy's need of a population capable of participating in its political life, could be satisfied by the pursuit of certain deliberate policies, but these choices in turn excluded others; the DeFunis case and the experiments with unrestricted admission to colleges had shown that broad policies of equalisation implemented for the benefit of groups whose grievances and deprivations were felt to give their individual members special claims on the community could clash with the equally fundamental rights of other

42. See in general Frederick Mosteller and Daniel Patrick Moynihan, eds., *On Equality of Educational Opportunity* (New York, 1972), containing essays resulting from a seminar at Harvard on the Coleman Report and its implications; Godfrey Hodgson, "Do Schools Make a Difference?", *The Atlantic*, March 1973.

individuals who were guiltless of causing these grievances—whose rights were derived from the same sources and ascertained by the same methods of enquiry. The prospect of such considerations, at the school level, had not escaped Coleman, whose original survey was based on a design which clearly showed that problems of social choice would arise from the outcome of the investigation. "Altogether it has become evident that it is not our role to define what constitutes equality for policy-making purposes", an internal memorandum explained to the team. "Such a definition will be the outcome of an interplay of a variety of interests, and will certainly differ from time to time as these interests differ. It should be our role to cast light on the state of inequality defined in the variety of ways which appear reasonable at this time".[43]

It may seem ungrateful, after two hundred years in which the principle of equality has been held as a moral truth given by fundamental law, to conclude that the concept should be considered as a beginning rather than an end. Yet this long period, during whose course the idea of equality has been reinterpreted to meet many different needs and contingencies, has yielded the perception that equality must itself be the result of social choice, effected by private or political decisions. This conclusion in turn represents a profound transformation from the moral ideas on which the Republic was based. The founders regarded equality as rooted in unalienable and immutable rights; though it might be the subject of changing policy, these rights were indestructible, and incapable of varying with different societies or periods.

Whatever the differences between eighteenth-century British and American views of sovereignty and representation, British and American theorists of the Republican and Whig traditions could agree about the permanence of the laws of nature, given by providence to be transmitted and enshrined in English constitutional law. The gifts of God were not thought to be susceptible to either deterioration or improvement. The history of two centuries has revealed, however, that the rights citizens could claim in their own society must be prescribed by that society rather than received directly from nature. In an ultimate philosophical sense the source of

43. James S. Coleman, "The Concept of Equality of Educational Opportunity", *Harvard Educational Review*, XXXVIII, no. 1 (winter, 1968), p. 17.

individual rights might be the same—nature, or the modern analogy of Rawls's "original position". In the earlier period, however, government had at the most a limited, protective part to play; and the rights in which people were equals were more likely to require protection against government than by it. This situation was entirely reversed when government became the central agency responsible for deciding what interpretation to place on the idea of equality in numbers of conflicting and inconsistent cases, and for enforcing their protection through policies constantly supervised and periodically reassessed. Government itself must decide how far it should promote equality of opportunity for specific individuals, equality of opportunity against equality of result.

Questions of this order were not answerable from criteria of equality alone since they arose, as has been seen, from imperfect or conflicting definitions of equality itself. They could be answered only by turning to the higher concept of equity or, in more common parlance, fairness. It was in this direction that the Supreme Court turned when it asked whether the grounds used for various forms of discriminatory legislation were rational or arbitrary, whether they would stand the test of objective standards. Fairness belongs to a higher order in ethics than equality, and equality can best be understood as a method of applying the mandate of fairness to specific circumstances. Yet when that has been said it is clear that fairness is in turn answerable to equality, in the sense that departures from manifest equality can be justified only when they correspond to the real differences in an objectively perceived situation. That conclusion has been reinforced—though it has not always been embraced—whenever the debate has been renewed since the time when the idea of equality escaped from the safekeeping of the law into the wider social context which it began to suffuse in the later eighteenth century. To perceive a situation objectively, or neutrally, it is necessary to establish objectively observable criteria, of which the one person, one vote principle is an example, and equal access to education, housing, and employment are others. Yet successive renewals of the debate, in which these criteria have in some measure been present, have revealed movement towards social equality as movement towards a vision but without a destination. To appear to have arrived at the answer is only to have reached the point where the problem has changed. To recognise this truth is not to admit that the journey should be discontinued or that the ideals were false. There is after all only one common destination in human affairs, and that one involuntary.

This point is one of general principle and will arise whenever legislation is used and public agencies are established to enact egalitarian purposes. The United States has become a troubled, in some ways privileged, but in any case an extraordinarily conspicuous testing ground for the issue of equality. The special character given to the American example by the existence of a federal Constitution enjoying pre-eminent authority adds some complexities to the case but in no way diminishes its general significance; without specific reference to the United States, Sartori made essentially the same point in observing, "We must now cease to speak of equality in the singular and proceed to deal with equalities in the plural. . . . Just as liberty actually comes down to the struggle to achieve particular liberties, so equality is defined, historically speaking, as the repudiation of certain differences instead of others. And the discourse on equality must bring us to reply to a precise question: What is the specific equality which has precedence in democracy?"[44] But American history has never yielded a single answer to this "precise question", and democracy cannot be so defined as to yield a specific answer: The answers have changed with time and circumstance. That was one inference at least to be drawn from the first two hundred years of American history.

The idea of fairness draws the guiding principles of political justice back towards the Aristotelian concept of proportion. But that does not mean that Aristotle, or the eighteenth-century's concepts of natural or common law or even the language of the American Constitution, can be expected to have the last word on the exact proportions proper to a continuously changing society. These can come only from constant reflection and repeated—in fact unending—application to changing circumstances. In the last analysis, equality as an end in itself ceases to be a tenable concept because it ceases to be a concept whose various aspects can be held in constant balance with one another. But in public life the last analysis is never arrived at, and there is always more to be done than has yet been achieved.

44. Giovanni Sartori, *Democratic Theory*, (New York, 1967), p. 334.

The first generally agreed rule of equality was equality before the law. The idea that justice required equality of procedure, though narrower than the wide range of claims that proliferated from the time of the American Revolution, was never in itself a merely procedural concept. It represented as a principle even of a stratified and unegalitarian social order that whenever people found themselves on common or on neutral ground, as they do when justice is sought among them, the condition of humanity demanded that the same procedures must apply to all: In short, to give preference to rank or wealth or sex or race could give no guidance in seeking the truth, and it is the essence of justice to seek the truth.

By an extension of this principle, it may be maintained that the principle of equality can never be less than a rule of procedure, a method of assessing the proportions that actually exist in relation to the proportions that would satisfy so far as is ever humanly possible the combined needs of individual aspirations and social aims. But this was the crux of the problem, not its solution. Individual aspirations, which have a rightful claim to the protection of society's rules, are not always in harmony and sometimes conflict with the same society's broad interest in achieving certain kinds of racial or group balance, to put the problem only in its most familiar terms. The problems posed for American legislators and judges during the years of the Incomplete Revolution since 1954 have dramatised one necessary paradox: It is that of finding in each instance a general principle on which to resolve microcosmic cases in a mass society. Egalitarian rules of procedure remain the indispensable point of departure and the essential method. It is possible that they may eventually yield an approximate equality of results throughout the population as a whole. But that aspiration rests on a hypothesis, not on a demonstrated syllogism; and if a changed society were to result from these procedures, that society would probably have different requirements, and possibly a different intuition of the demands of social justice with which to assess those requirements. In previous periods of American history there have been elements to challenge the prevailing consensus, in the hope of creating a new consensus in their own image; whether or not a consensus may be said to exist now, there is no reason to expect this process to cease. But a policy of imposing an absolute equality of results as the actual determinant of the measure of equal justice in social, economic, or educational policy would represent a substantial departure from earlier methods of assessment, and from all previous concepts of equality of opportunity. At the time of the struggle over the principle of desegregation the problem of race absorbed everything else, dramatising and simplifying the issue into a choice between equality and inequality; the outcome, however, left future generations to determine their preferences not between equality and inequality but between one concept of equality and another.

These refinements of meaning have done much to clarify the character of the choices that have to be made. Although that clarification cannot determine the choice in any particular case, the broader outlines of public policy, taking their roots in American principles of republican government, would always be justified in addressing themselves through the application of equal rules towards rather than away from the equalisation of results. To understand this reasoning it is crucially necessary to recognise that at any given historical period down to the present the distribution of goods, including education and the evidence of measured intelligence, represents a profound inequality of results, and therefore wherever this condition calls for a programme of action, the primary aim is rather to redress a gross imbalance than to create a preconceived plateau of attainments. Departures from equality of results are often both justified and necessary, but the Constitution requires that the burden of justification falls on those who demand such departures, while the Constitution's normal gravitation pulls in the direction of equalisation. This burden, however, contains several imperfectly reconciled ingredients of which the most important is that the Constitution extends its protection equally to all—to every individual on American soil—in his or her capacity as an independent and irreducible individual. No constitutionally acceptable outcome can conflict with that obligation. It is the individual whose rights are the object of the special solicitude of the Constitution and for whose protection the Republic had originally justified its claim to independent existence.

Index

Bradley, Justice Joseph P.: on civil rights, 189–90, 342–43; on social assumptions affecting women, 314
Bradwell v. *Illinois* (1872), 313–14
Brennan, Justice W. F., on religious establishment, 107
Brewer, Justice David J., on sex differences, 312–13
Brigham, Carl C., on Nordic superiority, 234
Britain: Abolitionists in, 157–58; anticlericalism in, 79–80; class and rank in novels of, 143; Glorious Revolution of 1688 in, 14, 20; immigrants from, 207–237; income tax in, 327; political reform in, 158; property in public office in, 144; treatment of American colonies by, 14, 17, 22–25, 39, 54–55. *See also* England
British Boundary Commission, cited by Frankfurter, 282
Brown v. *Board of Education* (1954), 269–71, 292
Brown, Justice Henry B., in *Plessy* v. *Ferguson,* 196–97, 199, 314
Brownson, Orestes, political views of, 137–38
Bryce, James, *The American Commonwealth* by, 88, 337–38
Buchanan v. *Warley* (1917), 259
Buffon, George Louis Leclerc: Jefferson disapproves of nominalist ideas of, 132
Bunche, Ralph, on gradualism, 253
Burger, Chief Justice Warren, on apportionment, 285–86
Burke, Edmund, denounces individualism, 132
Bushnell, Horace, on Protestantism and Republicanism, 89
Byllesby, Langdon, *Observations on Sources and Effects of Unequal Wealth* by, 128–28

Cabell, Joseph C., and finance of education, 120
Cady, Elizabeth, *see* Stanton, Elizabeth Cady
Calhoun, John C., *Disquisition of Government* by, 162–63
California: Asiatic contract labour in, 207; minorities in universities of, 346, 347; Negro population of, 254
Calling, Calvinist doctrine of, 9, 37

Calvinists, 52, 63, 90
Cantwell v. *Connecticut* (1940), 107
capitalism: as American creed, 89; collapse of (1929), 254; inequalities due to success of, 202, 206–8; and labour, 206, 225; Southern critics of, 162, 164
Capitalists, equality of opportunity for, 139
Cardozo, Justice Benjamin N., on all-white primary, 277
Carnegie, Andrew, 208, 218
Carpenter, Senator, of Wisconsin, on civil rights, 180
caste: attempts to create legal system of, 155, 168, 199; class not equivalent to (Cooley), 216; rejection of idea of, 166, 198, 240
Catholics, Roman: as Americans, 91–92; and education, 92–96; parochial schools of, 59, 101, 103, 104, 110; as group in social order, 200, 249; Irish, 151; question of interchangeability of, 293, 294; support Ives-Quinn Bill, 261
Catt, Carrie Chapman, leader of woman's movement, 310
Caucasian, as racial definition, 228, 259
censuses (1890, 1910), 242
Chase, Salmon P., Chief Justice of Supreme Court, 178
Chaucer, quoted, 298
Chauncy, Charles, on religious establishments, 76
Chevalier, Michel, on equality, 151
Chicano population of California, 346
Chinese, discrimination against, 187–8, 247, 338
Chinese Exclusion Act (1882), 242–43
Christianity: assumed to be American national religion, 81, 83, 88–89; and equality, 77, 337; and women, 297
Church and State, American doctrine of separation between, 85, 92; judicial problems of, 96–100; questioned by Catholics, 92–93, 96
Church of Christ of Latter-day Saints, *see* Mormons
Church of England, 80. *See also* Episcopal Church
Churches, *see* Baptists; Catholics, Roman; Congregational churches;

Design: Al Burkhardt
Composition: Heritage Printers, Inc.
Letterpress: Heritage Printers, Inc.
Binding: The Delmar Company

Text: 10/13 Palatino
Display: 18/21 Palatino
Paper: Glatfelter Book natural, basis 55